ALEXANDER
OF RUSSIA

OTHER BIOGRAPHIES BY HENRI TROYAT

Firebrand: The Life of Dostoyevsky
Pushkin
Tolstoy
Divided Soul: The Life of Gogol
Catherine the Great

ALEXANDER OF RUSSIA

NAPOLEON'S CONQUEROR

HENRI TROYAT

Translated by Joan Pinkham

NEW ENGLISH LIBRARY

Originally published in France under the title *Alexandre Ier: Le Sphinx du Nord*
by Librairie Flammarion © 1980 Flammarion

This English translation copyright © 1982 by E. P. Dutton, Inc.

First published in the United States of America by E. P. Dutton, Inc. in 1982

First published in Great Britain in 1984 by New English Library,
Mill Road, Dunton Green, Sevenoaks, Kent.
Editorial office: 47 Bedford Square, London WC1B 3DP

British Library Cataloguing in Publication Data

Troyat, Henri
   Alexander of Russia.
   1. Alexander I, *Tsar of Russia*
   Rn: Lev Tarassov   I. Title
   947'.072'0924   DK191

   ISBN 0-450-0641-1

Printed in Great Britain by St Edmundsbury Press
Bury St Edmunds, Suffolk

CONTENTS

LIST OF
ILLUSTRATIONS

TRANSLATOR'S ACKNOWLEDGMENTS

I want to express my thanks to Professor Andrée Demay of Smith College and Professor Elisabeth Arlyck of Vassar College for the help they so generously gave me with the translation of this book.

While M. Troyat's prose is modern and lucid, the many early nineteenth-century writers whom he quotes wrote a French that—because their language is now dated, because their native tongue was Russian or German, or because as diplomats they were deliberately ambiguous —presented special problems of interpretation.

For help in solving such problems I am grateful to these two distinguished teachers, who placed at my service their expertise as French scholars and their mastery of two languages.

JP

ALEXANDER
OF RUSSIA

I

MONSIEUR ALEXANDER

Among the many faces that leaned over his crib every day Alexander soon recognized one, which had only to appear and all others were eclipsed: a heavy face with a prominent double chin, blue-black eyes, and a tender smile, the face of his grandmother, Empress Catherine II of Russia. For this forty-eight-year-old woman the birth of her grandson on December 12/23, 1777,* had seemed like just compensation for the disappointments she had suffered in her family. In her youth she had

---

*Certain dates in this book are given in two forms: first according to the Julian calendar, which at the time of the events was used in Russia; then according to the Gregorian calendar, which was used throughout almost all of Europe. In the eighteenth century the Julian calendar was eleven days behind the Gregorian calendar. This discrepancy increased to twelve days in the nineteenth century and to thirteen in the twentieth. The USSR did not adopt the Gregorian calendar until October 1923. When a single date appears in this text it refers to the Julian calendar for an event that took place in Russia and to the Gregorian calendar for an event that took place elsewhere.

---

been so absorbed in political matters, love affairs, and building her reputation that she had neglected the education of her son, Grand Duke Paul. She had never even loved him. To her, he had very soon come to represent Prussian obstinacy, the craze for the military, blind mysticism, everything she detested. Alexander, she was sure, would be her consolation for his father the drillmaster. She skipped a generation, and saw the newborn infant as her true heir. The maternal instinct that had played so small a part in her feelings toward her own child suddenly awoke when she gazed upon the child of her daughter-in-law. Now, as if by delayed reaction, she was deeply moved, rapturously excited.

There was no question of leaving the infant to his mother. The poor girl would never be able to care for him properly. And Paul still less so. Only the Empress could educate the mind and strengthen the body of the sublime offspring. Besides, she had long been preparing herself for the task by reading and annotating the books of Locke, Rousseau, Basedow, and Pestalozzi. With the same enthusiasm she had shown in laying down laws, she laid down principles of childraising. Hardly had Grand Duchess Maria Feodorovna seen her son in the hands of the midwife than Catherine seized the child and bore him off to her own apartments. A hundred-and-one gun salute announced the news to all St. Petersburg. With their martial thunder mingled the joyous pealing of bells. The court poets, with Derzhavin at their head, immediately rushed to their writing desks to vie with one another in celebrating the appearance of "a new star," "a young eagle" in the Russian sky.

A week later the baptism took place in the church of the Winter Palace. The infant received the name Alexander, in honor of St. Alexander Nevsky, the national hero who in the distant past had vanquished the Swedes and the knights of the Teutonic order. He was still only a grimacing, wailing bundle, yet already his grandmother imagined him on the throne of Russia, pursuing the work she had undertaken. If necessary, she would remove her incompetent son Paul from the succession and offer it to her grandson, whose character she would have carefully formed. God would help in the noble task of making this substitution. Thrusting aside the inept parents, she would take responsibility for bringing up the child in her own way. No cradle, but a little iron bed with hard leather cushions. Around the bed, a railing to prevent visitors from approaching. No more than two lighted candles nearby, so as not to pollute the air. As nurse, the wife of a gardener at the court's summer residence, Czarskoye Selo—the doctors guaranteed her health and the abundance of her milk.

The child's chief governess was Sophia Ivanovna Benckendorff, the wife of a general. His official nanny was Prascovia Ivanovna Gessler, a careful, energetic Englishwoman who had married a Russian. "Monsieur Alexander," "the future wearer of the crown," as Catherine variously called him in her letters, was to sleep with the windows open, to grow accustomed to loud voices around him, and to take a cold bath every morning in a room where the temperature did not exceed fifty-nine degrees. Catherine herself closely supervised this Spartan upbringing. Without underestimating the contributions of heredity, she believed that with strictness and perseverance one could forge a man superior to his fellows. "[Alexander] never has a chill," she wrote in French to Franco-German critic and diplomat Friedrich Melchior Grimm. "He is big and fat, healthy and very cheerful." And a few months later: "For Monsieur Alexander, not a scrap of anxiety since he came into the world . . . . he is a healthy prince, and that's all there is to it. You say that he has the choice of imitating either the hero or the saint of the same name [Alexander the Great or Alexander Nevsky]. You are apparently unaware that this saint was a man of heroic qualities: He had courage, determination, and capability, qualities that raised him above his contemporaries, who were appanaged princes like himself. Now therefore I opine that Monsieur Alexander does not have a free choice, but has only to follow one or the other according to his natural bent, and in either event he cannot fail to be a handsome boy."

When the child was a few months old she had him brought into her study so she could enjoy watching him kick and play on the carpet. Every time she looked up from her files it was to rest her eyes affectionately on the object of all her hopes. She made toys for him, cut out pictures, designed a special costume "that can be put on all at once and closes behind with hooks." She proudly sent the pattern for this garment to the King of Sweden and the Prince of Prussia. Her letters to Grimm overflowed with details of the smallest doings of the "divine nursling." "He is beautiful as an angel. . . ." "His eyes are very lively. . . ." "I am making a delicious urchin out of him. . . ." But the "delicious urchin," she thought, needed a playmate. Furthermore, the empire would soon require several princes to rule jointly over new territories that the Russians would not fail to conquer. Pursuing her old dream of hegemony over the Byzantines, Catherine already envisioned the Turks driven from Europe and a sovereign of her own blood seated on the throne of Constantinople. The doting grandmother, eager for many offspring, coincided with the obstinate empress determined to enlarge her territories. She changed hats with ease—now the beribboned cap of grandma, now the bronze helmet of Bellona.

Once again her wishes were fulfilled, and so quickly that she herself was surprised. On April 27, 1779, the indefatigable Grand Duchess Maria Feodorovna gave birth to a second son. "The good old dames around him claim that we are as like as two peas in a pod," the delighted grandmother wrote in French to Grimm. "But he is more delicate than his older brother, and as soon as a breath of cold air touches him he buries his nose in his swaddling clothes. . . . Someone asked me who the godfather would be. I said, 'I know of no one it could be other than my best friend Abdul Hamid [the Sultan of Turkey]; but since a Christian cannot be baptized by a Turk, at least let us do him honor by naming the child Constantine.'* And everyone cried: 'Constantine!' And there he is, Constantine, no bigger than my fist, and here am I, with Alexander on my right and Constantine on my left."

As a symbol of Constantine's vocation to rule, Catherine had a medal struck showing a baby surrounded by Faith, Hope, and Love, and in the distance the imposing mass of the Church of St. Sophia in Constantinople. Nothing could have been clearer. Now her daughter-in-law could either rest or give birth to a few girls, as she pleased.† The succession of the dynasty was ensured.

For the early education of Alexander and Constantine, who were growing up rapidly, Catherine composed a "grandmother's primer" consisting of stories from Russian history, a collection of maxims "strung together," she said, "like pearls." She considered that she was constructing "an entire Alexandro-Constantinian library," for until that time, she felt, only incompetents had made an attempt to teach the young generations about their country's past.

When Alexander and Constantine reached the ages of six and five respectively, Catherine removed their maids and governesses and entrusted their upbringing to men. Strutting proudly in the first rank of this male team was General Nicholas Ivanovich Saltykov, a sickly, misshapen personage with a heavy head that seemed to crush his thin shoulders. An ignorant but wily courtier, he had no peer at filling his pockets while flattering the powerful. According to Colonel Masson, who taught arithmetic to the two young Princes, "Saltykov's chief func-

---

*By allusion to Constantinople, where Catherine hoped he would one day rule.

†Paul and Maria had ten children: the future Alexander I (1777–1825); Constantine, the future Viceroy of Poland (1779–1831); Alexandra (1783–1801); Helen (1784–1803); Maria (1786–1859); Catherine, the future Queen of Württemberg (1788–1819); Olga (1792–1795); Anne, the future Queen of the Netherlands (1795–1869); the future Czar Nicholas I (1796–1855); and Michael (1798–1849).

tion in connection with the Grand Dukes was to protect them from drafts and to make sure they kept their bowels open."[1] Nevertheless, Catherine had taken care to draw up a seven-point "Instruction" for this superintendent of studies. It was a jumble of recommendations concerning the need for good physical and mental health, nobility of character, and application in intellectual work. Although there was nothing very original about these principles, Catherine was so pleased with them that she displayed the document in her study and gave copies to visitors whom she wished to honor with her confidence. Some observers were surprised that her Majesty's program allotted no place to music. But Catherine had never appreciated that art. She wrote to Grimm: "No harpsichord. Messieurs Alexander and Constantine shall not learn music; they can scrape or play if they like, without apprenticeship." Runich, who had no love for the Empress, was to write in French in his *Souvenirs* that the Instruction "was a collection of commonplaces . . . all very philosophical, in bad Russian."

Grouped around Saltykov were a few ad hoc schoolmasters, including General Protassov (whom Masson described as "narrow-minded, mysterious, sanctimonious, and pusillanimous"), Masson himself, and Baron Osten-Sacken. Religious instruction was dispensed by the arch-priest André Samborsky. Catherine had chosen him because, though he was a Christian by conviction, his cosmopolitan education, open-mindedness, and disdain for traditions distinguished him from other Russian ecclesiastics. Having served a long time as chaplain of the Russian legation in London, he had married an Englishwoman there and returned with a British accent, looking like an Anglican pastor, with no beard or mustache and a frock coat instead of a cassock. It had taken all the Empress's authority to force the court to accept his unorthodox costume. The old dignitaries whispered that the souls of the young Princes were incurring the greatest dangers under the influence of the "heretic." But Catherine, who feared nothing so much as religious excesses, was relying on this progressive priest to inculcate in her grandsons both a respect for God's commandments and a hatred for narrow-minded piety.

Samborsky also proved to be a good language teacher, and Alexander and Constantine were quickly initiated into the subtleties of English. They were taught German by the son of Pastor Groot. Russian, by contrast, was much neglected in the beginning. Still, Catherine assigned the excellent writer Mikhail Nikitich Muraviev the task of awakening his young pupils' appreciation for their mother tongue. They resigned themselves reluctantly to this exercise, which seemed so

pointless. On the other hand, how fascinated they were by the stories
of the German geographer and explorer Pallas, who would talk to them
about his travels across Siberia, on the steppes of southern Russia, and
on the shores of the Black Sea.

Suddenly, in the midst of these sententious personages appeared a
young, ardent, cultivated man who was to assume an importance in
Alexander's life that the boy could never have guessed. Frédéric César
de Laharpe was twenty-nine years old and had been born in Rolle, on
the shores of Lake Geneva. He had been acting as mentor to the two
brothers of Alexander Lanskoy, Catherine's favorite, on a journey to
Italy, and Lanskoy had suggested that his imperial mistress make the
young Swiss the tutor of the Grand Dukes. Catherine was amused and
charmed by what she learned of Laharpe. She was told that he was a
disciple of Gibbon and Rousseau, a fierce republican, a friend of the
people, and an opponent of tyranny. The Empress flattered herself that
she, too, was up to date on liberal ideas. Convinced that this radical
would be able to awaken in his pupils an inclination for justice without,
however, undermining their natural disposition for autocracy, she
wrote Laharpe, officially inviting him to St. Petersburg. He accepted
enthusiastically. In due course he arrived in the capital of this country
about which he knew absolutely nothing but which he had no doubt
would be better governed thanks to his enlightened ideas. Having read
Catherine's famous Instruction, he declared himself in agreement with
the high-minded principles that had guided its author, and set to work
with a stout heart.

In the beginning his role basically consisted in teaching Monsieur
Alexander French. This was a bit tricky because the pupil spoke only
English, Russian, and a little German, while the teacher knew none of
those languages. Finding it impossible to make himself understood
when he was alone with the boy, Laharpe had the idea of drawing
different objects in a notebook and writing their names underneath in
French. This method amused Alexander. He began to enjoy the lessons,
which took place once a week, then every day, and finally twice a day.
The child made such rapid progress, his thirst for learning was so evident and his heart so open, that his tutor soon came to have quite a
fatherly affection for him. During his long walks with the little Grand
Duke, Laharpe taught him French words, of course, but what he most
wanted to teach him was French ideas: to move on from vocabulary to
philosophy and then to politics, to inspire the future absolute sovereign
with respect for the will of the people.

On June 10, 1784, Laharpe decided to stake everything on one

throw of the dice. He could no longer be satisfied, he said, with a
subordinate position. If he was not given final authority over the moral
education of the Princes, he would return to Switzerland. He wrote a
long memorandum setting forth his pedagogical ideas and gave it to
General Saltykov for transmission to the Empress. She read it with
astonishment: "One must never forget that Alexander of Macedon,
gifted with wonderful genius and the most brilliant qualities, laid Asia
waste and perpetrated so many horrors solely because he wished to
imitate the heroes of Homer, just as Julius Caesar, taking Alexander as
his model, committed crimes and went so far as to stifle liberty in his
native land."

Further: "Every good citizen needs to know the principles which
govern perfectly constituted societies, but it is particularly necessary for
a prince to be imbued with them from an early age. He will see that
at least there was a time when men were equal, that if things have
changed since, it can never have been in order to deliver up the human
race, bound hand and foot, to the caprices of a single man and that there
have been absolute monarchs sufficiently generous and truthful to
make this public admission to their subjects: 'We take pride in saying
that we exist only for our peoples.' "

Catherine was pleased by this frankness. If Laharpe wrote to her in
this vein, she thought, it was because he considered her to be a liberal
sovereign after his own heart. As a disciple of the Encyclopedists, she
could do no less than agree he was right. In the margin of the memorandum she wrote in a firm hand: "The man who wrote this surely seems
capable of teaching more than just French."

Thus armed with the approval of the Empress, Laharpe thought his
future assured. But a few days later, on June 25, 1784, his protector,
young Alexander Lanskoy, Catherine's latest favorite, died of diphthe-
ria. After having nursed him like a mother, Her Majesty sank into
despair, keeping to her bed, refusing to receive her entourage, renouncing all political activity. It was feared that she might have a
stroke. Laharpe could already see himself packing his bags. But Catherine got a grip on herself, returned to business, and confirmed him in his
new functions. Henceforth he would be charged with molding the
mind of Alexander in such a way that he would always be a man first
and a sovereign second.

From week to week the intimacy between pupil and teacher grew.
Alexander saw everything through Laharpe's eyes, hung on his words,
scarcely breathed apart from him. Later he would say, "All that I am
and all that I may be worth I owe to Monsieur Laharpe." Barely ten

years old, he listened with emotion and gratitude as his young mentor spoke to him of the inviolable dignity of the human person; of love for one's neighbor whatever his class; of the necessity of establishing a republic, with an enlightened, tolerant monarch at its head, one who would be a father to his subjects instead of their oppressor. Alexander delighted in these noble ideas as if they were music. He was not in class but at a concert. And Laharpe, too, let himself be deluded by the harmonious dreams he was composing. Two dreamers seated side by side, invoking Demosthenes, Plutarch, Tacitus, Rousseau, the Encyclo-pedia—but definitely not the Bible. Fundamentally irreligious, Laharpe dictated to his pupil the following definition of Christ: "A Jew from whom the Christian sect took its name."

The other teachers, relegated to the background, railed against the revolutionary Swiss under their breath. Some even went so far as to say that he was trying to make Alexander into a Marcus Aurelius, "when Russia needs a Tiberius or a Genghis Khan." But the chief thing La-harpe's detractors held against him was that he was a foreigner, igno-rant of Russian reality and incapable of opening his pupil's eyes to the country he would one day be called upon to govern. And indeed, in the artificial atmosphere of St. Petersburg and particularly Czarskoye Selo, Alexander was living in a bell jar, far removed from his people, sur-rounded by courtiers with powdered wigs and glittering decorations. He spoke French and English better than Russian, had never traveled, and imagined that nature was as pleasant everywhere as in the imperial gardens. He thought he knew the peasants because he had seen a few of them near the capital, at the entrance to a model village, dressed in their holiday clothes and singing folk songs to welcome him. He pitied them from a distance. They hardly seemed to him to belong to the human species. Besides, Laharpe, the friend of the humble, did not protest against the institution of serfdom. Impassioned in theory, he was prudent in practice. The ruler he wanted for the nation was an "enlight-ened despot"—that was all. They would see about the rest later.

Catherine never tired of praising the tutor she had chosen for Alex-ander. She told him in public, "The maxims you are inculcating in [Alexander] are well suited to strengthen his character; I read them myself with the greatest pleasure and am infinitely satisfied with your work." For his part, Laharpe wrote, "Providence seems at last to have taken pity on the millions of men who inhabit Russia, but it took a Catherine II who wanted her grandsons to be brought up like men." As to his pupil, Laharpe shared Catherine's view that he possessed every talent. And first among them, a talent for pleasing. Whatever he did, his grandmother was ecstatic. "It is a pleasure to play with him," she wrote Grimm. "If you could only see Alexander the shopkeeper, Alexander the cook, Alexander going through all the different classes of men, of trades, painting, papering, mixing and grinding colors, chopping wood, cleaning the furniture, being coachman and groom." One day when he was sick, shivering with fever, he wrapped himself up in a coat and posted himself on guard with a rifle outside the Empress's bedroom. Amused, she asked the meaning of this ceremony, and he replied, "It's a sentry who is dying of cold." Grimm, the captive audience, was immediately informed by letter of this sally. Another time Alexander demonstrated his gifts as an actor in a comedy his grandmother had written, *The Liar*. He took three different roles in the play and performed so brilliantly that Catherine "did not believe her eyes." Not for a second did it cross her mind that such skill in adapting his expression to the demands of a text might reflect a dangerous penchant for artifice and dissimulation.

In the meantime, Maria Feodorovna had given birth to three more children: Alexandra in 1783, Helen in 1784, and Maria in 1786. Since they were girls Catherine hardly paid any attention to them. But she did select a governess for her newest progeny, Madame Charlotte de Lieven, the widow of a major general.* This very dignified, very gentle, very firm person would also help with the education of Alexander and Constantine. The two brothers were united in a merry friendship. They got on as well together in their games as in their studies. When Catherine planned a triumphal journey across the southern provinces of Russia and especially the Crimea, she wanted to take them with her. Their alarmed parents begged her not to do so. She wrote them in French, "Your children belong to you, they belong to me, they belong to the state. From their earliest childhood, I have made it a duty and a pleasure to give them the tenderest care. . . . I reasoned as follows: It will be a consolation for me, when I am far from you, to have them near me. Of the five, three would remain with you. Am I to be the only one who is deprived, in my old age, for six months, of the pleasure of having some member of my family with me?"

Everything was ready for the journey when Constantine fell ill with measles. It was impossible to postpone the departure, so Catherine set

---

*Madame de Lieven, who was to remain at court for half a century, enjoyed the affection of the whole imperial family. For services rendered to the crown she was made Countess, then Princess.

out, furious and anxious, without her two grandsons. At each stage she corresponded with them, and they in turn sent her short, affectionate notes in French and Russian. "My very dear grandmother," wrote Alexander in French, "I feel how much you love me, and I love you as much as you love me. I thank you for having remembered me. I consider it a great honor that you call me friend. Today in the little theater I saw *The Barber of Seville* in Russian, played by great actors, and was greatly amused. I kiss your hands and feet. Your very humble and obedient grandson, Alexander."

When the Empress returned to Czarskoye Selo after more than six months' absence, Alexander and Constantine came to meet her on the road. The reunion was an explosion of laughter and tears. How the two brothers had grown! How handsome the elder was! His tutor Protassov had already noticed signs of puberty in him at the age of twelve. Two years later the same Protassov reported further observations. "For some time," he wrote, "Alexander Pavlovich has been observed to have very imperious physical desires which are reflected both in words and in nocturnal dreams. They seem to increase every time he has had private conversations with agreeable women." Informed immediately of these "nocturnal dreams" that troubled her grandson, Catherine sent word to her representatives abroad to inspect the stock of marriageable princesses. But how were they to find a young person worthy of this Prince with the crystal soul? "He is a deliciousissimus individual," she wrote to Grimm. Secretly, Protassov made a more discriminating judgment of his adolescent charge: "One observes in Alexander Pavlovich much intelligence and many natural gifts, but also an extreme laziness and a great indifference to events. Not only does he take no interest in the affairs of the country, the study of which would demand some effort, but he shows an aversion for reading the news and knowing what is going on in Europe. In short, his only desire is to enjoy himself and to live happily in idleness. Unfortunate dispositions for a man in his situation."

Nevertheless, indolence, insouciance, and a taste for pleasure were not the chief faults of this young man who had an imperial grandmother hovering over him and twelve tutors dogging his steps. The older he grew, the more he recognized the necessity of tacking every minute between the reefs of the false universe in which he was called upon to live. Frankness had never been his strong point. He very quickly understood that here it would be the ruin of him. The sumptuous court around him buzzed with lies, intrigues, and well-nursed hatreds. To avoid making enemies, he smiled at everyone, shared the most contra-

dictory opinions with equal graciousness, flattered people he would
have liked to slap in the face. Before an ever-larger audience, he continued to play *The Liar*.

Still imbued with the theories of Laharpe, Alexander witnessed the
arrival of the first French emigrés fleeing the Revolution. In their presence he could have defended the ideas of liberty and equality so dear
to his tutor and to himself. But he didn't want to hurt their feelings. So
he listened sympathetically while they recounted the trials they had
been through, pitied them sincerely, echoed their indignation as mo-
narchists. Some of them became his friends. With them he went boating
on the Neva, rode, swam in the ponds of Czarskoye Selo. According to
Count Esterhazy, they wore for these aquatic sports "a woolen costume
enveloping the whole body, and over this a very loose frock coat, likewise of wool"—the whole outfit having been especially designed and
ordered by the Empress. After he had left these garrulous, frivolous
Frenchmen, Alexander would return to his dear Laharpe and there, in
private, he would rediscover all his republican ardor. Once again, in low
voices, teacher and disciple would celebrate the era of justice and light
that was beginning for France now that she was delivered from the
tyrant.

But more and more emigrés poured into court, and the news of the
Terror discouraged the few liberals in Russia. Outraged by the excesses
of the Jacobins, Catherine herself recognized that the Encyclopedists,
of whom she had been so enamored in her youth, had set minds on fire
and that now the whole earth might go up in flames; therefore reasonable states must exert all their strength to extinguish the conflagration.
To begin with, she had the bust of Voltaire exiled to the attic. After the
execution of Louis XVI, she took to her bed, sick with indignation. She
recalled her subjects from Paris, closed Russian ports to French ships,
broke diplomatic relations with France, ordered all French residing in
Russia to take an oath of loyalty to her person, granted royal honors to
Louis XVI's younger brother, the Comte d'Artois, when he visited St.
Petersburg, offered asylum to the Prince de Condé, and contributed
funds to the army of the emigrés. Nevertheless, she kept her head and
refused to let herself be drawn into a war against France to reestablish
the monarchy. Prussia and Austria could see to that, while her own
troops were busy ensuring the definitive dismemberment of Poland.

At court Alexander heard nothing but venomous talk about the
France that was ruled by the guillotine. Laharpe, the personification of
gentleness and honesty, suddenly found himself with blood on his
hands. Although he had drawn in his horns considerably, he stood open

to the jibes of the emigrés and their Russian friends. One day Grand
Duke Paul came up to his son Alexander and, speaking of the permanently ensconced tutor, asked, "Is that filthy Jacobin still with you?"
Alexander dared not protest. He had to humor both his father, who
detested Laharpe, and his grandmother, who protected the tutor notwithstanding the crimes of the sans-culottes. Had she not recently told
the alleged tool of Robespierre, "Be a Jacobin, a republican, or whatever you wish; I know you are an honest man, and that is enough for
me"?

Moreover, if Grand Duke Paul had an aversion for Laharpe, he had
an even greater aversion for the Empress. Over time the animosity
between the son and the mother had grown so great that by mutual
consent they avoided occasions to meet. Caught between these two rival
entities, Alexander judged both coldly, in silence: In his father he found
an almost insane despotism, military discipline, obtuse harshness, madness; in his grandmother, majestic authority and licentious behavior.

As soon as he was old enough to take an interest in the life of the
grownups, Alexander understood the role of the favorites in the Empress's wake. This aging woman consumed young men at a furious rate.
To be Her Majesty's lover was equivalent to having an appointment at
court. One after another, men of handsome appearance succeeded
each other as minister of her heart and bed. She changed them as she
might have changed an official who had completed his period of service.
Some, like Potemkin, had dazzled her by their fiery spirit, their magnificence, their intelligence; others, like Lanskoy, had melted her by their
refined manners and delicate sentiments; still others, like the most
recent, Plato Zubov, had subjugated her by a charming profile, an
insolent carriage, and the radiant warmth of their skin between the
sheets. With Plato Zubov she felt, in her own words, "like a fly that has
been numbed by the cold and suddenly comes back to life."

Zubov was twenty-two years old, Catherine was over sixty. Blinded
by passion, she experienced once again the illusion of being loved for
herself. Overnight the new favorite, loaded with gifts, became the most
important personage in the empire. His functions were not limited to
pillow games. Very quickly he extended his overweening talents to
affairs of state. His antechamber was crowded with illustrious men
humbly come to beg favors. They laughed at his witticisms, bent their
backs as he passed, shamelessly entreated his protection.

Fourteen years old at the time when Plato Zubov began his ascent,
Alexander observed his grandmother's love-struck looks as she played
with her fan at table or withdrew to her apartments, heavy and short

of breath, Zubov at her heels. He was revolted by this senile passion, as by the upstart's growing arrogance. But faithful to his determination to remain neutral, he gave no hint of his anger. He even resigned himself to being Plato Zubov's companion on walks, at picnics, in parlor games. All the entertainments of the court brought them together, and they laughed side by side under the benevolent eye of the Empress, who was happy to see the cordial relations between her grandson and her lover. It was a family idyll. Even the virtuous Laharpe had no objections.

Actually, Laharpe had no cause for concern. The amorous excesses of Her Majesty did no damage to the innocence of the young Grand Duke. While Alexander judged his grandmother severely and dreamed at night of the pretty women he had met during the day, his purity was intact. Dreams were sufficient for him. His grandmother, surprised, wondered whether she should congratulate herself upon his chastity or fear that it was a sign of impotence. The Swedish envoy Jennings wrote to his government: "[Alexander] has retained all the natural graces of his age, and the flower of innocence which is first among them all."

Catherine no longer doubted that it was time to initiate her grandson. But she conceived of that initiation only within marriage. And remembering her own German origin, she thought the only safe match would be with a German girl. The information she had been able to obtain indicated that the court of Baden offered the best prospects for finding Alexander the ideal wife. She therefore instructed Count Rumiantsev, her diplomatic representative in southern Germany, to enter into negotiations on the subject. He went to Karlsruhe, examined attentively the two unmarried Princesses of Baden, and chose the elder, Louise. But she was still only a child. They would wait until she turned thirteen, then bring her to Russia, with her sister Frederika, on the pretext of a simple visit of protocol.

At last the little girls set out, terrified at the idea of meeting the Empress, who was said to be so imposing. "We await the two Princesses of Baden," wrote Catherine, in French, to Grimm. "One is thirteen, the other eleven. You can well imagine that in our country we do not marry children so young; that is not the purpose for the present, but I am providing for the future. In the meantime, they will become accustomed to us and to our ways and customs. As for our man [Alexander], he has no idea of all that; his heart is still innocent and it is a diabolical trick that I am playing on him, for I am leading him into temptation."

On October 31, 1792, the two travelers, exhausted by a long and difficult journey, arrived in St. Petersburg and fell at the feet of the

Empress. At the first glance Catherine judged Louise totally captivating in her childish freshness. That very evening she said to her private secretary Khrapovitsky, "The more one sees of the elder Princess of Baden the more pleasing she is. One cannot see her without being charmed." And the next day she wrote to Grimm: "Monsieur Alexander would be hard to please indeed if the elder escapes him." The members of the Empress's entourage shared her enthusiasm. Grand Duchess Maria Feodorovna, Alexander's mother, wrote to the Empress, "Not only do I find her pretty, but there is a charm about her whole figure that would induce the most indifferent creature to love her." "Her features were of a remarkable delicacy," said the Comtesse de Choiseul-Gouffier. "The profile of a Greek cameo, large blue eyes, a perfect oval-shaped face, hair of an adorable blond. A certain touching languor in her face and manners, eyes that were at once lively and full of feeling, a voice whose sweetness stole into one's soul." Countess Golovina wrote in the same vein in her *Souvenirs:* "A charming figure, ash-blond hair falling down the back of her neck in curls, a milk-white complexion, rose petals on her cheeks, a very pleasing mouth. There is something infinitely attractive, almost disturbing, in the sweet, animated expression of her blue eyes, almond-shaped and framed in black eyelashes and eyebrows." And the Swedish ambassador Stedingk noted laconically in a dispatch: "She is very pretty, with a sweet, interesting face, taller and more well formed than girls generally are at her age." Catherine thought there was no doubt that, faced with this perfection of nature, even Alexander the chaste would be set on fire.

Not so. Placed in Louise's presence, he remained icy. The young man's mother was anxious and wrote again to Her Majesty, "On seeing Alexander, she turned pale and began to tremble; as for Alexander, he was very silent and confined himself to looking at her, but he did not speak to her, although the conversation was general."

Alexander understood very well that his grandmother was setting a trap for him. All eyes converged on him and on this girl who was obviously intended for him. The face of every courtier showed the same tender sentiment, the same hope. Under such scrutiny, the adolescent was paralyzed by shyness. He would have preferred to choose the object of his affections himself and to contemplate her secretly, from a distance. His high birth prohibited so natural a pleasure. Everyone around the young couple was whispering and going into raptures. At last Alexander made up his mind to speak a few words. The girl replied. It was clear that she was by no means a fool. Was this the beginning of an idyll? On November 4, 1792, Catherine, radiant, said to her secretary

Khrapovitsky, "The Grand Duke shows every sign of loving the elder Princess, but the fiancé is shy and does not yet dare to approach her openly. As for her, she is very clever and knowing; she is nubile at thirteen."

A few days later it was Alexander's mother who celebrated victory in a short note in French addressed to the Empress: "I have the honor to inform you that in his letter of yesterday Monsieur Alexander tells us that 'he liked the amiable Princess of Baden more from day to day; that she had a certain sweetness, a certain modesty that were enchanting, and that one would have to be made of stone not to love her.' Those are the very expressions of my son; so I dare confess, my very dear mother, that I judge the satisfaction that this admission will give you by that which it caused me. . . . Our young man is becoming truly attached and is beginning to recognize the full value of the gift you mean to make him."

As for little Louise, she had made a close examination of Alexander out of the corner of her eye, while pretending to be looking elsewhere, and sent a detailed report, in French, to her mother: "Grand Duke Alexander is very tall and quite handsome; his legs and feet are especially well shaped, although his feet are rather big, but in proportion to his height. He has light brown hair, blue eyes that are not very large, but not small either, fine teeth, a charming complexion, a nice, straight nose. So far as his mouth is concerned, he looks very much like the Empress." Soon she began to take an interest in her own appearance, paying attention to the way her hair was dressed and rejoicing when she received as a gift from the Empress a gown "of purple velvet, embroidered in gold, with a skirt of straw-colored satin," which enabled her to shine beside the Grand Duke at the ball.

Catherine, on the watch for the least smile, the slightest friendly glance exchanged between the two young people, sent Grimm regular bulletins from the field: "Monsieur Alexander is behaving very sensibly and prudently. . . . He is beginning to be a little in love with the elder Princess of Baden, and I will not swear he is not perfectly repaid. . . . Never was there a pair more suited to each other, beautiful as the light of day, full of grace and wit; everyone takes pleasure in encouraging their budding love." But if she was touched by the girl, she was even more moved by her grandson. In the presence of Louise, she thought, he shone in a new light. Behind the adolescent, the enraptured grandmother suddenly discovered the man. She burst out in the enthusiasm of a woman in love. "You would be enchanted and astonished," she wrote Grimm in French, "to see this tall, superbly handsome, fine young man. Oh! what promise is there, what a personification of candor and depth, what health and principles, with an unequaled desire to do well! Oh! what an excellent fellow! Everyone is mad about him, and one really *can* be mad about him. He is the favorite of my heart, he knows that perfectly well and continues on his road. His head leans slightly forward, but it is a beautiful head! As soon as one sees him one forgets that the young man does not hold it absolutely straight but bends it a little forward. It has been called to his attention many times, yet when he dances or rides horseback and carries his head very erect, he recalls the Apollo Belvedere to all those who have had the honor of seeing the latter. He has the same nobility and grace, and for a young man of fourteen that is really a great deal. But enough, I must not say too much."

Catherine was not the only one who found Alexander a "superbly handsome, fine young man." Everyone who came near him agreed that he had a rare elegance of manners, that he was tall, slender, with noble features, an enchanting smile, and gentle blue eyes. The slightest emotion brought color into his face, which was of an almost feminine refinement. Even the spiteful Count Rostopchin wrote, in French, in a letter to Count Simon Vorontzov, ambassador to London: "Grand Duke Alexander, one may say it confidently, has not his equal in the world. His soul is even more beautiful than his body; never were the moral and physical aspects more perfect in one individual." As for his devoted tutor Protassov, he wept on hearing Alexander's confession and noted in his journal: "He told me frankly how agreeable the Princess was, that he had already been in love with our Russian women, but that his feelings for them were filled with fire and vague desires . . . with no other purpose than to delight in the sight of them and in their conversation. On the contrary, he feels for the Princess something special, composed of deference, tender friendship, and an ineffable pleasure in her company, something more satisfying, more calm, but incomparably more agreeable than those impulses of passion; in his eyes, she is more worthy of love than any other person here."

And little by little Alexander really was melting. He was yielding at the same time to Louise's charms and to the desire to gratify those around him. For once his grandmother and his parents seemed to agree about something; he was not going to disappoint them by opposing their wishes. "Alexander is beginning to fall in love with the Princess, insofar as his age [fifteen] and his calm nature allow," noted the Swedish ambassador Stedingk. "He has done violence to his timidity by writing a few words of declaration to his intended, and she has written him in the same vein and in the same tone."

Now that the affair was so well launched, it was at last possible to speak openly of marriage. The official consent of Louise's parents reached the court in January 1793. Like Catherine before her, the girl immediately began to study Russian and to listen to the lessons of a priest who came to prepare her for her new religion. On May 9 she was baptized Orthodox and traded her Protestant name Louise for the more Russian name Elizabeth Alexeyevna. The next day the engagement took place, and the Empress herself presided over the exchange of rings. After the ceremony she wrote in French to Louise's mother, "Everyone said that it was two angels who were being betrothed; one could not find a lovelier sight than this fiancé of fifteen and his fiancée of fourteen; besides, they are no little in love. As soon as the Princess was betrothed she received the title of Grand Duchess."

That evening there was a great dinner at court. Alexander and the new Elizabeth were enthroned under a canopy. The banquet was followed by a ball. The assembled courtiers, who had grown blasé from a surfeit of pleasures and intrigues, benevolently observed the movements of this young couple, who seemed to radiate purity. Watching them turn to the sound of the music, each had a sense of nostalgia for his or her own lost illusions. Baron von Goltz, the Prussian ambassador, wrote in French to his King, "Since I came to Petersburg, I have never seen the Empress show such great satisfaction as on the day of her grandson's betrothal; and she said she was enjoying a rare happiness. It is true that the young couple are in every respect worthy of the general admiration they inspire, for with their beauty they combine a gentleness which must win all hearts. Notwithstanding the great youth and timidity of this Princess, she performed perfectly, and the persons who come near her assure us that she does not lack character. Her sister, who is more lively, is pleasing and amusing, but it is said she will return home before the wedding."

As the days passed, Alexander permitted himself a few intimacies that astounded Elizabeth. The first kisses—of a purely Christian significance—were exchanged on the occasion of the Easter celebrations, with the authorization of the Empress and of Countess Shuvalova, Grand Mistress of the court. After Easter Alexander tried it again, touching her lightly with his lips. Elizabeth, both delighted and troubled, wrote to her mother, "When we were alone in my room, he kissed me and I kissed him. And now I think he will always do so. . . . You cannot imagine how odd it seemed to me to kiss a man who was neither my father nor my uncle. And what seemed even stranger to me, was that it didn't feel like when papa used to kiss me, he always scratched me with his beard."

Toward the end of summer, Frederika, Elizabeth's sister, left for Karlsruhe, and Elizabeth was in despair: "I shall be alone, alone, absolutely alone, without anyone to whom I can communicate my private thoughts." Alexander wept with her. He too felt very much alone. Now that the marriage had become inevitable, he wondered whether he had been right to yield. But how could one resist this terrifying grandmother with the coaxing smile and the steely glance?

For the moment, the court was preoccupied only with the festivities surrounding the signing of the peace with Turkey. These came to an end on September 15 with a display of fireworks. Immediately afterward came the solemn announcement of the wedding. It was celebrated on September 28, 1793, in the great church of the Winter Palace. At the last minute, some new dispute had broken out between the Empress and her son, Grand Duke Paul, and he had refused to attend the ceremony. It had taken all the insistence of his wife, Grand Duchess Maria Feodorovna, to make him change his decision. Standing under the nave in the first row of the family, he wore a sullen, scowling expression. It pained Alexander that this enmity was so blatantly displayed. He wanted everyone around him to be happy, but all he saw was jealousy, suspicion, calculation, muffled hatred.

For the occasion Alexander wore a silver caftan of glazed brocade, with diamond buttons, and the ribbon of the Order of St. Andrew across his chest. The bride's gown was made of the same silver glazed brocade and strewn with diamonds and pearls. Grand Duke Constantine held the ceremonial crown over the head of his brother Alexander, and Prince Bezborodko held the one over Elizabeth. After the ceremony the cannon of the Admiralty and the Fortress of St. Peter and St. Paul boomed out salvos of honor, while bells pealed in all the churches. The carillons rang for three days, the celebrations lasted two weeks. On the day following the wedding Elizabeth, still astonished by the event, wrote to her mother, "Grand Duke Alexander, or rather my husband (what a strange word, I cannot get used to it), wants to add a few words [to my letter]." "It is the union of Cupid and Psyche," wrote Catherine to the Prince de Ligne. Rostopchin noted, with more perspicacity, "If only this marriage does no harm to the Grand Duke. He is so young and his wife is so beautiful!"

II

GRANDMOTHER, SON, AND GRANDSON

As soon as Alexander was married, he felt the intoxication of early emancipation. It seemed to him that in taking a wife he had crossed the imaginary boundary that separated childhood, which was full of demanding studies, from adulthood, which was entirely given over to pleasures. For whatever it was worth, Laharpe continued to teach him, but the schedule of lessons was no longer respected. At Czarskoye Selo a chateau was being built for the young couple. In the Winter Palace sumptuous apartments were arranged for them. Pink, white, and gold predominated in the paneling and hangings of the bedchamber. The blue and silver drawing room had wide windows giving on the Neva, where boats slept at anchor. The Grand Duke and his wife were surrounded by a personal court, dominated by the scheming Countess Shuvalova and filled with frivolous, idle people who thought only of showing off and amusing themselves. Swept up in the whirlwind, Elizabeth wrote to her mother, "We are constantly busy doing nothing." And again: "We are spending this week dancing; since Monday there has not

been a day when we have not danced. On Tuesday we gave a ball, we
even danced 'walsers.' Yesterday there was a masked ball at the home
of one of the Empress's first ladies; this evening there is to be an amateur performance at the Hermitage."

Completely absorbed by the joys of this new life, Alexander slipped
into laziness. He no longer had either the leisure or the taste for reading. When Laharpe would recommend some serious work from which
he might benefit, he would promise to plunge into it that very evening,
then immediately after forget all about it. He was more interested in
clothes, gossip, and games than in the dull pages of books of history,
legislation, or politics. He paid great attention to stylish dress and liked
to strike refined attitudes. He took a fatuous pleasure in contemplating
himself in the mirror, his youthful narcissism blossoming under the
compliments received from every side. Disturbed by all this frivolity,
General Protassov noted in his journal: "During the months of October
and November, the conduct of Alexander Pavlovich has not been what
I had hoped. He clings to childish, especially military, trifles, and following the example of his brother he indulges in his dressing room in
unseemly games with his servants. These games, which are appropriate
to his age but unsuitable to his station, are witnessed by his wife. The
Grand Duke's conduct is equally childish with regard to her; he shows
a great attachment for her, spoiled by a certain brusqueness which is
unsuitable to the delicacy of her sex."

This "brusqueness" reflected Alexander's lack of experience as a
lover. Married too soon to a child too young, he did not know either how
to satisfy her or how to take pleasure in her. She for her part, with a
romantic soul and unawakened senses, was scarcely capable of responding to his caresses. Moreover, Alexander was not a passionate lover. He
was too much in love with himself to take an interest in the reactions
of the good little girl whom the Empress had slipped into his bed. If he
often sought the company of other women, it was primarily to see
himself mirrored in their eyes. He needed their admiration to retain
confidence in his own personal charm. His attentions to them went no
further. When he came back to his wife he willingly recognized that she
was affectionate, refined, intelligent, cultivated. No one at court could
hold a candle to her. But those very qualities that should have attracted
him disenchanted him in the end. When he was alone with Elizabeth
he didn't know what to say to her; he was bored. The courtiers who had
celebrated this quasi-mythological marriage now noticed that it was
already threatened with the worst disorders. Whatever the Empress
thought, the grand-ducal union, so often cited as an example, was hardly
better than the others—an observation that, given natural spitefulness,

gladdened the hearts of all who were in the same situation. They soon set about hastening the breakup of the couple. Countess Shuvalova took it upon herself to procure for both husband and wife tempting opportunities for infidelity.

The most dangerous trap was laid for Elizabeth by the Empress's own favorite, Plato Zubov. Weary of his nocturnal services to the Empress, he imagined other adventures. How could a man so long accustomed to gamy fare fail to be enticed by the tart freshness of the Grand Duchess? Convinced that his functions guaranteed him impunity, he did not hesitate to court Elizabeth in public. At the Empress's card table he made such eyes at her and heaved such sighs that everyone noticed. Elizabeth gently dismissed him. He affected despair, spending his days sprawled on a sofa and ordering his musicians to play melancholy airs to feed his despondency. At the same time he delegated Countess Shuvalova to go to the Grand Duchess and persuade her to yield. Pressed by so powerful a suitor, the young woman showed extraordinary tact in cutting short his compliments, avoiding a showdown, and maintaining her determination with a smiling face. Nor did Alexander, watching Plato Zubov maneuver around his wife, dare to put the Empress's all powerful lover squarely in his place. Although as a young husband he was outraged, he still preferred accommodation—anything rather than the scandal of an open quarrel. Tormented by anxiety, he wrote, in French, to his friend Count Victor Kochubey, the Russian ambassador to Constantinople: "We would have been very happy with my wife and we are still happy between ourselves, without Countess Shuvalova, who unfortunately has been placed with my wife. . . . Count Zubov has been in love with my wife since the first summer of my marriage, that is, for a year and some months. Imagine what an embarrassing situation that must be for my wife, who, really, behaves like an angel. But you must admit that it is exceedingly awkward to know how to conduct oneself toward Zubov. . . . If you treat him well, it is as if you approved of his love, and if you treat him coldly to discourage him, the Empress, who is ignorant of the situation, may be offended that you are not sufficiently honoring a man whom she favors. It is extremely difficult to keep to the middle course, as is necessary, especially before a public as malicious and as ready to do spiteful things as ours."

In truth, the Empress could not have been ignorant of her favorite's feelings toward the Grand Duchess, but she found this trifling infatuation diverting. She saw only its amusing side. A good lesson in life for her Alexander, who was still only a green boy. Catherine herself was almost ready to serve as go-between. "The Zodiac," as Plato Zubov was nicknamed, confided things to her that entertained and aroused her.

Only when he went too far did Catherine call him to heel; then he would slink back to his kennel, afraid of being dismissed.

In any event, it was an ill-chosen moment to try to seduce Elizabeth. It was said that she was pregnant by the Grand Duke. The young woman was angered by the public attention paid to her belly, especially since the news was false. "The Empress is firmly persuaded that I am pregnant; that gives her great pleasure," she wrote to her friend Princess Golovina. "Thanks to my dear husband, the Grand Duke senior believes it also; judge then what a shame it will be for me when everyone knows that that is not the case. And also, how awkward it will be: The Empress has told the Zodiac, who is consequently convinced of it; if I tell the Empress now that it is not so, she will repeat it to him. . . . You must confess that it is disagreeable for this Zodiac to be informed of everything that concerns me. And why must the Empress report everything to him? . . . He asks such stupid questions, which do not concern him in the least, on this subject, that I cannot abide him. What business has he to meddle in the state of my health?"

When the Empress learned that she had rejoiced too soon, she was keenly disappointed. Her daughter-in-law, Grand Duchess Maria Feodorovna, had shown from the beginning that she was an admirable brood mare; why couldn't her grandson's wife also produce the great-grandchildren she had a right to expect? What a pity for the dynasty! Who was at fault? Could it be that Elizabeth was sterile? That Alexander was impotent?

Increasingly obsessed by the question of who would succeed her, Catherine settled firmly on the idea of keeping the throne from her son Paul, whom she judged unworthy to inherit it, and substituting her grandson Alexander, of whom she expected miracles. But she still had to secure the consent of the chief interested party. Thanks to Laharpe, of course, Alexander was steeped in the liberal theories that Catherine had once admired but now rejected with horror. Had he not even been so irresponsible recently as to extol the provisions of the French Constitution before an audience of astounded courtiers? However, the Empress knew from experience that someone could profess democratic sentiments and at the same time act like a potentate. It was in fact not Alexander's political opinions that disturbed her but his reluctance to exercise power.

She was correct in thinking that he lacked all ambition to be a monarch. Brought up at the court, Alexander had come to detest it. Not only did he hate the intrigues, but he could no longer abide the woman who ruled over this universe of duplicity, servility, and envy. He condemned everything about his grandmother, the old woman in love and the despotic sovereign. To be sure, he showed every sign of respect and affection when he was with her. But behind her back he often gave vent to his anger and contempt. His brother Constantine joined in with unbelievably offensive remarks. Verbally the two ripped to shreds the authoritarian grandmother before whom the empire trembled. Writing to his friend Kochubey, Alexander made a long analysis of his difficult situation at court: "Yes, my dear friend, I repeat that I am not at all satisfied with my position; it is much too brilliant for a man of my temperament who cares only for tranquillity and peace. I am not suited to court life; I suffer every time I have to appear in public, and it makes me sick to see the things people stoop to every day to obtain distinctions that I wouldn't have given three sous for. I feel unhappy to be among people whom I should not wish to have as servants and who enjoy the most prominent positions here, like Zubov, Passek, Bariatinsky, the two Saltykovs, Miatlev, and a bunch of others who are not even worth naming. . . . In short, my dear friend, I feel that I am not at all made for the position which I occupy at present, and still less for the one which is reserved for me in future and which I have sworn to myself to renounce, one way or another. . . . Our affairs are in incredible disorder, there is corruption on every side, all the departments are badly administered. . . . My plan is that once I have renounced this difficult position (I cannot tell when that will be), I shall settle with my wife on the banks of the Rhine, where I shall live quietly as a private person, finding happiness in the society of my friends and in the study of nature."

With his new confidant Count Adam Czartoryski, a Polish gentleman who had been sent as a hostage to the court of St. Petersburg after the partition of Poland, Alexander was even more violent in his attacks on his grandmother's politics. During a long walk along the paths of the Palace of Taurida, the young Grand Duke declared, to the astonishment and delight of his interlocutor, that he hated despotism, that all men had a right to liberty, and that despite its excesses the French Revolution had accomplished something beneficial. Going further, he pitied Poland, which had been unjustly crushed, and said that he thought of Kosciusko as of a spotless hero and that he hoped for the rebirth of that noble country.* Such words were a total repudiation of the dream of

---

*Thaddeus Kosciusko, a Polish general who had helped defeat the British during the American Revolution, was the hero of insurrections against Russia. He had been taken prisoner by the Russians after the battle of Maciejowice in 1794 and brought to St. Petersburg.

Russian hegemony that had inspired Catherine throughout her reign. Reporting this conversation in his *Mémoires,* Adam Czartoryski concluded, "I confess that when I came away I was beside myself, deeply moved, not knowing whether it was a dream or reality. What! A Prince of Russia, the successor to Catherine, her beloved grandson and pupil, whom she would have wished to reign after her instead of her son, the Prince who people said would be the one to continue Catherine's work —that Prince repudiated and detested his grandmother's principles, he rejected Russia's hateful policy, loved justice and liberty passionately, pitied Poland and would have wished to see her happy! Was it not a miracle?"

Of course Czartoryski took these generous statements of Alexander's for true coin. And no doubt at the moment, talking to his friend, the Grand Duke was sincere. But he did not forget that he was addressing a Polish nobleman whose patriotic feelings had been wounded; to please him he overdid his indignation a little.

He never dared speak that way in front of Catherine. When she announced to him later that she meant to name him heir to the throne instead of his father, he merely stammered that he did not wish to rule. She insisted; he was evasive. He was not made, he said, for greatness and authority. His dream was family life in some quiet province, even perhaps abroad. If she loved him, Her Majesty should help him to leave the court. Wounded by this response, Catherine tried an indirect attack. She summoned Laharpe and instructed him to put pressure on his pupil to accept the crown. Grand Duke Paul would be excluded from the succession. The virtuous Swiss refused to lend himself to this immoral maneuver that would benefit a son to the detriment of his father. The Empress was shocked by such lack of comprehension on the part of a man she had loaded with benefactions. She suddenly remembered that he was a Jacobin, that he defended ideas she had abandoned, that his presence in the palace angered many people. After a few days' reflection, she let Laharpe know that she no longer required his services. He could pack his bags. Greatly shaken, the teacher broke the news to his pupil, who threw his arms around his neck. Together they wept over the cruelty of their fate. Alone in his room again, Alexander, overwhelmed with misfortune, gave vent to his grief in a letter: "Farewell, my dear friend. How much it costs me to write that word! Do not forget that you leave behind a man who is devoted to you, who cannot sufficiently express his gratitude to you, who owes you everything except his birth!"

Before leaving Russia, Laharpe, at Alexander's request, drew up a long "Instruction" on the best way for a prince to perform his functions with integrity. This document contained a little of everything—advice about hygiene and about morality, about government and correct eating habits. Of course Alexander forgot these recommendations as soon as he had read them, but he retained the greatest respect for their author.

Fortunately, the idle bustle of the court he condemned gradually distracted Alexander from his grief. Catherine tenaciously returned to the charge. He must accept the crown, she said, because if it fell to his father, that would be the end of the liberal dream for Russia. But if it was Alexander who ascended the throne, what benefits he could bring to the country by wisely applying Laharpe's precepts! To engrave these words in her grandson's head, Catherine confirmed them in writing. This time Alexander was shaken. But he was not one to give a definitive answer. Without either accepting or refusing, he sent Catherine a highly ambiguous letter, in French: "Your Imperial Majesty, never shall I be able to express my gratitude for the confidence with which Your Majesty has been pleased to honor me and her kindness in deigning to write with her own hand a document clarifying the other papers. I hope that Your Majesty will see by my eagerness to merit these precious kindnesses that I recognize their full value. It is true that I shall never be able sufficiently to repay, even with my blood, everything that Your Majesty has condescended to do for me and will be pleased to do in future. These papers clearly confirm all the reflections which Your Majesty was so gracious as to communicate to me not long ago and which, if I may be permitted to say so, could not be more correct. Placing once again at the feet of Your Imperial Majesty the sentiments of my liveliest gratitude, I take the liberty of being, with the most profound respect and the most inviolable attachment, Your Imperial Majesty's very humble and submissive subject and grandson—Alexander."

On reading this missive, Catherine would imagine that she had convinced her grandson, but if the letter fell into the hands of Paul, he would not be able to deduce from it that his son wanted to steal the scepter from him. Besides, to cover himself completely, Alexander also wrote to his father, addressing him with the title "Imperial Majesty." He would keep an equal balance between the two powers that watched over his destiny, protecting himself on both sides and waiting for events to decide for him.

Lately the two young Grand Dukes had drawn closer to their father. Paul, who refused to frequent Catherine's court, had transformed his estate into a veritable Prussian fiefdom. In the middle of a great park not far from St. Petersburg, the Palace of Gatchina rose, dark and severe. The buildings that surrounded it—stables, kennels, hospital, warehouses, workshops, barracks—had a Germanic look. The soldiers wore the German uniform, high boots, gloves up to the elbows, enormous three-cornered hats, oiled and braided hair. There were two thousand four hundred of them. Subjected to an iron discipline, they spent most of their time parading and drilling. The least fault in uniform or alignment was punished with a flogging. To Paul's mind, a strong army could only be composed of automatons. In a soldier, every human quality had to be combated and broken. In fact, the Gatchina troops were largely composed of rejects from the regular army. Most of the officers had been dismissed from their respective regiments for misconduct. They had limited minds and thick skins, and their chief virtues were that they would endure any insult and obey the most absurd orders without argument. "There were quite a number of vengeful spirits among them," wrote the memorialist Viegel. "From the marshes of Gatchina they watched jealously those who proudly marched along the road to glory, and already they were preparing their revenge." To Paul, who had chosen Frederick II of Prussia as his model, government was inseparable from the sound of fifes and drums. For any trifle the cannon thundered, and the successive salvos startled the women in the château.

Curiously enough, Alexander was attracted by this virile atmosphere. He and his brother would visit his parents three or four times a week. When he passed through the black-, white-, and red-striped gate that marked the border of the paternal domain, he changed worlds. At Czarskoye Selo, wearing a coat of the French fashion and buckled shoes, he conversed amiably with his grandmother and smiled approvingly when she made fun of Paul's "mania for soldiering." At Gatchina, buttoned up to the chin in his Prussian uniform, with spurs on his heels and a cane raised in his hand, he attended the endless drilling of the troops and echoed his father when Paul fulminated against the Empress's policies. He had often wondered why there was such hatred between his father and grandmother. There were some who whispered that Paul was an illegitimate son, not the child of Catherine's husband, Grand Duke Peter, but of her lover, Count Sergei Saltykov, and that consequently all the dynastic lines were in confusion.* Paul could not forgive

---

*Catherine's *Mémoires* support this thesis.

Catherine for having allowed this rumor to gain credence. He also resented the fact that she had at least accepted, if not directed, the conspiracy that had brought her to the throne in 1762. He even held her responsible for the murder of his father, because she had not seen fit to punish his assassins. He thought of himself as a second Hamlet, condemned to live side by side with a crowned criminal. To confirm a paternity that certain persons dared to question, he made a point of displaying, like his putative father, Grand Duke Peter, an inordinate passion for Prussian militarism. This passion only grew with the passage of time. He rejoiced to discover it in his sons Alexander and Constantine.

Actually, it was no strain for Alexander to join in his father's military pursuits. What boy doesn't love to play soldier? At Gatchina he swelled with importance, taught idiotic recruits how to handle a musket, keep in step, form a square, march and countermarch. Every day they made make-believe war. Alexander was indefatigable at the game. He who was so refined, so fastidious, liked nothing better than the cheerful uproar of the barracks and the foul language of the officers on duty. Having so long immersed himself in Laharpe's pleasant visions of liberty, equality, and fraternity, he now took pleasure in bullying the soldiers under his command. He would look on unmoved as one or another was beaten for clumsiness or negligence. From one extreme to the other, he gave free rein to all the contradictions of his nature, thus deluding himself with the notion that he was a "complete man." Fascinated by artillery, he liked to stand next to the cannons. He attended firing practice so assiduously that he became deaf in the left ear. "What makes the Grand Duke disagreeable in society," noted Rostopchin, "is his deafness. One has to shout, for he hears nothing with one ear." Despite this mishap, Alexander continued to be infatuated with the army. Like Constantine, he was proud to belong to the rough military fraternity surrounding his father. He would say with a superior air, "We Gatchina men. . . ." "The Grand Duke is surrounded by such people that the most honest man among them would deserve to be hanged without trial," wrote Rostopchin to Count Vorontzov. And Czartoryski wrote in his *Mémoires:* "The minute details of military service and the habit of attaching extreme importance to them warped Grand Duke Alexander's mind: He acquired an incurable taste for them."

A twenty-four-year-old captain, Alexis Arakcheyev, became the young Prince's confidant. What was it that attracted Alexander to this thin, dry man with the face of a monkey, whose gray eyes, set deep in their sockets, shone with cunning and ferocity? The incarnation of discipline, zeal, and hardness of heart, Arakcheyev seemed to his new friend to be a peerless leader. In his presence Alexander felt that he was covered not with tender skin but with a tanned hide; impervious to all human feeling; ready for the fierce battles life held in store for him.

But how delightful it was after the long maneuvers to spend the evening with the family in the chateau. When the young Grand Dukes returned with dusty uniforms and faces glowing from the fresh air, they would be joined by Elizabeth and by Julie of Saxe-Coburg, whom Constantine had just married. Elizabeth had become even more beautiful as she grew to womanhood. "Her complexion was not highly colored, but of a pallor quite in harmony with the expression of her face, which was of angelic sweetness," wrote Madame Vigée-Lebrun.* "Her ash-blond hair floated over her neck and forehead. She wore a white tunic caught by a belt that was tied negligently around a waist as slim and supple as a nymph's." Paul and Maria Feodorovna presided over the reunion. Through the open windows all the scents and sounds of evening came to them. Lilacs gave off their balmy fragrance; frogs croaked in the nearby ponds; the company played with the children or talked peacefully of warfare. Then the conversation would drift toward mystical matters. The violent Paul had a predilection for religious questions. He felt very close to the Freemasons and the Martinists.† During these rambling conversations Alexander, who had been raised in religious skepticism, nonetheless felt an agreeable attraction to the mysteries of the beyond. He repudiated the recent actions of the Empress: She had dissolved the Masonic lodges because they were suspected of revolutionary intrigue, imprisoned the great mystic Novikov in the Fortress of Schlüsselburg, and exiled to Siberia the courageous polemicist Radishchev, who had denounced the abuses of the regime in his *Journey from St. Petersburg to Moscow*. Why, at this late date, had these blows been struck against all the great minds of Russia by one who throughout her life had professed her admiration for talent and intelligence? Did old age invariably stifle the aspirations of youth?

When he was with his father, Alexander did not understand his grandmother; when he was with his grandmother, he doubted that his father was entirely in his right mind. From Czarskoye Selo, a few versts

---

*The celebrated French painter Elisabeth Vigée-Lebrun had been invited to court by Catherine II to execute some portraits.

†The Martinists were followers of the French religious mystic Claude de Saint-Martin (1743–1803). (Trans.)

away, Catherine sometimes heard faint echoes of the artillery practice
that was the joy of her grandsons.* She was vexed by the rapprochement between Alexander and Paul but not yet alarmed by it. Alexander
was much too intelligent, she thought, to persist for long in this ridiculous craze for the military. Besides, when she saw him again after his
excursions to Gatchina, he was still the same: elegant, attentive, submissive. At first sight, it did not appear that the courtier was losing ground
to the soldier.

Weary and worn out, Catherine planned more than ever to publish
a manifesto proclaiming Alexander as her successor. With this in mind
she had studied the archives, so as to be able to justify by the example
of Peter the Great himself the disinheriting of an unworthy heir and the
appointment of an heir of her choice. With the help of Vice-Chancellor
Bezborodko, she drew up the solemn text that would deprive Paul of
the throne in favor of Alexander. This document, locked in a chest, was
not to be made public until November 24, St. Catherine's Day in Russia.
Before that, the Empress wanted to settle a few important affairs. The
campaign against Persia, which she had rashly undertaken on the advice of Plato Zubov, had ended in failure, as the Russian troops were
unable to advance beyond Baku. On the other hand, she was relying
heavily on the benefits of a marriage between her granddaughter Alexandra, age thirteen, and young Gustavus IV of Sweden, who was eighteen.

After the wars and disputes of all sorts that had kept Sweden and
Russia enemies for so long, the proposed match made good sense politically. To be sure, Plato Zubov, who had been given the mission of
convincing the court of Stockholm that such a union could be concluded without the Orthodox Princess's having to renounce her religion, had encountered some reluctance. Nevertheless, it was decided
to celebrate the engagement on September 11, 1796, in St. Petersburg.
While all the dignitaries of the empire and the representatives of foreign powers stood gathered around Catherine in the throne room,
awaiting the arrival of the fiancé, Gustavus was in a neighboring room
still discussing with Plato Zubov the conditions of the contract. On the
Empress's right stood Grand Duke Paul, still officially her heir; on her
left was Alexander, who would be her heir as soon as she published the
manifesto; at her feet seated on a footstool was the young fiancée Alexandra, anxiously awaiting what would follow. Suddenly Plato Zubov

*A verst is about two-thirds of a mile, or slightly more than one kilometer. (Trans.)

reappeared, livid, without the King, went up to the Empress and whispered in her ear that everything was broken off: Gustavus IV had given up the plan and wanted to leave for Sweden again. Under the shock of the insult, Catherine felt her old heart fail. In a colorless voice she announced that His Majesty Gustavus IV had had an indisposition and that the celebration of the betrothal was postponed. Then she rose with difficulty and, leaning on Alexander's arm, left the hall between two rows of notables turned to stone. It was toward her grandson that she had instinctively turned for support, not toward her son. The courtiers noticed it. There was something symbolic in this couple of grandmother and adolescent: young Russia coming to the aid of old Russia, the future honoring and protecting the past.

Alexander was aware of the confidence his grandmother placed in him. And she for her part was counting the days until the fateful twenty-fourth of November, when she would make known her will. But on the morning of November 4 her servants found her collapsed and inert in her water closet: an apoplectic attack. The doctors did not believe she could recover. They even said the end was very near. People ran to look for Alexander. He was out on a sleigh ride with Constantine. Brought to the palace, he pretended to be in despair. But in his heart of hearts he felt no compassion for this dying woman of sixty-seven who had known every glory and who was struggling wretchedly, in the depths of her bed, against the darkness that was already closing in on her brain. Observing the young man's behavior, Countess Golovina even declared that he displayed, "to the point of indecency, his joy at no longer having to obey an old woman." In reality, Alexander found himself faced with a dilemma: Having known for a long time that the Empress had chosen him to be her successor, he could produce the famous manifesto and become Emperor instead of Paul. But acceptable as it would have seemed to him to be designated during Catherine's lifetime, it was repugnant to him to lay claim to the throne after her death. In the first case, he would only have had to obey; in the second, he would have to perform an act of will. In the first case, he would have been covered by the authority of his grandmother; in the sec 1, he would have to confront his father's anger by publicly taking a sacrilegious initiative. He did not have the courage to defy his father openly. He preferred to abandon himself to the flow of events.

Better yet, to signify his submission to the spirit of Gatchina he put on the Prussian uniform, which had never before been seen in the Empress's salons. Constantine did likewise. When he arrived to be present at his mother's last moments, Paul saw with satisfaction that his two sons were dressed in Prussian style, with pomade and powder in their hair, like worthy soldiers of Frederick II. He immediately understood that Alexander did not mean to take advantage of his rights to the crown. While the unconscious Catherine lay gasping out her last breath, Paul and Bezborodko hurried into the Empress's study, searched among her private papers, found the manifesto and burned it. The way was clear. There was nothing further to prevent Paul, who had been waiting for this moment for thirty-four years, from being proclaimed Emperor.

On November 6, 1796, toward the middle of the afternoon, the doctors informed Paul that Her Majesty was at the point of death. Alexander and Constantine accompanied their father to the Empress's bedside. Confronted with this pitiful face convulsed with pain, Alexander could not help thinking of the omnipotent, smiling grandmother of the last few years. As he had a tender heart, he almost fainted—or so it was said. Someone beside him was sobbing noisily. He glanced sideways and was disgusted to find Plato Zubov, who could not contain his despair, weeping not for his imperial mistress but for the position he had held at her side. There is always some risk attached to staking one's career on the life of an elderly person. For the favorite, it was the end of a dream of opulence, the signal of impending disgrace. Alexander turned his eyes from this puppet and looked at his grandmother, who was panting, with eyes starting from their sockets and pink drool at the corner of her lips. A sigh hoarser and shorter than the others: It was over. Everyone knelt down in the semidarkness. Then Paul made the sign of the cross, rose, and showed a triumphant face. The Procurator General, Samoïlov, declared to the crowd of courtiers massed in the antechamber that the Empress Catherine was dead and that her son, Emperor Paul, had ascended the throne. At these words, tears mixed with acclamations. The courtiers embraced each other and wept. Russia went on.

In the palace chapel a throne had been hastily brought for the swearing of the oath of allegiance. Seated under the gilt emblem of the two-headed eagle, Paul, his face wrinkled in the grimace of a bulldog, was unable to hide his satisfaction. His eyes shone with the light of revenge. One by one the courtiers knelt at his feet and kissed his hand. Bending his knee before the new sovereign, Alexander had mixed feelings: On the one hand, he had taken a great risk in delivering Russia up to this man of erratic moods; on the other, he had satisfied his conscience by not opposing the normal order of succession. Now it was his turn to be heir apparent. At the age of nineteen, with a father of forty-two, full of strength and determination, he had time. He would see what would happen. Was not the position of Grand Duke, safe from political cares, more enviable than that of Emperor?

Grand Duchess Elizabeth, for her part, was saddened and repelled to see how eagerly the whole court hastened to pay homage to a new sovereign who so little deserved it. "Again I had to go through abominable sensations, seeing all these people swear to be slaves, and slaves of a man whom, at that moment, I detested," she wrote to her mother afterward. "Seeing *him* in the place of that good Empress, seeing him look so satisfied, so happy to see all the contemptible things they were already doing—oh, it was awful!"

The ceremony of swearing the oath was hardly finished when Paul insisted on reviewing a regiment of the Guard. Standing beside him, Alexander saw him twitch his knee, tap his foot, and blow out his breath with annoyance because the soldiers did not parade past in perfect alignment. Immediately afterward the Emperor had his horse Pompom saddled and galloped off to meet his faithful troops of Gatchina, who entered the capital with the bugle corps at their head. Alexander gave an enthusiastic greeting to the officers of these regiments, who had formerly been kept in the background but whom he considered his "real comrades."

From one hour to the next the palace changed its appearance, as the Germanic spirit drove out the French. "A complete metamorphosis has taken place," noted Stedingk, "in the manner of dress and comportment. Wide cravats, straggling hair, and languid looks have disappeared. One sees nothing but gaiters, canes, and Swedish-style gloves." Every day was an excuse for parades. The changing of the guard, regulated to the last detail, became an affair of state. As for the memory of the Empress, it was sometimes cursed, sometimes mocked. "Oh! I was scandalized that the Emperor showed so little affliction," wrote Grand Duchess Elizabeth. "It seemed as if it were his father who had just died and not his mother, for he spoke only of the former, decorating all the rooms with portraits of him, and not a word about his mother, except to blame her and to disapprove highly of everything that had been done in her time."

From the beginning of his reign, Paul intended to take the opposite course from his mother in all things. He had the Freemason and mystic Novikov released from the Fortress of Schlüsselburg, recalled from exile the writer Radishchev, covered Kosciusko with gifts and gave him permission to leave for America, freed twelve thousand Polish prisoners and hostages dispersed in various Russian towns, and settled the former

King of Poland, Stanislaus Poniatowski, in superb accommodations in St. Petersburg.

The funeral of the Empress gave him the opportunity to make even clearer his hatred for his old mother, who had died three weeks before, and his veneration for his young father, who had been dead for thirty-four years. He insisted that the funeral ceremonies be performed simultaneously for Catherine and for the husband whom she had had assassinated. Peter's coffin was disinterred from the vaults of the Alexander Nevsky Monastery and deposited in the Winter Palace, in the hall of columns, beside the coffin of his "criminal wife." The expiation ceremony continued with the transfer of the bodies of Peter III and Catherine II to the Cathedral of St. Peter and St. Paul. By order of the Emperor, it was Alexis Orlov, the man chiefly responsible for the murder, who led the procession. Walking bareheaded, with the temperature below zero, he bore on a gilt cushion the imperial crown of his victim. His old accomplices, Passek and Bariatinsky, were pallbearers. Behind them, on foot, came the Emperor, the Empress, the Grand Dukes, the Grand Duchesses, the whole court, all the diplomats, all the military chiefs. In the crowded, icy cathedral priests in chasubles of mourning joined two enemy names in a single prayer. Standing in the nave beside his father, Alexander was filled with horror at the spectacle of the theatrical double catafalque toward which there rose holy words and clouds of incense. More than ever he was terrified by the idea of absolute sovereignty. Was there a single reign that was not spattered with blood? Must one renounce being a man in order to be able to govern men? Were not Laharpe's noble ideas fit only for the pleasure of conversation? The funeral chant of the choir fostered Alexander's melancholy reflections. Having become the second personage in the empire, he felt at once powerless to escape his destined role and incapable of assuming it.

III

THE REIGN OF PAUL

Observing his father, Alexander soon realized that the politics of the new Emperor were dominated by two ideas: to destroy everything that had been built by Catherine, whose memory he detested, and to consider Russia as the natural extension of Gatchina. Paul would have liked the entire country to maintain the strict order he had established on his private estate near St. Petersburg. Alexander the liberal was not opposed to a certain amount of discipline. If all his compatriots were in uniform, the nation would only be the better for it, he thought. He eagerly accompanied his father to Moscow for the coronation ceremonies, which were to take place on April 5, 1797. During the journey he discovered the true Russia, not that of the salons of St. Petersburg and the gardens of Czarskoye Selo but the country as it really was. Passing through towns and villages, he forgot about courtiers and looked at men.

In Moscow the streets were still covered with snow. A bitter wind blew on the procession as it slowly entered the city. The dignitaries were freezing on their horses, and among themselves they cursed the hard obligations of their office. Despite the cold, a large crowd had assembled along the route to greet the new sovereign. Horsemen at the head of the procession shouted to the spectators to remove their hats and gloves. Backs were bent. Paul bowed, hat in hand. As Alexander passed, a murmur of blessing rose from the multitude. High on his horse, he heard this hymn of praise. He knew he was handsome; he understood that he was admired, loved; and he was flattered to be so popular. The affection of the masses is a wine that goes straight to the head. Once one has tasted it, it is not easy to do without it.

At the time of the coronation, Paul settled the problem of succession by decreeing that the inheritance would go to male offspring in the order of their birth. This measure enhanced the prestige of Grand Duke Alexander. As if to increase his son's appetite for power, Paul then appointed him, successively, honorary Colonel of the famous Semeonovsky regiment, Inspector General of the cavalry, Military Governor of St. Petersburg, and President of the War College. Soon he would take his seat in the Senate. With so many different causes for satisfaction, Alexander gradually forgot his plan to withdraw with his wife to some solitary retreat in Switzerland or Germany.

He agreed with some of the Emperor's decisions. He thought an era of justice was dawning when he saw his father reorganize the Senate; create a fund to provide for years of famine; grant subsidies to daring manufacturers; forbid the importation of luxury items; found a school of medicine; decree that the serfs, whose status, of course, was not to be changed, did not belong to the lord but were "attached to the soil"; limit the peasants' corvées to three days a week; forbid the landowners to make peasants work on Sundays and holidays; reduce the price of salt; and install at the entrance to the palace a postal box for the grievances of the humble people. The Emperor kept the key to the box himself. He expected to learn a great deal from this private correspondence with his empire, but at the end of a year he had to admit disappointment and have the box removed. Too many insulting letters and satirical verses were deposited in it anonymously every day. If you authorized a Russian to open his mouth, instead of thanking you, he vomited. The nation had to be guided, not consulted.

After a few months' honeymoon with his country, Paul became increasingly irritated at the impossibility of satisfying everyone, nobles and peasants. His mind, which was already tolerably shaken, became unhinged. He no longer conceived of his subjects as anything but puppets subject to his will and whim. Suspicious in the extreme, he detected a hint of subversion even in modes of dress. Government functionaries were required to wear their uniforms at all times, and, by a ukase of January 13, 1797, Paul forbade the wearing of round hats, top boots, straight pants, and laced shoes. To enforce this regulation two hundred dragoons were sent out into the streets of St. Petersburg. They attacked passersby whose garb did not correspond to the imperial will, tore off hats, ripped waistcoats, confiscated shoes. With their clothes in rags the offenders, all members of the best society, went home to change. They reappeared with powdered hair, three-cornered hats, stand-up collars, knee breeches, and buckled shoes. Thus metamorphosed, they regained the freedom of the city.

Having regulated what his subjects wore, Paul naturally wanted to regulate what they read. By a ukase of February 16, 1797, he instituted lay and clerical censorship in St. Petersburg and Moscow. Private printing presses were closed down. He proscribed the waltz, which he considered a French dance, hence Jacobin. He deleted from the vocabulary the words *citizen, club,* and *society.* Professors could no longer speak in class about the *revolution* of the heavenly bodies. At night, after the nine o'clock curfew, main streets were closed off, the barriers being lifted only for doctors and midwives.

Increasingly haunted by the specter of revolution, Paul even came to distrust Freemasonry and Martinism, although as heir apparent he had declared himself sympathetic to their humanitarian theories. Certain great noblemen who were affiliated with these brotherhoods were suddenly ostracized by the very man who not long since had treated them as friends. Moreover, if one of his close collaborators had a personal idea of any kind, the Czar was irritated, as if it cast doubt upon his own genius.

Paul's capacity for work was equal to his appetite for reforms. Wanting to see everything and decide everything for himself, he set to work in his study at six o'clock in the morning and required all government officials to do the same. Long before daybreak, bureaucrats of every sort, their portfolios under their arms, hurried through the twilight darkness like needy phantoms toward their ministries, where chandeliers and oil lamps were already being lit. At the end of the morning, in high boots and a dark green uniform, Paul would go with his sons and aides-de-camp to view the military parade. A dalmatic of garnet velvet strewn with pearls covered his shoulders to distinguish him from the other generals. Bareheaded, balding, with frowning brows, one hand behind his back, the other waving a cane to mark the cadence of the parade, he made it a point of honor to brave the worst cold without the

protection of a fur. "Soon," Masson wrote, "the officers no longer dared
to appear in a pelisse; and the old generals, tormented by coughs, gout,
and rheumatism, found themselves obliged to gather around their master dressed like him." As supreme commander of the army, Paul decided that all transfers and promotions would be announced by himself
and that he alone would have the right to grant exceptional leaves and
to authorize marriages. He dismissed illustrious generals who displeased him and replaced them with uneducated men whose sole merit
lay in applauding his whims. The dismissals took place in public, before
the dismayed troops. Dissatisfied with a regiment of the Guard that had
not correctly obeyed one of his commands, he ordered it to set out at
once, in full dress uniform, for Siberia. Terrorized, the whole unit, with
the officers at the head, left for exile, while the Czar's advisers begged
him to revoke his decision. At last he consented reluctantly and sent a
courier with the countermand. The condemned soldiers, already several days' march from St. Petersburg, retraced their steps in the same
good marching order and with the same dull submissiveness.

One of Paul's first measures was to impose on the whole army the
Prussian uniform of the men of Gatchina, with gaiters and powdered
pigtails. The night before a review, hairdressers would labor over the
officers and men, covering their hair with grease and chalk so it would
braid well. Every man knew that he might be arrested, even deported,
for a lapse in duty, that his fate might well hang on a lock of hair or a
belt buckle. Before reporting to the rallying points, the noncommissioned officers got into the habit of saying farewell to their families and
providing themselves with money for a long journey.

The young noblemen in the Guard muttered angrily about the
"brutes" of Gatchina, the rough, dull-witted men who Paul said should
be examples to them. They regretted their handsome uniforms of Catherine's time, their epaulettes, sashes, and sword knots. They were
ashamed to have become "Prussian monkeys." Alignment, spacing, and
the goose step were the great principles of the new military regulation
of November 29, 1796. Certain terrifying remarks of the Emperor's
were repeated in the drawing rooms, in the barracks. He liked to say,
"That man is a gentleman to whom I speak and only while I am speaking to him." To Prince Repnin, who ventured to make a suggestion to
him, he shouted, "Monsieur Field Marshal, do you see these men of the
Guard? There are four hundred of them; I have only to say the word
and they will all be marshals." And to his sons Alexander and Constantine he said, "Don't you see, my children, that you must treat men like
dogs?" It really seemed as if it were Paul's pleasure to punish and

reward without reason, solely for the satisfaction of affirming his omnip-
otence.

Alexander, like the others, felt the repercussions of the Emperor's
sudden changes of mood. Although he had been granted a hundred
honorific titles, he was completely subservient to his father. Despite
appearances, he had no authority whatever and could make no decision
without special permission. Nothing depended on his own will, not
even his daily routine. Summoned repeatedly to the Czar's office, he
had to report to him on the least change in a sentry's station and, as
often as not, be abused for incompetence. At the age of twenty he
trembled before this potentate like a weak child who doesn't know
what to do to satisfy his master. One day, having made his father angry
over some trifle, he asked his mother, Maria Feodorovna, to draft a
letter of apology for him, in French, which he would copy out: "The
reproach you have given me, my dear father, cuts me to the heart. In
all my education only one sentiment has been inculcated in me . . .
respect, affection, submission to my beloved progenitor. As long as I
live, that will be my profession of faith, which my heart will continually
renew and which I shall sign with my blood."

But Maria Feodorovna was hardly capable of protecting her sons
from her husband's fits of anger, and naturally enough, Alexander
sought a more powerful ally. His choice fell upon Arakcheyev, the
"corporal of Gatchina," the man who was the incarnation of rules and
regulations. Here, he thought, was a lightning rod that would divert the
imperial thunderbolts. And indeed, Arakcheyev stood high in Paul's
esteem. Appointed Colonel, then Major General in the Preobrazhensky
regiment, he received the title of Baron, the Order of St. Alexander
Nevsky, and the estate of Gruzino with two thousand peasants. He was
to become in the end a Commander of the Knights of Malta and a Count
of the Empire. To protect himself, Alexander had all his decisions coun-
tersigned by this model servant who had the confidence of the Czar.
Arakcheyev's violence toward his inferiors did not disturb the conscience of Alexander, who was solely preoccupied with his own personal
tranquillity. He knew that Arakcheyev beat his soldiers, bit their noses,
and tore off their mustaches; that he slapped his officers; that he had
driven one of Suvorov's comrades in arms to suicide; yet he opened his
heart to him, begged his advice, and felt lost whenever the brute was
absent. When they were apart, he wrote him short notes full of humility
and affection: "I have just received many affairs to settle and I don't
know what decisions to make about them. So I am sending you the
relevant files, judging that it is better to ask for good advice than to take

the chance of doing something foolish. . . ." "Pardon me, my friend, for disturbing you, but I am young, I still need advice and I hope you will not refrain from giving me some. . . ." "Look after yourself, my friend, if not for your own sake at least for mine. I am very happy to note your feelings for me. I think you are aware of mine. Know that I love you with all my heart."

Thus Laharpe's fond pupil had no difficulty accommodating to a utilitarian friendship with a uniformed lout. True, for the exchange of ideas he turned to other friends, progressive young intellectuals whom he made his companions. At the center of this group was Prince Adam Czartoryski. The whole court praised the beauty, elegance, and broad culture of this Polish nobleman of twenty-seven, who came from the provinces that had recently been annexed, who remained bitter over Russia's conquests, and who courageously displayed his liberal sentiments. Another friend was Victor Kochubey, Alexander's correspondent abroad, who was now back from Constantinople and had resumed in person his role as confidant. Kochubey too was inspired by an ardent desire for justice in the conduct of public affairs. Nicholas Novosiltsev, who was more scientific in his approach to the problems of government, was the "thinker" of the group. His notions of law, political economy, and international history enabled him to dominate the discussions. The fourth member of the circle was the flamboyant young Paul Stroganov. His father, a Freemason of enormous wealth, had more estates and serfs than he could count, possessed the finest picture gallery in the country, traveled all over Europe, and made friends with the greatest minds of his time. On a sudden enthusiasm, he had entrusted the education of his son to a French schoolmaster, the future member of the National Convention Gilbert Romme, and given him permission to take the young man to France. When they reached Paris master and pupil found themselves in the midst of the Revolution. Fired by the new ideas, Paul —or "Popo," as his friends called him—gave up his title; frequented the Jacobin Club under the name of Paul Otcher (after one of his factories near Perm); founded a club, the Friends of Law; gave his French friends handsome subsidies; became the lover of Théroigne de Méricourt, "the unchaste Judith," and donned a Phrygian cap when he went out with her. Appalled by this behavior, the Russian ambassador to Paris, Simolin, wrote to inform Catherine II. She immediately sent Nicholas Novosiltsev to France with orders to bring "Popo" back to the fold at any cost. To punish the noble Russian sans-culotte, she exiled him to his estates, where he remained for several years before returning to favor. Having sobered down, he reappeared in the drawing rooms of St. Pe-

tersburg and married Princess Sophie Golitzina. In the meantime his
tutor, Gilbert Romme—having voted to execute the King, reformed the
calendar, asked that Marat be interred in the Pantheon, and protested
against the Thermidorian reaction—had put an end to his life with a
dagger. Emerging from this tragic tumult, Paul Stroganov wrote, "I
have seen a whole people raise the banner of liberty and shake off the
yoke; no, I shall never forget that moment. I cannot shut my eyes to the
fact that despotism exists in my country, and I look upon its hideous
specter with horror. . . . My blood and my fortune belong to my fellow
citizens."

Paul Stroganov readily repeated these strong words before his Russian friends, but in St. Petersburg he soon let himself be caught up again
in the refined pleasures of society. Married to one of the wittiest and
most cultivated women in the capital, he led the life of a great nobleman who was enlightened and idle. Knowing nothing about Russia,
hardly speaking the language, he regained a little of his revolutionary
ardor only when chatting with Alexander. Alexander meanwhile questioned his four liberal companions about the possibility of a change of
regime in Russia. In secret his friends drafted plans and submitted them
to the heir to the throne: abolition of all obstacles to liberty, equality of
citizens before the law no matter what their status, the advent of a just
and fraternal society. While Alexander expressed his passionate approval of these high-minded conceptions, he put the documents themselves away in a drawer and spoke no more about them. Disappointed
that so little consideration was given to the memorandum he had
worked on, Czartoryski wrote, "I do not know what became of that
paper. I believe that Alexander showed it to no one; in any case, he
never spoke to me about it again."

It was not long before Paul's suspicions were aroused by all these
secret meetings between Alexander and his too-intelligent friends. He
sniffed the scent of a democratic plot. Revolution always started with
childish nonsense; the prattlers had to be dispersed before they became
men of action. But the Emperor did not make any decision yet, preferring to let the boil come to a head. An atmosphere of mutual distrust,
of concealed hatred, developed between him and his son. On September 27, 1797, Alexander, in great distress, wrote Laharpe a long letter
in French, a profession of faith that he entrusted to Novosiltsev, who
was going abroad, to deliver:

"When my father ascended the throne, he wanted to reform everything. It is true that he began quite brilliantly, but his later actions have
not corresponded to the first. Everything has been turned upside down
all at once, and that has only increased the confusion of affairs, which

was already too great. The military waste almost all their time on
parades. In other areas, there is no coherent plan. An order given today
will be countermanded a month hence. No remonstrance is ever tolerated until the damage has already been done. In short, to speak plainly,
the happiness of the State counts for nothing in the governing of affairs.
There is only one absolute power, which does everything without
rhyme or reason. It would be impossible to enumerate to you all the
mad things that have been done.... My poor country is in an indescribable state: the farmer harassed, commerce obstructed, liberty and personal welfare reduced to nothing. That is the picture of Russia. Imagine
what I suffer in my heart. I myself—occupied with minute military
details, wasting all my time on the duties of a subaltern, and not having
so much as an instant to devote to my studies, which were my favorite
occupation before the change—have become the wretchedest of men."

Having described the disorders of the country under the senseless
reign of Paul, Alexander broached the most delicate part of his report.
For the first time, he who had always detested power envisaged the
possibility that he might one day govern Russia. His dream of a peaceful
existence, "in a chalet on the banks of the Rhine," gave way to the vision
of an imperial destiny, full of good deeds and enlightenment. He recognized his responsibilities and took the measure of his strength. Without
renouncing the principle of monarchy, he thought of tempering its
effects with a constitution. To him, the very word *constitution*, imported from France, had a magic power. He continued his letter, speaking sincerely, "You have always known my ideas, which inclined toward
settling abroad. At this moment I can no longer see a way of putting
them into execution, and besides, the unfortunate position of my country has made me turn my thoughts in another direction. I thought that
if ever it came my turn to reign, instead of settling abroad, I should do
far better to work to make my country free and thus prevent it in future
from serving as a plaything for madmen. That led me to a thousand
reflections which have convinced me that this would be the best kind
of revolution, being brought about by a legal power which would cease
to be such as soon as the constitution was finished and the nation had
representatives. This is my idea. I have communicated it to some enlightened persons who, for their part, had been thinking of the same
thing for a long time. We are four in all, that is Monsieur Novosiltsev,
Count Stroganov, young Prince Czartoryski, my aide-de-camp who is a
rare young man, and I*.... Once my turn comes, we shall have to work,

*Victor Kochubey was not mentioned in the letter.

gradually of course, to assemble representatives of the nation who, with guidance, will draw up a free constitution, after which my power will cease absolutely, and, if Providence favors our work, I shall retire to some corner and live satisfied and happy, seeing the good fortune of my country and rejoicing in it. That is my idea, my dear friend. . . . Ah! how happy I should have been if I could have had you beside me during this time! . . . Heaven grant that we may one day succeed in making Russia free and in safeguarding her against the injuries of despotism and tyranny."

While waiting for the dawn of this new political day, Alexander bent himself with distaste to the thousand petty tasks that his father imposed on him. His duties kept him from home all day and when he returned, sour and exhausted, he did not give his wife the affection or even the attention she wanted. Hurt by her husband's aloofness, she too cooled toward him. The moments they spent alone together grew increasingly rare and disappointing. When they came together in the evening, it was to go out in full regalia and attend official receptions, banquets, balls, performances, concerts. These requirements of court protocol were all the more trying to Elizabeth because she had to endure the public insults of her father-in-law. Although he had welcomed her graciously at first, he offended her by his crude remarks and brutal manners. "It is always something," she wrote to her mother, "to have the honor of not seeing the Emperor. In truth, Mama, I find that man *widerwärtig* [disgusting], just to hear him mentioned, and I find his society even more so, when everyone, no matter who it is, who says anything that has the misfortune to displease His Majesty may expect to receive an offensive remark from him. Thus I assure you that except for a few of his associates, in general the public at large detests him; it is even said that the peasants are beginning to talk. What were the abuses that I described to you last year? There are twice as many now, and cruel things are done, under the very eyes of the Emperor. Can you imagine, Mama, once he had an officer who was responsible for supplying the Emperor's kitchen beaten because the boiled meat at dinner had been poor; he had him beaten while he watched, and even made sure that a very strong cane was chosen. He has a man arrested; my husband informs him that the man is innocent, that it is another who is at fault; he answers: 'What's the difference, they'll straighten it out between them.' Oh! Mama, it is painful, horribly painful, to see acts of injustice and brutality every day, to see men made wretched (how many such does he not have on his conscience?) and to pretend to respect, to esteem such a man. . . . So I am the most respectful daughter-in-law, but in truth, not affectionate. In any case, he doesn't care if he is loved so long as he is feared, he has said so himself. And his wish is generally fulfilled, he is feared and hated. . . ."

Indignant at the humiliations that the Emperor had ordered inflicted upon the best officers and most valiant soldiers, Elizabeth dared hope that one day they would revolt. "Never were there better opportunities, but they are too accustomed to the yoke to be able to shake it off," she wrote. "The first order given with some force sends them back to their holes. Oh! if only there were someone to lead them!"

Was she thinking of her husband when she wrote those lines? Yes, no doubt, although she no longer felt anything for him but tepid affection born of the habits of married life. Unsatisfied, she had first launched into a girlish passion for the beautiful Countess Golovina, sending her lyrical notes in French: "I take no pleasure in life when I am separated from you. . . . You are constantly in my thoughts; you cause such a commotion in them that I am unable to do anything. . . ." "I love you. . . . Ah! if this goes on, I shall go mad. You occupy my mind every day until the moment when I fall asleep. If I wake up at night you immediately enter my head. . . ." "Heavens, all the sensations that the mere memory of those sweet moments brings back to me! . . . Ah! you can imagine, I hope, how dear to me is the date of the day when I gave myself to you entirely."

Alexander knew about the ambiguous intimacy between his wife and Countess Golovina, and he encouraged it. Elizabeth confessed as much in a letter to the young woman on December 12, 1794: "I shall love you in spite of all the universe. Besides, they cannot forbid me to love you, and I am authorized to do so by someone else who has just as much, if not more, right to order me to love you. You understand me, I hope." This liaison that was half love, half friendship with a woman of twenty-nine was not enough for Elizabeth. By her own admission she was not sensual, but she was very nervous. When her hair was combed it gave off sparks. "They almost no longer dared touch my coiffure," she said, "it had become so electric." When they put out the lights, her head was crowned with fiery plumes. Soon she looked elsewhere, to a man, for the impassioned, exalting love she had sought in vain at the beginning of her marriage. She did not have to look far for the man who would console her for being neglected: Alexander's best friend, the fascinating Czartoryski, with his sword-sharp wit and velvet eyes. She very quickly succumbed to the charm of the Polish gentleman. Amused by this affair, Alexander encouraged the two to be together. At the time of Plato Zubov's amorous advances he had already proved that he was not jealous. Elizabeth had remained faithful to him then. But this time she lost her head, wild with happiness and gratitude. No matter, Alexander closed his eyes. Perhaps he was indifferent to the betrayal; perhaps he took a perverse pleasure in sharing Elizabeth with his confidant. Whatever the case, he watched attentively over this liaison, which the whole court was whispering about. His wife's conduct relieved him of all obligation to her, and if he did not yet take advantage of the freedom, he congratulated himself upon it. For three years he was a complaisant witness to the development of the affair.

In fact, the licentious ways of the court encouraged easy virtue. Paul set the example. After long years of marital and extramarital fidelity, he wearied of both his wife, Maria Feodorovna, and his mistress, Catherine Nelidova. Moreover, after the birth of a tenth child (Grand Duke Michael), the doctors had forbidden the Empress to have sexual relations with her spouse. Immediately, Kutaïssov, a former barber and bootblack who had become His Majesty's intimate adviser, then Master of the Horse,* presented to the forty-four-year-old sovereign a young lady of sixteen, Anna Lopukhina, who captivated him with her freshness. Catherine Nelidova was unceremoniously repudiated in favor of the newcomer, a child who was "neither pretty nor amiable," but so innocent that Paul's heart was stirred. He showered her with presents, elevated men whom she recommended to him and struck down others, and to protect her from public spite had her marry Prince Gagarin, who would serve as a screen. As soon as the Mikhailovsky Palace was finished, he installed her in an apartment above his own. A secret staircase enabled him to join her every night without being noticed by the servants. But though he hid his goings and comings, everyone knew of them. Still, who would dare criticize him? Least of all Elizabeth, who since her adventure with Adam Czartoryski had been the focus of the court's curiosity.

On May 18, 1799, Elizabeth gave birth to a daughter, Maria. Everyone in the palace was soon laughing at the Grand Duchess's expense: The infant had black hair and black eyes. At the baptism, when Countess de Lieven presented the baby Maria to Paul, the Emperor asked in a dry voice: "Madame, do you believe that a blond husband and a blond wife can have a dark-haired child?" Flustered, she stammered: "Sire, God is all powerful."

By now Adam Czartoryski's career in Russia was definitively com-

---

*He was later made a baron, then a count.

promised. Paul gave him a diplomatic mission in Sardinia: "Send him as soon as possible," he ordered Rostopchin, who noted it in the journal of imperial decisions. The farewells of Adam Czartoryski and Alexander were heartbreaking. Then shortly after losing her lover, Elizabeth lost her daughter as well. "As of this morning, I no longer have a child, she is dead!" she wrote to her mother on July 27, 1800. "Mama, it is horrible beyond all expression to lose one's child; I cannot give you any details of this calamity today." A little later: "It is a long time since I have spoken to you of *Mäuschen* [Maria], but not an hour of the day passes without my thinking of her, and certainly not a day without my giving her bitter tears. It cannot be otherwise so long as I live, even if she were to be replaced by two dozen children."

Alexander too was stricken, but less by the death of the child than by the departure of the irreplaceable Adam Czartoryski. During this period, the whole little group of his friends had been disbanded: Kochubey, suspected of liberalism, had fallen into disgrace; Novosiltsev, threatened in turn, had left Russia of his own accord for England; Stroganov had been sent away from court. In his moral solitude, Alexander drew closer to his wife. Elizabeth, who had been the target of ill-natured gossip ever since her affair with Czartoryski, wrote to her mother: "I do not like to have to owe anything to the Emperor. . . . Certain persons who want to revenge themselves upon the Grand Duke and his friends through me are trying to give me an abominable reputation. What they gain by it I do not know, and I am as indifferent to it as one should be when one has nothing to reproach oneself for. If they want to make trouble between me and the Grand Duke, they will not succeed: He who knows every one of my thoughts and actions can never have any misunderstanding with me."

The truth was that any physical attraction between Alexander and Elizabeth had long since disappeared. "Yes, Mama, I do care for him," she wrote. "Some time back I was wild about him, but now that I am beginning to know him, I notice little trifles, really trifles . . . and there are a few of these trifles that are not to my taste and that have destroyed the *excessive* way in which I loved him. I still love him very much, but in another way." The two young people were no longer bound by desire but by friendship, common interest, and mutual trust. When they were alone together behind closed doors, away from indiscreet ears, they would talk quietly about the opportunities and dangers that lay in store for them. Paul's foreign policy seemed even more incoherent than his domestic policy. After ending the campaign that Catherine II had undertaken against Persia, he had become indignant over Bonaparte's

occupation of the island of Malta and had had himself elected Grand
Master of the Order. Then he had declared war on France and sent
three armies against her: one in Italy, another in Holland, and the third
in Switzerland. Despite Suvorov's brilliant successes in Italy, the expedition had failed. Paul was furious and had quarreled with his Austrian
allies and given up his intention of fighting the heirs of the Revolution.
But suddenly, in a complete reversal, the execrable Bonaparte became
a second Frederick II to him, an example to follow, a friend to cultivate.
Was not the First Consul bringing the rabble to heel? Impulsively, Paul
expelled from Mitau (Yelgava) the Bourbons to whom he had granted
asylum not long before, made a rapprochement with France, and quarreled with England for breaking its promise to restore the island of
Malta to his beloved Knights. British ships moored in Russian waters
were seized, their crews imprisoned. But that was not enough. To
punish proud Albion, the Emperor gave his troops the insane order to
march toward Orenburg (Chkalov), Bukhara, and Khiva, across thousands of versts, over the desolate wastes of the steppes, to conquer the
Indies. The first regiments to be dispatched were placed under the
command of General Platov, who had to be liberated for the purpose
from the Fortress of St. Peter and St. Paul where shortly before he had
been incarcerated for some peccadillo.

His Majesty's entourage was appalled by these harebrained decisions. In the salon of Olga Zherebzova, Plato Zubov's sister, a little
group of conspirators gathered to consider the best way of overthrowing the mad sovereign and replacing him with Alexander. Lord Charles
Whitworth, the British ambassador and Olga Zherebzova's lover, eagerly supported the enterprise, for the cabinet of St. James's hoped to
dethrone as soon as possible a monarch so opposed to British plans. But
the leading roles in the plot were taken by Vice-Chancellor Nikita
Panin, a great nobleman and a clever diplomat, the Zubov brothers,
and Ribas, a Neapolitan adventurer who had become an admiral in the
Russian navy. Although they worked with a will, they did not have time
to complete their plan. Once diplomatic relations with England were
broken, Whitworth was ordered to leave the capital with all his staff.
Not long after, Nikita Panin fell into disgrace, the Zubov brothers were
exiled, Ribas died of an illness, and Olga Zherebzova thought it prudent
to remove herself from the scene.

Just when everything seemed undone a man stepped out of the
shadows and took the affair in hand again. It was Count Peter Alex-
eyevich Pahlen, a cold, energetic, tenacious personage of pleasing appearance who knew the court inside out. Back from an important mili-

tary mission, he had hardly had time to resume his post as Governor of St. Petersburg when he decided to take action. Paul, he thought, was leading the country into a disastrous war against England. Should the British fleet, greatly superior to the Russian, appear tomorrow at Kronshtadt, Russia would have no choice but a shameful capitulation. Already, since the prohibition of trade with the United Kingdom, the landed gentry were complaining that they could no longer export their harvests.

In his four years in power the Emperor had only reinforced the reign of terror over a trembling population. From the least serf to the highest nobleman, everyone feared the despot's unpredictable whims, his ever-increasing bullying and persecution. Pathologically suspicious, Paul strengthened postal censorship, ordering that it be applied even to members of his own family. He became infatuated with a Jesuit, Father Gruber, and scandalized the court by considering a rapprochement between the Orthodox and Catholic Churches. Police spies attended all receptions and concerts in private residences. A decree was issued requiring every individual, man or woman, to get out of his or her carriage when the Emperor passed; most of the time, people simply hid when they saw him coming. Count Golovkin wrote, "This beautiful capital, in which people used to move about as free as air, which had neither gates nor guards nor customs officers, is transformed into a vast prison surrounded by guard posts; the palace has become the seat of terror, before which one may not pass, even in the absence of the sovereign, without taking off one's hat; these fine, broad streets have become deserted, the old nobility being unable to go to perform their functions at court without showing police passes seven times over." Countess de Lieven sighed, "The fortress was bursting with prisoners; in the last six weeks, more than a hundred officers of the Guard had been thrown into prison." Prince Eugene of Württemberg was to say a few years later, "The Emperor was not really insane, but he was in a state of tension and agitation even worse than true madness, which making its effects felt throughout the nation, every day subjected the lives and welfare of millions of men to his arbitrary will." Viegel noted in his journal, "We are cast into the farthest confines of Asia and we tremble before an Asiatic potentate wearing a uniform of Prussian cut, who has pretensions to French courtesy and a medieval spirit of chivalry." Young Osten-Sacken declared that "for a reasonable man, there remains only one solution: to die." And according to Adam Czartoryski, the whole country, without being aware of it, was already involved in a conspiracy against the Emperor, "by desire, by fear, by conviction."

The wily Pahlen, sure that his enterprise would be widely approved, first set to work to win the confidence of the man whom he wished to strike down. He steadfastly approved of the Emperor on every occasion and zealously carried out his most absurd decisions. When Pahlen's own son, an army officer, was placed under arrest, he was careful not to ask Paul to pardon him, saying instead, "Sire, you have performed an act of justice that will be salutary to the young man." Such remarks quickly earned him the esteem of his master. Changing from obsessive mistrust to ill-considered infatuation, Paul discussed the most important affairs with his new adviser. On February 18, 1801, he entrusted him with the management of the postal service. Two days later, Pahlen was made President of the College of Foreign Affairs. These honors, which might have gone to his head, did not make him lose sight of the goal he had set for himself. Taking advantage of his sovereign's favor, he suggested that Paul astonish the world with his generosity by proclaiming a general amnesty and recalling all the functionaries and officers who had been dismissed or exiled in the past four years. Delighted to show that he could be as magnanimous as he was fearsome, Paul yielded to his confidant's wishes. One after another, the "returnees" arrived in the capital, in carriages, in wagons, or on foot, according to their means. The Czar thought he could count on their gratitude, but in welcoming them home he had only increased the number of men around him who dreamed of revenge. It was from this troop of resentful men that Pahlen recruited his chief accomplices. For his second he chose his old comrade the German General Bennigsen, a gaunt giant of a man, dry and serious, who had a reputation for courage and a level head. The three Zubov brothers joined them as soon as they were back from exile. They had had their time of glory under the preceding reign. How could they be put back in the saddle?

Maneuvering skillfully, Pahlen suggested to Plato Zubov, Catherine's last lover, that he ask for the hand of the daughter of Kutaïssov, Paul's former barber, now his trusted adviser. As a parvenu, Kutaïssov was flattered by the prospect of such an alliance. He interceded with the Emperor for the Zubovs, who were back in the capital. His petition was heard: Prince Plato and Count Valerian Zubov were named honorary directors of two corps of cadets; Count Nicholas Zubov resumed his post as Grand Master of the Horse and was given command of the Sumsky dragoons. Once rehabilitated, the Zubovs' first thought was to invite the officers of the Guard to their homes and stir them up against Paul. Many of these officers were impetuous youths who didn't understand anything about politics and cared nothing for the constitution but who could not endure the rigors of Prussian-style military service. They criticized Paul the way they would have reviled a harsh instructor. One of the most hotheaded was Prince Yashvil from Georgia, an artillery officer whom the Czar had once struck with his cane.

Pahlen, for his part, was proceeding with extreme caution, first gaining the support of certain generals who held key posts in the capital —Talyzin, the commander of the Semeonovsky regiment; Uvarov, the commander of the *chevaliers-gardes;* Argamakov, commander of the guard at Mikhailovsky Castle—then others, too. Soon there were more than fifty men whose anger boiled over during the secret meetings, amid the smoke of the pipes and the flame of the punchbowl.

It still remained to obtain the consent of the heir to the throne. At the time of the earlier conspiracy under the aegis of Olga Zherebzova, Panin had informed Alexander of his plan and had met with a timid refusal. Wrapping himself in filial respect, the Grand Duke had not wanted to know anything about the unsavory intrigues of his partisans. Later Panin was to write to Alexander: "I shall carry to my grave the deep conviction that I served my country by being the first to dare place before your eyes the distressing picture of the dangers that threatened to destroy the empire." Would Pahlen, leader of the second conspiracy, which was far better prepared than the first, likewise fail to overcome Alexander's resistance?

At first, events seemed to be playing into his hands. At the beginning of 1801 Paul summoned from Germany the young Prince Eugene of Württemberg, Maria Feodorovna's nephew, took a fancy to the thirteen-year-old boy, and said to anyone who would listen, "Do you know that that little scamp has won my heart?" Other less innocuous remarks sent shudders through the Czar's entourage. It was said that he intended to marry his daughter Catherine to Eugene, adopt the Prince, and designate him as heir to the crown instead of Alexander. Or even that he had decided to imprison all the members of the imperial family in a fortress. "For, after all, I am master in my own house!" he cried. Pahlen hastened to report these words to Alexander, who turned faint with dread but still would not make up his mind. One day, as if to corroborate the fears of his informer, the Grand Duke's father burst into his room and seized the book that lay open on his table. It was the tragedy *Brutus* by Voltaire, in which Brutus condemns his own son to death for conspiring to betray Rome to the Etruscan tyrant Tarquin. As Paul read the last line, "Rome is free: that is enough. . . . Let us give thanks to the gods," a spasm of anger passed over his face. Without a word, he went back up to his apartment, took from his library a life of

Peter the Great, opened it to the page describing the death by torture of the Czarevich Alexis, who was guilty of having disobeyed his father, and bade Kutaïssov take the volume to the Grand Duke and make him read the instructive passage.[1]

This time Alexander was so shaken that the conspirators found him a receptive listener. With unctuous cunning Pahlen represented to the heir to the throne that Russia was racing to destruction, that the people were driven to desperation, that there was danger of a war with England and that it would be an act of patriotism for him to remove the Emperor from power. Pahlen stressed that there was no question whatsoever of making an attempt on the sovereign's life. Paul would simply be asked to abdicate in favor of the heir apparent, and when he had done so, he would be guaranteed a peaceful retirement on one of his estates near St. Petersburg. He could settle there with his wife, Maria Feodorovna, or with his mistress, Anna Lopukhina, now Princess Gagarina, or with both. This idyllic prospect reassured Alexander somewhat. If there was no violence, he would only be half guilty. Besides, he was not being asked to participate in the action, only to let others act without denouncing them. Once the way was cleared, he would ascend the throne and return happiness to the people, while continuing to honor his father. No one would have anything to reproach him for. So he gave in, but he refused to know anything about the preparations for the coup d'état.

Meantime, the whole imperial family had moved into the sinister Mikhailovsky Castle, which had only recently been built. The plaster in this vast habitation was not yet dry, and the walls were still sweating quicklime, oil, and varnish. Despite the objections of the doctors, who warned that the environment was unhealthy, Paul declared himself enchanted with his new residence. He had sent out three thousand invitations to the nobility of the city to celebrate his installation with a supper and a masked ball. Hundreds of candles had been lit to illuminate the rooms. But the fog was so thick that their reddish, flickering flames could hardly be distinguished. The dancers moved slowly in the semidarkness, the mirrors infinitely reflecting their ghostly bows. Seeing this vision from beyond the grave, Alexander was tormented by a horrible sense of foreboding. It seemed as if all of Russia were dancing there with languid abandon, in an atmosphere of death, before being swept away by a gust of wind.

A few days later, the Emperor summoned Pahlen to Mikhailovsky Castle. When he was shown into the sovereign's study, Pahlen found him with a black look on his face. Paul had been warned of a plot against his person. Shooting an inquisitorial glance at the Governor of St. Petersburg, he asked him abruptly if he knew of a conspiracy involving members of the imperial family. Pahlen, in no wise disconcerted, broke out laughing and replied, "But, Sire, if there is a conspiracy, I am part of it. I hold the strings of everything and nothing escapes my knowledge. Set your mind at ease; no conspiracy is possible without me. I'll stake my life on that."

Half reassured, Paul sent a courier to recall urgently to St. Petersburg his faithful friend Arakcheyev, whom he had recently exiled. Now *there* was a man, he felt sure, who was devoted to him to death. While awaiting the arrival of the fierce watchdog, he took a series of measures to protect the approaches to the castle. The sentries were doubled, official receptions canceled.

It was cold in the oversize rooms. Although fires were kept constantly burning, humidity attacked the interior walls. The velvet hangings mildewed. The painted frescoes peeled. The air was full of vapor. To combat the dampness it was soon necessary to cover the walls with wooden laths. The imperial family lived in an atmosphere of gloom and uncertainty, withdrawn from the rest of the world. Empress Maria Feodorovna wrote to a confidante, "Our existence is not cheerful, because our dear master is not at all so. In his soul there is an underlying sorrow that preys upon him; his appetite suffers; he no longer eats as before and rarely has a smile on his lips."

For that matter, all of St. Petersburg seemed to be standing still in shivering expectation. The relentless rain had a melancholy effect on the spirits of all. "The very weather is strange," wrote one contemporary. "It is always dark, weeks pass without our seeing the sun; one has no desire to go out. Besides, one does not go out without danger. It is as if God had turned away from us."[2]

Pahlen felt that the time had come for action. The conspirators met to choose the date for the coup d'état. The night of March 11 seemed particularly auspicious, for during those few hours guard duty at Mikhailovsky Castle was assigned to the third battalion of the Semeonovsky regiment, which was under Alexander's command. It was he himself who had mentioned this fact to Pahlen. Without being party to the plot, he wanted it to succeed. Only a few more days to wait, and Alexander was consumed with impatience and fear. Behind his back, in the shadows, he divined secret meetings of rebel generals, goings and comings of officers transmitting final instructions throughout the city, a whole bustle of vengeful activity, and with a mixture of malice and pity he watched his father, against whom the hatred of the nation was secretly gathering.

Sunday, March 10, 1801, ended with a concert that bored the Czar despite the efforts of Madame Chevallier, a French singer with a fine voice and a pleasing face. On leaving the concert hall to go to supper, Paul stopped in front of his wife, looked her up and down with a sneer, crossed his arms on his chest, and noisily blew out his breath with his nostrils distended, his pupils small and hard—his usual manifestation of anger. Then, turning to Alexander and Constantine, he gave them the same look. Finally, rushing on Pahlen, he hurled abuse at him in a low tone, with a twisted mouth.

During supper the guests were oppressed by a deathly silence. Paul hardly ate anything and rolled his eyes with fury. When members of his family tried to thank him at the end of the meal, according to Russian custom, he repulsed them rudely, gave a sarcastic smile, and left the hall without saying good night to anyone. The Empress burst into tears. Her sons comforted her.

The next day, March 11, the third battalion of the Semeonovsky regiment, loyal to the conspirators, assumed its assigned guard duty outside the castle. Inside, sentries supplied by the Preobrazhensky regiment and the Horse Guards took their places. As was his habit, Paul reviewed the troops and criticized the soldiers' conduct. At the Emperor's orders Pahlen summoned the officers and announced that His Majesty was dissatisfied with their performance; if they did not take their men in hand he would exile them all to distant lands "where even the crows wouldn't find their bones."

That evening there was a change of mood. Nineteen persons joined the imperial family at supper and Paul beamed with affability. He said that he was delighted with the new porcelain dinnerware, decorated with views of the castle, but remarked that every mirror in the room had a defect. "Look at this one, for example," he said to General Kutuzov, "it shows me with my neck crooked." Suddenly he gave his elder son so intense a look that Alexander lowered his head. Knowing what was about to take place that night, he could not hide his anxiety. His father asked him in French: "What's the matter with you this evening, Monseigneur?" "Sire," stammered Alexander, "I do not feel very well." "Well, consult a doctor and look after yourself," grumbled the Emperor. "One should always stop indispositions as soon as they begin, so they don't become serious illnesses." And as Alexander sneezed into his handkerchief, he added, "Bless you."

At nine-thirty, as soon as supper was over, Paul left the dining room without saying good-bye to his guests and passed in front of the sentries of the Horse Guards, who stood motionless as statues at the entrance to his private apartment. Seeing Colonel Sablukov in command of the detachment, he said to him in French, "You are Jacobins!" Taken aback, the Colonel replied without thinking, "Yes, Sire." In a furious voice Paul specified, "Not you, but the regiment." Sablukov, having collected his wits, murmured, "Call me what you will, Sire, but you are mistaken about the regiment." The Emperor, standing before him in his green uniform with red facings, threw out his chest. Under the powdered, braided hair his face, with its flat features like a Kalmuk's, wore an expression of distrust. He said, not in French this time but in Russian, "I know what's what. Dismiss your men." Sablukov gave the order: "Right face, forward march!" When the thirty men of the picket had left, the clatter of their heels echoing on the parquet floor, the Emperor announced to his interlocutor that he had decided to transfer the regiment of Horse Guards to the provinces, with the exception of Sablukov's squadron, which would be billeted at Czarskoye Selo. Then, catching sight of two of the castle lackeys dressed in hussars' uniforms, he ordered them to take the place of the sentries. "You will stay here tonight," he told them. And he went into his bedroom, with his little dog Spitz barking at his heels.

That same night, around eleven o'clock, the conspirators made their way in separate groups to the sumptuous apartment of General Talyzin, in the barracks of the Preobrazhensky regiment, contiguous to the Winter Palace. In the vestibule liveried servants collected coats and three-cornered hats and invited the guests to mount the grand staircase. Upstairs in the salons was a great assemblage of uniforms, sashes, swords, and decorations. Grenadiers, artillerymen, naval officers, Horse Guards, chevaliers-gardes—all the regiments of the garrison were represented—some fifty men in all. Their faces were flushed with alcohol and patriotic enthusiasm. They drank champagne and punch and criticized the sovereign in violent terms. Plato Zubov and his two brothers, Nicholas and Valerian, set the tone. Alexander, they said, was ready to ascend the throne as soon as his father was removed from it. They must go to the Emperor at once and demand his abdication. According to the latest report, Arakcheyev, recalled from exile by Paul to be his protector, had been arrested on Pahlen's orders as he entered the city. At that moment the double doors swung open and Pahlen appeared in person, buttoned up in his uniform with the blue cordon of the Order of St. Andrew across his chest. At his side stood General Bennigsen, thin as a skeleton. The guests gathered respectfully around the two men, who looked stiff and resolute. "We are among ourselves, gentlemen," said Pahlen, "and we understand one another. Are you ready? We are going to drink a glass of champagne to the health of the new sovereign.

The reign of Paul I is over. We are not guided by a spirit of revenge, but we wish to put an end to outrageous humiliations and the shame of the motherland. We are Romans. We all know the significance of the Ides of March. . . . All precautions have been taken. We can count on the assistance of two regiments of the Guard and the regiment of Grand Duke Alexander." At that point, a thick voice was heard from the audience: "And if Paul resists?" Pahlen answered imperturbably: "You all know, gentlemen, that to make an omelet one must break eggs."

Pahlen then divided the officers present into two groups, and taking command of the first, placed Bennigsen and Plato Zubov at the head of the second. The night was black. A light snow swirled over the city. On the broad street leading from the Preobrazhensky barracks to Mikhailovsky Castle, two battalions advanced in step through the darkness. From the Nevsky Prospect quarter, a battalion of the Semeonovsky regiment was hurrying toward the same point. The soldiers did not know what was expected of them. It was not their business to understand but to obey. Still, this nocturnal commotion made them uneasy. The column from the Preobrazhensky regiment, led by Plato Zubov and Bennigsen, reached its destination first. Pahlen and his men had lingered on the way. Perhaps the Governor of St. Petersburg was not eager to intervene personally in the coup d'état; by playing for time, he hoped to keep his hands clean. In any event, they could not wait for him. As the troops surrounded the castle, the Zubov brothers and Bennigsen, followed by all the officers, approached a side drawbridge and gave the password to the sentry. The drawbridge was lowered. Walking stealthily, the conspirators entered the castle through a service door, climbed a narrow spiral staircase, and slipped into a library that served as antechamber to the Emperor's apartment. Instead of the picket of Horse Guards, whom Paul had dismissed a few hours before, there were only two drowsing lackeys. Awakened by the noise, one of them uttered a cry and collapsed under the stroke of a saber; the other fled in terror. The path was clear.

But now suddenly, as if sobered by the prospect of committing a sacrilege, most of the officers beat a retreat. Only some ten followed the Zubov brothers and Bennigsen into the bedchamber. By the feeble light of a candle they saw before them large paintings in gilt frames, a Gobelin tapestry, the gift of Louis XVI, a narrow guardroom bed. The bed was empty. Doubtless the Emperor had fled by another door when he heard the cry of the lackey. Plato Zubov exclaimed furiously, "The bird has flown!" But Bennigsen, very calm, felt the sheets and concluded, "The nest is still warm, the bird cannot be far!" As the officers ferreted in all corners, their giant shadows broke on the cornices of the ceiling. Suddenly Bennigsen noticed bare feet sticking out under a Spanish screen placed in front of the chimney. Sword in hand, he rushed forward, pushed the thin screen aside, and discovered the Emperor in a white shirt and cotton nightcap, his face distorted by fear, his eyes wild. Faced with this crush of officers covered with decorations, he stammered, "What do you want of me? What are you doing here?" "You are under arrest, Sire," replied Bennigsen. Paul still tried to overawe the inebriated band: "Under arrest? Under arrest? What does that mean?" Plato Zubov interrupted him, "We come in the name of the motherland to beg Your Majesty to abdicate. The security of your person and suitable maintenance are guaranteed to you by your son and by the State." Bennigsen went further: "Your Majesty can no longer govern millions of men. You make them unhappy, you should abdicate. No one wants to make an attempt on your life; I am here to defend you. Sign the act of abdication." The Emperor was pushed toward the table, an officer spread before him the document of renunciation, another held out a pen. Paul dug in his heels. Mastering his terror, he shouted, "No, I will not sign this!" Plato Zubov and Bennigsen left the room in exasperation, perhaps to look for Pahlen, the only one who might persuade the obstinate monarch. While they were gone, an uproar was heard in the antechamber. Was it new conspirators arriving, or followers of the Emperor? They must act quickly. The officers remaining in the room urged Paul to make up his mind. Crowded around him, they gesticulated, shouted, threatened. The angrier they became, the more fiercely he resisted, pitiful and grotesque in his nightclothes.

In the midst of the scuffle, the candle end was overturned and went out. Only the flame of a night light that was kept burning in front of an icon dimly illuminated the room. In the semidarkness it was hard to distinguish faces. Was it Nicholas Zubov, the colossus, who had just raised his hand against the Czar? A solid gold snuffbox thrown by a strong arm struck Paul on the temple. He collapsed, and the band of conspirators, trembling with fear and hatred, threw themselves upon him. To quiet him as he struggled and screamed at the top of his lungs, an officer seized a commander's sash, threw it around Paul's neck, and drew it tight. Half strangled, the Emperor glimpsed among his tormentors a young man wearing the uniform of the Horse Guards. Thinking he recognized his younger son Constantine, who led that regiment, he implored him with a dying rattle, "Mercy, Monseigneur! Mercy, for pity's sake! Air, give me air!" A few instants later, Bennigsen came back into the room and found the hideous corpse of Paul in his white shirt, lying at the feet of the circle of officers. Pahlen arrived in turn to take note of the demise. Everything had happened as he had foreseen. By delaying his appearance on the spot, he had avoided participating in the murder.

A disheveled woman ran toward Paul's bedroom. It was the Empress Maria Feodorovna. She had heard the echoes of the struggle. She had to know. *"Päulchen, Päulchen!"* she screamed in German. Guards dispatched by Bennigsen barred her way with crossed bayonets. She threw herself on her knees before the commanding officer and begged him to let her see her husband. He refused. In the bedchamber they were busy arranging the body so as to hide, as much as possible, all traces of violence.

During this time Alexander, who had taken refuge in his ground-floor apartment, was waiting, more dead than alive, to see what would happen. He had not closed his eyes all night. Ready for any eventuality, he had not even taken off his uniform. Listening for every sound, he had heard overhead the clatter of boots, shouts. Now all was silent. What had happened? Had his father signed the act of abdication? Had he left for Gatchina or some other residence outside the city? Was he still alive at least? Overwhelmed with remorse, he sat down next to his wife, embraced her tenderly, forehead to forehead, hoping for a comfort she could not give him. It was in this position that Pahlen found them when he came to announce the terrible news. He had uttered only a few words when Alexander, stricken with horror, burst into sobs. He had not wanted that, yet he felt guilty. What others had done, he had hoped for. Now, forever, he was branded with ignominy. However innocent, he was a criminal. A patricide with clean hands. The worst kind. While he wept, Pahlen looked at him coldly and wondered if he had not been wrong to place his bets on this weak reed. Finally, with a sort of disdainful commiseration, in the stern voice of a schoolmaster, the Governor of St. Petersburg said in French: "That's enough childishness. Go reign. Come show yourself to the guards!" Elizabeth too exhorted Alexander to overcome his prostration. By the account of all witnesses, she revealed in this ordeal as much strength as he did weakness. "A disorder like that of a dream," she was to write to her mother. "I asked for advice, I spoke to people to whom I had never spoken before and to whom I shall perhaps never speak again in my life. I entreated the Empress to be calm, I did a thousand things at once, I made a thousand decisions. It was a night that I shall never forget."

With difficulty Alexander stood up, and guided by Pahlen, walked to the interior courtyard of Mikhailovsky Castle, where the troops who had been on guard that night had gathered. Livid and staggering, he drew himself up when he saw the rows of soldiers ranged before him to do him honor. Pahlen, Bennigsen, the Zubov brothers were at his side. His accomplices. And he even had to thank them. Struggling to overcome his revulsion, grief, and fatigue, he shouted in a voice choked with tears, "My father has died following an attack of apoplexy. During my reign, everything will be as it was during the reign of my beloved grandmother, the Empress Catherine." He was answered with thunderous hurrahs. "Perhaps it's all better this way," thought Alexander, while the officers who had killed his father congratulated him. Shortly afterward he received the congratulations of Constantine, a harsh, hot-tempered man who was overjoyed at his older brother's accession to the throne. Only the Empress Maria Feodorovna wept sincerely for the end of a hated monarch.

IV

THE
SECRET COMMITTEE

Public notices posted in the streets announced to the inhabitants of St. Petersburg that they had changed sovereigns, Paul I having succumbed to an "attack of apoplexy." That excuse had been used so often in obituaries of the Romanov dynasty (including, not too long since, to cover up the assassination of Peter III) that on hearing the news Talleyrand said, "The Russians should invent another illness to explain the death of their emperors." In Russia, however, there was such a feeling of relief that in spite of the official mourning the people could not contain their manifestations of sacrilegious joy. Everywhere people embraced each other—in drawing rooms, in hovels, and on the public streets—blessing the name of the new Czar. The day after the murder, when he appeared at the traditional changing of the guard, Alexander was greeted with cheers from a delirious crowd. How handsome he was, how tall, how young, how grief-stricken! With him, Russia at last had an enlightened, benevolent monarch. After four years of nightmare they were emerging into a sunlit future. Three days after the regicide Elizabeth wrote to her mother, "However real my sorrow over the sad way in which the Emperor died, I cannot but confess that, together with all of Russia, I can *breathe* again."

Alexander's first decisions delighted the very persons who had doubted his competence. He stopped the Russian expeditionary force that had been sent out with the mad intention of conquering India, recalled to service twelve thousand officers and functionaries who had been disgraced, gave permission for foreign books to be imported, reopened the private publishing houses, lifted the ban on passports to the various European countries, brought back the famous polemicist Radishchev whom Catherine II had exiled to Siberia,* ordered officers and men to cut their pigtails and don Russian instead of Prussian uniforms, abolished the dread police unit known as the "Secret Expedition," created a commission to draft laws, and had the gallows taken down from public squares. "There remains no trace of the least constraint in anything," wrote the Swedish diplomat Stedingk. "All of Paul's institutions have perished with him. A host of people are arriving every day. All the persons who played a role under Catherine II have come back."[1] The Austrian consul Viazzoli reported to his government: "I no longer recognized St. Petersburg. Joy, contentment, satisfaction, tranquillity are depicted on every face; animation and brilliance have reappeared; everything is going well, wonderfully well. . . . The great number of exiles and of Russian noblemen who had retired to their estates have hastened hither, and the city is swarming with inhabitants of every rank, sex, and age, enchanted to be enjoying a just, mild, moderate government." The young men again wore their hair short, in the style of the Roman emperors; round hats, long pants and waistcoats reappeared on the streets. The Fortress of St. Peter and St. Paul was emptied of its occupants. "Now, thank heaven, Russia is going to be like the rest of Europe," wrote Empress Elizabeth to her mother.

But the enthusiasm that surrounded Alexander did not cure him of his malaise. Through all his triumphs he dragged behind him the disfigured corpse of his father. To Prince Adam Czartoryski, who tried to comfort him, he said, in French: "No, it's impossible. There is no cure for that! I must suffer. How do you expect me to stop suffering? It cannot change."[2] Empress Elizabeth went further: "His sensitive soul will be forever racked by it. . . . To sustain him he needs the idea of restoring the welfare of his country; there is no other motive that can give him determination. And determination he needs, for dear God! what a state

---

*Despite the fact that he had been restored to favor, Radishchev was to commit suicide in September 1802.

this empire was in when he received it. . . . All is calm and tranquil, except for an almost uncontrollable joy that reigns from the humblest member of the populace to the entire nobility."[3]

And Alexander really did need to drown himself in work in order to forget the night of the tragedy. Only total devotion to the cause of the empire, he thought, could rehabilitate him in his own eyes. But the wound was still too fresh not to open again at the least occasion. Even his mother tormented him: For a brief time she had made the extravagant claim that she should succeed to the throne of her deceased husband, and she now suspected her eldest son of having instigated the murder. Already consumed with remorse, Alexander had to defend himself, justify himself before her. He met the scrutinizing look of the Empress Dowager with a mask of innocence and affection. It was true that he was used to dissembling. Throughout his whole adolescence he had played a role. But what earlier had been only an actor's exercise, well suited to his changeable nature, now became a torture to him. His appearances in public were so many ordeals. Sometimes, unable to bear it any longer, he fled society. "He would often lock himself up in the most hidden corner of his apartment," wrote Countess Edling, "and there, abandoning himself to his grief, he would utter muffled groans accompanied by floods of tears."[4]

Alexander had always wept copiously. This time he thought he was Orestes pursued by the Furies. It seemed to him that a curse hung over his family. All her life his grandmother Catherine II had had on her conscience the death of her husband Peter III, which she had desired but not ordered, and now *he* bore the responsibility for the assassination of his father, even though he had remained in his room while the regicide was being committed. How much treachery, how much violence in the Romanov line since Peter the Great!

When Alexander tried to analyze himself, he could no longer tell precisely whether it was because of weakness of character, personal ambition, or a political ideal that he had allowed himself to be won over to the conspirators' cause. Most likely all three factors had played a part. Still, he preferred to tell himself that he had been raised to the throne against his wishes, by the will of the army and the people. To convince the world of that, he would at least have to bring the guilty parties to justice. But he could not, on the morrow of his accession, strike the men who had made that accession possible. Only a person as naïve as Laharpe would have dared advise him to do so, in a moving letter: "The assassination of an emperor in the midst of his palace, in the bosom of his family, cannot go unpunished without trampling underfoot all laws, both human and divine, and compromising the imperial dignity. . . . It is for you, Sire, who ascended the throne of Russia only with regret, henceforth to consolidate that throne, which has been shaken by successive revolutions. . . . It is by impartial, public, stern, and timely justice that such outrages can and must be repressed."

Alexander shrugged his shoulders. Off in his native Switzerland, Laharpe reasoned like a philosopher, not a statesman. To listen to him would mean provoking a scandal that would echo throughout Europe. In the course of the interrogations, the accused would of course protest that the present Czar had encouraged them in their action—and they would have evidence to prove it. No, once again the course of wisdom was to play for time, to lie, to smilingly prepare the disgrace of the most embarrassing witnesses. Having welcomed old Nikita Panin, the leader of the first conspiracy, with tears in his eyes, Alexander now had his police spy on him. In the end he was sent back to his estates. Pahlen, overwhelmed with kindnesses, was soon relegated to his property in Kurland. Plato Zubov was invited to travel abroad, Bennigsen was ordered to stay away from St. Petersburg for a time. Other accessories to the crime were assigned to regiments of the line stationed in the Caucasus or Siberia—thus, gently and firmly, Alexander rid himself of his troublesome accomplices. His ingratitude toward them was as much a question of prudence as of revulsion. By removing them from his path, he hoped both to free himself from their influence and to wipe out the memory of the crime they had perpetrated for his benefit.

He took the measure of his popularity at the celebration surrounding his coronation in Moscow. True, Elizabeth found herself a bit ridiculous, "in a carriage as big as a lantern, with four little pages hanging on to the coachman's seat opposite me." But she was the only one who found the situation amusing. When Alexander passed through the crowd on horseback, he was greeted by murmurs of veneration. The people called him "our little father," "our bright sunshine." Strangers fell to their knees, made the sign of the cross, kissed his boots, his stirrups, his horse's croup, as they might have kissed a holy icon. For the coronation he refrained from wearing the bishop's dalmatic in which his father had presumptuously outfitted himself. Similarly he refused to exercise the Czar's prerogative of taking communion bread and wine with his own hands, receiving them instead from the officiating priest, like any obedient son of the Orthodox Church. The audience was greatly moved.

During the magnificent receptions organized in the greatest houses of the city, the Russian aristocracy showed their affectionate devotion to the imperial couple. Unanimously they admired Alexander's tall stature, his delicate features, the soft dreamy blue eyes, the wavy chestnut hair, the dimple in his chin, and the charming smile he had inherited from Catherine. He had simple, elegant manners; never raised his voice; bent his head a little because of his deafness, the better to hear his interlocutors; affected graciousness to the humble and knew how to inspire the confidence of the arrogant. Infatuated with his own person, he loved the noble gestures and theatrical words that captured the imagination of the public and enhanced his image. In earliest childhood he had acquired the habit of hiding his feelings. Now, though he was no longer caught between Czarskoye Selo and Gatchina, between Catherine and Paul, between the hammer and the anvil, he still felt at ease only in dissimulation, evasiveness, falsehood. He refused to make a clearcut choice between the two currents of thought that attracted him, rationalism and sentimentalism. He took sides in turn, now with Voltaire, now with Rousseau. A materialist, but given to idyllic dreams. He aspired at one and the same time to political power and to retirement on the banks of the Rhine. His split personality was a constant bafflement to the people around him. Some felt as if they were dealing with an androgynous creature comprising both masculine strength and feminine sensitivity. But the mixture was so delightful that there were few who criticized it.

In Moscow there was one ball after another. The ladies spent fortunes on clothes. Neither fatigue nor aching feet could dampen their enthusiasm as they swirled gracefully around the twenty-four-year-old Czar whom they called "our angel clad in purple." Alexander never went to bed before three in the morning. But he was not without scruples. He wrote a severe note to himself, in French, about amusing himself in this way while the nation waited for him to institute decisive reforms: "You are sleeping, wretch, and countless matters await you. You neglect your duties to devote yourself to sleep and pleasures, and poor unfortunates are suffering while you loll on your mattresses. What shame! You have not the courage to overcome the laziness that has always been your lot. Rise, shake off the yoke of your own weaknesses, become again a man and a citizen useful to your motherland."

Back in St. Petersburg, Alexander conscientiously resumed his studious routine. Epistles containing extravagant eulogies continued to pile up on his table. Derzhavin, the most famous Russian poet of the time, addressed an ode to him inviting him in pompous verses to show himself "a man on the throne." Another poet, Chichkov, wrote, "Alexander reigns, the hand of God is with us. . . . Having the soul of Catherine, he will be great like Peter in justice and in battle." Karamzin, a historian and novelist whose star was rising, greeted in the person of the young Czar "the coming of spring which will make us forget the dark fears of

winter." Even in Germany, old Klopstock, author of *The Messiah,* celebrated the advent of the new Russian Czar, whose humanitarian sentiments would vanquish the forces of evil and wash away the shame that
had tarnished the beautiful name of Alexander ever since the King of
Macedon. An anonymous young Russian sent the Emperor a long letter
of adoration and prayer, begging His Majesty to renounce despotism, to
grant his country national representation, and to improve the lot of the
serfs. In conclusion he wrote, "Peoples are always what the government
wishes them to be. Czar Ivan Vasilyevich [Ivan the Terrible] wanted to
have silent slaves . . . he had them. Peter I [Peter the Great] wanted us to
be blind imitators of foreigners; we became such. The wise Catherine
began to make us into Russians. Alexander, the idol of the people, will
complete this great work." Alexander was moved and gave orders to
seek out the author of the anonymous message. It was readily discovered
that he was a young functionary named Karazin. Brought before the
Emperor, he expected to be reprimanded for his audacity. But Alexander clasped him to his breast and declared, "Continue to tell me the
truth; I would that all my subjects were like you!" Alexander no doubt
pronounced these words with an eye on the gallery, but there was an
element of sincerity in the remark, nevertheless.

Having been unexpectedly thrust into affairs of state, the new Czar
felt the need to be enlightened and assisted, whether or not he heeded
the counsel he received. True, he had experienced politicians in the
Senate, but those old men belonged to another era, to "grandmother's
day," and he wanted to go forward. So he used them only to handle
ordinary business, showing them great deference and making fun of
them behind their backs. Of course he could have called on his dear
Arakcheyev. But Arakcheyev personified all the faults of the preceding
reign. To take him as adviser would be to give up all pretense of being a
providential innovator, and Alexander was bent on appearing in that
light.

To assist him in the elaboration of his vast plans, he summoned the
personal friends who had been sent away by Paul not long before. They
were of his generation and shared his ideas. Stroganov, Czartoryski,
Kochubey, Novosiltsev—the little group was again assembled, no
longer around the Grand Duke but around the Czar. Before leaving
Dresden, where he had been in exile, Kochubey wrote in French to
Count Alexander Vorontzov, brother of the ambassador, "I am leaving
because I believe that all good men should gather around [the Czar] and
do all they can to heal the countless wounds which his father inflicted
upon the country. And after that, if he should wish to employ me, I shall
serve him to the best of my ability, preferably in some branch of inter-

nal administration." On arriving in St. Petersburg Kochubey wrote Vorontzov, again in French: "All the actions of our new master bear the stamp of wisdom, moderation, and a restraint astonishing for his age."

When Alexander met his old companions again, it was a reunion of brothers. Like the Czar, they knew little about Russia or about politics, and based their convictions on their reading. They admired the English constitution and revolutionary France, and dreamed of establishing social justice and individual liberty in their country. Presided over by the young sovereign, whom they called their "gentle obstinate one," they formed a private circle which they themselves jokingly called the "Secret Committee" or the "Committee of Public Safety." The old dignitaries, bitter over being kept outside their deliberations, referred to the four newcomers as "Alexander's little confidants."

The Secret Committee had no official existence. Its meetings were surrounded with a certain mystery, inspired perhaps by Masonic rites. Two or three times a week the members of the little brotherhood would come to the palace to dine with Alexander and after the traditional cup of coffee would gravely pass through a secret corridor to His Majesty's study. There they discussed noble principles, drafted reports, scribbled plans. There was no agenda. Each one made his own passionate speech. They jumped from one subject to another on the slightest pretext. Everything came under discussion, the "reforms in the shapeless edifice of the empire," as Stroganov put it: foreign policy, the appointment of officials and of ladies-in-waiting, the abuses by an agent of the secret police, or the mysterious circumstances of the death of a Spanish lady during a night of debauchery. In the heat of conversation, the members of the Committee did not hesitate to contradict the Emperor. If he persisted in his opinions, as often happened, they raised their voices. Speaking of the nobility, Stroganov cried, "It is composed of a quantity of people who became gentlemen only by virtue of service, who have received no education and who have been led to think that there is nothing above the power of the Emperor. . . . It is the most ignorant class, the most debauched and the one with the dullest wits!"[5]

One day, having been disrespectful to His Majesty in the course of a stormy debate, Stroganov wrote him in French, "I must, Sire, apologize to you for having allowed myself to be carried away yesterday in the discussion that occupied us; I know that you are indulgent and even sometimes to excess, but I know that what I did was wrong and that the propriety which should characterize one's conduct is entirely lacking in mine. Thus, if you have the goodness not to condemn me, I must do so myself and inform you that I find the heat with which I spoke very reprehensible. . . ." Not in the least offended by his adviser's free language, Alexander replied, again in French: "My dear friend, I think you have gone quite mad! How is it possible to point out and accuse yourself for something that is the best proof of your interest in me and your love for the public good? . . . While I argue with you, I must do justice to the sentiments that inspire you. For pity's sake, no more of these apologies that are so out of keeping with the friendship that unites us. What would be unseemly in public can be very much in place when we are alone, and the greatest proof of friendship that you can give me is to scold me well when I deserve it. Farewell, my dear friend. Yours for life. Alexander."

There was another person who was burning to participate in the work of the Secret Committee. Alexander's former tutor, Laharpe, having become a member of the Swiss Directorate, felt more than ever that he was just the one to guide the young sovereign in his decisions. He wrote to his former pupil that he would like to see him again to assure him in person of his devotion. Alexander could do no less than invite him to St. Petersburg. Laharpe arrived proudly wearing the uniform of his office, with an embroidered belt and a saber slapping against his calf. From the start of his visit, Alexander distrusted this man whose high-flown rhetoric had once fired him with so much youthful excitement. He wisely kept him out of the meetings of the group, all the while assuring him that a chair was always reserved for him in his study. It did not take Alexander long to discover that there had been a curious change in Laharpe in the period of a few years. This man who had always recommended the simplicity of the common man was now advising him to combat his natural shyness and at all times to strike the firm attitude of an eagle-eyed leader. Laharpe mingled with the throng of courtiers, observing his former pupil's bearing in society, then wrote him letters pointing out his errors. He all but gave him marks for conduct. On such and such a day, he said, the Czar had entered the salon with too hesitant a step; another time, he had blushed inappropriately and bowed to those present too rapidly, too nervously; for this or that grand occasion it would have been better if he had shown himself in public with the Empress at his side. Summing up his general impression, the incorrigible mentor wrote to Alexander: "It seems to me that it is of the highest importance for you to *act the Emperor*, whether you are appearing in public or dealing with men to whom you have entrusted some department. . . . When the head of a nation presents himself, speaks or acts in that capacity, he should, in the picturesque words of Demosthenes, clothe himself in the dignity of his country. . . . Your youth, Sire, commands you perhaps even more imperiously not to be lax on this point. . . . Let those whom you have placed at the head of administrative departments become accustomed to the idea that *they are only your delegates,* that you have the right to hear about everything and to know everything, and that you mean to use it. Let there be no sharing of that right."

As for the government of the country, the democrat Laharpe conceived of it only in the form of uncompromising absolutism. "In the name of your people, Sire," he wrote, "keep intact the authority that is vested in you. . . . Never let yourself be carried away by the *aversion that absolute power inspires in you. . . . Have the courage to retain it whole, without partition,* since the constitution of your country grants it to you legitimately." Elsewhere, Laharpe declared that "any limitation of the imperial authority in favor of an assembly of men would be frowned upon by the nation." Lastly, forgetting the theory of the separation of powers that he had taught his pupil, he advised him to exercise "strict surveillance over the courts," if they did not function as it suited him.*

These firmly stated principles offended Alexander as a reader of Montesquieu and Voltaire but satisfied him as the inheritor of the crown of Russia. While he invoked republican morality, he never forgot for a second that he was monarch by the grace of God, accountable to no one. He loved liberty, but as a subject of conversation that could be infinitely expatiated upon. The beauty of the idea lay in the very impossibility of making it a reality. A few years later Prince Czartoryski would say of Alexander, "He would gladly have consented to everyone's being free, providing everyone voluntarily did as he alone wished."

For that matter, the other members of the Secret Committee, even when they envisaged a social upheaval, thought of it only as being supervised and controlled by a sovereign with an iron fist. Disinterring the memorandum that Bezborodko had once drawn up, Stroganov praised its merits to Alexander. In this document Bezborodko had said, "Russia should be an autocratic State. The slightest impairment of the autocracy would lead to the detachment of several provinces, would weaken the State, and be the source of innumerable public calamities." Despite this straitjacket imposed by the quasi-religious respect for the Czar, the Lord's anointed, the symbol of national unity, Alexander's advisers did try to institute partial measures to improve the lot of their contemporaries. But these efforts were hampered by their master's

---

*Emphasis in the text is Laharpe's own.

habit of reversing himself, of refusing to promulgate today what had
been decided upon yesterday. It was as if the Czar's fear of taking action
was another aspect of his lack of frankness. Just as he hated to say either
yes or no, so he hesitated to place his signature at the bottom of a
document: He felt comfortable only in the nebulous realm of sentiments and words.

Nevertheless, a few decisions did come out of the interminable
nocturnal discussions. On September 8, 1802, the Emperor fixed the
powers of the Senate. In Alexander's opinion, this high assembly, which
was responsible for publishing imperial decrees, overseeing the administration, and serving as a supreme tribunal, should be an independent body. Accordingly, he was angry when he read on the document
that was presented to him the consecrated salutation: *To our Senate*.
"What! To *our* Senate?" he exclaimed. "The Senate is the august guardian of the laws. It was created to guide and instruct us. But it is not our
servant!" An impressive show of indignation, by which Alexander once
again proved his talents as an actor.

An imperial manifesto published on the same day as the decree
reforming the Senate announced the creation of eight ministries to
replace the colleges that dated from the time of Peter the Great. Seven
portfolios were entrusted to old, declining dignitaries whom Alexander
despised. Of one of them, Zavadovsky, the Czar said, "He is a nonentity
and the only reason he is in the ministry is that he would make such an
outcry if he were excluded." The only one of his friends to be included
was Kochubey, who received the eighth portfolio, as Minister of the
Interior. The three other members of the Secret Committee would
have to content themselves with the rank of deputy ministers. Always
wavering and elusive, Alexander hoped that giving places of honor to
a few fossils would disarm their criticism and keep the real management of affairs in the hands of his young friends. Later they would try
to quietly rid themselves of the venerable, incompetent survivors. Alexander's habit of trying to run with the hare and hunt with the hounds
disturbed Stroganov, who wrote, "I cannot fail to notice how confused
our young Emperor's ideas are." And Vorontzov noted, "Monsieur Kochubey was struck with the lack of order that reigned in all the Emperor's projects. He had made no plan and knocked at every door, so
to speak, not knowing his own mind."

Other decisions that were laboriously worked out reformed public
education and created six circumscriptions, each with its own university, secondary schools, and lower schools. However, Alexander was
opposed to the idea of opening military schools in the provinces or

training officers in the secondary schools, because he intended the future leaders of his army to receive their instruction in St. Petersburg, under his eyes, as in the time of his ancestors. As always he oscillated between initiative and tradition, between the desire to forge ahead and the fear of losing an ounce of his authority.

But the Czar's great concern was to bring about profound social reform and especially the reform of serfdom. Serfs represented nine-tenths of the Russian population. To be sure, they were not actually slaves, since the peasants were attached to the soil and had retained a certain village autonomy through the centuries. But they had no civil rights. Completely subjected to the will of the landowner, they were the human chattel that guaranteed his prosperity. He could sell them with the land, send them off to military service for twenty-five years, have them punished according to his whim, or marry them to anyone he pleased. Only the power to impose the death penalty was denied him. Since the time of Peter the Great, the male serf had constituted a new taxable unit, the *soul*. What finer gift could a sovereign make to those who served the throne than a bunch of souls chosen in some corner of his empire? Catherine II had distributed to her favorites 800,000 of those souls, Paul I 115,000 in four years.

Vast fortunes in land and serfs had thus been built far from the capital. A high-ranking nobleman almost never visited his estates, knew nothing about his *muzhiks*, and entrusted the administration of all his property to intendants, who were often absent themselves. In many cases the farmers, lacking directives, tended their fields lazily, incompetently, for better or worse. Fifteen hundred landed proprietors shared one-third of the total number of serfs in Russia, each master having at his disposal an average of 2,500 souls. Below these magnates reigned 2,000 lesser landowners with about 700 souls to their credit. Seventeen thousand small landowners contented themselves with 200 souls and lived modestly in the provinces. At the bottom of the scale, some 200,000 debt-ridden members of the decayed nobility vegetated on their plots of land, surrounded by groups of half-starved peasants.[6] But whatever their financial situation, none of these nobles considered himself to be of the same human essence as the serfs. The landowners, dressed in European fashion, lived in the time of Czar Alexander; the serfs, clothed in rags, lived in the time of Peter the Great. An unbridgeable chasm separated the two: They had nothing in common but the language they spoke and the religion they professed. And even at that, many of the provincial gentry expressed themselves more easily in French than in Russian. The happiness of the peasant depended entirely on the character and wealth of his master. Under a benevolent master he felt as if he belonged to a vast family and was affectionately protected against all the blows of fate, starting with famine. Under a cruel master, his life was a hell marked by forced labor and corporal punishment. It was the domestic serfs whose condition was the most wretched, and in the great houses there were countless numbers of them. Nearer to the nobleman than the peasants, they were directly subject to his despotism. Idleness, drunkenness, and debauchery reigned among the valets and serving girls. They were bought and sold, traded, lost at the gaming table. The newspapers published announcements of this kind of commerce: "For sale: a cook, a girl who knows how to sew, an old armoire."

In the Czar's opinion it was necessary to deal once and for all, and as soon as possible, with the thorny question of serfdom, which neither Peter the Great nor Catherine the Great had succeeded in settling. The members of the Secret Committee unanimously condemned the anachronistic institution. Czartoryski declared, "Serfdom is a thing so horrible that no consideration should prevent its being rooted out." Kochubey regarded it as a "great infamy" of which Russia could only be ashamed. Novosiltsev concurred. And Stroganov, whose vast estates in the Urals were peopled with forty-six thousand souls, cried out during a meeting of the group with Alexander, "Millions of men feel the weight of their slavery. Hatred reigns between them and their born oppressors; yet it is through their industry that the greatest part of the wealth of the empire is produced and we must be careful not to discourage them!"

With a fine burst of enthusiasm the young legislators threw themselves into the work, guided by the principles of equality and justice. But their ardor cooled very quickly, as they were seized by fear of the cracks that this reform would produce in the social edifice. Soft-pedaling his enthusiasm, the impetuous Stroganov stressed the necessity of "handling the landowners gently" and of leading them to the proposed goal "without shocking them, by imperceptible degrees." In his opinion, the most important thing was to avoid spreading news of the affair, so as not to stir up the muzhiks. Laharpe advised that they should "proceed quietly, without touching property, without speaking of liberty or of liberation." Kochubey, too, drew back before the magnitude of the obstacle. In his view, although serfdom was to be condemned, it "belonged to an order of things which it was delicate to touch."[7]

In the end, they all agreed that a sudden reform should be avoided. They were willing to abandon their seignorial rights over the peasants, but not over the lands those peasants tilled. To liberate a peasant without giving him the means of buying back the land was inconceivable, but to deprive a landowner of a part of his domain in favor of his serfs was even more so. The landowner considered the land part of his capital, the foundation of his wealth and prestige, the natural source of his revenues. The serf considered that that land his people had cleared and cultivated for centuries, from father to son, had become his own property. "We belong to you," they said to the nobles, "but the land belongs to us." After long deliberation, Alexander gave up on the only solution possible: to emancipate the peasants without allotting them land. In short, everything would remain as in the past. One more hot-air balloon deflated. To salve their consciences, the members of the Secret Committee nevertheless took a few minor measures, feeble palliatives for a situation they allegedly found repugnant: There would be no more distribution of lands and serfs for services rendered to the State; it would be forbidden to publish announcements in the gazettes concerning the purchase or sale of human beings; merchants and the middle classes would be able to acquire lands and serfs, a privilege formerly restricted to the nobles. In Alexander's mind, this last provision would enable commoners to establish small properties. Finally, a ukase of March 4, 1803, supplementing an imperial decree of February 20, 1802, set forth the conditions under which a nobleman could free his serfs, if he wished, so as to create a new class of "free farmers." However, the administrative procedures for this emancipation were very complicated and (always the same stumbling block!) no provision had been made for the serfs to buy back their plots of ground. Liberated, they were condemned to starve unless they could arrange to be taken on as servants. Few serfs would benefit from this hasty and incomplete measure, and by the end of Alexander's reign there were only forty-seven thousand free farmers.

The Secret Committee was out of breath. They no longer even talked about a constitutional monarchy. After thirty-six sessions in two and a half years, their meetings ceased of themselves, without Alexander's having requested it. In the meantime, Laharpe, disappointed, had returned to Switzerland.

Tired of his advisers, the Czar became increasingly stubborn and conscious of his imperial prerogatives. When the old poet Derzhavin, now the Minister of Justice, dared to contradict him over some trifle, he replied sharply, "You're always trying to lecture me! Am I an autocrat or not? Well, I do as I please!"

Nevertheless, he was extremely agreeable in the bosom of the family. He surrounded his mother with considerations and even had her take precedence over his wife in official ceremonies. His wife he treated affectionately and respectfully even as he deceived her. Fickle by temperament, he liked to pass from one conquest to the next, often contenting himself with pleasing the lady without pursuing his advantage. Thus he courted the wives of his two friends, Stroganov and Kochubey, had a brief affair with a French singer, Mademoiselle Phillis; succumbed to the charm of another French artist, Madame Chevallier; sighed at the feet of a third, the famous Mademoiselle George; took a passing fancy to Mesdames Bacharach, Kremmer, Severin, and Schwartz, whose husbands looked the other way; and cherished for his very young sister Catherine a passion that was ambiguous, to say the least. According to Karamazin, Catherine had "eyes of fire and the figure of a demi-goddess." Princess de Lieven wrote that she had "a dazzling freshness of complexion and the most beautiful hair in the world." In the general opinion she had much charm and an incisive mind, was well read but haughty, with abrupt manners and on occasion even insufferable impudence. Her influence over Alexander increased with the passage of time. He loved her for her buxom grace and her sparkling conversation. How far did their intimacy go in the languorous tête-à-têtes they delighted in? Alexander wrote her, in French: "Farewell, charm of my eyes, adoration of my heart, lamp of the age, phenomenon of nature, or better than all that, Bissiam Bissiamovna with the flat nose." "What is that dear nose doing, the nose I love so to flatten and to kiss?" "If you are mad, at least you are the most delightful madwoman who ever existed. . . . I am mad about you." "I love you like a madman! . . . I rejoice like a maniac to be seeing you again. After having run like a man possessed, I hope to take delicious rest in your arms." And in a postscript: "Alas, I cannot take advantage of my former prerogatives (I refer to your feet, you understand?) to apply the tenderest kisses in your bedchamber."

But this incestuous inclination was not enough for Alexander. He had a need to fire the hearts of the women around him. "You do not understand the charm of conversation with women," he said to one of his companions, "you always want to push things too far." But he himself pushed "things" pretty far when he chose for his mistress Maria Naryshkina, the wife of a splendid court dignitary and the daughter of a great Polish nobleman, Prince Tchetvertinski. According to the contemporaries, Maria Naryshkina eclipsed all the other women at court. "Her beauty," wrote Viegel, "is so perfect that it appears impossible, supernatural: the ideal lines of her face and her flawless silhouette stand out with particular clarity." General Kutuzov declared that "women are worthy to be loved since there is among them a creature as fascinating as Madame Naryshkina." The poet Derzhavin, who not many years earlier had celebrated "Psyche" in the person of the future Empress Elizabeth, now celebrated "Aspasia" in the person of the favorite. He praised "the fire of her black eyes" and "the roundness of her voluptu-

ous breast." Dresses of a studied simplicity set off the lines of her body
and the radiance of her face. At court receptions she invariably appeared wearing a white gown with soft folds, without jewels of any sort.
Her example was Madame Récamier.* Behind all this grace lay hidden
a keen appetite for pleasure and a limited mind not the least interested
in politics. Having no ambition to become the power behind the throne,
Maria Naryshkina never wearied the Czar with her requests or advice.
With her he didn't think, he didn't worry, he relaxed. Joseph de Maistre,
the representative of the King of Sardinia, described the new favorite
as follows in a letter to his sovereign: "She is not a Pompadour, she is
not a Montespan; she is rather a La Vallière, except that she is not lame
and will never become a Carmelite."†

The wealth of the Naryshkins being incalculable, Maria Naryshkina
never needed to beg a favor of her imperial lover; she already had
everything she could desire. Her husband was Master of the Royal Hunt.
For a century the name of the Naryshkins had figured in the annals of the
Russian court. No one could forget that a Natalya Naryshkina had given
birth to Peter the Great, and that a Leon Naryshkin, nicknamed the
Harlequin, had been Catherine the Great's official court jester. When
the Naryshkins traveled they were accompanied by troops of intendants,
secretaries, lady's companions, and salaried artists. When they entertained, an orchestra of forty musicians amused the guests amid a profu-
sion of flowers and exotic fruits; and they had three dinners served:
Russian, French, and Italian. These receptions took place not only in
Russia but abroad. The Naryshkins possessed a castle in Florence, a villa
in Fiesole "to enjoy the fresh air," a palace in St. Petersburg on the
Fontanka, and a summer residence on Krestovski Island. This last house,
a huge structure with a green cupola and a Roman portico with white
columns, was very near the summer residence of the Czar, which was
located on Kamenny Island, on the other side of a tributary of the Neva.
Alexander had only to cross a wooden bridge to be at his mistress's. The
salons were immense, with allegorical paintings on the ceilings, heavy
damask hangings, massive furniture, and dim mirrors. When there was a
reception His Majesty would open the ball by a polonaise with Maria

---

*Juliette Récamier was a celebrated French beauty of the time, the hostess of a
fashionable salon, and the longtime mistress of Chateaubriand. The famous reclining
portrait by David shows her dressed in the Neoclassical manner described. (Trans.)

†Louise de La Vallière and Françoise de Montespan were successive mistresses of
Louis XIV; Jeanne de Pompadour was the mistress of Louis XV. While the latter two
exercised powerful political influence, La Vallière played a role only in the private life
of her royal lover. (Trans.)

Naryshkina, while the Master of the Royal Hunt sadly shook his head. On other evenings the Emperor retired with her immediately to a boudoir that she had arranged for their meetings. There, everything was simple, intimate, cozy. Maria Naryshkina said that in this secret place she was at last *at home* and persuaded her lover that he was at home, too. In this second home he found something warm and appealing that was missing from the conjugal hearth. Alexander, who was of a rather frigid temperament, was grateful to his mistress all the more for awakening in him bursts of feeling that surprised him.

Elizabeth, meanwhile, bore the betrayal with dignity, although she wrote to her mother, "I pardon everything in a woman except the seduction of a married man, for one cannot calculate its disastrous consequences." When Alexander learned that Maria Naryshkina was at last pregnant by him, he was exultant. It was the favorite herself who informed the Empress of her "interesting condition." Elizabeth, who still had no child, was hurt and indignant. "Did I tell you, dear Mama," she wrote to her mother, "that she [Maria Naryshkina] has had the impudence to be the first to inform me of her pregnancy, which was so little advanced that I could very well have been ignorant of it. I think that to do that, one must have an effrontery that is inconceivable to me. It was at a ball, and the thing was not yet common knowledge as it is now. . . . She knew very well that I was not ignorant of the way in which she might have become pregnant. I don't know what will become of all that and how it will end, but I do know that I shall not ruin either my disposition or my health for a creature who is not worth it. . . . Add to that that the Emperor is the first to ridicule virtuous behavior and that he makes remarks on this subject that are really revolting on the lips of the man who should be the guardian of order, the guardian of morality, without which there is no order." Indeed Alexander, proud as could be of this paternity, went strutting about like a peacock. When the child was born she was given the name Sophie. From the house with the green cupola the Czar wrote a note to his sister Catherine: "It is from *home* that I write you, and my companion and my child are at your feet and thank you for remembering them. . . . The happiness that I enjoy in my little household and the affection that you show me are the only charms of my existence." Yes, in the arms of the beautiful, not over-bright Maria Naryshkina, Alexander forgot the pomp and constraint of the court, the walls of the imperial palace haunted by the bloody memory of his father, even the wife who had been at his side on the night of the murder and who, knowing everything about him, was unable to help him shake off his obsession. Whether she liked it or not, she was his accomplice. She shared in his remorse. It was only when he was away from her that he could be another man. A new man, without a memory.

Yet he did not abandon Elizabeth completely, did not make a choice; he led two complementary lives at once. As in the past, he took almost all his meals with the Empress and was very attentive to her in public. From time to time he even visited her bed. While he was delighted when Maria Naryshkina gave him several more bastard children—who would die at an early age—he still hoped that Elizabeth would give him a legitimate heir. Meanwhile, Elizabeth abandoned herself to her own tender feeling for a handsome officer of the Guard, one Alexis Okhotnikov. He died mysteriously, stabbed as he left a theater, and the Empress had a mausoleum erected over his grave. The monument represented a woman weeping at the foot of an oak split by lightning. Alexander was not disturbed by all the talk about this affair. Having long espoused the theory of reciprocal freedom in their marriage, he even encouraged his wife to be unfaithful; that would, after all, justify his own conduct. According to Baron de Barante, the couple had even made a compact in writing "to agree upon this emancipation."

Besides, for Alexander such diversions of the drawing room and the bedroom were only a distraction from his real passion—politics. The disbanding of the Secret Committee did not mean he had lost his taste for power. Quite the contrary. Reshuffling the ministerial posts, he removed the old servants of the state and replaced them with his young friends. But, as before, it was he alone who made the decisions. Vacillating and reversing himself, he satisfied no one. Like the men of "grandmother's day," the new men realized that they could exercise no influence on him. He exasperated the former by his deference to the latter and the latter by his friendship for the former. He would listen with glowing cheeks and tears in his eyes to the democratic speeches of one of his confidants. Then he would find himself with his aides-de-camp— Uvarov, say, or Peter Dolgoruky—dyed-in-the-wool reactionaries who begged him not to venture too far down the path of progress, and he would nod his head, agree with them entirely, and thank them for their disinterested advice. He adopted the same attitude when he visited his mother, the Empress Dowager, who bristled at the prospect of any reform. The antagonism he felt around him increased his native indecisiveness. Pulled in every direction, he could get out of his difficulties only by resorting to half-measures and equivocation. Soon coming to doubt the results of his own domestic policy, he began to think of making up for it with diplomatic successes on the world stage. He forgot the wretched fate of the serfs in his country and dreamed of the international fame of Catherine the Great.

V

THE BAPTISM OF FIRE

One can love parades and hate war. That was the opinion of Alexander, who had a passion for handsome uniforms, impeccable alignments, and skillful maneuvers executed with pomp and precision—and a repugnance for military adventures in the field. His great idea was to establish peaceful relations with all his neighbors. If he agreed to incorporate the kingdom of Georgia into Russia, it was only because Georgia itself, torn by dynastic struggles, had asked to be placed under his protection. To all other states he declared his intention of not seeking to expand Russian territory. The first measure the Czar took to ensure peace was to sign an agreement with England, on June 5, 1801. He also reestablished diplomatic relations with Austria and assured France that he was favorably inclined toward her.

France intrigued him above all. It was a strange nation: After the bloodbath of the Revolution and the disappointing experience of the Directorate, it seemed to have had such a need for order and stability that it had given itself over to a dictator. And in fact only one of the three Consuls who were now governing the country was in control, holding all real powers while the others served merely as his advisers: the glorious General Napoleon Bonaparte. And Bonaparte, as soon as he had been nominated to this supreme position, had proved his administrative and political genius. He had reestablished internal peace by liquidating his last opponents; he had recalled the emigrés, signed a Concordat with the Pope and, through his most recent victories, forced Austria and England to grant him respect. He had as his diplomatic counselor the astute and supple Talleyrand, whose cunning, culture, and gentlemanly manners formed a striking contrast to the impetuosity and coarseness of his master. Without doubt, thought Alexander, in future one would have to reckon with this Bonaparte, this thirty-two-year-old general as versed in issuing laws as in winning battles.

When the First Consul of France sent General Duroc to congratulate him on his accession, the Czar displayed great curiosity to make the acquaintance of this specimen of postrevolutionary fauna. He strolled with Duroc down the paths of the Summer Garden, said countless gracious things to him, and addressed him as "citizen," not suspecting that the term had long since been abandoned in Bonaparte's entourage. Annoyed, Duroc finally made a respectful protest. But Alexander, more republican than his guest, went right on enthusiastically calling him "citizen."[1]

For a while Duroc believed that his interlocutor, who was so cordial, was amenable to the idea of a Franco-Russian alliance. But when he alluded to the advantages that Russian maritime trade would gain from French protection in the Mediterranean, Alexander replied, "I want nothing for myself. I only want to contribute to the tranquillity of Europe." And when Duroc was getting ready to take his leave without having obtained any precise answer, Alexander added gently, "Tell Bonaparte that it must not be thought of him that he wants to invade." Soon the Russian ambassador to Paris, Kolychev, was replaced by Count Morkov, who was unfavorably disposed toward the First Consul.

In St. Petersburg Count Alexander Vorontzov was dismissed as Minister of Foreign Affairs and replaced by his assistant, Adam Czartoryski. For a long time Alexander had considered Czartoryski his best adviser on diplomatic matters. But he also knew that his friend, a prudent, honest man, had one major failing so far as the Russians were concerned: his immoderate love for Poland. Devoted with all his soul to the land of his birth, he hoped that someday the Czar would rectify the injustice of the partition of that wretched country and reestablish it

within its historic boundaries. But although Alexander believed in eq-
uity in foreign policy, he knew that Russia, Austria, and Prussia would
never of their own free will give up the Polish provinces they had
annexed. Obsessed with his unrealistic project, Czartoryski wanted to
prevent a rapprochement between Russia and the German states, while
the Emperor thought only of reaching an agreement with them in
order to achieve a better balance of power in Europe. He had quickly
realized that the Treaty of Amiens represented only a precarious truce
in the conflict between England and France. Furthermore, as the son
of a Princess of Württemberg and the husband of a Princess of Baden,
he could not but take an interest in the fate of those two small countries,
which were always threatened by France. Looking farther afield, he
encompassed in a sort of admiring affection the other Germanic states,
Russia's natural ramparts against French ambitions. The Empress Dowager, who was sensitive to everything German, exercised a moral pressure on him that further helped him to oppose the views of Czartoryski.
He wrote to Morkov in Paris, "You will represent to the French government on my behalf how advisable it would be not to drive the court of
Vienna to extremities and not to give it the advantages that always
accrue to offended justice. At this time it is more indispensable than
ever to establish justice and moderation everywhere."

Still carried away by his admiration for Germany, he dreamed of
making the acquaintance of the descendant of the great Frederick and
of watching the superbly trained Prussian grenadiers on parade. Without informing either Czartoryski or Kochubey, he took advantage of a
stay on the western frontier of his empire to make a visit, on May 29,
1802, at Memel, to King Frederick William III and Queen Louise of
Prussia. The ceremony with which he was welcomed and the ardor of
the sentiments expressed exceeded all his hopes. For a week parades,
maneuvers, dinners, balls, excursions into the countryside, were so
many opportunities for him to charm his hosts. Countess Voss, Grand
Mistress at the court of Queen Louise, noted in her journal: "The Emperor is a very handsome man, he is blond and has an attractive face,
but he carries himself ill. He probably has an excellent heart, sensitive
and affectionate. In any case, he is extremely considerate and obliging."
And a few days later: "The Emperor is the most agreeable man one can
imagine. His thoughts and feelings are those of a gentleman. Poor man,
he has been completely conquered and bewitched by the Queen."

And indeed, Alexander was captivated at once by this beautiful,
intelligent, emotional woman of twenty-six, who told him straight out
that to her he represented perfection on earth. "I have never seen the

Alps, but I have seen men, or rather one man in the full meaning of the word," she wrote of Alexander to her brother George. Louise, who was quick to catch fire, had such a taste for coquetry that, according to Count Simon Vorontzov, she would have been "proud and happy to make a lackey or a beggar fall in love with her." Faced with the Czar of Russia, she could not contain herself. Her boring, clumsy husband, Frederick William III, encouraged her, thinking of the political advantages of this sentimental conquest, and Alexander cheerfully entered into the game. There was nothing he liked so much as the exchange of flirtatious remarks, amorous glances, compliments that had a double meaning. Intoxicated by his success, he forgot the far-off Maria Naryshkina. Still, despite this light fencing, he did not mean to go all the way. "It was very seldom," wrote Czartoryski, "that the virtue of the ladies with whom this prince was occupied was really in danger."[2] When Queen Louise became too forward, he retreated into his customary diffidence and coldness. Fearing a nocturnal intrusion into his bedchamber, he even barricaded his door: an unnecessary precaution, for the "enchantress" was clearly too romantic to be sensual. She was content to have kindled a flame in the Emperor, as he was content to have kindled a flame in her. Their liking for each other was reinforced by the Platonic nature of their encounter. Henceforth Alexander would have one more woman to "adore" without having touched her. For him she would be the incarnation of Prussia with all its charm. He would no longer be able to separate politics from sentiment. He had only one disappointment: the Prussian army, whose maneuvers he had watched, seemed far inferior to his own. "I have come back cured of the opinion I had of the Prussian troops," he said later to Baron von Stutterheim, the Austrian military attaché.

Naturally, in the course of Alexander's idyllic conversations with Queen Louise, the two had also discussed Europe. The sovereigns had not yet come to any decisions. But that did not prevent Czartoryski from writing to the Emperor, in French, after his return: "I regard this interview [at Memel] as one of the most unfortunate things that has happened to Russia. Because of the intimate friendship which Your Imperial Majesty contracted there with the King [and by implication, with the Queen], Your Majesty no longer considers Prussia as a political State but as a person who is dear to him and toward whom Your Majesty believes he has particular obligations to fulfill." Count Simon Vorontzov echoed these sentiments, proclaiming that the journey was "the rashest step one can imagine in the world," because it destroyed the balance between Prussia and Austria and encouraged the latter to accede to all

the demands of Bonaparte as the price of peace. "All the sovereigns of
the earth came to visit the late Empress," he wrote to his friend Stroganov. "Now it is the Emperor of Russia who goes to visit others."

Indifferent to the protestations of his entourage, Alexander continued to think that by being nice to everyone he could steer clear of
a generalized conflict. But then Bonaparte became Consul for life, and
his ambition seemed to grow with the honors he received. The Treaty
of Amiens was broken and both France and England resumed preparations for war. Preoccupied by the position of the straits that gave access
to the Baltic and the North Sea, the Czar wrote to Ambassador Morkov
in Paris: "The Emperor, satisfied with the portion Providence has assigned to him, has no thought of expanding in any direction; he intends
that no one shall expand at the expense of Turkey." Bonaparte turned
a deaf ear; then, as Morkov became too pressing, he demanded that the
envoy be recalled. Alexander did as Bonaparte wished but bestowed
upon Morkov the insignia of the Order of St. Andrew and replaced him
with a mere chargé d'affaires, Monsieur d'Oubril. On both sides there
were as yet only minor vexations. Yet Alexander confided in a letter to
Laharpe: "Like you, my friend, I have revised my opinion of the First
Consul. Since he became Consul for life the veil has fallen from him,
and since then things have gone from bad to worse. He has begun by
depriving himself of the greatest honor a man can attain and the only
one that remained for him to pluck down, that of proving that he had
worked for the happiness and glory of his motherland without any
personal ambition and, faithful to the constitution to which he himself
had sworn, of returning after the ten years the power he held in his
hands. . . . Now he is one of the most famous tyrants that history has
produced."[3]

Notwithstanding this opinion he expressed in private, the Czar had
no intention of doing anything rash because of the disturbing rise of
"the Corsican." In January 1804 General d'Hédouville, who represented France in St. Petersburg, could still write to Talleyrand, "The
rumors that are being spread about Russia's hostile intentions seem to
me to lack any foundation; they spring solely from the military boasting
of the English party."

But not long afterward, a piece of news exploded in St. Petersburg
like a bombshell: The Duc d'Enghien had been kidnapped from Ettenheim, on Badenese soil, despite the law of nations, and summarily executed on March 21, 1804, in a trench near the chateau of Vincennes.
Since the Duc d'Enghien belonged to the Bourbon-Condé family, in
Alexander's mind he was a personage who could not be touched. The

solidarity of monarchy united the whole court of Russia to the young prince. Besides, he had visited St. Petersburg under the reign of Paul I and had charmed the Czar, the Czarina, and the Grand Dukes during his brief stay on the banks of the Neva. By raising his hand against him, Bonaparte had committed sacrilege. "First of all I must speak to you of a matter that everyone has been talking about here for the last three days and which I cannot get out of my mind; it is the death of that poor Duc d'Enghien," Empress Elizabeth wrote her mother. "I have been upset about it all day." And Joseph de Maistre wrote, "Indignation is at its height. The good Empresses wept. The Grand Duke is furious and His Imperial Majesty is no less strongly affected. The French legation is no longer received. . . ." The Emperor immediately ordered seven days of mourning. A funeral service was held in the Roman Catholic church of St. Petersburg, in the presence of the imperial family, the court, and the diplomatic corps. On the cenotaph erected in the nave were inscribed the words: *Quem devoravit bellua corsica* ("To the victim of the Corsican monster"). That evening there was a reception at Prince Bielosselski's. Everyone present was in mourning. When Madame d'Hédouville appeared the guests were shocked to note that the wife of Bonaparte's representative had put on a colored dress. By common accord, both men and women turned their backs on her.

On April 17 the Emperor called a special meeting of the Council of State at the Winter Palace to discuss the attitude that should be adopted in the face of "Bonaparte's revolting highhandedness." In a burst of anger, he had dictated to Czartoryski the following note: "His Majesty would find it detestable to maintain relations any longer with a government which knows neither restraint nor duties of any kind and which, stained with an abominable assassination, can no longer be considered as anything but a den of thieves." But in the course of the deliberations Alexander calmed down again and recognized that this spectacular declaration might provoke a war for which Russia was not ready. After all, he had not been directly offended by Bonaparte's action. Russia's policy should not be hampered by sentiment. A compromise solution was unanimously adopted. The council drafted a note of protest that Monsieur d'Oubril would deliver to the French government and another addressed to the Diet of Ratisbon. The note sent to Paris read: "His Imperial Majesty has learned, with as much astonishment as grief, of the event that took place at Ettenheim, the circumstances that accompanied it, and the distressing result that followed. . . . Unfortunately, His Majesty considers it to be nothing but a violation of the law of nations and the rights of a neutral territory, a violation which, to say the least, is as gratuitous as it is manifest, the consequences of which are difficult to calculate and which, if one were to regard it as permissible, would reduce to nothing the security and independence of sovereign States. . . . His Majesty is persuaded that the First Consul will hasten to lend an ear to the just demands of the German States and that he will feel the urgency of employing the most effective means to calm the fears that he has just aroused in all governments and to put an end to this state of affairs, which is too alarming for their future security and independence."

Bonaparte, whose pride was offended, ordered Talleyrand to reply in kind to this note, which all things considered was moderate in tone. But Talleyrand allowed himself to be carried away and on May 16, 1804, wrote, "If the present object of His Majesty the Emperor of Russia could be to form a new coalition in Europe and begin war again, what use are vain pretexts and why not act openly? However deeply grieved the First Consul will be at the resumption of hostilities, he knows no one on earth whom he wishes to allow to intervene in the internal affairs of the country and, as he does not meddle in the parties or opinions that may divide Russia, His Majesty the Emperor has no right to meddle in the parties or opinions that may divide France. . . . The complaint which Russia raises today leads one to wonder if, when England was planning the assassination of Paul I, and it was known that the authors of the plot were within a league of the borders, any move was made to have them seized."

The last part of the note was published in the widely read newspaper *Le Moniteur*. For the Czar it contained a threefold insult: the affirmation that, contrary to the statement of the manifesto, Paul I had not died from an attack of apoplexy but had been assassinated; the absurd insinuation that England had mounted the conspiracy; the reproach to the son for having failed to punish his father's murderers. Thus after three years of respite, of thinking that time was effacing the memory of the patricide from all minds, Alexander found himself publicly accused as an accomplice in a crime that had not been expiated. With perfidious cunning Talleyrand had aimed his thrust at the most sensitive point of the Czar's conscience. And to cap it all he recalled the French ambassador, General d'Hédouville, from St. Petersburg. In Paris, meanwhile, the Russian chargé d'affaires Monsieur d'Oubril was trying in vain to find a compromise. Having been shown the door in cavalier fashion, he soon found himself obliged to ask for his passports.

In the meantime, the Empire had been proclaimed in France. On May 18, 1804, Bonaparte had become Napoleon. He had even permitted himself the luxury of being anointed by the Pope, amid extraordinary pomp. To the dismay of the old monarchies, a new sovereign, full of strength and arrogance, thrust himself upon the scene. To Alexander, this unscrupulous adventurer had no right to the mystical respect that traditionally surrounded crowned heads. He thought the parvenu capable of anything—crimes, violation of treaties, contempt for the given word—to satisfy his ambition. "That man is growing more reckless in proportion as the French grow more pusillanimous," he said to Baron von Stutterheim. "I think he will go mad." To contain the madman the reasonable nations had to unite. Although he did not have any particular sympathy for the English, the Czar was inclined to think it was from them that he would obtain the most effective support. England, he thought, being already at war with France, could not but be favorable to the idea of concerted action. The Anglophiles around him pushed him in that direction by pointing out the common interests of the two countries. "The production of each of our two countries is necessary to the other, and each finds in the other the best and most advantageous markets in the universe," wrote Simon Vorontzov. "We are formidable because of our land forces, and England is the greatest maritime power in the world." Echoing this assessment, William Pitt, who had returned to power, declared to the Czar's ambassador that "a good Englishman should be a good Russian and a good Russian should be a good Englishman," for the two nations united were destined sooner or later to topple "the colossus of power, ambition, and despotism."[4]

In September 1804 Alexander and his associates decided to move into action. Czartoryski and his Italian secretary, Abbé Piatoli, prepared an Instruction designed to enlighten the cabinet of St. James's on the Russian plan: the return of France to its former limits and revision of the Prussian and Austrian borders; and in case of the partition of Turkey, allocation of certain territories to Russia and Austria and establishment of a federation of separate states on the ruins of the Ottoman Empire, under the aegis of Russia. While setting forth this grandiose plan, Alexander stressed the fact that he "had nothing against the French nation but only against its government." The proof? According to the terms of the Instruction, the peoples delivered from Napoleon would be accorded a liberal regime inspired by the gains made by the French Revolution. The document was categorical on this point: "Far from attempting to reestablish, in the countries that must be freed from the yoke of Bonaparte, former abuses and a state of affairs to which minds that have tasted forms of independence could not become accustomed, we shall on the contrary make every effort to secure them liberty on a genuine basis." In addition, Alexander recommended that all countries accept a kind of international law founded on "the obligation never to start a war until they had exhausted the means that mediation by a third party could offer." Borne on the wings of imagination, he even envisaged the creation of a "European federation" of states of good will: "After so many alarms, after having felt the disadvantages of a precarious or illusory independence, most governments will probably wish to join a league which would guarantee their tranquillity and security to the highest degree. . . . It is above all the intimate bond between the courts of St. Petersburg and London that would guarantee the durability of this state of affairs."[5]

Armed with this Instruction, Novosiltsev left on a secret mission to England. When William Pitt learned of Alexander's plan, he could not help smiling at so much naïveté. Napoleon was at Boulogne pressing forward with preparations for debarkation on the English coast, the only conceivable future for England lay in relentless war against France, and here the Czar's envoy came to talk to him about a pact according to which a nation would, in short, have to wait to be attacked and conquered before fighting back! In order not to discourage Novosiltsev directly, he told him that "in future" such a measure would be salutary and that England would naturally subscribe to it. But everything in its time. For the moment, the problem was to bring Austria and Prussia into the league of nations of good faith. This concept of "good faith," declared the English, was extensible, and could be applied as well to a just war as to an honorable peace. In other words what counted in any situation was not the "good faith," but the "league." The label was only to save appearances. To overcome the reluctance of Russia as well as of Austria and Prussia, Pitt did not hesitate to imply that Great Britain could subsidize its allies heavily. After the victory, he said, they would reorganize the world on sound foundations and a congress of well-intentioned sovereigns would create a reign of peace among nations.

Russia signed a treaty of alliance with Austria in November 1804; another with Sweden in January 1805; and a third with England in April 1805. Thus all that was lacking was the agreement of Prussia, over whose territory part of the Russian troops must pass. But the King of Prussia wavered between the desire to participate in the coalition so as to rid himself of Napoleon and the hope that if he remained neutral Napoleon would let him have Hanover. These hesitations were just what Czartoryski needed, for he had not abandoned his Polish project. To put an end to all the shillyshallying of a questionable friend, he said, they must "pass over the body of Prussia," take Warsaw and Poznania away from her, and reconstitute Poland "under the scepter of Alexander." "That is the only way," he added, "to bring Poland, which has been forgotten even by France, back to life."[6] But this plan was not favorably received at court. Alexander himself found it brutal and risky, while at the Emperor's table young Prince Peter Dolgoruky violently criticized Czartoryski to his face: "You speak like a Polish prince and *I* speak like a Russian prince!" Czartoryski blanched and bit his lips. The Czar didn't turn a hair. Which of his two advisers did he approve of? However much Czartoryski and Dolgoruky disagreed over Prussia, they were of one mind about France. Only vigorous military action could force Napoleon to revise his aggressive policy. To galvanize her allies, England gave Austria three millions pounds sterling and promised the same amount to Prussia. Russia had already received her share.

Two Russian armies were concentrated on the western border: One of fifty thousand men commanded by General Michael Ilarionovich Kutuzov was ready to join the Austrian forces; the other, consisting of ninety thousand men commanded by General Mikhelson, was destined, if necessary, to march against Prussia. On the home front patriotic enthusiasm was at its highest pitch. Elizabeth wrote to her mother, "At present I confess, Mama, that I feel the deepest love for Russia, that however pleased I should be to see Germany again, and however much I like to think of it, I should be very distressed to leave Russia forever, and that if, through some imaginary circumstance, I found myself alone and mistress to choose the place where I should live, it is in Russia that I should go to settle."

Alexander was preparing to join Kutuzov's army. Just in case, he made a visit to a *staretz*,* a mystic, Sevastianov, to ask for his blessing. One could admire Voltaire and still listen to mystical predictions. The staretz begged him not to fight against "the accursed Frenchman," for God would not deliver up Napoleon until much later. Impressed by this prophecy, Alexander only prayed the more fervently when the "Te Deum" was celebrated in the Cathedral of Kazan.

He left St. Petersburg troubled in mind, dreading the thought that he would no doubt have to send his troops to invade recalcitrant Prussia, the country of the delightful Queen Louise. Was it not possible to avoid distressing so charming a person? When he reached Brest

---

*Staretz: old monk reputed for his piety and wisdom.

Litovsk he sent his favorite aide-de-camp, Peter Dolgoruky, to Berlin with orders to try every means to overcome the reluctance of Frederick William III. If the King did not wish to join the coalition, let him at least grant the Russian troops passage over his territory. While awaiting the results of this last attempt, Alexander agreed to honor Czartoryski's relatives with a visit to Pulawy. As his minister wished, he would go from there to Warsaw where—why not?—he would have himself crowned King of Poland. The Poles rejoiced at the prospect of the forthcoming renaissance of their motherland. For nearly two weeks, however, Alexander remained in Pulawy indulging his hosts' nationalism but making no move to carry out this plan. Then suddenly, on October 4, he declared that he would go directly to Berlin without stopping in Warsaw or signing any resolution regarding Poland. Czartoryski's hopes crumbled. He was disappointed not only as a Polish patriot but also as a Russian politician. For the first time the Czar went his own way overtly, in opposition to his minister.

The failure of Czartoryski's ambitions delighted the traditionalist Russian clan, including Peter Dolgoruky. Chance had served Alexander's envoy to the King of Prussia. While he was pleading the Russian cause in Berlin, Napoleon had simply invaded the territories of southern Germany. Frederick William III, furious, had immediately authorized the Russian troops to cross the border to fight the common enemy. What a load off Alexander's heart! At the invitation of Frederick William III, he hurried to Berlin to consider what action should be taken. Never mind the Poles and Czartoryski, he thought. What he had to have was an alliance with Prussia, which if need arose would make available an army of 150,000 men.

A brilliant reception awaited him in Berlin on October 25. Louise appeared before him with a crown on her head, radiantly beautiful. While the young woman watched them with a tender smile, the King and the Emperor heaped shame upon France. On November 3, 1805, at Potsdam, they signed a treaty providing that Prussia would join the coalition, without specifying the exact nature of its assistance, in exchange for the assurance that it would receive Hanover after the victory. To seal the good relations between them, Alexander, who was always inclined to theatrical gestures, expressed the wish to do homage to the shade of Frederick the Great. On a freezing night he, Frederick William III, and Louise crossed the deserted courtyards of the castle of Potsdam to the church of the garrison. By torchlight, the three of them descended to the crypt. The Queen, very pale, had put on a black cloak. In the silence of the vault the Czar placed a kiss on the tomb of the great captain who had been so much admired by his father Paul I, his grandfather Peter III, and his grandmother Catherine II. Lifting up his voice to the departed, he invoked his aid against Napoleon. Then, pressing his friends' hands, he exchanged with them a solemn oath of eternal fidelity.

Meanwhile, Napoleon was acting with his customary speed and vigor. After the capitulation of Ulm, the Austrians were beaten under the walls of Vienna and fell back to Olmütz (Olomouc), where the main body of Kutuzov's army was already gathered. It was to that little town in Moravia that Alexander now hastily made his way.

As soon as he arrived there, on November 18, he realized that his presence was not enough to galvanize the troops. Despite the fact that he was the first Russian sovereign since Peter the Great to appear on a battlefield, none of the soldiers appeared moved. The Comte de Langeron, a French emigré who had become a general in the service of Russia and was an eyewitness to the campaign of 1805, wrote, "I was stunned, as were all the other generals, by the coldness and the gloomy silence with which our troops received the Emperor." Ill fed, lacking warm clothes and boots, the men had only one thought: to plunder the neighboring villages. Discipline was lax. Fights broke out between Russians and Austrians. The noncommissioned officers had trouble controlling this army of men "living on frozen potatoes without salt."[7] The officers too were disaffected. The Emperor neglected them. "He had little consideration for them," wrote Langeron; "he rarely received them, seldom spoke to them, and reserved all his favors for five or six young favorites, his adjutants, the Lievens, Volkonskys, Gagarins, Dolgorukys."

The Emperor's entourage was in a swaggering, vainglorious mood bordering on recklessness. Young aides-de-camp with aristocratic names, buttoned up tight in brand new uniforms with gilt shoulder knots, sashes around their waists, and chests blazing with decorations, swore to inflict on Napoleon a defeat from which he would never recover. They begged His Majesty to be present at, even take command of the military operations in person. In vain did Czartoryski advise against it; the Czar haughtily refused to listen. He also refused Kutuzov's wise advice that they wait for reinforcements, that by accepting a decisive battle they were in fact playing into Napoleon's hands. To Alexander this excessive caution verged on cowardice. With the Czar at its head, the Russian army was capable of every heroism; to doubt that was to doubt Russia.

Old General Kutuzov, bloated and one-eyed, bowed before his

young master. A man of the preceding reigns, he had an almost religious respect for the imperial will. Besides, since the arrival of Alexander and his Austrian ally Emperor Francis, Kutuzov had been commander in chief in name only. No one listened to him. One day when he ventured to ask His Majesty's intentions regarding certain troop movements, he received the reply: "That's none of your business!"[8] "The young men around the Emperor," wrote Langeron, "ridiculed Kutuzov and called him General Slowpoke; he had no power and was accorded no respect."

As a military adviser, Alexander openly preferred the Austrian general Weyrother, a dull-witted, conceited flatterer. Weyrother's ingratiating manners had gained him the esteem of the band of young aides-de-camp at headquarters, of whom Peter Dolgoruky was the most restless and ambitious. At meetings of the council of war they stood in awe of this new chief of the armies, who was a pure representative of Viennese military science.

In the meantime Napoleon, who was quartered in Brünn (Brno), decided that prolonging the war would entail unnecessary risks. On November 25 he sent General Savary to Olmütz with a double mission: to deliver a letter of welcome to Alexander and to gather information on the sly about the size of the enemy force and the state of mind of both officers and men. No one in the Russian camp thought to stop Savary at the outposts. Conducted to headquarters, he gave Napoleon's letter to Alexander, chatted with the officers, surreptitiously observed the men, and withdrew convinced of the weakness of the Russo-Austrian position. The French had a good laugh over the adventure. The thirtieth *Bulletin des Armées*, dated December 3, 1805, reported that "after three days of conversations with some thirty conceited fops who, under different titles, surround the Emperor of Russia, [Savary] readily understood that presumption, imprudence, and thoughtlessness reigned in the decisions of the military cabinet, as they had reigned in those of the political cabinet."

Savary brought back from his incursion behind the Russian lines a letter from Alexander addressed to the "Head of the French Government." There was no mention of the possibility of an armistice, but the note was courteous in tone: "I have received with much gratitude the letter of which General Savary was the bearer, and I hasten to express my thanks to you. I have no other wish than to see peace reestablished in Europe with fairness and on a just basis. At the same time I hope to have the opportunity to be able to oblige you personally. Please accept my assurance of that desire, as well as of my highest consideration— Alexander."

No sooner had Alexander delivered this missive to Savary than he ordered the allied armies to go meet the enemy. At his insistence all the regiments marched in step, as on parade. On November 28, near Wischau, a skirmish took place during which the Austro-Russians, who greatly outnumbered the enemy, routed a few French squadrons. It was there that Alexander, bursting with youthful enthusiasm, received his baptism of fire. He conducted himself bravely throughout the affair and as soon as the shooting was over rode over the battlefield. Through his binoculars he observed from a distance the dead and wounded left on the field. Greatly shaken by the sight of the blood, he felt too sick to eat his dinner and went to bed. But next day he was again full of valor and presumptuousness. He thought the successful engagement at Wischau foreshadowed many more to come, and everyone around him loudly concurred.

Thinking that this first contact with the Russian troops would have given his adversary pause, he sent the impetuous Peter Dolgoruky to Napoleon with a proposal for an armistice. But Napoleon had the Czar's envoy stopped at the outposts and talked with him in the open air, on the road. The arrogance of this "conceited young puppy," as he called him, enraged him. "He spoke to me as he might have spoken to a boyar who was being sent to Siberia," he later wrote the Margrave of Württemberg. And indeed, Peter Dolgoruky was not in the least impressed by his august interlocutor. Not once did he call him "Your Imperial Majesty." "Are we going to fight for a long time?" Napoleon asked him. "What do you want of me? Why does Emperor Alexander make war on me? He has only to extend the borders of Russia at the expense of his neighbors, especially the Turks, and then all the disputes with France will come to an end."[9]

To these words Peter Dolgoruky replied sharply that the Czar did not seek any territorial advantage for Russia and that if he had taken up arms it was solely to defend the independence of the other European states that were constantly threatened by France. Napoleon, irritated, cut him short: "Russia should follow an entirely different policy and attend only to its own interests." And he added curtly: "Well, we shall fight! Leave me! Go, Monsieur, go tell your master that I am not in the habit of allowing myself to be insulted in this way! Leave this instant!" Peter Dolgoruky remounted his horse and rode off.

Back behind Russian lines, he drew up a report for the Emperor making it clear that the French army was afraid to confront the allied armies at Austerlitz: ninety thousand Austro-Russians against seven thousand French. "We are certain of success," wrote Peter Dolgoruky; "we have only to go forward, as we did at Wischau."

During the night of December 1–2, Weyrother held a meeting of the council of war to brief the commanders of the various units on his plans for the morrow. His long exposition in German was translated by Colonel Toll for the Russian officers, who soon got lost in the muddle of villages, rivers, and heights cited as reference points. "It was like a schoolmaster reading a lesson to young pupils," wrote Langeron. No objection was allowed. In the light of the candelabra, above the maps spread out in disorder on the table, the faces looked anxious and deferential. Kutuzov, not daring to protest against a plan that had already been approved by the Emperor, pretended to fall asleep. According to the plan, the allied armies were to abandon the heights of Pratzen, descend into the plain where the French army was massed, and passing around it to the right, bottle it up in Brünn and cut off the road to Vienna.

At dawn Alexander, as brisk and elegant as if he were on parade, rode with a few aides-de-camp to the Pratzen plateau to inspect the troops who would soon evacuate their position to surround the French. A red sun was rising on the horizon, but the plain was still bathed in a heavy, milky mist that concealed the movement of the enemy. Seeing Kutuzov, who was peering anxiously into the distance, Alexander said to him enthusiastically, "Well, do you not think things are going perfectly?" The old one-eyed general smiled and replied with the prudence of a courtier, "Who can doubt our success when it is Your Majesty who is in command?" "No, no," exclaimed the Czar, "it is you who are in command here, *I* am only a spectator!" Kutuzov bowed his head, but when Alexander had left he said to General Berg, "Now that's just perfect! I am supposed to command, when I didn't give the order to attack and didn't even want to make this attack!"

Toward eight o'clock in the morning, the Austro-Russian army moved into action, voluntarily abandoning the Pratzen plateau by degrees, in accordance with Weyrother's risky plan. When the mist dissipated, Napoleon ordered his forces assembled in the plain to attack all along the line and to take this very Pratzen plateau, which, in his opinion, was the key to the battle. At that moment dazzling sunshine flooded the countryside. Understanding Weyrother's enormous mistake, Kutuzov tried to keep as many troops as possible on the heights to resist the French assault. Alexander was angry at the old general's refusal to comply with the instructions he had received the night before and spoke sharply to him: "Why don't you advance?" Hoping to gain time, Kutuzov answered, "I am waiting for all the troops in the column to be assembled." "But we're not on the parade ground at Tsaritsyn, where we don't begin the review until all the regiments are present!"

retorted the Emperor. "Sire, it is precisely because we are not on the
parade ground that I am holding back the offensive. However, if you
insist . . . With the help of God . . ." And Kutuzov gave the order to his
troops to march. The flanking movement failed. Napoleon seized the
undefended Pratzen plateau, and installed his artillery there. From this
vantage point the French batteries easily bombarded their adversaries
below. The allies' lines broke. An hour later they were in full flight.
Pressed by the French, the Russian soldiers streamed back on the run,
a torrent of haggard faces, lurching banners, and disordered bayonets.
The swelling flood submerged the officers, who cried in vain to the
panicked troops to stop. Gunners abandoned their cannons. The
wounded dragged themselves along, begging their fleeing comrades to
help them. No one heard them. It was every man for himself. Stampede!
The French were everywhere. A belated intervention by the Russian
Imperial Guard, ordered by Kutuzov, could not save the situation. In
the midst of the general confusion, Alexander tried vainly to keep calm.
Several of his suite's horses were killed before his eyes, a cannonball fell
a few feet away, splattering dirt in his face. His aides-de-camp had
dispersed. "A deep sorrow could be read on his face," General Ermolov
said later; "the remnants of all the regiments were passing before him
and he had tears in his eyes."

Later, in the evening twilight rent by flashes of light and detona-
tions, Alexander rode away from the battlefield, followed by his English
physician, James Wylie, and an equerry. The Czar, an indifferent rider,
could hardly keep his seat and the equerry had to help him cross a
shallow ditch. He dismounted, exhausted, sat down under a tree, and
covering his face with a handkerchief, wept bitterly. He had been so
certain of victory. In his grief were mixed impotent rage against his
fleeing regiments, compassion for all the men who had died in vain, and
guilt, a feeling of horrible responsibility. Colonel Toll, who passed by,
tried to comfort him. Alexander dried his eyes, embraced him,
mounted his horse again, and resumed his way through the cold, misty
night, to escape possible pursuit. Czartoryski joined him on the road.
They passed through villages full of drunken soldiers who didn't even
recognize their sovereign. Utterly worn out, they arrived at last in a
small town where, traveling faster, his Austrian ally Emperor Francis
had already taken refuge. With great difficulty a hut was found for
Alexander's lodging. Without saying a word, he dropped onto a bed of
straw, shivering with fever. He had an upset stomach. Dr. Wylie wanted
him to drink a little wine as a tonic, but His Majesty's baggage train had
been lost, and all provisions for the road had disappeared with it. Dr.

Wylie hoped Emperor Francis could give him some wine. But the Emperor was fast asleep and the Grand Marshal of his court, Lamberti, refused either to wake his master or to dispense supplies without permission. In desperation, the doctor went to beg wine from some Cossacks who were bivouacked nearby. They proved understanding. James Wylie heated the wine, mixed in a few drops of opium, and made his patient, whose teeth were chattering, swallow the potion.

The next day, after a good night's sleep, Alexander showed himself hale and hearty to his cheering troops: It had been rumored that he had been wounded, perhaps even taken prisoner. But the acclamations that rose from a crowd of men with dirty faces and uniforms awry could not cure him of his humiliation. "The Corsican" had already moved into the castle of Austerlitz. On December 4, 1805, Emperor Francis met Napoleon to sign an armistice, which directed Russian troops to leave Austrian territory without delay. Five days later, Alexander had a final interview with his former ally, at Holitsch; then, with head hanging, started back on the road to St. Petersburg. Before leaving he sent a message to the King of Prussia: "In every circumstance and forever, I am ready to support [Prussia] with all my strength, and my very person is at her orders." But Frederick William III had no use for the promises of a defeated man and hastened to present his congratulations to the victor.

To Kutuzov fell the thankless task of repatriating the remnants of the army across Hungary. The hard battle of Austerlitz had cost the Russians twenty-five thousand men. "For Russia, that is only a drop of blood," wrote Joseph de Maistre to the King of Sardinia. Yet this "drop of blood" weighed heavily on Alexander's conscience. He could not help associating all these deaths, which he had not desired, with the assassination of his father in which he had not participated. After the battle Rostopchin said, "God could not grant his support to the forces of a bad son."

The persons around Alexander were struck by the change that had come over him in so brief a time. Suspicious, morose, silent, he seemed to have lost his youth in a single day. He consoled himself with the thought that from the disaster of Austerlitz he would at least have learned the true measure of Napoleon's strength. Henceforth, made prudent by experience, he would be wary of enthusiasm and prepare his moves better. But in the meantime, he had to find an excuse for the Russian defeat. The Russian people, hundreds of leagues away from the theater of operations, as yet had only a very vague idea of the magnitude of the disaster. Officially, the Austrians were responsible for everything. "Their infamous conduct, to which we owe this reversal, has caused me inexpressible indignation," wrote Empress Elizabeth to her mother. "There are no words to tell what one feels at the sight of an entire nation that is cowardly, treacherous, foolish, and has, in short, all the vilest qualities. . . . Despite their reverses and the betrayal all around them, our excellent troops have acquired a new glory even in the eyes of their enemies and inspire the liveliest enthusiasm in their compatriots. These soldiers are angels, martyrs, and heroes at the same time. They were dying of hunger, collapsing on the spot from starvation, and asked only to fight, while convoys of provisions were reaching the enemy and those wretched Austrian troops were supplied with everything."

As soon as he arrived in St. Petersburg Alexander went with the two Empresses, who had come to meet him, to the Cathedral of Kazan. After giving thanks to God for having spared his life through so many dangers, he reviewed his troops on the square of the Winter Palace. The people thronged to see him, hailing him like a conquering hero. "They all rushed after him," an eyewitness wrote in French. "The press around him was so great that he could not advance; people prostrated themselves, kissed his feet and hands; the joy was like delirium. This sovereign, so rightfully adored, wept with emotion and declared that this moment fully compensated for all the sufferings he had endured, that he would consent with all his soul to endure even more if he were again to be greeted with marks of affection so dear to his heart."[10] And Countess Stroganov wrote, "People were drunk with joy at seeing him again. He arrived at night; next morning all the rooms and corridors of the palace were so crowded that it was difficult to pass and the square in front of the palace was black with people. When he appeared they rushed to kiss his hands, his feet, and even his coat."

Although Alexander was somewhat embarrassed by this mistaken admiration, those around him advised him to give an entertainment in the Hermitage theater, with a ball and supper, so as to disarm any who did not share in the general rejoicing. The evening was a perfect success. "The whole place glittered with finery, ornaments, crystal, and decorations," wrote Admiral Chichagov. "All the men were in full dress uniform and the ladies were covered with diamonds. You would have thought you were in Paris, in the camp of the victor." Commissions and decorations were distributed in abundance. Even Kutuzov, who was still out of favor with Alexander, received the cordon of the Order of St. Vladimir. (He was also sent away from the capital to become Governor of Kiev, a sort of honorable disgrace.) Punitive action *was* taken against a few generals, including Langeron, who was allowed to retire. As for Alexander, he kept his head and refused to accept the cordon that the Order of St. George wanted to confer on him for gallantry. Besides, people around him were gradually recognizing their mistake. As the troops returned to the capital, tongues began to wag, the truth dawned on public opinion. Joy was succeeded by consternation. On January 6, 1806, Nicholas Novosiltsev wrote in French to Paul Stroganov, who was on a diplomatic mission to London, "You know that when we parted you left us exceedingly troubled about the figure we should cut in Petersburg. Our anxiety and shame at appearing there increased as we approached the capital. . . . Judge of our astonishment when we learned that the Emperor had been received with indescribable enthusiasm . . . that all the good city of Petersburg was in seventh heaven over the distinguished way our army had conducted itself in this affair, that it was composed exclusively of heroes . . . that it asked nothing better than to begin over again immediately after the battle but that the Austrians had not wanted to, and that in order to prevent us from doing so they had concluded an armistice unbeknownst to us; that in short these Austrians were real traitors sold out to France and that we had lost the battle only because they had communicated our plans to the French, and their whole army had immediately gone over to the French. . . . You can readily imagine that tales of that sort cannot be believed for long: People from the army were arriving continually to correct the ideas of the public. They soon found out what had happened, what was the true cause of the defeat, and how we had behaved afterward. . . . Thus soon after our arrival we saw the Emperor go down in public opinion in a really alarming way; there was no more talk of betrayal, but all the disasters were attributed to him and to him alone."[11]

Though at first Alexander was affected by this drop in popularity at home and abroad, he pulled himself together. Perhaps the battle of Austerlitz had not ended his struggle against Napoleon, but only begun it. Now that the Emperor of the French had become uncontested master of half of Europe, could he resist for long the temptation to broaden his hegemony? If Russia did not want to find itself one day under the thumb of the "crowned Corsican," it would have to reconstitute its decimated regiments as soon as possible, change commanders, tighten or renew its alliances. Through all his efforts at diplomacy, Alexander knew that the best way for him to avoid war was to prepare for it. His sincere desire for peace was accompanied by a disturbing rattle of arms.

VI

TILSIT

Disconcerted by his recent diplomatic and military defeats, Alexander did not know what course to follow. The instability of his mood was almost pathological. He acted only on nervous impulse, passing from enthusiasm to prostration, from courage to fear, from selfishness to generosity, from openness to trickery, from superficial pleasures to profound meditation. Napoleon would say of him to Metternich, "No one could have more intelligence than the Emperor Alexander, but I find that there is a piece missing in his character, and I cannot discover what it is."

Immediately after Austerlitz the Czar—at the same time stubborn and indecisive, energetic and wavering—advised the King of Prussia to be patient and sent Paul Stroganov to England to meet with Fox, the successor to William Pitt who some said had died of despair after the collapse of the coalition. Having reorganized his army Alexander ventured into negotiations with Napoleon, hoping to extract from him the promise of an honorable peace. Monsieur d'Oubril was dispatched to

Paris ostensibly to prepare an exchange of prisoners but in reality to discuss the conditions for a solid agreement between the two empires. The Czar's emissary had been given full powers, with only one order: to maintain a zone of protection around Russia so as to ward off any danger of invasion.

As soon as he arrived in France, Monsieur d'Oubril fell sick. Hardly recovered from his illness, he did his best to hold his own against Talleyrand, Clarke, and Napoleon himself through a long series of talks. But he was in a position of inferiority, while the negotiators opposite him had all the prestige of victory.

Napoleon had just published the Act of Confederation of the Rhine, confirming the dissolution of the German Holy Roman Empire, extending his protectorate over a good part of Germany. At such a time he found the claims of Russia excessive. Monsieur d'Oubril, intimidated, was only too happy to be able to sign a treaty that to him represented an acceptable last resort. The document he signed, in panic, called for Russian evacuation of Germany, independence of the Ionian Islands and the Republic of Ragusa from France, and maintenance of a Russian garrison at Corfu. France, for its part, kept the rest of Dalmatia, which placed Napoleon at the gates of the Ottoman Empire, and obtained Cattaro (Kotor) on the Adriatic, which had been occupied by the Russians not long before. Worst of all, d'Oubril abandoned Russia's Neapolitan ally Ferdinand, agreeing that Napoleon's elder brother Joseph, already King of Naples, should also become the King of Sicily, where Ferdinand and his wife Marie Caroline had taken refuge. Ferdinand would receive a monetary indemnity in exchange.

Monsieur d'Oubril had hardly initialed this document when he regretted having done so. On sober reflection he realized that he had gone too far. "I find it necessary to think how I shall justify myself in St. Petersburg for having done the opposite of the orders furnished to me," he wrote to Paul Stroganov. "I go there today to present both my work and my head so as to be punished if I have done wrong."

His fears were justified. The treaty raised a storm of protest at the Russian court. Paul Stroganov wrote, "I find it impossible to bear a Russian name and not to die of shame on reading this extraordinary act." And also: "It is time for us to decide if we are going to become a French province, following the example of Prussia, Austria, etc., or if we still retain something of our former glory." "Under Peter and Catherine we were wounded by temporary reverses, but never and nowhere have we endured humiliation," protested Rumiantsev. Only General Kutuzov and Admiral Chichagov dared say that the army, bled

white, needed a few years' rest and training before going into combat
again. The other dignitaries vied with each other in a chorus of praise
for the valor of the Russian soldier and his impatience to return to battle
to avenge the honor of the motherland. Overwhelmed by his advisers,
Alexander breached diplomatic custom and refused to ratify the treaty
that had been signed in his name by an emissary who, he claimed, had
exceeded his authority. Monsieur d'Oubril was disavowed and sent back
to his estates. The prospect of peace with France grew dimmer.

Meanwhile, Alexander's closest friend and associate Adam Czartoryski had found himself in disagreement with the Czar on too many
points and had asked to be replaced as Minister of Foreign Affairs.
"Prince Adam is hampered by the Emperor in everything he proposes
to do," wrote Novosiltsev. "The Emperor wants only half measures; the
Prince seizes every opportunity to ask him to appoint another in his
place and to let him depart . . . but the Emperor will not hear of it."
Czartoryski himself analyzed the situation in a letter to Paul Stroganov:
"The Emperor is still the same; fear and weakness are still at their
height. We are afraid of everything, we are incapable of making a firm
decision; it is even impossible to advise him, for fear that the advice will
not be accepted. The Emperor wants to keep us so as to avoid the
trouble of making a change, but in any event he only wants to do as he
pleases. . . . He is a combination of weakness, uncertainty, terror, injustice, and incoherence that drives one to grief and despair."[1]

Finally, after many protestations of friendship, the Czar accepted
Czartoryski's resignation and replaced him with the Baltic baron Budberg.

In the first rank of the enemies who had brought about Czartoryski's
downfall stood the Empress Dowager Maria Feodorovna. Not content
with denouncing the incompetence of "that Pole," whom she held
responsible for "all the calamities of last autumn," she put Alexander on
guard against his own blind friendship for Prussia. "I can never tire of
repeating to you that the attachment of your grandfather [Peter III] for
the court of Berlin caused his ruin, that the attachment of your father
for that same court was disastrous for him, and that yours, dear Alexander, has been sufficiently so until now," she wrote her son, in French.
"I shall confine myself to entreating you to take good care that you
cannot be accused of sacrificing to that attachment the interests and
glory of your country."

But although Alexander had satisfied his mother by changing his
Minister of Foreign Affairs, he refused to listen when she attacked his
policy toward Prussia. Since his meeting with Queen Louise, he felt a

moral obligation to protect that unfortunate country. In the month of July 1806, through an exchange of secret declarations with Frederick William III, he committed himself to guaranteeing by force of arms the independence and territorial integrity of Prussia. In return the King of Prussia promised not to help France in case of a war with Russia. But Prussia was already allied with France. Frederick William III had two strings to his bow: In St. Petersburg they believed he was firmly devoted to the Czar, and in Paris they considered him on Napoleon's side— especially since he had been promised Hanover as the price of his submission. But now Napoleon changed his mind and decided to restore Hanover to England in order to soften the British negotiators. At once Frederick William III indignantly denounced his alliance with France and appealed to Russia for military assistance in accordance with the secret treaty. "Tell me, Sire, I beseech you," he wrote to Alexander in French on August 8, 1806, "if I may hope that your troops will remain within reach to come to my aid and if I may count on them in case of aggression."

Despite his mother's exhortations and the advice of his friends, Alexander chivalrously kept his word. The defeat at Austerlitz had not sufficed; he had yet to be convinced of Napoleon's genius. Confident of his troops' valor, he was not afraid to measure himself against the Emperor a second time. On October 1, 1806, with the agreement of the Czar, Frederick William III sent an ultimatum to Paris demanding that French forces stationed in Germany be withdrawn and that France consent to a Confederation of Northern Germany that would include all the German states not part of the Confederation of the Rhine. In reply Napoleon ordered his troops to march on Prussia. One week was all it took the French to crush the proud Prussian army ignominiously on the battlefields of Saalfeld, Jena, and Auerstedt. On October 27 Napoleon made a triumphal entry into Berlin. Driven from their capital, the King and Queen with a few faithful followers fled before the advance of the invader and took refuge on the borders of eastern Prussia.

Meanwhile, Russia, which had not yet taken part in the military operations, was feverishly preparing to intervene. Some of its troops were at that moment engaged against Persia and others had to move against Turkey, which Napoleon had just persuaded to enter the conflict. To fight France Alexander declared a national war and levied an army of 612,000 men. All classes of society were taxed for money and supplies. But there was a shortage of rifles, and barely one-fifth of the militia received them. The others were armed with pikes and lances. One hundred sixty thousand firearms were ordered from manufacturers in London and Vienna. To galvanize the public, the Holy Synod prescribed that after mass on Sundays and holy days a solemn anathema should be read against Napoleon, who was accused of being a disturber of the sacred peace of the world, an enemy of Orthodox Christian religion, a shameless supporter of the Infidels, a convert to the cause of the Koran, a propagator of the cult of idols, and a builder of synagogues who wanted to gather the Jews together and declare himself their Messiah. These fiery words left the Russian people unmoved. Everything that went on beyond the borders seemed unreal to them. So long as they had not seen the enemy soldiers in their own fields, among their own villages, they could neither hate them nor quite believe in their existence.

Alexander was greatly preoccupied with choosing a new commander in chief. Not for anything in the world would he take Kutuzov again —the man was a nuisance, and he reminded him of the blunders at Austerlitz. His entourage extolled the virtues of Marshal Michael Kamensky, age sixty-nine. The old man protested, terrified by the responsibility the Emperor was planning to lay on his shoulders. Obliged to give in, he was dragged from his country estate and welcomed in St. Petersburg as a savior.

The Empress Elizabeth had just given birth to a daughter, also named Elizabeth, on December 3, 1806. The birth augured well for events to follow. She wrote to her mother: "I am well, my good Mama, as is my little Elise, who begs you to forgive her for not being a boy." Then, overcoming her fatigue, she personally received Generalissimo Kamensky and in a voice choked with emotion told him of all the hope the nation placed in him.

Anxious to consolidate his reputation as a man of great originality, Kamensky aped Suvorov's hearty bonhomie to the point that some said he looked like a clown. During the months of November and December 1806 a Russian army of 100,000 men crossed the border into Prussian territory. This time Alexander refrained from going to the theater of operations. Kamensky himself had been seized with uncontrollable panic by the time he reached Vilna (Vilnyus). He wrote to the Emperor begging to be relieved of his command: "I am too old for the army. My sight is growing so dim that I can no longer see the name of a single town on the map. My eyes hurt and my head aches. I can hardly sit a horse. I venture to beg you to find a replacement for me, a trusted friend, a son of the motherland, so that I may turn the command over to him. . . . I sign without knowing what I sign."

At three o'clock on the stormy morning of December 14 Kamensky, worn out with fatigue and anxiety, summoned Bennigsen and ordered him to take the army back to Russia. Then he climbed into a cart and left camp to go home. Instead of obeying him, Bennigsen went into battle with the French at Pultusk. The engagement turned to his advantage. After long hesitation, Alexander appointed him commander in chief. To reach this decision he had had to overcome his repugnance for a man who had played a decisive role in the murder of Paul I. As Joseph de Maistre put it, the new commander in chief was in reality "assassin in chief." In any case, the Czar awarded Bennigsen the Order of St. George and sent him a few lines in French: "The superior talents which you displayed [at Pultusk] are a further justification of the confidence which you have already inspired in me." Under the preceding reign Bennigsen would have also been rewarded with lands and peasant serfs. An improvement in customs, according to some; injustice toward a servant of the regime, according to others.

On February 8, 1807, Bennigsen confronted the French near the village of Eylau in eastern Prussia. "It was not a battle but a slaughter," Napoleon said afterward.[2] On the Russian side the dead and wounded numbered twenty-six thousand. Each of the two adversaries claimed victory, but since on the evening of the battle Bennigsen had ordered his troops to fall back on Königsberg (Kaliningrad), Napoleon remained master of the field. That did not prevent Alexander from sending his commander in chief his congratulations, in French: "It is you, General, who were destined to have the glory of vanquishing the one who has never yet known defeat." And Bennigsen was honored with the Order of St. Andrew, while he continued his retreat across the country through mist and snow.

Toward the end of February, the Imperial Guard was sent to swell Bennigsen's army. They left the capital amid cheering throngs. "There will remain in St. Petersburg," Alexander wrote to Bennigsen, "only a single battalion of the Preobrazhenskys to guard the palace and a squadron of Cossacks for patrols." For three days old Count Stedingk saw marching past under the windows of his embassy on St. Isaac Square "those superb troops composed of the elite of the army, whose handsome appearance leaves nothing to be desired."[3] The Emperor, the Empress, and Grand Duke Constantine bowed to the departing regiments as they passed with flags unfurled. At the gates of the city sledges were waiting to rush the infantry battalions to their new cantonment, where they were to take up winter quarters and prepare for the decisive encounter.

Alexander himself soon left to join the army. Passing through Mitau he stopped to visit the Comte de Lisle—otherwise known as Louis XVIII— chatted amiably with him, judged him to be insignificant and

even incompetent, but promised to help him ascend the throne of
France. Then he hastened on to Pollangen, a little town on the Baltic
Sea, where the King of Prussia had come to welcome him. Together
they went to Memel, where they found waiting the charming Queen
Louise, whose fate had been so much on Alexander's mind. Living with
her husband in modest lodgings, she was consumed with melancholy
and bitterness. "The climate is terrible here," she wrote. "Nothing but
snow and ice. Not the least flower, not the least violet. But my heart is
still in bloom and my hope in God will never die."⁴ When she saw the
handsome Alexander again she sighed, "Ah! my cousin!" and held out
her hand to him with infinite sadness and grace. She had, she said, no
other support in the world but him. He replied that he had not come
only as an ally but as a friend and that Russia would make every sacrifice
to aid Prussia. Then, as the troops paraded before them, he turned to
Frederick William III and exclaimed, "Neither of us two will fall separately. We shall fall together or neither will fall!" "The Emperor is still
the same superiorly agreeable man, full of kindness and graciousness,"
Countess Voss noted in her journal. "He is a man who has not his equal
in the world." The next day she gave this further detail: "Nevertheless
[he is] a little more artificial than he used to be, perhaps. He pays more
attention to the young ladies."

While Alexander was charming the "young ladies" around Queen
Louise, the Russian and Prussian plenipotentiaries at Bartenstein (Bar-
toszyce), Bennigsen's headquarters, signed a treaty that strengthened
the ties between the two countries and provided for the reconstitution
of Prussia, the dissolution of the Confederation of the Rhine, and the
return of France within its borders. Neither England nor Austria sub-
scribed to these conditions, and many of the officers in Alexander's own
army were critical. Even Grand Duke Constantine urged his brother to
make peace with Napoleon. But Alexander was stubborn. He waited
impatiently for good weather to return so that operations could be
resumed.

On June 14, 1807, the battle of Friedland (Pravdinsk) took place.
Despite their numerical superiority, the forces of Bennigsen, who had
"vanquished the invincible," gave way under the violence and precision of the French attacks. The Russians were obliged to retreat after
losing a third of their men. News of the disaster reached Alexander on
June 16, at his headquarters in Olita (Alitus) far behind the lines. Two
days later, a young officer, Denis Davydov,* aide-de-camp to General

---

*He was later to become the leader of the partisans during the Russian campaign.

Prince Bagration, arrived there to find the general staff in utter disarray. "I reached headquarters on June 18," he wrote in his *Mémoires*.
"There was a miscellaneous collection of people of all kinds: Englishmen, Swedes, Prussians, French emigrés, Russians in the civil and military services, common people without either civil or military employ-
ment, parasites, schemers; in short a regular *bourse* of speculators on
politics or the war, ruined in their hopes, their plans, and their ambitions. . . . And so tense, all of them! One would have thought it was half
an hour before the end of the world. Only Bennigsen remained impas-
sive: He was visibly suffering, but with silent sorrow."

Not even the most bellicose of the Czar's advisers dared invite him
to continue the struggle. The army was disorganized, supplies were low,
the new recruits were insufficiently trained. Many veterans had fallen
in combat, and many capable officers had disappeared. England, disappointed by the failure of the operations, forgot its promise to send a
landing force of ten to fifteen thousand men and haughtily refused to
provide a new credit of six million pounds, thus placing the Russian
treasury in the greatest difficulties. "Every good Russian," wrote Czartoryski, "must be struck by the distressing truth that Russia is in very
nearly the same situation as Prussia found herself in last October.
. . . The enlightened politician and the determined soldier alike will
wonder why we should not try political overtures rather than obdu-
rately persisting in a struggle the danger of which is evident." And
Grand Duke Constantine exclaimed, in French, to his brother: "Sire, if
you don't want to make peace with France, well, give a loaded pistol
to each of your soldiers and ask them to blow their brains out! You will
achieve the same result as you will obtain from another and final battle
which will unfailingly open the gates of your empire to the French
troops, who are experienced in combat and always victorious!"

Feeling that he had tried everything in his power to save Prussia,
Alexander himself saw no alternative but negotiation. On June 22, 1807,
he sent his aide-de-camp Prince Lobanov to Tilsit (Sovetsk) to work out
a truce and suggest a meeting with Napoleon. The Emperor of the
French received the Russian plenipotentiary with extreme courtesy,
signed the proposed armistice with him, invited him to dinner, offered
a toast in champagne to the health of the Czar, inquired after the health
of the Czarina Elizabeth, and noticing that his guest's eyes were wet
with emotion, turned toward General Duroc and exclaimed, "Look,
look, Duroc, how the Russians love their sovereigns!"[5]

Once Alexander approved the provisions of the armistice, an interview between the two Emperors was set for June 25, 1807, at eleven
in the morning on the border river, the Neman. Napoleon, who was

fond of dramatic settings, had had a great raft anchored in midstream bearing two superbly decorated pavilions of white canvas. The larger structure, in which the sovereigns were to meet, had a gigantic *A* painted on the Russian side and on the French side an *N* of the same size. Napoleon had deliberately omitted the initials of the King of Prussia, who, naturally enough, took offense at the slight. When they reached the water's edge in a line of barouches the Czar, Frederick William III, Grand Duke Constantine, and their escort sat down in a half-ruined cottage to await the appearance of Napoleon. Alexander was wearing the green uniform with red facings of the Preobrazhensky regiment with gold shoulder knots on the right shoulder, white knee breeches, white gloves, a big hat with white and black plumes, short boots, and a sword at his side. His chestnut hair was powdered; the light blue cordon of the Order of St. Andrew crossed his chest. To witnesses he appeared very calm, but a solemn dread was weighing on his heart at the idea of finding himself face-to-face with this legendary personage who had just taught him a hard lesson. How would he manage to overcome his feeling of inferiority before the "Corsican ogre"?

While Alexander recognized the military capacities of his future interlocutor, he did not despair of reaching an agreement with him. After all, he thought, Napoleon had no desire to conquer the world. What he wanted was that Russia stop contesting his domination over southern and central Europe. In exchange he would probably agree to leave the Czar a free hand in the east of the continent. In short, it would be a question of clearly delimiting the zones of influence, of fixing the border between the empires of West and East, and of ensuring Russia's security by the definitive annexation of the principalities of the Danube and the reestablishment, even if only partial, of the kingdom of Prussia. With the historic meeting only a few minutes away, Alexander took comfort in the certainty that his antagonist wanted his collaboration in completing the pacification of central Europe, and in imposing an effective blockade on England. He desperately wanted to believe that Napoleon needed him just as he needed Napoleon. An aide-de-camp ran up and cried, "He's coming, Your Majesty!"

Alexander slowly picked up his hat and gloves and came out of the crumbling cottage. On the opposite bank he saw a rider approaching at the head of a brilliant escort, before a line of cheering troops. The shouts of the French reached the Russian camp. Simultaneously, on either side of the river, the two Emperors each climbed into a large boat. Aides-de-camp and advisers ranged themselves behind them. The King of Prussia, uninvited, remained in disgrace on the right bank of the Neman, his eyes fixed on the tent in which his fate was to be decided. He urged his horse down the bank and breast-deep into the water, and sat there motionless, in dismay.

The boats slid slowly over the water. White-shirted rowers pulled at the oars. Napoleon was first to set foot on the raft; he walked quickly forward. Alexander saw before him a thickset, rather rotund man with an energetic face, a prominent chin, and steely eyes. The Emperor of the French was wearing the uniform of the Guard decorated with the red cordon of the Legion of Honor. His big, legendary hat was pulled down over his forehead. He held out his hand. Alexander took it. The two men embraced. "I hate the English no less than you do and I shall second you in anything you undertake against them," said Alexander. "In that case, everything can be settled and peace is made," replied Napoleon.[6] Alexander was no doubt struck by the Corsican accent of his former enemy. As a pupil of Laharpe, the Emperor of Russia spoke a more musical French than the master of France.

Shortly afterward, they both entered the pavilion. From the outset Alexander realized that his analysis had been correct: Napoleon ardently desired a peace that would enable him to strengthen his European position and to destroy England's power permanently. He denounced the treachery of Russia's allies, extolled the courage of the Russian troops in combat, and envisaged a division of the world between the two empires. Behind the words Alexander sensed a man who was rough, virile, practical, convinced of his lucky star. By contrast Alexander felt himself becoming more pliant, delicate, evasive. Yes, he who had been born on the steps of the throne, in the shadow of Catherine the Great, had nothing in common with this plebeian whose eyes were bigger than his stomach. And yet he could not resist his interlocutor, who was pacing rapidly back and forth under the tent. After two hours of friendly conversation, the sovereigns came out arm-in-arm. Alexander conducted Napoleon back to his boat. On the following day the raft received, in addition to the two Emperors, the King of Prussia, who saw a first faint hope of recouping a piece of his territory.

Napoleon proposed that for the rest of the negotiations they meet at Tilsit, which would be declared neutral territory. The modest town, lost in the fields, was divided into two sectors. On the day when Alexander arrived the password, given by Napoleon, was *Alexander, Russia, greatness.* The next day it was Alexander who chose the password *Napoleon, France, gallantry.* On the Russian side, the Czar's security was ensured by a detachment of hussars from the Guard and a battalion of the Preobrazhensky regiment. The commander of that battalion was

Michael Vorontzov, the son of Count Simon who only recently had been the Russian ambassador to London. Sharing his father's hatred for the French, Michael Vorontzov reported in sick to avoid witnessing a meeting he could not endure. The other Russian officers were not so intransigent. Every day they met for lunch with the French aides-de-camp at Marshal Berthier's. All officers of the Russian army spoke French with ease, so it was not hard to fraternize. Since it was forbidden for any soldier who was not a member of the garrison to enter Tilsit, many officers billeted on the right bank dressed as civilians and slipped into town to try to catch a glimpse of Napoleon.

Every morning General Duroc came to inquire after Alexander's health, while Count Nicholas Tolstoy went for news of Napoleon. Then the two sovereigns would review the Russian and French troops and go on excursions on horseback accompanied by the King of Prussia, a "troublesome and unhappy" witness. Almost always they dined at Napoleon's, on gold plates, under the guard of a double rank of grenadiers. In the presence of the King of Prussia, Alexander and Napoleon avoided discussing important questions. Napoleon despised this unwanted guest and never passed up an opportunity to needle him. Looking at the King's Prussian uniform, he asked him ironically, "How do you manage to button so many buttons?"[7]

As soon as Frederick William III had withdrawn, serious conversation resumed. The two monarchs would talk privately together until past midnight. "I shall be your secretary and you will be mine," said Napoleon to Alexander. In words, they seemed close to an agreement. They rebuilt the world with resounding phrases. To elaborate the details of the accord, Napoleon called upon the able Talleyrand, while Alexander appointed Prince Lobanov and Prince Kurakin, one as ill qualified as the other for this delicate task. In the course of the drafting the treaty gradually departed from its original conception. By slow degrees Talleyrand pulled the covers over to his own side of the bed.

To soften Napoleon's intransigence, Frederick William III decided to bring to Tilsit his wife, the irresistible Queen Louise. She fell to her knees before the Emperor of the French, begging mercy for Prussia: "Will you not leave us Magdeburg and Westphalia?" "You are asking a great deal, but I promise I shall think about it," said Napoleon, raising her up with cold courtesy. "That's a lovely gown you are wearing. What is the material, Madame? Is it crepe or Italian gauze?" That evening at dinner she tried again to captivate him with her light remarks and velvet smile. But Napoleon remained unmoved and only asked her ironically, "Why are you wearing a turban? Not in homage to Emperor

Alexander, since he is at war with Turkey!"[8] Not long afterward he wrote to Josephine, "The Queen of Prussia is really charming, she is very flirtatious with me, but don't be jealous, I am a piece of oilcloth and it just slides over me. It would cost me too dear to play the gallant." And to Count Nicholas Tolstoy he said, "I shall not do for the sake of the Queen of Prussia's beauty what I could not do for the sake of your Emperor's friendship."[9] To Alexander he expressed himself even more bluntly: "He's a contemptible king, it's a contemptible nation, a contemptible army, a country which has deceived everyone and does not deserve to exist. Everything [Prussia] is keeping, she owes to you."[10]

For her part Queen Louise, humiliated as a woman and as a sovereign, felt a physical repugnance for "the monster," "the son of the Revolution." She thought him cruel, conceited, and uncommonly ugly, with his puffy face, pasty complexion, prominent stomach, and short legs. And to think that her destiny, the destiny of her country, depended on this dwarf! She went sighing and weeping from one Emperor to the other. Alexander consoled her and casting his eyes up to heaven murmured, "Have faith in the future!"

While the details of the treaty were being worked out, Alexander became better acquainted with the man he now proclaimed his friend. This is how he described him to Czartoryski: "He is a man who in the midst of the greatest excitement always has a calm, cool head; all his rages are only for others and most often they are only calculated. One of his favorite sayings is that in all things one must first find the method, that there is nothing so difficult that it cannot be accomplished at last...."

Duplicity accompanied Alexander's clearsightedness. His show of liking and admiration for Napoleon was only an act. At Tilsit he was on a stage, playing a part, fooling his public. In reality Alexander, who had a vindictive, dissembling nature, would never forgive Talleyrand's reply, three years before, to the Russian note on the execution of the Duc d'Enghien—the letter that had reminded the Czar in very harsh terms of the assassination of his own father. To be sure, he told General Savary, "I shall confess to you that no one ever had more prejudices against a person than I had against [Napoleon]; but after three-quarters of an hour of conversation with him, they all disappeared like a dream and I never remembered them, so deeply was I struck by what he said to me." And speaking of Napoleon on another occasion he exclaimed, "If only I had seen him sooner! . . . The veil has been torn asunder and the time of error is past." But his real feelings he confided in letters written in French to his favorite sister Catherine: "God has saved us: Instead of making sacrifices, we are emerging from the struggle with a kind of added luster. But what will you say to all these events? I, passing my days with Bonaparte, spending hours on end in private conversation with him?" And to his mother: "Fortunately, with all his genius, Bonaparte has a vulnerable side: It is vanity, and I have decided to sacrifice my pride for the salvation of the empire." He even went so far as to write to the King of Prussia: "Have patience. We shall take back what we have lost. He will break his neck. In spite of all my demonstrations of friendship and my external actions, at heart I am your friend and I hope to prove it to you by acts."[11]

Napoleon, meanwhile, believed in the Czar's sincerity. "My dear," he wrote to Josephine, "I have just seen the Emperor Alexander; I was very pleased with him; he is a very handsome, good young emperor; he is cleverer than is commonly thought." And also: "He is a hero out of a novel. He has all the manners of an agreeable Parisian." Not long after, refining his judgment, he was to consider Alexander tenderhearted, changeable, accessible to flattery. But France might have much to gain from an understanding with this emotional, inexperienced, malleable sovereign.

Thus each of the two Emperors thought he was deceiving the other in an atmosphere of theatrical cordiality. For Napoleon, Tilsit was the assurance that he would have a free hand elsewhere; for Alexander it was an honorable way of gaining time. Though each declared that this treaty promised lasting peace, neither of them was really convinced of it.

The "treaty of peace and friendship" signed on July 7, 1807, with seven secret clauses, was supplemented by a "treaty of offensive and defensive alliance" between France and Russia. In spite of Alexander's efforts and Queen Louise's sighs, Prussia, an indispensable barrier for the security of Russia, was only partially reconstituted. Reduced to four provinces (Pomerania, Brandenburg, Old Prussia, and Silesia), she lost those territories between the Elbe and the Rhine that were destined to become the kingdom of Westphalia and be given to Napoleon's brother Prince Jerome. The region of Bialystok was allotted to the Czar. The rest of Poland would constitute the grand duchy of Warsaw, and was provisionally awarded to the King of Saxony. The secret articles stated that Cattaro, previously ceded to Austria, and the independent Ionian Islands would be eventually restored to France. In addition Alexander promised Napoleon not to interfere in western Europe but obtained freedom of action in the Baltic, the eastern part of the Balkans, in the Dardanelles and Asia Minor. Mediation by the French in Constantinople would establish peace between Russia and Turkey, while mediation by the Russians in London would strive for peace between France and

England. If the Russian mediation failed, the Czar would give military support to France and join the continental blockade. If the French mediation failed, Napoleon would make common cause with Russia against the Ottoman Empire.

Obviously, the agreements contained many points that were not clearly settled. Notwithstanding his promise to support Russia against the Porte, if necessary, Napoleon had no intention of ever ceding Constantinople to the Czar. "Constantinople represents world empire," he said. Similarly, so far as the principalities of the Danube were concerned, all he gave Alexander was hopes. Finally, the solution of the Polish problem was also unfavorable for the Russians. The grand duchy of Warsaw ruled by the King of Saxony would surely join the Confederation of the Rhine, and thus the great Napoleonic empire would have a common border with Russia, something Alexander had wanted to avoid at all costs.

Nevertheless, for the moment the two Emperors were satisfied with what they had accomplished. Alexander charged Prince Kurakin to deliver to Napoleon the insignia of the Order of St. Andrew, for himself and for four members of his suite. In exchange, Napoleon had General Duroc bring the Czar five badges of the Legion of Honor. Shortly afterward Alexander, wearing the cordon of the Legion of Honor, and Napoleon, wearing the cordon of the Order of St. Andrew, reviewed together the regiments of their personal guards. On seeing the battalion of the Preobrazhensky regiment standing at attention, Napoleon asked the Czar, "Will Your Majesty permit me to give the Legion of Honor to the bravest man, the one who conducted himself best in this campaign?" Touched, Alexander consulted the colonel in command, who designated, somewhat at random, the grenadier Lazarev. Lazarev, flabbergasted, saw the Emperor of the French detach a cross from his coat and pin it on his, Lazarev's uniform. The pale, well-kept hand hardly brushed the cloth. "You will remember that this is the day when we became friends, your master and I," said Napoleon.[12]

Not to be outdone, Alexander ordered a Russian decoration bestowed upon the most gallant of the French soldiers. The two sovereigns embraced in front of the cheering troops. Alexander promised Napoleon to visit him in Paris. At last they separated. Seated in his boat, the Emperor of Russia watched as the bulky figure of the Emperor of the French, who had remained on the bank to see him off, diminished in the distance.

VII

EMBRACES AT ERFURT

As soon as he returned to St. Petersburg, on July 4, 1807, Alexander noticed that the atmosphere had changed. The city was illuminated to receive him, but there was no joy in people's hearts. The clergy had been ordered to stop pronouncing the anathema against Napoleon and to celebrate the peace that had at last been restored, but people prayed with shame and rage. The very ones who had forgiven the Czar for the defeats of Austerlitz and Friedland could not forgive him for the alleged success of Tilsit. They did not understand how their sovereign could embrace today the man whom yesterday he had sworn to strangle. For some time already Alexander had ceased to be the darling child of Russian high society that he had been immediately after his accession. Now his popularity hit bottom. Simon Vorontzov declared openly that the signers of the Treaty of Tilsit should have returned to St. Petersburg mounted on asses. Count Stedingk, the Swedish minister in Russia, reported to King Gustavus IV: "The dissatisfaction with the Emperor is increasing, and the remarks one hears on all sides are frightening. The good servants, the friends of the Emperor, are in despair, but there is not one of them who knows how to remedy the evil and who has the courage to inform the Emperor of the excessive danger he is in. They say that they can see no remedy, that the Emperor is obstinate, that he is not unaware of the bad things people are saying but that he attributes them to outside agitation, to the millions the English are spending to win supporters (which is entirely false and something said by Savary), and that, desiring only the welfare of his subjects, he has nothing to fear from them. It is only too true, however, that in private gatherings and even in public assemblies there is often talk of a change of reign and that people so far forget their duty as to say that the whole male line of the reigning family should be proscribed, and that since the Empress Dowager and Empress Elizabeth do not have the requisite qualities, Grand Duchess Catherine must be set upon the throne." And General Savary, Napoleon's envoy to St. Petersburg, described the situation in these terms: "Nothing could have equaled the irreverence with which the Russian youth dared to discuss their sovereign. For a time I was anxious about the possible consequences of this license in a country where palace revolutions were only too common."[1] One day Novosilt-sev screwed up his courage and whispered in Alexander's ear, "Sire, I must remind you of the fate of your father." Not at all disturbed by the remark, the Czar replied, "Good heavens, I know, I see that, but what can I do against the destiny that is leading me?"[2]

Perhaps he was secretly relieved at the idea of falling under the blows of conspirators as his father had. If that was the price of moral redemption, should he not accept it with serenity? A mystical fatalism tempted him in that direction, for all that he still called himself a disciple of the Encyclopedists. In any case, the growing animosity he felt around him did not turn him from the course he had chosen. During an audience granted to General Savary he alluded to the threats that hung over him personally and exclaimed, "If they want to dispatch me, let them make haste, but let them not think they can drive me to weakness or dishonor. I shall push Russia toward France as long as I can. Don't mistake for public opinion the views of a few wretches whom I don't use and who are too cowardly to undertake anything. They are not clever enough or resolved enough for that. . . . I know that people are plotting, that England is still at work, and that what you have seen is the result of those intrigues. I am not afraid of them; despite everything, I shall reach my goal. Have no anxiety on that account. They will have no choice but to give in. I am working for change, but I can only bring it about slowly. . . . I love my relatives very much, but I am reigning and I mean to be treated with respect."[3]

Alexander sustained this tough frame of mind with a regular, austere way of life. Up at five in the morning, he would dress, write or dictate his correspondence, and at nine o'clock attend the changing of the guard. After a short walk he would talk with his ministers for three or four hours at a stretch and then lunch soberly with only a few companions. "His evenings," wrote Stedingk, "he spends in retirement or at home, with one or two persons with whom he is intimate and who come to his rooms or whom he goes to see with no attendants." The nocturnal visits Stedingk mentioned were those of the Emperor's official mistress, Maria Naryshkina. He continued to seek relaxation and pleasure with her without, however, showing any disrespect to his wife. But he still devoted the best part of his attention to work, to politics. Disliking large gatherings, he avoided balls and galas. On the rare occasions when His Majesty gave a reception, the diplomats would line up, frozen at attention, in the audience room, facing the Grand Dukes and Grand Duchesses; the Emperor, the Empress, and the Empress Dowager would pass slowly before this assembly, greet each one with a nod of the head, say a few gracious words to the chief ambassadors, and withdraw, leaving behind them an icy chill. This extreme reserve, the rarity of entertainments, the monotony of the court routine antagonized the high society of the capital. "The Emperor does not make sufficient public display," wrote Hédouville. "His kindness and economy are not appreciated by the Russians, and especially by the nobles who want to be dazzled, are avid for riches, and need to be led with a firm hand."

Like her husband, the Empress liked nothing so much as simplicity and solitude. A resigned sadness hung over her life. She had made her peace with Alexander's infidelity. Had he not even had the impudence to talk to her proudly about Maria Naryshkina's pregnancy? But "the child of adultery" died not long after birth. Alexander was profoundly affected, and Elizabeth offered sincere condolences to her husband's mistress. She could not bear to see him suffer. "As soon as I have a hint that he might become unhappy," she wrote, "I cling to him with all the warmth of which my heart is capable: I forget all grievances. I identify with his fate, whatever it may be." To be sure, her behavior was not blameless, but her sentimental adventures were so disappointing that in her own eyes she almost seemed excused. After the tragic death of her lover Okhotnikov she felt more abandoned than ever and poured out all her affection on her only child, little Elizabeth, "Lisinka," born in December 1806. Fifteen months later the little girl died suddenly of an infection brought on by teething. "Now," wrote Elizabeth to her mother, "I am no longer good for anything in this world, my soul has no more strength to recover from this last blow." And a little later: "I have the illusion of spring in my apartment, the illusion of sunshine, flowers, singing birds, the birds that belonged to Lisinka. She was often amused by her bullfinches: One of them whistles perfectly an air which I should never forget if I lived to be a hundred." When Dr. Wylie tried to console the Emperor by telling him that at her age the Empress could still hope to have another child, Alexander answered sadly: "No, my friend, God does not love my children."

Immured in her grief, Elizabeth found pleasure only in reading, walking, and chatting with a few intimate friends. When she looked in a mirror her beauty, blooming as she approached thirty, seemed to her bitterly useless. "It is difficult to describe all the charm of the Empress," wrote Rosenweig, the ambassador of Saxony. "Features of extreme refinement and regularity, a Greek profile, large blue eyes and hair of a ravishing blond. There is an atmosphere of elegance and majesty about her, and her step is as light as air. In short, she is without doubt one of the most beautiful women in the world." Count Golovkin lauded "her tact, her sagacity, her knowledge of the human heart." But he added that she was very unhappy. "Her children are dead," he wrote, "her husband no longer pays attention to her; as for her family, she is separated from them forever. The court scarcely sees her, the nation is not at all attached to her, all the interests of life have disappeared for her." Joseph de Maistre made a more subtle comment on her situation: "No one can judge these wrongs between a married couple. They themselves would not be able to say which of them was first at fault. But in the meantime, the mistress is there with her kindness, her beauty, her adroitness, her graces, the power of habit, and the power of a relationship which is no doubt very guilty, very unfortunate, but which is very natural and does not exist in another quarter."

With her retiring, private ways, Elizabeth was increasingly disappointing to the courtiers who liked to see pomp and ostentation. In contrast to the dullness of the sovereign couple, the Empress Dowager, Maria Feodorovna, did everything she could to prove that she, by herself, incarnated the splendor and authority of monarchy. On the death of her husband she had hoped to govern the country with the consent of her son, but he had slipped from her control and now she had to be content with acting behind the scenes. Thanks to Alexander's benevolence, she had a place in the highest ranks of the empire, managed all the great charitable establishments, controlled the Bank for Loans and the spinning mill of Alexandrovsk, and enjoyed an annual income of one million rubles. This substantial sum made it possible for her to live in grand style. Her personal court eclipsed the Czar's. While the imperial couple was content with a team of two horses, she demanded six for her private carriage and never left her palace without an escort of hussars and pages. Perpetuating the tradition of Catherine II, she attended parades in military uniform, the cordon of an order across her breast. Her elegant, gay receptions, at which she appeared sumptuously dressed, surrounded by ladies-in-waiting and chamberlains, were in sharp contrast to the dreary exercises in protocol of her son and daughter-in-law. "Her whole apartment, which was furnished with great taste and richness, was open," wrote Stedingk. "The greatest gaiety reigned at this ball, together with much magnificence and dignity. The supper was served on round tables, the table of the reigning Empress being in the center—it had eighteen place settings. There was much dancing after supper." And Savary wrote Talleyrand, "The Empress Mother is the one who displays her imperial state. Every external honor, every homage is directed to that point. In public ceremonies, Maria Feodorovna often takes the Emperor's arm; the Empress Elizabeth walks behind her, and alone. I have seen troops under arms and the Czar on horseback waiting for his mother to arrive. Not a favor is granted in Russia, not a single appointment is made, but the beneficiary goes to pay her his respects and to kiss her hand in thanks, without her having taken the least part in obtaining the favor; but he does not go to say anything to the Empress Elizabeth. It is not the custom. The great personages of St. Petersburg are careful not to let two weeks pass without making an appearance at the Empress Mother's. Elizabeth almost never appears there, but the Emperor dines there three times a week and often sleeps there."

Conscious of the prestige she enjoyed in Alexander's entourage, the Empress Mother tried to influence her son's politics. She was as haughty and categorical as he was gracious and dissembling. Sometimes she succeeded in convincing him, as in the case of Czartoryski's removal from office; sometimes she ran into a wall, as in the case of the unfortunate alliance with Prussia. But she was most strongly opposed to any rapprochement with "the Corsican parvenu." Her court soon became a center of anti-Napoleon sentiment and a hotbed of criticism of the Czar. Elizabeth was pained that this campaign of systematic disparagement of Alexander was being led by her mother-in-law. On August 29, 1807, she wrote, in French, "The Empress who, as a mother, should support and defend the interests of her son, from thoughtlessness, from pride (and certainly for no other reason, for she is incapable of evil intentions), has succeeded in becoming like the leader of an insurrection; all the malcontents, of whom there are a great number, rally around her, praising her to the skies, and never has she attracted so many people to Pavlovsk as this year. I cannot express to you how indignant it makes me."

Of course, Elizabeth herself had no affection for the Emperor of the French, who seemed to have bewitched her husband "by magic." But despite her repugnance for Napoleon, she thought it was essential to maintain "a necessary peace." Her feeble voice was lost in the chorus of recriminations. Every day the enemies of France gained new adherents. When General Savary appeared at a social gathering all faces froze. In the eyes of Russian society, he was "the executioner of the Duc d'Enghien," the man who had given the firing squad the order to shoot, who had had the victim's grave dug in advance. Elizabeth wrote her mother, "The more attachment to his new ally [Alexander] shows and the more he honors him in the person of Savary, the louder the outcry, to the point where it has become frightening."

The next ambassador to St. Petersburg, General de Caulaincourt, was given an even more hostile reception. *He* was accused not of having assassinated the Duc d'Enghien but of having kidnapped him from Ettenheim. The rumors circulating on this subject were so slanderous that he felt the need to justify himself before Alexander. He exhibited papers, cited irrefutable testimony. The Czar replied politely, "I already knew through my ministers in Germany that you had nothing to do with the horrible affair you speak of. . . . I am pleased to tell you so."[4] But while he received Caulaincourt with marked kindness, he appointed as ambassador to Paris Count Peter Tolstoy, who was fiercely opposed to the French alliance.

To overcome Russian society's reservations about him, Caulaincourt gave a series of receptions, dinners, entertainments of all kinds, spent more than his salary, contracted debts. "Must I sell my shirt?" he wrote Napoleon. His table was open to all and the renown of his chef, Tardif, spread throughout the city and attracted guests. At one supper for four hundred persons, in the middle of the month of February, he served pears at three hundred francs apiece, which dazzled Joseph de Maistre. "I find it very amusing to observe Caulaincourt," he wrote. "He is well born and plumes himself upon it; he represents a sovereign before whom the world trembles; he has an income of six or seven hundred thousand francs; he is first everywhere. . . . Yet under all his embroidery he has a very common look; he is as stiff as if he had brass wire in his joints. The general opinion is that he looks like a provincial at court."

Indeed, Caulaincourt's lavish entertaining was not enough to disarm public opinion. Alexander might say to Napoleon's envoy, "You have had a great success in high society; you have conquered the most rebellious," but in reality the criticism of France, its representative, and the Czar, who persisted in taking "the wrong road," was becoming increasingly harsh. The animosity of the Empress Dowager reached its peak when she learned of the marriage of Jerome to Princess Catherine of Württemberg, a union that made the Czar's mother the aunt of a common Bonaparte. The many French royalist emigrés who had become officers in the Russian Guard and the envoys of sovereigns who had been despoiled by Napoleon fanned the flames. "It is certain," wrote one of them, Roger de Damas, "that today Bonaparte runs this empire and directs its affairs as if it were one of the provinces of France. The Czar is no longer anything but a prefect." Among Napoleon's detractors must also be counted Alexander's subjects in the Baltic countries, who though nominally Russian had retained sentimental ties with Germany, and the Prussian officers who had enlisted under the banners of Alexander after the dissolution of the army of Frederick William III. In September 1807, when the Czar decided to change the uniform of his troops, replacing the tight, Austrian-style tunics with more comfortable and elegant ones modeled on those of the Napoleonic army, the Guard muttered against "the French livery." Everything that came from Napoleon was suspect. The Russians might speak French in the salons, read French books with delight, imitate French fashion in dress and coiffures, and applaud the excellent French artists who performed in Russian theaters, but they cursed "Bonaparte," the unworthy heir to French culture.

While court and army protested from a sense of honor, merchants, landed proprietors, and industrialists protested out of self-interest. After his offers of mediation had failed, Alexander had been obliged to break relations with England and, as he had promised at Tilsit, to join the system of continental blockade devised by Napoleon. Up until then, however, it had been to England that Russia exported most of its raw materials: iron, hemp, wood, flax, tar, tallow, wheat, potash, leather, wax, horsehair, and so on. Of a total of thirty million rubles' worth of merchandise that had left the port of St. Petersburg in 1802, the English had bought seventeen million rubles' worth and the French only a half a million. That same year, of 986 merchant vessels that had entered the port of St. Petersburg, 477 had been English and 5 French.[5] This disproportion explains the anxiety of the businessmen when the profitable British outlets were closed. They were right to be alarmed. Economic and financial stagnation very soon set in. Wheat exports diminished by four-fifths, banking transactions became difficult, paper rubles lost 50 percent of their value, prices rose and the purchasing power of wage earners dwindled. The slight increase in French purchases was not enough to make up the enormous deficit in the balance of trade. Even contraband, under the American or Swedish flag, could not remedy the situation, for the price of commodities brought in illegally—sacks of sugar, bales of cotton—was prohibitive. Many manufactured products disappeared from the market. People were obliged to cut back. Social gatherings—the balls, suppers, and masquerades—went on against a background of sullen resentment against Alexander, who was now blamed both for the difficulties of daily life and for the submission of Russian politics to the wishes of Napoleon.

For the elite of St. Petersburg, the enemy was not France but the French emperor, but for the elite of Moscow all France was to blame. The Czar's ideas were rejected in the old capital not for subtle political reasons but out of visceral nationalism. Moscow, the city of Russian tradition, had always wanted to be different from St. Petersburg, the city of the European future. In Moscow everything reflected the empire's Asiatic past. The city, which had grown up haphazardly around the red brick wall of the Kremlin, was only a collection of wooden manor houses nestled in the depths of immense parks, of tumbledown cottages surrounded by vegetable gardens, of churches with multicolored cupolas, of open-air markets, waste ground, and palaces with the façades of Greek temples. The twisting streets, most of which had neither pavement nor sidewalk, were crowded with a heterogeneous population in which bearded muzhiks wearing boots and peasant women in ample, bright-colored dresses with kerchiefs on their heads rubbed elbows with elegant young men wearing powder and pomade and fine ladies with short hair and little flat curls on their foreheads. While St. Petersburg was the gathering place of dignitaries and functionaries, Moscow was the gathering place of men who had left the service because they were tired or out of favor and who preferred the pleasures of a peaceful, patriarchal, independent existence to the myriad constraints of court. St. Petersburg was ambition. Moscow was nonchalance and joie de vivre.

There were no limits to hospitality in Moscow. The great families were surrounded by innumerable servants. The Sheremetyev household had three hundred, the Stroganovs six hundred. The doors were open at all hours. At Alexis Orlov's, dinner was laid for one hundred fifty to three hundred guests, and any gentleman was welcome at his table provided he wore a uniform. Every evening in one or another of the great houses of Moscow there was a supper, a ball, or a masquerade. The musicians in the excellent orchestras were serfs. "In Moscow," Viegel noted in his *Memoirs*, "the whole winter is one perpetual Carnival." Bulgakov gave details: "Balls follow balls, and I cannot understand why they don't drop dead from fatigue. If this sort of folly continues all winter, everyone will finally collapse and for next season we shall have to declare a mass campaign to recruit more ladies." Fourteen private mansions possessed their own theaters. Mademoiselle George and her Russian rival Semionova appeared at Count Apraxin's. But most of the time it was amateurs who performed tragedies, comedies, vaudevilles, always in French. Other distractions were sleigh rides on the frozen Moskva River, cock fights, gatherings at the English Club, and hunting parties in the surrounding countryside.

When fine weather came Moscow emptied, the nobles and their retinues returned to their estates. Almost all the servants moved with their masters in a caravan of barouches and wagons. When they halted, cooks bustled about preparing meals. At midday they took tea by the side of the road. The children would scatter to play and their tutors and governesses would reprimand them in French, German, English. After a few weeks in the country they would all return to Moscow with a fresh appetite for pleasures, and the balls, suppers, and performances would start over again.

So, too, the political discussions. The most indulgent of Alexander's critics accused him of being inconsistent. Formerly the Czar had said he supported the revolutionary principles of 1789; today he was aligning himself with Napoleon. Why did he always seek models abroad? Wasn't there enough in Russia's rich past to inspire a monarch who was concerned about the happiness of his people? More and more Muscovites thought Russia's only salvation lay in a return to ancestral values: French tutors lost their prestige among the noble families and some were dismissed, their services suddenly deemed unnecessary. People continued to speak French in the drawing rooms but from time to time slipped a Russian phrase into the conversation. A movement grew for the purification of the language—it was said to have been infected with too many foreign words—and for the glorification of the literature of the Middle Ages, a blessed time when imitation of the West had not yet stifled the Slavic genius. The patriotic craze spread from Moscow to literary circles in St. Petersburg. Plays were produced there exalting the exceptional virtues of the people in adversity and war. Admiral Chichkov, Derzhavin, the playwright Chakhovskoy, and many others founded a society of friends of Russian *(Besseda)*, aimed at restoring the prestige the national language had lost during preceding reigns.

Of course, most of the provincial gentry did not trouble themselves over these considerations. They preferred hunting, wine, and cards to more intellectual pursuits. But they had all been touched by the slump in agricultural products and the unsteadiness of the ruble. Logically enough, they held France responsible for their financial difficulties. And behind France stood Alexander.

As for the simple muzhiks, who had been sorely tried by the levies of fresh troops in 1806, they wept for the dead who had given their lives for nothing, pitied the maimed who had come back to hobble about the villages, and wondered how the "Antichrist Napoleon," who had spilled so much Russian blood on the battlefields, had been able in a few hours to win the friendship and confidence of the Czar. They counted up their comrades who had fallen in vain. They doubted the sanity of the nobles who had commanded them. They sought an explanation for the meeting at Tilsit. Prince Viazemski recorded in his notebooks a conversation between two peasants: " 'How could our little father, the Orthodox Czar, bring himself to meet with this accursed Antichrist?' said one. 'Isn't it a great sin?' 'I'm surprised you don't understand, little brother!' replied the other. 'Don't you know they met in the middle of a river? Our little father had asked for a raft so Bonaparte could be baptized in the river before he appeared before the pure eyes of the sovereign.' " And Viegel wrote in his *Memoirs:* "This is a time when all the affection that subjects can have for their monarch has been transformed into something worse than hostility, into a feeling of disgust. I do not flatter myself that I am very wise, but in this circumstance I have seen the cruel injustice of the Russians. I have been ashamed for them. They have acted like the Cheremiss and Chuvash whom they so despise, who beat their gods when the latter have not fulfilled their wishes."

Alexander was kept well informed of what was being said at court and among the people. To keep a closer watch on his subjects' mood, in January of 1807 he had reestablished a kind of secret police, the "Committee for General Security." He who needed so much to be loved felt misunderstood, hated, despised. Yet for the immediate future he could see no other solution than the one he had chosen. The only thing he could do to give the illusion of political progress was to change the personnel around him. At Foreign Affairs General Budberg, who was a wretched diplomat, was replaced by Count Nicholas Rumiantsev. This great aristocrat was much interested in art and literature and was peculiar in that he was both a nationalist and a Francophile. Czartoryski, Novosiltsev, and Kochubey were relieved of their duties and went abroad. To head the Ministry of the Interior Alexander appointed

Kochubey's former associate Michael Speransky, a cultivated, flexible, intelligent man who had long been quietly preparing himself for this task. On January 13, 1806, the Ministry of War was entrusted to the fearsome Arakcheyev. The public could not understand why so narrow-minded, cruel, and cowardly a person had been elevated to an important post. It was said that he had refused to participate in the battle of Austerlitz because his sensitive soul could not endure "the sight of slaughter"—but this same sensitive soul was unmoved by the corporal punishments inflicted on soldiers at his orders and in his presence. In his youth at Gatchina Alexander had had an opportunity to appreciate the organizational capacities of the man whom he had then called friend. With this uniformed brute at the head of the troops, he was sure that discipline would be respected. It would take nothing less than an Arakcheyev, he thought, to forge the invincible army Russia needed.

For the time being, that army intervened only in matters of secondary importance. At Tilsit Napoleon had suggested that Alexander focus his legitimate territorial ambitions on the Baltic. "The lovely ladies of St. Petersburg," he had said, "must not hear from their palaces the cannon of the Swedes. Sweden is your geographical enemy."[6] Thus encouraged, the Czar sent his troops against Finland, then a Swedish province, at the beginning of 1808. He occupied the country, pushed on to the eastern shore of Sweden, and once King Gustavus IV was overthrown, imposed on the defeated adversary the profitable peace of Fredrikshamn (Hamina). By this treaty Russia obtained the Aland Islands and all of Finland, which was to be established as a grand duchy with a constitution, an army, and a reigning grand duke—none other than the Czar himself. But in St. Petersburg public opinion was hardly touched by this victory and was not impressed by the gift of so cold and barren a country. The resumption of the war against Turkey, on the other hand, made it possible to ensure that Russia would seize the rich lands of Moldavia and Walachia to the south. Displeased at this extension of Alexander's influence to the Black Sea, Napoleon suggested that he exchange those two principalities for Silesia. The Czar replied at once indignantly, "I should give up [Silesia] rather than possess it at the expense of Prussia. I should not want the whole Ottoman Empire at that price: I make it a point of honor."

The two Emperors disagreed even more sharply on the subject of Poland. Both were convinced that the old kingdom must be restored. But Napoleon envisaged the country as being completely French-dominated, while in Alexander's mind Poland would be closely tied to Russia and serve as an outer bulwark. Every consideration of politics, strategy, and history encouraged the Czar to defend that thesis. "In case of war," he said to Czartoryski, "it would surely be advisable for me to declare myself King of Poland, so as to rally people to my cause." And to Caulaincourt he exclaimed, "Poland is the only question on which I shall never compromise. The world is not big enough for us to reach an accommodation on the affairs of that country."[7] Since relations between Russia and France were deteriorating, Alexander finally yielded to Napoleon's requests for a second meeting, in September 1808, at Erfurt.

As soon as the court learned of his intentions there was a general outcry. The Empress Mother once again spoke on behalf of the opposition. Erfurt, she said, was a fortified town held by a "bloody tyrant" who again only recently had aroused world indignation when the Spanish sovereigns abdicated in his favor at Bayonne. This meeting was a trap from which Russia, like Spain, would emerge humiliated. "Alexander, stay away from it!" she wrote, in French. "You will ruin your empire and your family. Turn back, there is still time. Listen to the voice of honor, to the prayers and supplications of your mother. Stop, my child, my friend." He answered her very respectfully, also in French, that for the moment he must pretend to share Napoleon's views: "Let us not hasten to declare ourselves against him; we would run the risk of losing everything. Rather, let us appear to consolidate the alliance so as to lull him into a sense of security. Let us gain time and prepare. When the time comes, we shall look on serenely at Napoleon's downfall."

These explanations convinced no one, and Alexander left St. Petersburg amid unanimous censure. Since this time, too, he was Napoleon's guest, he was accompanied by only a small retinue, including Grand Duke Constantine, Speransky, Rumiantsev, and Caulaincourt. On the way to Erfurt, whether he liked it or not, he had to stop at Königsberg, where he met those two living reproaches, the King of Prussia and Queen Louise. After listening to their grievances he was even more ill disposed toward Napoleon, which did not prevent him from telling Marshal Lannes, who welcomed him to Friedberg, "I have much affection for the Emperor Napoleon and I shall prove it to him at every opportunity."[8]

Napoleon rode out to meet his friend on the road, and on seeing the procession of barouches dismounted, while the Czar stepped down from his carriage. They embraced fraternally, as at Tilsit. Then an equerry led up to Alexander the mount his host was giving him, caparisoned Russian-style with a housing of white bearskin. The two sovereigns made their entrance into Erfurt riding boot to boot, greeted by artillery salutes and the pealing of bells. Alexander was wearing the dark green tunic of a Russian general, Napoleon the uniform of the chasseurs of the Guard. They were cheered by a crowd of curious spectators. The residence that had been prepared for the Czar was the most sumptuous in the city. The following days were equally divided between private conversations and public ceremonies. The two Emperors were inseparable. Together they visited the French camp; together they watched the army maneuvers through field glasses; together they visited the battlefield of Jena, scene of the defeat of Prussia, the country so dear to Alexander's heart; together they attended a great ball at the castle of Weimar, where the Czar danced with the ladies while Napoleon watched him, motionless, with ironic benevolence; together they received the Kings of Bavaria, Westphalia, and Württemberg and other reigning princes of Germany who had hastened to pay homage to their supreme protector.

All these petty sovereigns trembled before the man on whom their survival depended. Not one of them would have dreamed of rebelling against the humiliations inflicted on them. According to the master's orders, they had a right only to a picket of "ten men of the Guard and no men on horseback." Mounted guards were reserved for the two Emperors.[9] In the course of a ceremonial gathering, as King Maximilian Joseph dared to raise his voice in his corner, Napoleon snapped at him, "Hold your tongue, King of Bavaria!" Goethe himself was summoned to Erfurt, bowed before Napoleon, and was rewarded with the cross of the Legion of Honor.

In the evening, having dined at Napoleon's table, the monarchs and their entourages met again at the theater. The most celebrated actors of the Comédie Française appeared before "a *parterre* of kings and princes." "A *plate-bande,*" corrected one sarcastic witness.* It was hard to tell whether the show was on the stage or in the hall. The Czar was particularly eyeing the actress Antoinette Bourgoin, nicknamed "the goddess of joy and pleasures." As he mentioned his interest in this engaging young person to Napoleon, the Emperor of the French replied, "I do not advise you to make advances to her." "You think she would refuse?" said the Czar. "Oh no!" exclaimed Napoleon, "but to-

---

*The pun is lost in translation. In French (as in English) *parterre* can mean not only the front rows of spectators in a theater but also an ornamental arrangement of flowers, grass, and shrubbery in a park or formal garden. A *plate-bande* is a flower bed, but *plat* (flat) also has the meaning of abject or obsequious, and *bande* (strip) can also be a group. The witness is thus referring to the "servile band" of kings and princes around Napoleon. (Trans.)

morrow the post leaves, and in five days all Paris would know the details of Your Majesty's figure from head to toe..... And then, I take an interest in your health. So I hope you will be able to resist temptation."[10] The Czar prudently restrained his amorous impulses. On Tuesday, October 4, 1808, Talma, acting in Voltaire's *Œdipe,* put special feeling into his reading of the meaningful line, "The friendship of a great man is a gift of the gods!" At these words, Alexander rose and shook the hand of Napoleon, who was seated beside him in the box. The audience gave an ovation to the two Emperors, who bowed. On which side of the footlights were the actors? Alexander wrote to his sister Catherine, "Bonaparte claims that I am only a fool. He laughs best who laughs last. As for me, I place all my hope in God."

In reality these brilliant demonstrations hid a growing misunderstanding. Curiously, the Czar was encouraged in his obstinacy by Talleyrand, who was working cunningly against the interests of his master. Taking Alexander aside, Talleyrand said to him, "Sire, what did you come here for? It is up to you to save Europe, and you will succeed in doing that only if you hold your ground against Napoleon. The French people are civilized, their sovereign is not. The sovereign of Russia is civilized, his people are not. The sovereign of Russia should therefore be the ally of the French people. The Rhine, the Alps, the Pyrenees are conquests of France. The rest is the conquest of the Emperor, France doesn't care about it."[11] These words revived hope in Alexander, who already foresaw the decline of French hegemony. With even deeper treachery, Talleyrand suggested that Alexander should not try to pacify bellicose Austria, whose military support he might need in case of a new confrontation with Napoleon.

From their first conversations the Emperor of the French noted that Alexander was not so "easy" as he had been at Tilsit. Having urgent need to send his armies from Prussia to Spain, Napoleon wanted a formal pledge that the Czar would join him against Austria; but Alexander found the most varied pretexts to avoid committing himself. The discussions dragged on and grew acrimonious, and Napoleon complained to Caulaincourt: "Your Emperor Alexander is as stubborn as a mule. He plays deaf to whatever he doesn't want to hear. This confounded business in Spain is costing me dear!" During one altercation stormier than the others, he flung his hat on the ground and stamped on it. Unimpressed by this display of southern temper, Alexander said with a cold smile, "You are violent, I am stubborn. So anger will get you nowhere with me. Let us talk, let us reason, or I shall leave."[12] And he started for the door. Napoleon called him back and the conversation resumed in a pleasanter tone.

But the roles were reversed when Alexander asked Napoleon to demonstrate his peaceful intentions by evacuating Prussia. Then it was Napoleon who became indignant and obstinate. "Is it my friend, my ally," he cried, "who proposes that I abandon the only position from which I can threaten Austria's flank if she attacks me while my troops are in southern Europe, four hundred leagues from home?"[13] Similarly, he said to some of his close advisers who were counseling conciliation: "It is a system of weakness that you are proposing to me. If I agree to it, Europe will soon be treating me like a little boy."[14]

With great difficulty they reached a compromise. Napoleon accepted Russia's annexation of Moldavia and Walachia, providing the Porte consented. In exchange, he obtained the promise of military cooperation against Austria if that power should initiate hostilities. But in the meantime Alexander had reassured Baron Vincent, Austria's representative at Erfurt, that this latter commitment was entirely theoretical. Having thus duped each other, the two Emperors officially declared themselves satisfied at the strengthening of the ties between them. During one of these meetings Alexander started to remove his sword and noticed that he had forgotten it. Napoleon, who had just taken off his own, begged him to accept it. Alexander, his eyes shining with false gratitude, exclaimed, "I accept it as a token of your friendship. Your Majesty is very certain that I shall never draw it against him."[15] Napoleon wrote to Josephine, "Everything is going well, I am pleased with Alexander. He must be pleased with me! If he were a woman, I think I would make him my sweetheart." They also decided to present joint offers of peace to England. Peter Tolstoy, who was too outspoken, would be replaced as ambassador to Paris by Prince Alexander Kurakin, who it was hoped would be more accommodating. In fact, according to Rostopchin, he was "a beast who should be a German prince driven from his State or an idol among the savages."[16] Lastly, Napoleon instructed Talleyrand to inform the Czar officially that he planned to repudiate Josephine and ask for the hand of one of the Grand Duchesses, "so as to consolidate his work and found his dynasty." The Czar had long since been alerted to the matrimonial intentions of his "friend." Grand Duchess Catherine, the only one of his sisters who was of an age to marry, would not be averse to the prospect of becoming Empress of the French. "She would accommodate to it very well, I think," Empress Elizabeth wrote to her mother. "All she needs is a husband and freedom, although I doubt she would have complete freedom with this one." But Alexander could not deliver up his favorite sister to be devoured by "the Minotaur." He was horrified at the mere idea of a Grand Duchess of Russia replacing "that whore Josephine" in Napoleon's bed. He could imagine the indignant reaction of his mother and the whole court. However, he mastered his feelings and said to Talleyrand, "If only I myself were concerned, I should gladly give my consent, but mine is not the only one that must be obtained. My mother has retained an authority over her daughters which it is not for me to contest. I can try to give her some guidance; it is probable that she will follow it, but I dare not vouch for it. All that, inspired by true friendship, should satisfy the Emperor Napoleon."

This dilatory response did not discourage the illustrious suitor but it gained Alexander time to take countermeasures. No sooner had he returned to St. Petersburg than he hastened to engage Catherine to a petty German prince, the Duke of Oldenburg. "His appearance is not very agreeable," Elizabeth wrote her mother, "and is even frankly disagreeable. . . . I shall never believe that he could inspire love, but Grand Duchess Catherine assures me that he is the husband she must have and that she sets no value on appearance."

Unable to obtain the hand of Catherine, the "Corsican ogre" proposed to fall back on her younger sister, little Anne, who was barely fifteen. In a panic over this fearful possibility, Alexander sought his mother's advice: "If Napoleon has this idea and approaches me about it, how is he to be answered? The consequences of a refusal will be acrimony, ill will, and wrangling, for you must know the man who will be wounded."[17] Maria Feodorovna examined the situation coolly and wrote to her daughter Catherine, "My first reaction was to tell Alexander that everything we had done to save you from that misfortune [marriage to Napoleon] should be our rule now. . . . Let us begin with the possibility of consenting to the union and see what favorable consequences it would have for the State. They are the following: 1) The hope of prolonged peace with France. . . . What will be the unfavorable consequences if we refuse this union? . . . 2) Embittered as he will be by a refusal, Napoleon's ill humor, his rage against us will increase. . . . He will haggle with us until he is in a position to fall upon us. Our nation, informed by him that there have been proposals of marriage which might have preserved us from the scourge of war with him, will be angry with the Emperor, and with me, for having refused them. . . . 3) As for my poor Annette, we must think of her as being sacrificed for the good of the State. For what a miserable existence the child would have united to a scoundrel to whom nothing is sacred and who knows no restraint because he does not even believe in God! . . . What would she see, what would she hear in that school of wickedness and vice? . . . Katya, I shudder to think of all that. . . . The State on the one hand, my child on the other, Alexander sovereign, a refusal likely to bring troubles and misfortunes down upon him! . . . Shall I, Annette's own mother, dictate her unhappiness? . . . If that man [Napoleon] should die united to Anne, the poor unfortunate will be exposed to all the horrors of the disturbances that will follow in the wake of his death, for how can we suppose that that man's dynasty will be respected? We have debated over various answers to be given to Caulaincourt and have decided upon this one: The youth of my daughter, who is not even formed, in view of the irregularity of certain periods. . . ."[18] After a final family council, Caulaincourt was informed that as Grand Duchess Anne was barely nubile, she could not be given in marriage to the Emperor of the French who was already forty years old. Nevertheless, to avoid an open quarrel between the two courts, it was hinted that in a few years, when little Anne had reached full development, this plan of marriage would be favorably reconsidered by Russia.

Napoleon took this phony excuse like a slap in the face, especially since in January 1809, on the occasion of the wedding of Grand Duchess Catherine, the King and Queen of Prussia were given an exceptionally splendid welcome to St. Petersburg. Alexander meant this to be Russia's answer to Napoleon's magnificent display at Erfurt. During a ball at Princess Dolgoruky's, Caulaincourt said in vexation to the company at large, "There is no mystery about this journey: The Queen of Prussia has come to sleep with Emperor Alexander." The remark made the rounds of every drawing room in St. Petersburg. While they did not believe this slander, most observers were surprised at the extravagant gifts that Queen Louise found in her apartment in Mikhailovsky Palace: a toilet set made of solid gold, Persian and Turkish shawls, a dozen dresses embroidered with pearls, rare jewels . . . Doubtless Alexander had wanted to refurbish the wardrobe of the unfortunate sovereign who had lost almost everything in her country's disaster. The trials she had been through had somewhat dimmed the young woman's freshness. Joseph de Maistre said of her, "She has often been compared to the reigning Empress [Elizabeth]. The Queen may be a more beautiful woman, but the Empress is a more beautiful sovereign." And Elizabeth wrote her mother, "It is impossible not to consider the Queen a beautiful woman. But she must not grow any stouter. She is in the early stages of a pregnancy which makes her feel ill most of the time and gives her lackluster eyes." Queen Louise herself noted in her diary: "January 8,

1809: Bed without sleeping; I am ill and I fear I am pregnant; I suffer a great deal and am frightful to see. . . . January 10: Sleepless night; fever, toothache, nausea. . . . January 12: Dead tired; if this goes on I shall be buried in St. Alexander Nevsky cemetery. . . . January 13: Dog tired. . . . January 16: At the Hermitage theater Mademoiselle George, celestial, beautiful, terrifying; it gave me a fever all evening. . . . January 20: Bad chest cold. . . ."

In spite of her drawn face, "lackluster eyes," and weak legs, Queen Louise heroically forced herself to appear at all the festivities to maintain her reputation as an international beauty. The court admired her and was astonished at her daring décolletages, but Alexander remained insensible to this bountiful provocation. He even seemed to be avoiding opportunities for a half-sentimental, half-political conversation with the indefatigable coquette. At a reception where she appeared with bare shoulders and a low-cut bodice, bejeweled like a reliquary, she found the Czar looking at her as she stood next to Maria Naryshkina, with whom, it was said, he was about to break off. As was her custom, Maria Naryshkina was wearing the simplest of white dresses, and her sole ornament was a bunch of forget-me-nots nestled in her jet-black hair. Alexander compared the two women and smiled at his mistress. Louise murmured, "I go away as I came. My kingdom is not of this world."[19] In her letter of farewell she said to the Czar, "I embrace you in thought and beg you to believe that in life and death I remain your grateful friend. . . . Everything was superb in St. Petersburg. Only I saw too little of you."

The royal couple had hardly left St. Petersburg when Alexander received a visit from Prince Schwarzenberg, who had been sent by the cabinet of Vienna to try to persuade him to remain neutral in case of conflict between Austria and France. Alexander replied proudly, "If you make a move, I march [meaning, at France's side]. You will set fire to Europe and you will fall victim to that fire."[20] But in his heart of hearts he was by no means resolved to take joint action with Napoleon. It seemed to him that the Emperor of the French was in a poor position: in contention with the Holy See, involved in the difficult and discreditable Spanish affair. The imperial eagle was dragging its wing. Was not this the moment to abandon it? Supported by funds from England, Austria was arming to the teeth. There was talk of 400,000 men ready to crush Napoleon's troops, who were worn down by too many successive campaigns.

From the first engagements the Austrians were routed. On May 13, 1809, Napoleon entered Vienna, and Alexander told Caulaincourt, "I

have done everything to avoid war, but since the Austrians have provoked it and begun it, the Emperor will find in me an ally who will
march boldly; I shall do nothing by halves." To Schwarzenberg, however, he spoke quite differently. The Austrian envoy reported to
Vienna, in French, "The Emperor assured me that nothing would be
neglected that was humanly possible to think of to avoid striking blows
at us; he added that his position was so strange that although we found
ourselves in opposite camps, he could not help wishing for our success."[21]

Reluctantly, the Czar gave the order for thirty-two thousand men
to cross the Bug and enter Austrian territory. Using every means possible, the Russian army brought off a miracle: It avoided contact with the
troops it had come to fight. The casualties in the most serious encounter
amounted to two Cossacks killed and two officers wounded.[22] Russia's
true adversaries were not the Austrians but the Poles who had rallied
to the French forces. Prince Poniatowski wrote Napoleon, "I am loath
to accuse the Russian generals of such perfidy, but I cannot conceal
from Your Majesty that there is perfect concert between them and the
enemy."[23]

The hard battle of Wagram—in which the Russians, of course, did
not participate—settled the outcome of the war, to Alexander's great
disappointment. He was officially on the side of the victor, yet he deplored the downfall of the vanquished. Napoleon had once said to
Rumiantsev, "In the end our alliance will be a shameful one." Now he
said, "You have been colorless. The saber was not drawn a single
time."[24] By the Treaty of Vienna, signed on October 14, 1809, Russia
obtained some crumbs: the minuscule district of Tarnopol, in southeast-
ern Poland.* Public opinion was disgusted at this piece of charity. "Napoleon has humiliated Alexander," wrote the publicist Gretch, "by giving him, out of the lands taken from Austria, not some province but
400,000 souls, the way our czars used to reward their accomplices."

A more serious fact to Alexander was that the same treaty awarded
Krakow and western Galicia to the grand duchy of Warsaw, thus almost
wholly reconstituting Poland under French protection. At Tilsit Napoleon had suggested ceding to Russia all of Prussian Poland, that is, all
the territory between the Neman and the Vistula, but out of respect for
his friends the sovereigns of Prussia Alexander had declined the offer.
Now he regretted it. In his eyes the expansion of the grand duchy of

*In 1815 it was returned to Austria. Now it is a western subdivision of the Ukraine.

Warsaw increased the French threat to his borders. Of course, Napoleon claimed that he had never had any intention of reestablishing the kingdom of Poland. He even declared himself ready to "eliminate the words *Poland* and *Poles* not only from all political transactions, but also from history." These assurances made no impression on Alexander, who understood perfectly the artful game his partner was playing. He considered Napoleon's stirring speech to the French Legislative Body, beginning with the words, "My ally and friend the Emperor of Russia," as a pompous excuse for a dirty trick. He thought that if he had taken a more active part in the war against Austria, his wages might have been all of Galicia. He had made the mistake of being too timid, and blamed himself for it. Another "deplorable" fact: Without waiting for the definitive answer of the Russian court concerning his possible marriage with Grand Duchess Anne, Napoleon announced his intention of marrying Marie Louise of Austria. "Austria has sacrificed a beautiful heifer to the Minotaur," said the Prince de Ligne. At the Russian court, however, it was no laughing matter. No member of Alexander's entourage wanted to see little Anne sent to France to be the victim of a barbarian, but rejection by the said barbarian, who had made his move first, was taken as an affront.

Events were moving fast for the French: Pope Pius VII was taken prisoner, Holland and the Hanse Towns were annexed . . . Among the territories swept up by Napoleon was the little duchy of Oldenburg, whose present Duke was none other than the father-in-law of Alexander's beloved sister Catherine. "It's like a public insult," said the Czar, "a slap in the face of a friendly power." Napoleon moved borders, cut pieces out of nations, made and unmade dynasties. No human feeling, it seemed, could deflect him from his political designs. Alexander regretted that he himself was sometimes accessible to pity, friendship, affection. "The Corsican" was made of sterner stuff. Perhaps if he had been in Napoleon's place he would not have had the cold courage to repudiate Josephine. Break a man? Yes. But a woman? . . . And yet he had to admit that he had points in common with this monarch whom he admired and detested at the same time. As an autocratic czar, educated by a Jacobin, he was fond of invoking democratic ideas while jealously defending his prerogatives as a sovereign. For his part, Napoleon, a product of the Revolution, might be guilty of the worst excesses of authoritarianism, but he nonetheless represented a new social order based on liberty and equality. Despite their good intentions, neither of the two Emperors could make his acts accord with his principles.

Meanwhile, Alexander thought he had found the ideal associate to assist him in his ambiguous aspirations as a reforming despot: Michael Speransky. With this indefatigable and ambitious worker he hoped to take up again the program of renovation that had been outlined by his friends of the Secret Committee. The son of a simple priest in the village of Cherkutino, Speransky (whose real name was merely Mikhail Mikhailovich) had been educated at Vladimir Seminary, then at St. Alexander Nevsky Seminary in St. Petersburg. When he became secretary to Prince Alexis Kurakin, he was still so conscious of his humble background that he declined the offer to sit at his master's table. Soon, however, when he saw that he was held in high regard, he gained self-confidence. Freed by his patron from his commitments to the Church, he flew from one post to the next, made himself indispensable everywhere, participated in the work of the Secret Committee, went with Kochubey to the Ministry of the Interior, drafted imperial decrees and manifestos, won the confidence of the Czar and accompanied him to Erfurt. Speransky was thirty-seven years old at the time. In the presence of Napoleon he felt an almost religious admiration. He saw the Emperor of the French not so much as the victor of Wagram but as the author of the Civil Code, the reorganizer of the country, the creator of an administration that was said to be unequaled. Back in St. Petersburg, Speransky dreamed of changing the political structure of Russia from top to bottom, taking France as a model. He spoke of "adopting drastic measures" and "taking bold action." Alexander liked that sort of talk. He sensed that his new Secretary of State was a "Westerner" like himself. An Anglophile, Speransky dressed in London fashion, lunched at eleven o'clock on eggs, roast beef, and tea, and went riding every morning on a horse with a short-cropped tail. But if he followed fashion, he also had more serious concerns. Very widely read, familiar with the great philosophical systems of Europe, he soon discovered, through Saint-Martin and Swedenborg, "the antechamber of God." His belief in Freemasonry strengthened his leanings toward social Christianity. In his view, problems of political economy and public law were also matters that could be discussed in the spirit of the Gospel. Tall and stooping, with a pale complexion, a balding forehead, a long delicate nose, thin lips, and deep, moist eyes, he attracted everyone's attention by the intelligence and sweetness expressed in his face.

In the course of many conversations with Alexander, Speransky set forth a vast plan for legislative, economic, and fiscal reforms that would reconcile the Russian people with their sovereign. Inspired by the idea that the legislative and executive powers must necessarily be separate, he envisaged the creation of a high assembly, the Council of State, which would be composed of thirty-five members chosen by the Czar and would have a consultative voice in the field of legislation. Parallel to the Council of State would be the Imperial Duma, a legislative chamber including three degrees of elected representatives of the nobility and the middle classes. The Duma would be the organ of popular will. As for the Senate, it would become a High Court of Justice. A special committee would be charged with elaborating a civil code modeled on the Napoleonic Code. The ministers would be responsible to the Imperial Duma, which would study law drafts submitted to it.

For administrative purposes Russia would be divided into provinces, which in turn would be divided into districts and again into townships. At each level there would be a duma composed of representatives of the landowners. The representatives of the provincial dumas would send delegates to the Imperial Duma. In the judicial sphere township, district, and provincial courts would be created that would be subordinate to the Senate, the "supreme court."

At his minister's suggestion, the Czar issued a ukase providing that henceforth the titles of nobility awarded to those who had served the empire would be purely honorific and would not confer any rank in the civil service. Another ukase stated that promotion to the higher ranks of the service would be dependent on a certain level of education. Many functionaries and noblemen were indignant over this quite reasonable restriction.

But the most important part of the plan dealt with the definition of individual rights in Russia. For purposes of clarity, Speransky divided the citizens into three hierarchical groups: the nobility, the middle classes, and the workers. Individual rights were likewise divided into three categories. To the nobility alone Speransky granted all rights, including political rights, provided the beneficiaries were landed proprietors. In addition nobles retained the possibility of "acquiring inhabited lands," so long as they "administered them in accordance with the law." The document did acknowledge the "common civil rights" of the peasants, but still referred to those peasants as "serfs." It was nonetheless a first, very timid step toward mitigating serfdom. In the same way, while the author spoke of representative government, he continued to consider the supreme power as being essentially autocratic. As it stood, Speransky's liberal program was so hemmed in with precautions that its implementation was not likely to shake the monarchic foundations of Russia.

Nevertheless, Alexander was afraid of the storm that these innovations he had desired in theory might raise in practice. Of all Speransky's proposals, he adopted only the one relating to the creation of the Council of State. Starting on January 1, 1810, he regularly attended the weekly meetings of this body with Speransky, who had been promoted to the rank of "Imperial Secretary," seated on his right. While awaiting the problematical implementation of the other parts of his program, Speransky took certain urgent financial measures: amortization of the promissory notes in circulation by means of a fund derived from an increase in taxes, establishment of a new customs tariff, elimination of copper coins. Although designed to save the State from bankruptcy, these compromises united all the representatives of the possessing classes against their author. Speransky was accused of trying to ruin the noblest families. His idea of an Imperial Duma, in which elected deputies would arrogate to themselves the right to criticize measures taken by those in power, seemed to represent a revolutionary utopianism worthy of the sans-culottes. Lastly, it was muttered that Speransky was contemplating the abolition of serfdom, the ancestral foundation of Russian society. Even Alexander, though he had granted Finland the semblance of a constitutional regime, thought that Russia was not ready for the same experiment. He explained his position frankly to General Baron Armfelt: "I swear to you that I like these [constitutional] forms much better than the exercise of free choice based only on my own will. [In Finland] I cannot make a mistake because advice of all kinds is available to me; [in Russia] I am surrounded only by uncertainty and almost always by customs that have stood in the stead of laws."[25] Thus, after applauding the proposals of his Imperial Secretary, Alexander lent a complaisant ear to the criticisms that bombarded Speransky. The great nobles could not forgive this parvenu, this "son of a village priest" for his dizzying ascent to ever greater honors and responsibilities. "His office," one of them said, "is a Pandora's box, out of which fly all the ills that overwhelm our country."[26]

During a visit by Alexander to Tver (Kalinin), where his brother-in-law the Duke of Oldenburg was Governor General, Grand Duchess Catherine gave him a treatise by the famous historian Karamzin entitled *Dissertation on Old and New Russia.* On the flyleaf was inscribed: *To my brother alone.* In this work Karamzin drew up a bitter indictment of the ideas of the reforming minister. "They complain about him in palaces and in cottages," he declared. He insinuated that the recent financial measures had been "worked out by people who are deliberately trying to destroy the credit of the State." Pretending to believe that Speransky was seeking to abolish serfdom immediately, he fulminated, "I do not know whether Boris Godunov did well to take freedom from the peasants, but I do know that it would be difficult to return it to them: It is less dangerous for the security of the State to enslave men than to free them at the wrong time." And he made his fiercely nationalistic position clear: "Since Peter the Great we have become citizens of the world but we have ceased to be citizens of Russia. . . . The foreigners have taken control of our education, our court has forgotten the Russian language; fascinated by European luxury, our nobility has allowed itself to be driven to ruin. . . . It is dangerous to meddle with the structure of an old State. . . . Russia has existed for a millennium in the form of a great empire, not a savage horde; yet still they speak to us of new institutions and new rules, as if we had just emerged from the virgin forests of America." Even the drafting of a code of laws according to the French example seemed sacrilegious to this fanatical defender of custom: "Russia really does not need to solemnly admit her stupidity before all Europe and to bend her graying head over a book concocted by a few former lawyers and Jacobins." In conclusion, an appeal to God: "Our political principles are not inspired by the Encyclopedia published in Paris but by another Encyclopedia infinitely older, the Bible."[27]

On reading this diatribe Alexander was distressed to realize how isolated he was in the face of the conservative opposition. Was it wise to pursue a policy of reform that was opposed not only by those privileged in terms of wealth but also by those privileged in terms of faith and education? And besides, was this a good time to be occupied with the internal organization of the country when Napoleon, doing exactly as he pleased, had just appropriated the duchy of Oldenburg? Russia's timid proposals for a joint settlement of this affair and of the Polish question received a stinging reply from the Emperor of the French: "Even if your armies were to camp on the heights of Montmartre, I would not yield you one inch of Warsaw territory."

A veritable plot was taking shape at court to overthrow Speransky, who was denounced as a friend of France, an admirer of Napoleon, and a traitor to the country. General Baron Armfelt, who favored breaking with Napoleon, told Alexander: "Speransky should be sacrificed, guilty or not. That is indispensable to rally the nation around the chief of state. The war we are going to make on Napoleon is not an ordinary war; if we are not to succumb, we must necessarily make it a national war. . . . See how fiercely the public attacks him; let them discover a conspiracy, that is exactly what we need!" Balashov, the new Minister of Police, reported to the Czar some disrespectful remarks made by his chief associate. "You know how suspicious the Emperor is," Speransky was supposed to have said. "Everything he does, he does halfway. He is too weak to govern and too strong to be governed." The postal censorship office intercepted a letter from Speransky in which he mentioned Alexander's forthcoming inspection tour of fortifications on the western border and, alluding to the Czar's fair complexion, called him *"notre Vauban, notre veau blanc."** This insolent pun was not enough to make Alexander angry. As usual, he hesitated to make a quick decision.

Although Speransky was vilified on all sides, he continued to exercise his high functions. But now he had a rival for Alexander's esteem. General Arakcheyev, "that watchdog of the Russian throne," "that terrible bugbear," as Joseph de Maistre called him, was once again in favor at court and was stirring up suspicions about the Imperial Secretary. Alexander kept a balance between these two confidants who hated each other. A past master at playing double games, he would meet them separately in great secrecy, hide from one what the other had said, pretend to believe the one who had spoken last, and wait for circumstances to dictate his course of action in the end. In reality, Speransky, the flexible, enterprising liberal, and Arakcheyev, the believer in discipline and custom, represented the two aspects of Alexander's own complex nature, two caricatures of himself. He moved forward supported by these two men. He found their reciprocal animosity amusing. Arakcheyev twice offered his resignation and withdrew to his estate at Gruzino so as not to have to rub shoulders with "that son of a village priest," then came back with rage in his heart, recalled by Alexander who had need of his counsel. Speransky despised this uncouth, illiterate personage who, he said, had "the mentality of a drill sergeant." The refined Alexander shared this point of view but felt that Arakcheyev, with his limited mind, brutal manners, and reactionary ideas, was a servant of exemplary devotion, reliable in all circumstances. Speransky, on the other hand, was so intelligent, so cultivated, so astute, that in a way his very virtues amounted to a failing: He gave the Czar a sense of inferiority. Alexander liked Speransky and mistrusted him. Nevertheless, he made him responsible for organizing a kind of intelligence network in France. Young Count Karl Nesselrode was selected to go to Paris, get in touch with French political circles, and send Speransky secret reports on the situation in France. According to Alexander's

---

*"Our Vauban, our white calf," the two expressions rhyming in French. The Marquis de Vauban (1633–1707) was a French military engineer famous as an expert on fortifications. (Trans.)

instructions, neither the Russian ambassador to Paris, Kurakin, nor the Minister of Foreign Affairs, Rumiantsev, both of whom were pro-French, was to be informed of this correspondence.

As soon as he arrived in Paris Nesselrode made contact with Talleyrand, whom ever since Erfurt the Czar had trusted as an ally against Napoleon. Although imbued with the deepest devotion to the Russian cause, Talleyrand hastened to ask reward for his betrayal. "I am in need of fifteen hundred thousand francs," he wrote Alexander on September 15, 1810, "and it would be important for me to have them in the month of November. Although it is a simple matter in itself, I must exercise great care in choosing the means to procure the sum. If Your Majesty finds that in making so bold as to address myself to him I have only paid homage to the generosity with which he is endowed . . . I beg Your Majesty to have a letter written to Monsieur Bentham saying that Your Majesty gives Monsieur Labinski, Your Majesty's Consul General in Paris, a credit of fifteen hundred thousand francs on him, Bentham, in Frankfurt." Alexander replied with a polite refusal, "I ask you yourself, Prince, can I accede to this request without doing you a complete disservice? . . . If I do you this service, how and by whom can I do it without its coming to light? It is therefore with regret, Prince, that I deny myself the pleasure that I shall always take in obliging you."

Talleyrand nonetheless remained Russia's preferred political informant. The letters that Nesselrode sent the Czar through Speransky as intermediary contained chiefly information and advice from "my cousin Henry"—that is, from Talleyrand. He was also sometimes called "handsome Leander" or "Anna Ivanovna." Fouché figured in the correspondence as "the President" or "Natasha," the Czar was "Louise," Caulaincourt "Holchinsky." When a letter spoke of the "love affairs" of Monsieur Butiagin, a secretary at the Russian embassy, it was understood as a reference to the general discontent in France.

These mysterious documents—of no great value—were all submitted to the Emperor; but to be in better control of the situation, Speransky exceeded his authority and, unbeknownst to Rumiantsev, had two of the more credulous employees of the Russian Ministry of Foreign Affairs, Beck and Gervais, communicate to him the secret files of the Ministry. The Minister of Police, Balashov, immediately exploited this conspicuous bit of imprudence. Soon Speransky's numerous enemies were declaring the leak a scandal, if not an act of treason. They openly accused Speransky of maintaining criminal relations with Napoleon's agents. They demanded his head. With one word Alexander could have exonerated his associate whose only fault, he knew, had been to read the diplomatic dispatches of the chancery, to which he should not normally have had access. But this time the wave of hatred against Speransky was too violent. The court, the city, the whole country needed a scapegoat. Alexander himself felt little more than profound embarrassment, but in response to the wishes of persons around him, he feigned anger. Summary executions were repugnant to his limp, formless character, but he decided to act anyway and quickly—if not from personal conviction, at least from expediency.

On Sunday, March 17, 1812, a messenger from the cabinet brought Speransky an order to present himself before the Emperor at eight o'clock that evening. As there was nothing unusual in this, he proceeded calmly to the Winter Palace. A general and two ministers were waiting in the antechamber when he arrived. He was ushered into the sovereign's presence before them. The audience went on for two hours. At last the door opened again and the two men appeared on the threshold. Speransky was livid; the Emperor himself, with tears in his eyes, seemed greatly shaken. Which man had done more to hurt the other? Speransky held his portfolio nervously clutched against his chest. The officers on duty heard Alexander say with emotion, "Once again, farewell." When Speransky reached home he found Balashov, the Minister of Police, in person, waiting for him. His papers were placed under seal. In the middle of the night, without having had the courage to say good-bye to his family, the great legislator, the friend and confidant of the Czar, cast down from the height of his splendor, left St. Petersburg under police escort to go into exile in Nizhni Novgorod. One of his assistants, Magnitsky, was also arrested and sent away. A few days later the two officials of the Ministry of Foreign Affairs who had committed the folly of communicating secret documents to Speransky were placed under lock and key. Thus the interpretation of the affair as a plot against the security of the State was confirmed.

Speransky's sudden disgrace was greeted by the public as a first victory over the French. "The death of a tyrant could not have provoked such general rejoicing," noted the memorialist Viegel. "What a great day for the country and for us all that March seventeenth was!" wrote a contemporary, Barbe Bakunina. "God has shown us his benevolence, and our enemies have fallen. An outrageous crime, an infamous piece of treachery has been discovered in Russia. . . . It is probable that Speransky was ready to deliver up our country and our Emperor to our worst enemy."[28] "The whole empire is going to resound with this adventure," declared Joseph de Maistre. As the former minister's family left to join him, the people along the way hooted after them.

As for Alexander, having banished Speransky from his sight on a poor pretext, his heart was heavy. The day after his minister's departure for exile, he confided to Prince Alexander Golitzin, "If they cut off your arm, you would cry out with pain, wouldn't you? Well, last night they took Speransky from me; he was my right arm!" To Nesselrode, a few days later: "Only the present circumstances have forced me to make this sacrifice to public opinion." Lastly, to Novosiltsev: "[Speransky] is really guilty only toward me alone, guilty of having repaid my confidence and friendship with the blackest, the most abominable ingratitude. But that would not yet have driven me to harsh measures if certain persons who for some time have taken the trouble to follow his words and actions had not seen and denounced circumstances which made one suspect the most malevolent intentions." He reported to Novosiltsev the words he had spoken to his minister before dismissing him: "The enemy is knocking at the gates of the empire, and in the situation in which you have been placed by the suspicions you have drawn upon yourself by your conduct and the remarks you have permitted yourself to make, it is important to me not to appear guilty in the eyes of my subjects, in case of calamity, by continuing to repose my trust in you."

But as always, Alexander confided different thoughts to different persons. To some he declared that it had pained him to have to sacrifice Speransky to public opinion without even being able to verify the accusations heaped upon him; to others he swore that he was so angry with the minister that he envisaged the worst punishment for him. In a conversation with Parrot, the Rector of the University of Dorpat, he claimed that on learning of Speransky's "treachery" his first impulse had been to have him shot.

With Speransky far away in Nizhni Novgorod, then in Perm, Alexander began to regain his composure. The congratulations he received on the occasion of this sudden dismissal, this "clean sweep," as some put it, soon allayed his scruples. He had the feeling that by sacrificing his best collaborator he had rebuilt national unity around himself. He said philosophically, "Sovereigns cannot be judged according to the same standard as private persons. Politics requires them to perform certain duties which the heart condemns." Was he thinking of his father when he advanced this proposition? Yes, no doubt. If he wanted to forge ahead he had to knock down everything in his way: relatives, friends, confidants, ministers . . . The series of necessary sacrifices had begun for him long before, at Mikhailovsky Castle, during the bloody night of

March 11–12, 1801. A night from which he had never completely escaped.

Now the figure of a new adviser loomed up in the shadow of His Majesty: Baron von Stein, the former minister of the King of Prussia. An open enemy of France, he had been pursued by Napoleon first in Germany, then in Austria, before coming to settle in St. Petersburg at the invitation of the Czar. With this defector at his side, Alexander once again drank deep at the springs of suspicion, fear, and hatred. From day to day the rupture of diplomatic relations with France seemed more alarming and more inevitable.

VIII

THE PATRIOTIC WAR

Every time he bent over the map of Europe Alexander had the same sense of inevitability. A single glance was enough to convince him that the history of his country was the direct consequence of its geography. With its flat spaces and open borders, Russia was a permanent temptation to the invader. In the distant past the attackers had been the nomads of the steppes—Khazars, Pechenegs, Polovtsy. They had been followed by the Tatars of the Golden Horde, who for three centuries had dominated the entire territory. Then it was the Poles who had pushed their advance as far as Moscow, and the Swedes, whose repeated incursions had finally been broken by Peter the Great at Poltava. Was it now the turn of the French? Ever since Erfurt Alexander had been persuaded of it. On December 26, 1810, he wrote to his sister Catherine, "It seems that blood must flow again: At least I have done everything that was humanly possible to avoid it. . . . If I am not sanguine, I am not downcast and I submit to the will of God with confidence in Him." And on November 10, 1811: "We are on a continual alert; all the circumstances are so ticklish, things are so tense, that hostilities may begin from one moment to the next. It is impossible for me to leave my center of administration and activity." Lastly, on December 24, 1811: "The political situation is going from bad to worse and the infernal creature who is the scourge of humankind is becoming more detestable by the day."[1]

In the meantime the "infernal creature" had delivered a thundering tirade to the Czar's ambassador, Prince Kurakin: "Don't think I am stupid enough to believe that it is Oldenburg you are concerned about. I see clearly that it's a question of Poland. I'm beginning to believe it is you who want to seize Poland, thinking perhaps that there is no other way of securing your borders on that side. . . . You know that I have 800,000 men, that every year 250,000 fresh conscripts are placed at my disposal, and that consequently in three years I can increase my army by 750,000 men, which is enough to continue the war in Spain and to make war on you."

These words were faithfully reported to the Czar, who was not surprised by them. He said to Count Saint-Julien, Austria's representative at the court of St. Petersburg, that he considered the occupation of part of northern Germany and of the duchy of Oldenburg as an intolerable violation of the Treaty of Tilsit "by a power whose aim is continual expansion." "It is possible that everything will be settled again," he went on. "I ask nothing better, but I hold myself in readiness for anything. . . . As soon as a French army crosses the Oder—for I can no longer establish myself on the Elbe, since they are already astride that river—I think I have a right to consider the war as begun, and Providence will decide what the outcome will be."[2]

To the Czar's mind, there were economic considerations no less imperious than these strategic ones. In claiming the right to forbid Russia to trade with neutral states, Napoleon had condemned the country to suffocation. Pushed to the wall by France's demands, Alexander confided his grievances and his intentions to Czartoryski in a letter, in French: "A break with France is inevitable, it seems," he wrote. "Napoleon's goal is to destroy, or at least to humble, the last power that remains standing in Europe, and to achieve that goal he makes demands that are inadmissible and incompatible with the honor of Russia. 1) He wants all trade with the neutrals stopped, which would deprive us of the only trade that still remains to us. 2) At the same time he demands that, deprived of all means of exporting our own products, we should do nothing to hinder the importation of French luxury items, which we have prohibited, no longer being rich enough to pay for them.

As I can never consent to such proposals, it is probable that war will ensue in spite of everything Russia has done to avoid it. It is going to cause torrents of blood to flow, and poor humanity is going to be sacrificed again to the ambition of a man who seems to have been created for its misfortune."

Alexander's advisers, led by Armfelt, encouraged him to take a firm stand against France, which was entangled in affairs in Spain. Everyone who came near the Czar noted a new determination in his attitude. "The Emperor has regained some of the assurance which, since the Friedland affair, had totally abandoned him," Count Saint-Julien wrote Metternich. And he added that public opinion promised "the greatest voluntary sacrifices of men and money if the Czar wants to shake off the yoke—so humiliating for this proud nation—of dependence on the plans of the court of the Tuileries."

As the days passed, Alexander felt his people drawing closer to him, as if the French threat constituted the best cement for national unity. No longer did anyone dream of challenging his leadership of the country. At his orders, immediately after Tilsit Arakcheyev had undertaken the reorganization of the army. Supply depots were prepared, the weaving of cloth for the military was accelerated, as was, especially, the manufacture of rifles and cannon. Troops from Moldavia, Finland, and Siberia went to join the units already gathered on the western border. A few extra regiments were hastily formed in the Moscow region.

This intensive mobilization was matched by diplomatic activity in all directions. Alexander's first concern was Austria. He knew that Napoleon's victory and his marriage to Marie Louise had placed that country once and for all under the thumb of France. But he also knew that, in spite of all the treaties, Vienna felt closer to St. Petersburg than to Paris. Even when Austria signed a convention, on March 14, 1812, committing her to place thirty thousand men at Napoleon's disposal, Alexander's confidence was not shaken. He was convinced that for friendship's sake Austrian troops would avoid contact with Russian troops, just as for friendship's sake the Russians had avoided contact with Austrians in 1809. "I demand, I expect nothing of Austria," he said to Count Saint-Julien. "I only want to know that she is remaining passive." And to convince his interlocutor that in case of conflict he would pursue the struggle resolutely, he added, "I expect initial failures, but they will not discourage me; by falling back I shall place a desert between his army and mine: men, women, children, cattle, horses, I shall take everything away, and the Russian light cavalry is unrivaled for that."[3]

Moreover the King of Prussia, although he had been delivered up to France bound hand and foot, also wanted to keep in Alexander's good graces. While assuring Napoleon of his entire cooperation, he sent the Czar a secret emissary, General Scharnhorst, who bore a touching letter written in the King's own hand: "If war breaks out, we shall do each other only such harm as is strictly necessary. We shall always remember that we shall be united, that one day we are to become allies again and, while yielding to irresistible necessity, we shall preserve the freedom and sincerity of our feelings."[4]

On April 5 an offensive and defensive alliance was signed with Sweden. Alexander wrote to his plenipotentiary Suchtelen, "The war that is going to break out is a war for the independence of nations." Stockholm declared in return that the Czar "could send his armies against Constantinople, Vienna, and Warsaw without fear of Sweden's making a move." Prince Bernadotte, the heir to the throne of Sweden, even gave the Czar some experienced advice on how to conduct the campaign against the Grand Army, of which he had once been one of the most brilliant marshals: "You must avoid big battles," he wrote on April 24, "work the enemy's flanks, force him by so doing to detach troops and tire him out with marches and countermarches, which is the thing the French soldier dislikes most and the situation in which he is most vulnerable. Let there be plenty of Cossacks everywhere!"

A few days later Kutuzov signed the Treaty of Bucharest with Turkey, putting an end to a long and costly war. By the terms of this agreement, Russia kept Bessarabia but was to evacuate Moldavia and Walachia. This territorial sacrifice made available to Alexander all the forces engaged in that sector, forces he would badly need against Napoleon.

At the same time Alexander tried to butter up the Poles by promising them that in case of victory he would restore their country to its old borders by adding to it all of Lithuania. And as a token of his good intentions toward the Catholic population, he transformed the Jesuit college of Polotsk into an academy. Lastly, he resumed negotiations with England, which on June 18, 1812, resulted in the Treaty of Stockholm. What Alexander wanted from the cabinet of St. James's was that it should supply "maritime armaments and act as treasurer."[5]

These various transactions, pursued with cunning and method, demonstrated a perseverance on the part of the Czar that bordered on obsession. Irresolute at first, he would let himself be driven back and forth between opposite solutions for a long time; then, like a marble that has found a groove, he would never deviate from his path. It was as if his stubbornness were the natural consequence of the difficulty he had experienced in coming to a decision. His strength was born of weakness, his persistence was the result of previous vacillation.

Caulaincourt was still blind to the imminence of war and transmitted to Paris the reassuring words of Chancellor Rumiantsev, "In the [Franco-Russian] alliance Russia is as honest and pure as a virgin." Dissatisfied with his ambassador, who was far too pro-Russian, Napoleon recalled him and appointed Lauriston in his place. During a final audience, Alexander told Caulaincourt, "If Emperor Napoleon makes war on me, it is possible, even probable, that he will beat us if we accept combat, but that will not bring him peace. The Spaniards have often been beaten, and they are neither defeated nor subdued. Yet they are not so far from Paris as we; they have neither our climate nor our resources. We shall not place ourselves in jeopardy. We have space and we shall preserve a well-organized army. . . . I shall not be the first to draw my sword, but I shall be the last to put it back in its sheath. . . . If the fortunes of war were to go against me, I should retreat to Kamchatka [in northeastern Siberia] before I should give up provinces and sign treaties in my capital that were merely truces. The Frenchman is brave, but long privations and a bad climate are trying and discouraging to him. Our climate, our winter will fight for us. Your miracles are accomplished only where the Emperor is, and he cannot be everywhere at once and far from Paris for years."[6]

A few weeks later Alexander spoke along the same lines to Napoleon's aide-de-camp General de Narbonne: "I have no illusions; I know how great a general Emperor Napoleon is. But, you see, I have space and time on my side. There is no remote corner of this territory, hostile to you, to which I shall not retreat, no distant post which I shall not defend before consenting to a shameful peace. I shall not attack, but I shall not lay down my arms so long as a single foreign soldier remains in Russia."[7] And placing his finger on a map he added, "If Napoleon goes to war and fortune smiles upon him, notwithstanding the legitimate goal pursued by the Russians, he will have to sign the peace on the Bering Strait."[8]

To the Rector Parrot he wrote, "This terrible struggle will decide the fate of my empire. I do not hope to triumph over the genius and strength of my enemy. But in no case will I sign a shameful peace, and I shall choose rather to bury myself under the ruins of the empire. If fate decides that it be so, say this to posterity for me. I have opened my heart to you."

Meantime, through Ambassador Kurakin the Czar informed Napoleon that he was still prepared to "return to the Treaty of Tilsit," but

that he posed a preliminary condition: that the French armies evacuate
Prussia, Swedish Pomerania, and all the territory they occupied beyond
the Elbe. He knew that these demands were unacceptable, but by
forcing France to reject them, he meant to lay the responsibility for
aggression on Napoleon.

On April 9, 1812, Alexander left St. Petersburg for Vilna, the capital
of Lithuania, so as to be near his army; despite his unfortunate experience in the past, he wanted once again to take command. Nevertheless,
before he left he asked Lauriston to tell Napoleon that he considered
himself "his friend and most faithful ally." The Czar was accompanied
by a brilliant retinue, composed chiefly of foreigners. Of course there
were the inevitable Arakcheyev, Chief of Staff Prince Volkonsky, Count
Nicholas Tolstoy, and General Balashov, but they were supplanted in
the sovereign's favor by Armfelt, Bennigsen, Colonel Michaud, Gneise-
nau, Paulucci, Diebitsch, Toll, Stein, Clausewitz, Pfuehl, and many others. Whatever their nationality, all these advisers shared a common
hatred for Napoleon, who had driven them from their homelands. They
were counting on Alexander's bayonets to destroy the power of the
tyrant, the son of the Revolution. Each of them had his own plan,
discussions grew acrimonious, feuds and factions developed, and the
few generals who were native Russians cursed the conceited emigrés
for meddling in everything and thinking themselves entitled to lead the
army into combat, an army of which they were unworthy. Of all these
armchair strategists, the one whose opinion carried the most weight
was without question the Prussian general Pfuehl, who modeled his
military methods after those of Julius Caesar and the great Frederick,
was totally ignorant of the political and military organization of Russia,
held no official post, and did not even speak the language of his soldiers.

Between conferences with his generals, Alexander set about winning the hearts of the Poles, and especially the Polish ladies, with receptions, balls, distributions of sundry rewards, and exemptions from taxes.
One of these Polish noblewomen, the future Comtesse de Choiseul-
Gouffier, née Tiesenhausen, fell under his spell. He danced with her ten
times, drew her apart to a window recess, bewildered her with compliments, and gave her a jeweled medallion bearing his emblem, with the
result that she thought him an angel in human shape. She would never
forget his resemblance to a classical statue—a resemblance somewhat
endangered by stoutness—his eyes "the color of a cloudless sky," his
perfect nose, his "small and pleasing" mouth, and even his incipient
baldness, which she said gave his face "a serene and open look."[9]

It was during one of these balls, at Bennigsen's suburban estate, on

June 12/24, 1812, that Alexander learned that the Grand Army had
crossed the Neman. He had been expecting the attack for a long time,
yet at that moment he had the chill feeling that it was a decree of fate.
God had shaken the dice in a box and thrown them on the table. From
now on it was forbidden to dream. He had to act. Mastering the dread
in his heart, he ordered that the ball should continue. But next morning
he wrote to Napoleon direct: "Monsieur my brother, I learned yesterday that in spite of the faithfulness with which I have kept my commitments to Your Majesty, his troops have crossed the borders of Russia.
. . . If Your Majesty does not intend to spill the blood of his peoples for
a misunderstanding of this kind and if he agrees to withdraw his troops
from Russian territory, I shall consider what has happened as if it had
never occurred and it is still possible for us to come to terms. In the
contrary case, Your Majesty will force me to see him henceforth only
as an enemy whom nothing on my part has provoked. It depends on
Your Majesty to keep humanity from the calamities of another war. I
am Your Majesty's good brother—Alexander."

Alexander gave this letter to Balashov with orders to take it to
Napoleon. Russian headquarters had been moved from Vilna to Svent-
ziani, and the Emperor of the French was now installed in the old
Lithuanian city, occupying the very house that had been vacated by the
Czar. Napoleon received Balashov graciously, invited him to dinner,
and launched into a long speech that no one dared to interrupt. He was
aggressive, conciliatory, surly, haughty, good-humored by turns. "I
have made great preparations," he exclaimed, "and I have three times
as many men as you . . . I have more money than you . . . No, Monsieur,
I cannot fail to have the best of it! I have good information. What can
you expect from this war? The loss of your Polish provinces. If you
continue the war, if you continue the campaign, you will lose them at
once. I have conquered a whole province without fighting. If only out
of regard for your sovereign, who had made Vilna his imperial headquarters, you should have defended it. . . . Now that all Europe is behind
me, how can you resist me?"

Unimpressed by this tirade, Balashov guessed that behind Napoleon's boasting lay a surprising indecision. Taking advantage of a silence
around the table, he ventured, "We shall do what we can, Sire." But
Napoleon resumed his monologue, without listening: "I am already in
Vilna and I don't yet know why we are fighting. Emperor Alexander
takes upon himself total responsibility to his people for this war, and in
what a way! . . . Emperor Alexander will be the cause of the King of
Prussia's final misfortune. I shall annex Prussia to France. . . . Tell

Emperor Alexander that I assure him, on my word of honor, that I have 550,000 men on this side of the Vistula, that the war has begun, but that I am not against peace." And after a pause, "Emperor Alexander is getting very bad advice. . . . How can we help being disgusted when we hear that Armfelt and Stein, men who are ready to pull the cord that may cut off his life, have free access to his office and that he receives them in private. . . . They say that Emperor Alexander receives Stein at his table! How can one place Stein at the table of the Emperor of Russia? . . . Is it possible that he imagines that Stein could be attached to him? . . . Good Lord, good Lord, what a fine reign he would have if he didn't break with me! You would have seen what that would have accomplished at the end of ten years. . . . But after all, I'm not angry with him on account of this war. One more war is one more triumph for me."

Finally, with bitter irony, Napoleon asked his guest, "Which is the road to Moscow?" Not in the least disconcerted, Balashov replied, "Sire, that is a question which is rather hard for me to answer. The Russians, like the French, have a saying that all roads lead to Rome. One can take whatever road one likes to Moscow. Charles XII took the one through Poltava."* After dinner Napoleon, pointing to Caulaincourt, exclaimed, "Emperor Alexander treats ambassadors well. He thinks he can gain something politically by coaxing and flattering. He's turning Caulaincourt into a Russian."[10]

On bidding farewell to Balashov the Emperor of the French gave him a letter for Alexander. In this final message he declared that "God himself being unable to cause that which has happened not to have happened," he refused to retrace his steps, but that he "kept his ears open to words of peace" if the Czar acknowledged he was in the wrong. "A day will come," he wrote, "when Your Majesty will admit to himself that he lacked perseverance, confidence, and, permit me to say so, sincerity. Your Majesty has spoiled his whole reign."

This letter was to remain unanswered. Alexander was not at all intimidated by the French threat. The information he received from Vilna indicated that there was serious disorder among the disparate regiments that made up the Grand Army. And indeed, the Lithuanians

---

*According to Balashov's report, reproduced by Tatishchev in *Alexandre Ier et Napoléon*, referring to the definitive rout of the Swedish army that marked Russia's emergence as a world power. It is quite possible that in recounting this incident Balashov credited himself with an acid retort he never made.

were appalled at the insubordination and lack of discipline of the troops
camping on their territory. "Six hundred thousand men of all the European nations politically subject to Napoleon were marching in two
columns, without stores, without rations, in a country impoverished by
the continental system [blockade] and only recently ruined by heavy
requisitions," wrote the Comtesse de Choiseul-Gouffier in her *Mémoires*. "In the town and in the countryside, unheard of disorders.
Churches looted, the sacred vessels, even the cemeteries were not
respected, the unfortunate women outraged. . . . The looters were shot.
They went to execution with incredible insouciance, their little pipes
in their mouths. What difference did it make to them if they died now
or later. . . . The army had been without bread for three days. At Vilna
they gave the soldiers bread that was not properly kneaded or baked,
a kind of biscuit; there was no fodder for the cavalry, and they fed the
horses wheat cut in the fields at the end of June. They were dying like
flies and their carcasses were thrown in the river."

The Russian regiments were no better provided for. "The troops
have no shoes and their greatcoats are full of holes," wrote Rostopchin,
who had recently been appointed Governor of Moscow. "Rations are
short. Miloradovich's men have had no bread for five days. Morale is
very low. A great number of soldiers and even some subordinate officers
spend their time robbing and looting. It is impossible to punish everyone." But Alexander refused to take the wretchedness of his army into
consideration. Such as it was, he thought, it could still defeat the Napoleonic hordes. Determined to fight only a defensive war, he lent a willing
ear to those who urged him to draw the enemy deep into the interior
of the empire. He particularly liked the way Rostopchin put it in a letter
to him: "I do not fear reverses. Your empire has two powerful defenders
in its size and its climate. . . . And even if unfortunate circumstances
made you decide to retreat before a victorious enemy, the Emperor of
Russia will still remain formidable in Moscow, terrible in Kazan, and
invincible in Tobolsk."

What was fine in theory, however, was intolerable in practice. In spite
of the best arguments, Alexander could not make up his mind to abandon
a large part of Russia without a fight. He finally adopted Pfuehl's plan,
which represented a compromise between a tactical retreat and a coun-
teroffensive. According to this plan, the main body of the Russian forces
would fall back on the fortified camp of Drissa, at a bend in the Dvina,
while the rest of the troops would attack the enemy's rear. Unfortunately, this maneuver proved impracticable because of the numerical
weakness of the Russian army. Against Napoleon's 400,000 combatants

(French, German, Polish, Dutch, Italian, Austrian, Swiss . . .) the Russians could muster only 220,000 divided into three armies: The first, commanded by Barclay de Tolly, numbered 127,000; the second, commanded by Bagration, 48,000; while the third, of 43,000, commanded by Tormassov, was sent far away to the south to protect the Austrian border. Thus the first and second armies alone would have to bear the brunt of the attack. Alexander ordered them to meet at Drissa, but the famous entrenched camp could not be held because of inadequate defenses and the lack of provisions. Furthermore, the French easily went around Drissa, heading south of the direction foreseen by Pfuehl. The Prussian strategist thus became the object of unanimous disapproval among his comrades in arms.

Alexander's confidence was shaken. He no longer knew whom to trust and doubted his own abilities as a commander. Balashov, Arakcheyev, and the Imperial Secretary Chichkov, who had replaced Speransky, urged him to leave the army. In the field they said, he was risking his life needlessly, while in Moscow or St. Petersburg he would be able to arouse the enthusiasm of the entire nation. The decisive argument was supplied by Grand Duchess Catherine, who exhorted her brother to be head of state before being head of the army. "I believe you to be as capable as your generals," she wrote him, "but you have not only the role of captain to play, but also that of ruler. If one of them does wrong, punishment and blame await him; if you make mistakes, everything falls on you, and for confidence to be destroyed in the one on whom everything depends and who, as sole arbiter of the destiny of the empire, should be the support upon which everyone leans, is a greater evil than lost provinces. Your character is such that if you have a mistake to blame yourself for you will suffer more than a thousand other men would. . . . A tormented soul preoccupies the mind. . . . You may condemn me, but I cannot lie to you. Perhaps I should have kept silent!"[11] He answered, "I gather that you want to drive me out of the army, but I am nonetheless touched by the stirring sentiments that prompt you. How happy I should be if I had a few more people like you! Your ideas do as much honor to your head as to your patriotism and your heart."[12]

At last he ordered Chichkov to draw up a manifesto proclaiming national war against the invader, sent forward a train of barouches, and left by night for Moscow. On July 12, at nine o'clock in the morning, he appeared at the top of the Kremlin's staircase of honor, the famous Red Steps, and saw at his feet a sea of heads. All Russia was there before him, united in religious veneration. Shouts rose from the crowd, mingled and grew louder: "Hurrah!" "Lead us where you will!" "Guide us, our father!" "We will die or conquer! . . ." As the Czar descended the steps hundreds of hands reached out to touch him. The people laughed, wept, tried to kiss the edge of his uniform. With great difficulty he cleared himself a path to the cathedral, where the bishops welcomed him with a ringing speech: "God is with you. Through your voice He will command the tempest, and calm will return, the waves of the deluge will subside." In a burst of patriotism the merchants of Moscow, assembled in the Palace of Sloboda, contributed millions of rubles to the common cause, the nobles proposed that eighty thousand men be levied immediately from their estates, and a few of the wealthiest promised to equip whole regiments.

After spending a week in Moscow Alexander returned to St. Petersburg with cheers ringing in his ears and moved into his palace on Kamenny Island. The delirious welcome he had received in the former capital had made him realize what reserves of courage, sacrifice, and faith the Russian people had. The pupil of Laharpe, the enthusiastic reader of Voltaire, now suddenly felt he had been chosen by the Almighty for a supernatural task. But was he capable of responding to the wishes of the nation and the orders of God? He agonized over that question. "I am convinced," noted Joseph de Maistre, "that he thinks he is of no use to his people because he does not feel capable of commanding armies; it is a great sorrow to him, yet it is as if he wept because he was not an astronomer." In the course of a conversation with Mademoiselle Stourdza, one of Elizabeth's ladies-in-waiting, the Czar sighed, "I regret that I cannot respond to the devotion of this admirable nation as I should like to do. The country needs a leader capable of guiding it to victory, and I, unfortunately, have neither the experience nor the necessary gifts. My youth was spent in the shadow of a court; if I had been entrusted to Suvorov or Rumiantsev, they would have trained me for war and perhaps I might have been able to parry the dangers which threaten us now." Then, noticing his companion's worried look, he added, "No discouragement, and all will be well."[13]

But the "discouragement" that he found unacceptable quickly spread among those around him. The advance of Oudinot's troops, which had been detached from the Grand Army, represented a serious threat to St. Petersburg. In the palace there was panic, despite the patriotic expression on every face. The Empress Dowager was preparing to pack her bags, and Grand Duchess Catherine, pregnant and nervous, fled to Jaroslaw. From there she wrote her brother, begging him once again not to take personal command of the army, "for it is

essential to have without delay a leader in whom the troops have confidence, and on that score you can inspire none."

Amid this pitiful disarray, Alexander and Elizabeth were the only
ones who kept their heads. Events proved them right, for General
Wittgenstein soon halted the progress of the French on the route to
Pskov. He was immediately hailed as the "savior of St. Petersburg" and
received the cross of the Order of St. George. People breathed again
in the capital. Madame de Staël had recently arrived in Russia, fleeing
Napoleon, who she said was persecuting her and pursuing her across
Europe. When she met Alexander, she was enchanted by his rectitude,
courage, and conscientiousness, and predicted victory for him. Then,
alluding to the lot of the common people in Russia, she cried, "Your
character is the best constitution that Russia could hope for!"

Notwithstanding these flattering words, Alexander grew increasingly anxious about the turn of events. The Russian troops were falling
back in haste, the peasants were burning the harvests, Vitebsk had been
abandoned, Smolensk fell in spite of a heroic resistance and the retreating defenders set fire to the city. The road to Moscow was open. The
soldiers were losing confidence in their leader. Barclay de Tolly had
now assumed command, but he had a cold, reserved manner and was
not liked by the men. His rival Bagration, a Georgian prince with a fiery
temperament and a limited grasp of the situation, stirred up discontent
in military circles against the man he held responsible for the shameful
Russian retreat. "The enemy attacks and not a shot is fired," he wrote
Arakcheyev in French. "We begin to retreat, I don't know why. No one
in the army or in the country will believe that we are not sold out. I
cannot defend Russia all by myself. . . . Why should we offer no resistance to the enemy when we could make an end of him so easily?
Forward along the whole line, a cavalry reconnaissance and a general
attack! There lie honor and glory! . . . A retreat is all right for a hundred
versts, but not for five hundred! . . . To think that we have abandoned
the most important position when there was no necessity to do so!
. . . I swear to you on my honor, Napoleon was in a sack as never before.
He could lose half his army but never take Smolensk. . . . It is shameful,
a blot upon our army, and as for [Barclay de Tolly] I think he should not
remain alive. . . . This is no way to fight. We are going to lead them to
the very gates of Moscow. . . . We must hasten to get ready some
hundred thousand men at least, so that when [Napoleon] approaches
the capital the whole country will fall upon him. Conquer or fall beneath the walls, that is my opinion! . . . Your minister [Barclay de Tolly]
may be fine in his ministry, but as a general he is worse than bad,

detestable, and it is to him that the fate of the whole country has been entrusted! I shall go mad with despair. . . . I should rather be a common soldier than commander in chief with Barclay!"

The criticism became so strident that Alexander decided to sacrifice Barclay de Tolly to public opinion as he had done before with Speransky. But who should replace him? The entire nation turned to Kutuzov. He had done the Emperor the greatest service by signing the peace with the Turks, his soldiers loved him for his simplicity and bravery, the nobility recognized him as a true Russian devoted to his country, and the clergy looked upon him as a respectful son of the Church. But although Alexander had given him a seat on the Council of State and had conferred upon him the title of Prince and Most Serene Highness, in his heart he detested the fat, one-eyed, courteous old man. With egregious bad faith he held Kutuzov responsible for the defeat at Austerlitz and for the loss of Moldavia and Walachia in the deals made at Bucharest. In addition to these unspoken grievances, he had a kind of physical repugnance for the man. Finally, however, he overcame it. On August 5 he called together a committee composed of Count Saltykov, President of the Council of State, Prince Lopukhin, Count Kochubey, and Generals Viazmitinov, Arakcheyev, and Balashov. After four hours of discussion the committee chose Kutuzov as single generalissimo. Three days later Alexander summoned Kutuzov and officially granted him full powers, on condition only that he should never enter into negotiations with the enemy. That same evening he wrote in French to his sister Catherine, an ardent admirer of Kutuzov, to inform her of the appointment: "The bickering between [Barclay de Tolly] and Bagration was growing worse by the day so that I was obliged, after having explained the whole situation to a special little committee which I formed for the purpose, to appoint a commander in chief for all the armies. . . . In general, Kutuzov is in great favor here and in Moscow." The letter showed how little enthusiasm Alexander had for this choice, which had been imposed on him from outside. He confided his real feelings to his aide-de-camp General Komarovski: "The public wanted Kutuzov to be appointed, I appointed him; as for me, I wash my hands of it!"

Immediately afterward Alexander left for the town of Abo (Turku), where he met Bernadotte and obtained new guarantees that enabled him to bring all the garrisons in Finland back to Russia. A month before, a treaty of alliance had been signed with Spain, and the peace of Orebro with England. Though armed with these promising treaties, Russia was in fact standing alone against Napoleon. Her general staffs swarmed with foreign generals, but the soldiers were Russian. In the opposite camp, the general staffs were composed of French generals, but most of the soldiers were foreigners.

On his return from Abo on August 22, the Czar was host at dinner to Sir Robert Wilson, a British officer attached to Russian headquarters. Wilson had come, allegedly on behalf of his comrades in arms, to demand the dismissal of Chancellor Rumiantsev and the renunciation of any notion of accommodation with the enemy. He made so bold as to say that if the order came from St. Petersburg to suspend hostilities, the army would consider that order as not expressing the imperial will, and would refuse to obey it. Outraged at the Englishman's insolence, Alexander turned pale then flushed, got hold of himself at last, and said in a loud voice, "That I, the sovereign of Russia, should hear such talk! You are the only person from whom I can allow it!" As for Rumiantsev, he declared that he would never part with that faithful servant, "the only one who in all his life has never asked for a personal favor and who has never advised that we submit to Napoleon." Nor could there be any question of a premature peace: "So long as there is an armed Frenchman on this side of our borders I shall keep my word, come what may."

No sooner was Kutuzov named to his supreme post than he prepared to leave for the army. Before setting out he met one last time with Madame de Staël. The new generalissimo, who had been soundly educated in Strasbourg and was deeply interested in French literature, admired this capable, talented woman. She for her part saw him as the champion of resistance to the invader. "He was an old man with the most graceful manners and animated expression, although he had lost an eye by one of the many wounds he had received in the fifty years of his military career," she wrote. "Looking at him, I was afraid he would not be equal to the struggle against the strong and ruthless men who were swooping down upon Russia from every corner of Europe; but the Russians, who are courtiers in St. Petersburg, become Tatars again in the army. . . . I was moved when I left this illustrious Marshal Kutuzov; I did not know whether I was embracing a conqueror or a martyr, but I could see that he understood all the greatness of the cause for which he was responsible."[14]

At this time Kutuzov was sixty-seven years old. He had grown even stouter since Austerlitz. He walked heavily, was soon out of breath, had difficulty sitting his horse and even on campaign preferred to travel in a little carriage drawn by four horses. Lazy, fond of good food and sensual pleasures, he indulged himself at table, enjoyed himself with his mistress, a big Moldavian peasant whom he dragged with him everywhere disguised as a soldier, and very often fell asleep in the middle of a discussion, with his chin on his chest and his potbelly protruding. But in spite of his tendency to be drowsy or absentminded, his judgment was still very keen. He was cunning, patient, and endowed with a rough common sense that always showed through the polish of Western culture. Russian to the marrow of his bones, he spoke French and German with ease in drawing rooms and at headquarters but addressed the common soldiers in their own language, with an earthy accent. While Alexander, who was steeped in European delicacy and elegance, was annoyed by Kutuzov's affectation of good-natured simplicity, the troops gave an enthusiastic welcome to the new generalissimo the Czar had given them. They regarded him as a true patriot, valued him as a former officer of Catherine the Great, as a brave man who had proved his courage in battle a hundred times over, as a fervent believer in the Orthodox faith, and as a leader who did not trifle with discipline but who was at the same time concerned about the welfare of his men. They had been orphans, now they had found a father. And miraculously that father was of their blood, their religion. He would strike down the Antichrist who had planted his claws in the flesh of Russia. Passing the regiments in review, Kutuzov said, "I've just come to see if you lads are in good health. On campaign a soldier doesn't have to be bothered about elegant dress. He should rest and prepare himself for victory." Another time, speaking as if he were talking to himself but loudly enough to be heard by the honor guard that had been sent to meet him: "How could one retreat with hearty fellows like this?"[15]

In reality, from the moment he assumed command of the army Kutuzov was firmly convinced that retreat was necessary; he had even envisaged abandoning Moscow. But the Emperor and the entire country had placed such hope in him that he could not allow himself to avoid combat again. Barclay de Tolly had been dismissed for incompetence because of his evasive tactics, and he, Kutuzov, must renounce those tactics lest he face the same accusation. Whether he liked it or not, he thought, only an engagement before the old capital, the sacred heart of Russia, could raise the morale of the troops, justify their confidence in him, and perhaps, by bleeding the enemy, prepare his speedy decline. Yet when he counted up the forces on either side, he had no great hopes. To be sure, he had about 120,000 men against 130,000 of Napoleon's, which made the two armies almost equal. But in his opinion only a crushing numerical superiority would enable him to vanquish so seasoned an adversary. His own regiments were worn out from the repeated marches by which they had drawn back. The ill-fed troops were living off looting, their horses were exhausted. Nevertheless, from the highest officer to the least soldier, they all dreamed of doing battle to save the old city. Against his better judgment, Kutuzov decided on a general engagement with Napoleon outside Moscow, around the village of Borodino on the banks of the Kalotcha, one of the tributaries of the Moskva River.

The decisive battle took place on August 26/September 7, 1812. The artillery went into action at dawn. Throughout the day the French threw themselves against the Russian positions in successive waves. Suffering enormous losses they succeeded in taking some fortifications, Bagration's famous entrenchments. During one of these attacks Bagration was mortally wounded. The whole left wing of the Russian army fell back. The battle entered its second phase. Assured of success on their right flank, the French forces now struck the center of the Russian troops and tried to surround "the great redoubt." They entered it after a desperate struggle, but the Russian front was not broken. Napoleon refused to order the Guard into action to win a decisive victory. The cannon fell silent. When night came each side camped on its positions. Cossack patrols harried the enemy in the darkness. For a moment Kutuzov considered resuming battle as soon as day broke. But on learning the great number of casualties he decided that it was better to withdraw and save the remainder of his army from utter disaster. In the heroic butchery of Borodino (or of the Moskva) he had been forced to sacrifice fifty-eight thousand men dead and wounded, or one half of his troops. Napoleon had lost nearly fifty thousand, including forty-seven generals. Beside this mountain of corpses each one claimed victory. "My dear," Napoleon wrote Marie Louise, "I write you from the battlefield of Borodino. Yesterday I beat the Russians, their whole army. . . . The battle was hot. . . . I had many killed and wounded." And at the same moment Kutuzov was writing his wife, "I am well, my dear, and am not beaten: I have won the battle with Bonaparte."

While the Russian army was withdrawing in good order, Kutuzov held a council of war at Fili on the outskirts of Moscow. Determined to abandon the "holy city" without another useless battle, he told his associates, in French, "You are afraid of the retreat through Moscow, but for my part I consider it providential, because it will save the army. Napoleon is like a torrent that we cannot yet stop. Moscow will be the sponge that absorbs it." And after a heavy silence he concluded, "I feel that I shall have to pay the piper, but I sacrifice myself for the good of my country. I order retreat." During the night in the wretched isba where he had taken shelter, his staff heard him sobbing as he turned over and over on his pallet.

At that time the exodus from Moscow had already begun. For weeks hundreds of vehicles loaded with varied assortments of baggage had been setting out on the road in slow, jolting convoys. The noble residences were being emptied. Balls became rare events, the orchestra of the Nobles' Club now played only for a few wounded officers and loose women. French nationals were suddenly shipped off to Nizhni Novgorod. Confectioners' shops and the stores that sold French fashions were abandoned, chanceries hastily packed up their files, and over the heads of the panicked population Governor General Rostopchin, drunk with patriotism, exploded into action. He forbade lynching, then had a certain Vereshagin lynched for having predicted that Napoleon would be victorious inside of six months. He covered the walls with patriotic broadsides, distributed old weapons to the people, paraded icons through the streets, ordered "all the brave" to assemble on the Three Mountains for a decisive battle, countermanded the order for no reason, dismissed the two thousand firemen with their pumps and firehoses, called a crowd together for an outdoor prayer in the Kremlin square, closed the vodka shops and opened the prisons. Immediately after Borodino the headlong flight accelerated. Following the high-ranking nobles, now the lesser gentry, the government officials, tradesmen, everyone who owned a vehicle and a horse cleared out of town. The streets echoed with the clatter of wheels. Carriages, barouches, landaus, telegas, wagons followed each other in single file. On the walls of the abandoned houses could be read inscriptions in French: *The word adieu, that terrible word!* Or: *Farewell, delightful haunts that I leave with so much sadness!* Soon, of the 250,000 usual inhabitants of the city there would remain only some 15,000, the seriously wounded who were unable to leave their hospital beds, common-law criminals released from their dungeons, servants forgotten by their masters.

When they entered the gates of Moscow, Kutuzov's soldiers, worn out from a long day's march, thought they were entering a dead city. Suddenly they heard a joyous fanfare. Two battalions of the garrison were coming out of the Kremlin with fifes and drums at their head. They were led by a swaggering colonel. "What scoundrel asked you to play music?" General Miloradovich roared at him. "According to the military code of Peter the Great," the colonel replied, "the garrison should abandon the fortress to the sound of music." "Did the code of Peter the Great provide for the surrender of Moscow?" the general retorted furiously. On the bridge over the Iaouza Rostopchin, wearing a military redingote, on horseback with a crop in his hand, watched as the troops marched past. Kutuzov pretended not to notice him. And the procession went on, a broad river of haggard faces and dusty greatcoats.

The French vanguard was treading on the heels of the Russian rear-guard. By tacit agreement between the two commanders, the Cossacks withdrew slowly while Murat's cavalry followed them at a short distance without intervening. One might have thought two allied armies were marching together through a conquered city. "Sometimes," wrote Montesquieu, "we were obliged to halt to give them time to march, and if a few straggling soldiers or baggage porters remained among us, we sent them back to them."

In the depths of his dejection Kutuzov had an inspiration, and abandoning the route to Ryazan, which led east, he turned down the old road to Kaluga. In a few days, executing a skillful flanking maneuver, he brought his troops to the camp of Tarutino, south of Moscow. Ensconced there, he received all the necessary supplies from the rich central provinces, reorganized and reinforced his regiments, and had his Cossacks intercept convoys to prevent the French from obtaining provisions in the countryside surrounding the old city. In addition, from Tarutino he threatened the route that the enemy might take for a possible retreat to Smolensk. Finally, if Napoleon decided to march on St. Petersburg, the Russian troops at Tarutino could quickly move north and attack him from behind, while Wittgenstein's forces held him in check from in front. Thus, Kutuzov thought, Moscow would not have been sacrificed in vain.

Meanwhile, some hundred versts away, Alexander waited in the greatest anxiety for news from the front. A courier who arrived on August 29/September 10 told him that a great battle had just been joined near Borodino. He could not sleep all night. Next morning, on his saint's day, he received a rather optimistic report from Kutuzov. Rejoicing prematurely, he had the document read aloud after the "Te Deum" in the cathedral of St. Alexander Nevsky Monastery. News of the "victory" spread rapidly through the city. On their return to the palace the Czar and his family were acclaimed by the crowd that had poured into the streets. When he heard these cheers Alexander wondered if he had not been wrong to arouse the people's enthusiasm before he knew more about the results of the fighting. But it was too late to turn back: Kutuzov was immediately elevated to the rank of field marshal, his wife was made a "portrait lady,"* the corps commanders

---

*"Portrait ladies" were persons who, by reason of their relationship to the imperial family or their exceptional merits, were authorized to wear on their court gowns a miniature of His Majesty, set in diamonds.

were rewarded with honorific titles, and every soldier was given a bonus of five rubles.

The rejoicing was soon over. Before long the Czar received a letter from Rostopchin and other messages informing him that while his army had conducted itself admirably, it had been obliged to abandon Moscow. The public euphoria was replaced by consternation, indignation, and rage. The people were in such a hostile mood that when it came time to celebrate the anniversary of the coronation, Alexander's advisers begged him not to ride to the Cathedral of Kazan on horseback, as was his custom, but in the Empress's carriage. He gave in reluctantly. "Our windowed carriages moved slowly through an immense crowd whose very silence and angry faces contrasted with the festive occasion," wrote Mademoiselle Stourdza. "So long as I live I shall never forget the moment when we ascended the steps of the cathedral, between two ranks of common people who uttered not a single cheer. One could have heard the sound of our footsteps, and I have never doubted that one spark would have been enough, at that moment, to produce a general conflagration. A glance at the Emperor told me what was going on in his mind and I felt my knees buckle under me."

At court everything was in confusion. "Moscow has been taken," noted Joseph de Maistre. "Excellent reasons are given for that, but reason nonetheless says that, barring a miracle, there is no more Russia. Until now we could fall back, but at this time there is nothing behind us but Spitsbergen [in the Arctic Ocean]." That was also the opinion of Rostopchin, who wrote his wife on September 14, "I regard Russia as lost forever." The Empress Mother, Grand Duke Constantine, Chancellor Rumiantsev, Arakcheyev, and Volkonsky were in favor of early negotiations. But Grand Duchess Catherine, who according to her brother Constantine "doesn't even know where she will give birth," was in an increasingly bellicose mood. From Jaroslaw she sent Alexander scathing letters: "You are openly accused of having brought disaster upon your empire, of having caused general ruin and the ruin of private individuals, lastly, of having lost the honor of the country and your own personal honor. . . . You need not fear a catastrophe of the revolutionary sort, no! But I leave it to you to judge the state of affairs in a country whose leader is despised. . . . The idea of peace, fortunately, is not widespread; far from it, for the feeling of shame following the loss of Moscow gives rise to the desire for revenge."[16]

With the country divided between those who were hoping for an honorable compromise and those who preferred ruin to capitulation, Alexander knew that his reputation in the eyes of posterity was at stake

and perhaps his throne as well. Even those who favored peace at any
price would not forgive him for the conditions he would be forced to
accept to obtain it. A second Tilsit would seal the condemnation of his
reign. So he must fight on to the last man, in spite of all advice to the
contrary. He had said to Caulaincourt, "Once war has begun, one of us
—either he, Napoleon, or I, Alexander—must lose his crown." He answered his sister Catherine, "Of course there are things that it is impossible to imagine. But be persuaded that my resolve to struggle is more
unshakeable than ever; I should rather cease to be what I am than
compromise with the monster who is the curse of the world. . . . I place
my hope in God, in the admirable character of our nation, and in my
steadfast determination not to bow under the yoke." And a few days
later, on receiving Colonel Michaud, a messenger from Kutuzov, he
made the following statement to him, in French, to be transmitted to
the army: "Tell all my good subjects, wherever you go, that when I have
not one soldier left, placing myself at the head of my dear nobles, of my
good peasants, I shall use up the last resources of my empire. But if ever
it is written in the decrees of Divine Providence that my dynasty is to
cease to reign on the throne of my ancestors, after having exhausted all
the means at my disposal, I shall let my beard grow down to here and
go eat potatoes with the least of my peasants in the farthest confines of
Siberia, rather than sign the shame of my beloved country, whose sacrifices I fully appreciate. Colonel Michaud, do not forget what I say to
you here: Perhaps one day we shall remember it with pleasure. . . .
Napoleon or I, he or I; now we can no longer reign together. I have
learned to know him, he will not deceive me again!"

A gratuitous statement, for Alexander was still anxiously wondering
what Napoleon meant to do now that he was master of Moscow. The
general opinion was that the Grand Army would soon march on St.
Petersburg. That would be the logical next step in the campaign. To
provide for this contingency, the Czar ordered preparations to be made
for evacuating the archives, the imperial treasury, the schools and hospitals, and he negotiated the sending of the Russian fleet to England.
Learning of these measures, the inhabitants themselves made ready to
leave the capital. Everyone looked for a place of refuge in the provinces. People discovered distant relatives who were hospitable, packed
up their belongings, assembled the greatest possible number of vehicles
and boats. On the Neva and its canals a flotilla of boats loaded with
furniture and baggage awaited the first alert to weigh anchor. "Everyone has already packed his bags, starting with the court," noted Joseph
de Maistre. "During the last month more paper has been burned in St.

Petersburg than it would take to roast all the cattle in the Ukraine."

But Napoleon still did not move. When he entered Moscow and learned that the city was almost deserted, he cried, "That's unbelievable! Go, bring me the boyars!" But since Peter the Great there had been no boyars in Russia, and the nobles who had replaced them were already far, fleeing the invader. In the vast city of empty houses, released criminals broke down the doors of cabarets, famished soldiers looted shops and wine cellars, people jostled each other in the streets, this one dragging a clock, that one a sack of flour, another a basket full of bottles. Suddenly during the night the first flames rose. The fire sprang up at several points at once and roared into the heart of Moscow. Who had started the conflagration? According to Napoleon, the monstrous act had been "conceived and prepared by Rostopchin." Had not the Governor General of Moscow sent the firemen away and removed the pumps before the French entered the city? Had he not incited the population to the supreme sacrifice by the notices he had posted? Had he not had the example of Vitebsk, Smolensk, and Gzhatsk, which had been given to the flames before they fell into the hands of the enemy? Besides, Rostopchin at first boasted that he was "the incendiary of Moscow." Later he retracted his claim, saying that it was Napoleon's soldiers who had caused the catastrophe "by visiting houses at night and making light with candle ends, torches, and fagots." No doubt the truth lay in a combination of the two explanations. The fire had been started both deliberately and accidentally, by the will of one man and by the carelessness of countless others. Rostopchin was not the only person who had a hand in the disaster, but he was the one principally responsible. In any case, at the time the Russians thought differently: The unanimous opinion was that the French had burned the old capital, the cradle of Orthodox civilization, in a spirit of revenge. After that sacrilege there could be no question of negotiating with them. They were hardly to be considered Christians, or even men.

In the turmoil of the fire, disorder and looting took on nightmare proportions. "The desire for food was so great that several of our men braved all dangers and entered burning houses," wrote von Kalkreuth, an officer in the hussars. "We dismounted and ran to the cellar. It was full of Frenchmen of all branches of service. . . . At every moment new bands of soldiers came from the courtyard shouting to us to leave because the whole house was in flames." "Soldiers, *vivandières*, convicts, and prostitutes," Captain Labaume wrote, "ran through the streets, entered the deserted palaces and snatched everything that could gratify their greed. Some covered themselves with stuffs woven of gold or silk; others put over their shoulders, without choice or discernment, the most highly prized furs; many covered themselves with women's and children's pelisses, and even the convicts hid their rags beneath court garments. The rest, flocking to the cellars, broke down the doors and drinking the most precious wines, staggered off with their immense booty." The streets were strewn with broken furniture, trampled clothes, smashed chests, slashed paintings. In vain did the authorities have some of the looters shot—the disorders continued. The flames of the burning city could be seen in the sky for a radius of three hundred versts. People in the countryside thought it was the Apocalypse. At last, after four days, the conflagration subsided. As almost all the buildings in the city were made of wood, only two thousand houses out of ninety-three hundred remained intact.

In St. Petersburg the thousands of refugees from Moscow and the devastated provinces recounted and exaggerated the crimes of the invaders. It became obvious to everyone in the empire that Napoleon wanted to annihilate Russia, its strength, its tradition, its religion. People spoke with horror of the horses that the French had herded into the city's churches, turning them into stables. Even gentle Empress Elizabeth wrote to her mother, "So now the horde of barbarians is lodged on the ruins of that beautiful capital. They acted there as they have done everywhere else. Our people began to set fire to the object of all their affections rather than let it fall undamaged into the hands of the enemy, and the *great nation* [the French] will not stop sacking, looting, and destroying so long as there is anything left to destroy. In the meantime, our army has gone around Moscow and is posted in the vicinity of the road by which the enemy came and is already beginning to disrupt his communications. When Napoleon entered Moscow he found nothing of what he hoped for. He was counting on a public, there no longer was one, everyone had left; he was counting on resources, he found almost nothing; he was counting on the moral effect, the discouragement and prostration he would cause the nation, he has only aroused rage and the desire for vengeance." And also: "Every step that [Napoleon] takes in Russia brings him nearer to the abyss. We shall see how he endures the winter!" A young functionary, Alexander Turgenev, even looked beyond the present nightmare to the future apotheosis: "Moscow will be born again from her ashes," he wrote his friend Viazemsky, "and the feeling of revenge will be the source of our glory and our greatness. Her ruins will be the pledge of our moral and political atonement. Sooner or later, the glow of the Moscow fire will light our way to Paris."[17]

This time the whole country joined together in hatred for the occupier. A few persons of taste gave up drinking French wines. Nurses told children that the Emperor of the French was "the sorcerer Apollyon" and that he ruled over an army of monsters "with gaping maws and hooked beaks." A very fashionable parlor game consisted of inventing methods of execution for Napoleon. Each player made his own sadistic proposal. At one of these gatherings, the future Comtesse de Choiseul-Gouffier made a great hit by saying, "I should like Napoleon to be drowned in the tears he has caused to be shed." Certain provincial towns were overwhelmed by an influx of refugees, who camped several together in small, unfurnished rooms. Accustomed to comfort and consideration, the emigrants suffered from their new poverty. But Russian hospitality knew no constraint. Those who had been able to salvage some part of their fortunes were already giving dinners and balls for their less fortunate compatriots. At these balls young ladies in French dresses danced French quadrilles and anathematized in French the enemy of the motherland. It was Nizhni Novgorod that welcomed the greatest number of "emigrés" as they called themselves. "All Moscow gathers at the Arkharovs', or rather all of Moscow's unfortunates," wrote the poet Batyushkov. "Some have lost their houses, others their estates, still others have nothing left but a crust of bread. . . . They all complain and insult the French in the French language, and their patriotism is summed up in these words: *Point de paix* [no peace]."

More and more young men enlisted in the various militia. It became shameful for anyone old enough to bear arms to hang back. Even peasants came to swell the ranks of the partisans. Wonderful leaders arose to lead into combat these groups armed with pikes, sickles, and bayonets.

Under the orders of a Denis Davydov or a Tchetvertakov, the militias at first restricted themselves to attacking the enemy foragers who roamed around Moscow. Exasperated by the operations of these guerrillas, Napoleon considered for a moment the possibility of rallying the rural population to his cause by proclaiming the abolition of serfdom, but he immediately recoiled from the disorders that such a measure could not fail to provoke. Moreover, he was reluctant to offend the Russian nobles, who he still hoped would finally persuade the Czar to make peace. Actually, European-style emancipation would have done nothing to change the muzhiks' loathing for the invader, who had been cursed by the Czar and the Church. They had an instinctive hatred for the notion of a foreigner's setting foot on their soil. They would rather suffer under a Russian nobleman than be freed by a Frenchman. "Slavery does not exclude national enthusiasm," noted Joseph de Maistre. Suddenly Napoleon felt as if in Russia he was faced with another Spain, this one gigantic, fierce, Asiatic, polar.

As for Alexander, he was astounded to discover the existence of popular opinion in his country. How was it that the obscure Russian multitude, which had no means of expressing its views on affairs of state, had been able in these exceptional circumstances to assure the Czar of its support and perhaps even to dictate his conduct? It was a miracle of spontaneity, of illegality almost, a mysterious plebiscite without ballots, a word of hope flying from mouth to mouth. For the first time the autocrat, who had always made his decisions without consulting his people, felt himself borne forward by an irresistible mass movement. The voice of his subjects drowned out the voice of his ministers. With a mixture of happiness and anxiety, Alexander sensed that the Emperor of Russia was about to become Emperor of the Russians.

Entrenched in camp at Tarutino, Kutuzov was biding his time. Would the French winter in Moscow, march on St. Petersburg, or beat a retreat along the road back to Smolensk? To be ready for any eventuality, the field marshal ordered the conscription of 180,000 recruits. Soon he had at his command 80,000 foot soldiers and 35,000 well-equipped cavalry, with 200,000 militiamen alongside them as a reserve, deployed in a circle around Moscow. His artillery, meanwhile, had been increased by 216 cannon. Nevertheless, he remained deaf to the pleas of the English general Wilson, who was pressing him to launch a decisive attack. "It will all collapse without me," he replied imperturbably. Rostopchin, furious at the inaction of the field marshal he detested, wrote in French to Alexander, "Kutuzov is an old biddy who has lost her head and thinks she is doing something by doing nothing." And he recommended that "the old imbecile and obsequious courtier" be relieved of his command. Alexander was not far from sharing Rostopchin's resentment of the somnolent Kutuzov, but knowing how popular the field marshal was with the soldiers, he did not dare remove him from supreme command.

In the meantime, Alexander had received a letter from Napoleon, dated September 8/20, 1812, which struck him as a disguised admission of weakness: *To my brother, the Emperor Alexander. The proud and beautiful city of Moscow is no more. Rostopchin has had it burned. Four hundred arsonists were arrested in the act; all declared that they were setting the fire on orders from the Governor and the Chief of Police; they were shot. . . . I have made war upon Your Majesty without animosity: a note from Your Majesty before or after the battle would have* halted my advance, and I might have been able to sacrifice the advantage of entering Moscow. If Your Majesty still retains some remnants of his former feelings, he will take this letter in good part."

The Czar did not deign to reply. When he had learned of the burning of Moscow, he had wept. When he read this message, he smiled coldly. Informing Bernadotte of "Bonaparte's" note, he spoke of "bluster." It was perfectly clear that Napoleon feared the prospect of his troops' wintering amid the ruins, the lack of provisions, and the relaxation of discipline that would result from prolonged inaction. The time had come to strike him a mortal blow. Still Kutuzov hesitated. On September 23/October 5, despite strong opposition from Wilson, he even agreed to receive Lauriston, sent by Napoleon to Tarutino to initiate "friendly talks." "Is this singular war, this incredible war to go on eternally?" asked Lauriston. "The Emperor, my master, has a sincere desire to end this dispute between two great and generous nations and to end it forever." "I have no instructions on that subject," answered Kutuzov. "When I left for the armies, the word peace was not mentioned a single time. . . . I should be cursed by posterity if I were regarded as the prime mover behind any kind of accommodation, for such is the present mood of my nation. . . . The Russian people look upon the French as if they were the Tatars of Genghis Khan." "But there is a difference!" exclaimed Lauriston. "The Russian people see none," retorted Kutuzov.[18] Lauriston nevertheless asked for a safe-conduct to go to St. Petersburg with a view to possible negotiations. Kutuzov left him no great hope but promised to submit the matter to His Majesty. On reading his report, Alexander exploded. How dared the field marshal receive a plenipotentiary sent by Napoleon? "All the news that you will receive from me," he wrote Kutuzov, "all my exhortations, all the ukases addressed to you, in a word everything convinces you of my firm resolve: at the present time no proposal from the enemy will persuade me to cease combat and, by so doing, to fail in the sacred obligation to avenge the offended motherland."

After a second fruitless approach by Lauriston to Kutuzov, Napoleon understood that Alexander would remain adamant. A hard engagement at Vinkovo near Tarutino, which turned to the disadvantage of the French, helped bring Napoleon to a decision. After thirty-two days' occupation of Moscow, he ordered the retreat. Kutuzov heard the news on the morning of October 11/23 in the isba where he had spent the night. Afinkov, the officer of the Guard who brought him the latest reports, found him sitting on his bed with his uniform unbuttoned, his single eye shining with a glint of hope. "Tell me, my friend," he said,

"has Napoleon really abandoned Moscow? Tell me quickly, don't keep
me in suspense!" "When I had finished," wrote Afinkov, "the venerable
old man turned toward the icon of the Saviour and cried: 'God, my
Creator, You have heard our prayers at last! From this moment, Russia
is saved!' "

Leaving Moscow pillaged, desecrated, and burnt, the Grand Army,
still 100,000 strong, descended toward the south. But it bore no resemblance to the powerful, disciplined troop that had crossed the Neman
a few months earlier. The weather was mild; the road was muddy;
across the plain stretched an interminable caravan of pedestrians,
barouches, telegas, horsemen. Civilians had joined the soldiers. Each
one had his personal wagon stuffed with precious objects snatched from
the flames. Even the common soldiers, victims of their greed, bent
under the weight of their sacks. Military wagons rolled wheel to wheel
with elegant tilburies. Peasants who had been requisitioned drove
herds of cows before them. Rigged out in women's pelisses and fur
bonnets, the officers looked as if they were in costume. People accosted
each other in French, Spanish, German, Italian. They were not regiments on the march but twenty tribes of nomads, weighed down with
booty and united by fear, dragging themselves across the steppes.

Napoleon first tried to head for Smolensk, going south through
Kaluga to avoid his former route, which would take him through devastated regions. But Kutuzov cut him off near Maloyaroslavets. A heavy
battle began. The town changed hands eight times. Although the
French finally remained masters of it, Napoleon feared a stronger attack. Turning north, he decided to march for Smolensk by the road he
had first wished to avoid and which, while it was guarded by many
French posts, offered no real possibility of reprovisioning. That was
what Kutuzov had hoped and even foreseen. Now the Russian army was
advancing parallel to the French army. It did not seek contact, however. The old field marshal was counting on fatigue, lack of discipline,
and privations of all kinds to wipe out his enemy's combat effectiveness.
Already, except for a few regiments of the Guard, the French troops
were like marauding bands who thought of nothing but procuring food
in the surrounding countryside. The first snow fell. Platov's Cossacks
harried the starving, freezing troops in their flight. They would fall
upon them by surprise, shouting their terrible "hurrah!," massacre the
men, sweep up the provisions, and disappear like phantoms in the milky
mist. The peasants took up arms and supported the regular troops. The
French were cruelly short of food. Each man's only thought was to
survive. They would kill each other for a piece of horsemeat. They shot

prisoners, useless mouths to feed. They stole clothes from the dead to cover themselves. The cold grew more intense. "We continued to advance without knowing where our steps were taking us," wrote G. de Faber du Faur. "A raging storm drove into our faces the snow that was falling from the sky in large flakes, together with that which it swept up from the ground, and seemed to desire with all its might to oppose our progress. The horses could no longer move forward over the frozen ground and collapsed; the convoys and, for the first time, the cannon remained behind for lack of teams to draw them. The route over which the Grand Army was hurrying to Smolensk was strewn with frozen corpses. But the snow had soon covered them like an immense shroud, and little mounds, like the tombs of the ancients, showed us only faint traces of our buried comrades in arms."

The survivors dreamed of Smolensk as of a promised land where they would find food and warmth. But the city was only an inhospitable ruin. They would have to push on, drag themselves as far as Vilna. They would not pass by way of Vitebsk as they had on the way to Moscow, since that town had fallen into Russian hands, but by way of Orsha, which meant they would have to cross the Berezina, a tributary of the Dnieper. After violent fighting at Krasny the French, exhausted, numb from cold, with empty stomachs, halted at the edge of the river. The armies of Chichagov, Wittgenstein, and Kutuzov, which had also suffered from the cold, were preparing to join forces and crush the enemy troops now concentrated in a space of fifteen square leagues, with their backs to the water. One hundred twenty thousand men on the Russian side, thirty thousand on the French side. The trap could not fail. But deceived by Napoleon's movements, Chichagov had set no watch over the approaches to the village of Studyanka, and that was precisely the place where General Eblé's pontoniers, up to their shoulders in the icy water, were working frantically to build their trestles. The bridges were hardly complete before there was a rush for the opposite bank. Once again Napoleon escaped his pursuers.

It was 18 degrees below zero as the horde of survivors of Berezina limped toward Vilna. Their faces had turned blue, black, their breath froze on their lips, they bled from the nose and fell. The corpses piled up along the route. Wolves attacked the wounded lying on the plain. Peasants captured the stragglers. They pushed files of prisoners ahead of them with clubs and pitchforks. Sometimes they tortured and killed them, sometimes they took pity on them and gave them bread. At Smorgonie Napoleon left his troops to return to France at top speed. The remnants of the Grand Army, some twenty thousand men, under the orders of Murat, reached Vilna with great difficulty, but were unable to hold out there and moved on toward the Neman.

"It makes one's hair stand on end to think of the account [Napoleon] will have to render before God," Empress Elizabeth wrote her mother. "Already, it is said, what troops he has left are heaping imprecations upon him, and it is thought that he has crossed the border alone. . . . In time to come people will not believe the tale of this unprecedented flight of the French army. It clearly shows that the great man of the century is only a charlatan whose genius evaporates as soon as he meets firm resistance." And again: "I used to say to you, speaking of Russia: 'Let him who touches her beware!' With a little presumption, I could claim to have the gift of prophecy, so entirely has the event justified that prediction."[19]

Kutuzov entered Vilna on November 30/December 12, 1812. Not long after, on December 11/23, Alexander himself arrived in the city. Dissatisfied with his field marshal's dilatoriness, he had decided to remain with the armies to keep a closer watch on him and impose his own views on him. Kutuzov, in ceremonial uniform with all his decorations pinned on his chest, greeted his Emperor on the steps of the palace. The two men embraced before the troops. The Czar had named Kutuzov Prince of Smolensk after the victory of Krasny and now presented him with the cross of the Order of St. George. But during a ball given by the generalissimo he said to a dancing partner, "We have to be nice to the old man." And when Kutuzov, following a custom dating from the time of Catherine the Great, had the enemy's captured flags placed at the feet of His Majesty, Alexander frowned and muttered a few words that sounded to those near him like, "The old actor!" Not long after, abandoning his reserve, he confided to Wilson that he had no respect for the military capacities of the new Prince of Smolensk and that if he honored him with that title it was solely "out of consideration for the feelings of the Moscow nobility."

At Vilna Alexander discovered the seamy side of his triumph. He had spent the entire Russian campaign studying maps in the gilded halls of the Winter Palace, and suddenly the horror of war assaulted his eyes and nostrils. It was said there were 430,000 dead on the ground that had been traversed by the two armies between Moscow and Vilna. At the monastery of the Basilians alone, 7,500 rotting corpses were piled up. In the houses with broken windows and gaping cracks, chunks of human flesh stopped up the apertures to protect the living against the cold. Amid the rubble, in spite of the icy wind, the air was stinking. Alexander visited the wounded in the hospitals. The sight of their suffer-

ings shook his delicate nerves, but he controlled himself. He said to the
future Comtesse de Choiseul-Gouffier, "I have suffered a great deal, I
have been very worried. . . . I don't have Napoleon's cheerful philosophy, and this wretched campaign has taken ten years off my life."

Since his sensitive nature had been so sorely tried, it was logical that
he should desire a speedy end to the hostilities. There were many in his
entourage who urged him to lay down his arms now that the enemy had
been driven from Russian territory. Kutuzov, especially, was loath to
send his troops beyond the borders after so much fighting and so many
hardships. To him this war was patriotic and not political, Russian not
European. He respectfully said so to the Czar, but ran into a stone wall.
Alexander was determined to pursue the struggle so as to crush Napoleon once for all. "If we want a stable and lasting peace, it must be
signed in Paris," he said. Baron von Stein supported him in this view,
as did all the Prussian officers, whose prime hope was to see their
country liberated and restored. Alexander was their man. They were
not going to let him go until he had destroyed the source of aggression,
France.

Events soon proved them right. The Prussian general York deserted
the Grand Army with his troops, forcing the French to accelerate their
retreat. Not long after, the King of Prussia himself, abandoning Napoleon, signed the Treaty of Kalisz and made common cause with Russia.
Only recently Alexander had been fighting to liberate his country; now
he was going to fight to liberate Europe. In this new war he was determined not to present himself as a conqueror but as a peacemaker. He
would not demand territories for himself but justice for all. "The Moscow fire has shed light in my soul," he said, "and filled my heart with
a faith I never knew until today." Before his departure from St. Petersburg Empress Elizabeth had given him a Bible. He read it in his spare
time, underlining in pencil the passages that seemed relevant to his
present preoccupations. He had been an agnostic, then had slipped
toward deism. Now he wondered if he was not a Christian.

On Christmas Day 1812, all the churches of Russia solemnly celebrated the liberation of its soil, which "twenty peoples" had come to
ravage. What exactly were the causes of this victory over Napoleon?
Certainly not the rigors of the Russian winter, thought contemporaries.
At the beginning of the retreat and until the French reached Borisov,
the cold had been bearable. It was only after Berezina that the bitter
weather had completed the destruction of the Grand Army, which was
already exhausted by fatigue, hunger, and lack of warm clothing. The
Russians, who were better supplied, better equipped, and more accus-

tomed to the climate, had borne the cold without suffering too much damage. Thanks to Kutuzov's tactical skill, Napoleon had been drawn ever deeper into the interior of a region that had been previously emptied of its resources. The Russian general had left the Grand Army to disintegrate in idleness and banditry amid the ruins of Moscow and then had pursued it in retreat with increased forces, compelled it to take the already ravaged route to Smolensk, engaged it successfully at Maloyaroslavets, Vyazma, and Krasny, and harried it constantly, even in its temporary encampments, with attacks by the partisans. A great upsurge of popular resistance had helped him in his task. He had counted on the patriotism of all classes of the society and he had been right. Having become national, the war was incarnated in the person of the Czar. Little by little, Alexander felt himself transformed into a legendary hero. He thought his inflexibility had paid off, that he, usually so irresolute, deserved credit for having resisted all those who had urged him to make peace. Far from attributing the success of the campaign to his field marshal's plan, Alexander continued to criticize him. The victory had been achieved not thanks to Kutuzov, he thought, but in spite of him, by the entire Russian nation grouped around their sovereign. Now the invasion had been repulsed, the most important task still lay ahead: to finish off Napoleon.

By order of the Czar, the main body of the Russian troops left Vilna, made its way to the border by forced marches, and entered the grand duchy of Warsaw. When the "liberators" arrived, the Poles did not know whether to rejoice over the departure of the French or to bemoan the return of the Russians. In either event, their country's independence was compromised. Fearing for his compatriots who had supported Napoleon in his march on Moscow, Czartoryski wrote the Czar to implore his clemency. He also suggested that Alexander name his fifteen-year-old brother, Grand Duke Michael, King of Poland. Alexander replied magnanimously in French on January 23, 1813, "Revenge is a feeling that is unknown to me and my sweetest joy is to return good for evil. My generals have been given the strictest orders to act accordingly and to treat the Poles as friends and brothers. . . . I am going to speak to you in all frankness: In order to make my ideas on Poland prevail, I have to overcome certain difficulties, despite the fact that my intellectual position is splendid. First, opinion in Russia. The manner in which the Polish army conducted itself here, the sack of Smolensk and Moscow, and the devastation of the whole country have revived old hatreds. Second, if my intentions regarding Poland were made public at this time it would throw Austria and Prussia completely into the arms of France, a result which it is very essential to prevent, especially because those powers are already indicating that they are most favorably inclined toward me.... You yourself must help me to make my plans palatable to the Russians and to justify the predilection I am known to have for the Poles and for everything related to their favorite ideas. Have some confidence in me, in my character, in my principles, and your hopes will no longer be disappointed. . . . I should inform you definitely, however, that the idea of my brother Michael cannot be accepted. Do not forget that Lithuania, Podolia, and Volhynia have hitherto been considered Russian provinces and that no logic could persuade Russia to see them under the rule of a sovereign other than the one who governs Russia."

Once again Alexander postponed the settlement of the Polish question, ostensibly to avoid offending the cabinets of Berlin and Vienna. In reality, his mind was made up: Russia, having vanquished Napoleon, had ipso facto acquired the grand duchy of Warsaw.

Alexander had set up his headquarters at Kalisz; there the principal military leaders, with Wittgenstein and Blücher at their head, urged him to carry operations beyond the Elbe. As was his habit, Kutuzov, "the Grandfather," countered their enthusiasm with his prudence, somnolence, and slow calculation. Before acting he wanted to strengthen the army and give it time to rest. "Nothing is easier," he exclaimed, "than to cross the Elbe now. But how shall we return? With blood all over our faces."[20] Despite this reluctance, in the end he came round to his sovereign's opinion. He was too faithful a courtier to resist the imperial will for long. Besides, for the last few days he had been feeling ill, definitely weaker, and his ideas were no longer very clear. Nevertheless, he decided to take part in the new campaign. He would travel in a barouche.

On March 26/April 7, Alexander set out at the head of his troops. In an order of the day he proclaimed to the army, "We are defending faith against unbelief, liberty against tyranny, humanity against savagery." A week later he crossed the Oder at Steinau and entered Saxony. The population cheered him. He was given a crown of laurels. He sent it to Kutuzov, saying, "These laurels belong to you." The field marshal's illness had taken an alarming turn, and Alexander redoubled his attentions to him, as if by these last tokens of esteem he were trying to make amends for his former lack of understanding. At Bunzlau (Boleslawiec) Kutuzov, exhausted, gave up the expedition. Others would complete his work. He died on April 16, 1813. His body was transported to St. Petersburg and buried in the crypt of the Cathedral of Kazan. "You are not the only one who weeps for him," Alexander wrote to the field marshal's widow. "I mourn with you and all of Russia mourns."

At first Alexander considered taking command of the army himself, to fight Napoleon sovereign to sovereign. Then, perhaps fearing a reversal that would tarnish his reputation, he appointed Wittgenstein to replace Kutuzov. By not being directly in charge of military operations, he thought, he would be better able to devote himself to his providential mission. Thanks to him, for the first time in the history of the world, light would come not from the so-called civilized West, but from allegedly barbarous Russia.

IX

THE FRENCH CAMPAIGN

On April 24, 1813, a sunny spring day, Alexander made his entrance into Dresden, the capital of Saxony, with the King of Prussia at his side, both of them on horseback and in full dress uniform, followed by a large prancing escort. The Russian and Prussian troops presented arms to the sound of fifes and drums. The crowd massed along the route shouted for joy. But the King of Saxony, Frederick Augustus, did not share his subjects' enthusiasm and, doubting that Alexander and Frederick William would be successful against Napoleon, preferred to withdraw prudently to Bohemia to await the outcome of the fighting.

What Alexander had learned of recent events in France made him hopeful. Malet's abortive conspiracy, which had broken out in Paris during Napoleon's absence, was evidence, he thought, of definite discontent in a nation exhausted from incessant wars. According to his secret agents, the French as a whole longed only for peace: Further large-scale conscription had angered the people to the point of revolt, the finances of the empire had touched bottom, and the birth of the

Eagle's son had not sufficed to make relations between France and Austria any the more cordial. Of course Emperor Francis, the father of Marie Louise and grandfather of the infant King of Rome, could not openly express the wish to see his son-in-law's downfall. But behind the scenes Metternich was dragging out the negotiations with Napoleon and drawing closer to Russia by imperceptible degrees.

By the end of April Napoleon was in Weimar. On taking command of his army, he said, "I shall conduct this campaign not as the Emperor but as General Bonaparte." At a wave of his hand, 125,000 men, supported by quantities of artillery, set out toward Leipzig. Alexander and the King of Prussia, meanwhile, left Dresden on April 29 and joined their troops (39,000 Russians and 33,000 Prussians), just in time to see them attack the enemy near Lützen. In the midst of the excitement and firing, the Czar said to those who were urging him to take cover, "There is no bullet for me here!" He remained on the field. Beaten back at first, the French recovered and gained the upper hand, and the allies had to fall back toward the Elbe. Napoleon could not pursue them for lack of cavalry. That night, greatly distressed by this defeat, the Czar went to the house where the King of Prussia was resting after the hard day, woke him up, and told him what he had concluded: After the heavy losses sustained by their troops, there was no question of resuming the fighting on the morrow. Furious and mortified, Frederick William sat up in bed and growled, "I know how it's going to be! If we start to retreat we'll cross not only the Elbe but the Vistula, too. If we do that I can already see myself back in Memel." And jumping out of bed he added, "It's Auerstedt all over again!"*

Nevertheless, the two sovereigns thought it politic to consider the battle of Lützen a success for the allies. Wittgenstein was decorated with the Order of St. Andrew and Blücher with the Order of St. George, second class. Napoleon, meanwhile, had a strongly worded proclamation read to his soldiers: "We shall hurl these Tatars back into their fearful climate which they ought never to leave. Let them stay in their frozen deserts, places of slavery, barbarism, and corruption, where man is reduced to the level of a brute."

The allies withdrew in order beyond the Elbe and took up a good strategic position near Bautzen on the Spree, while the Emperor of the French entered Dresden to the sound of the same bells that had re-

---

*At Auerstedt, near Weimar, on October 14, 1806 (the same day as Napoleon's victory at Jena), French Marshal Davout had defeated the Prussians. (Ed.)

cently celebrated the arrival of the Emperor of Russia. Installed in the royal palace, Napoleon invited the King of Saxony to return to his "liberated" capital. Then, on the strength of his victory, he sent Caulaincourt to Alexander, offering to begin peace negotiations unbeknownst to Austria, whose duplicity he denounced. But the Czar refused to receive Napoleon's plenipotentiary and informed him that he would not consider any negotiations that did not include Austria. The master of France, whom he had once called "that great man," had become "the modern Attila." Napoleon, not to be outdone, called Alexander a "Greek of the Byzantine Empire."

Meanwhile, the allies were receiving reinforcements. Barclay de Tolly arrived in Bautzen after taking Thorn (Torun) on the Vistula, bringing the Russo-Prussian army to 100,000 men. Under these conditions, how could they resist the temptation to deal the enemy a fatal blow? It would be a second Borodino. Whatever happened, they would not retreat. But the encounter began badly. By evening of the first day the Russians had lost some forward positions. On the second day Alexander never left the battlefield. Wittgenstein remained at his side. Through his field glasses Alexander could make out Napoleon's gray greatcoat and big hat across the battlefield. At four o'clock in the afternoon, seeing the Russian and Prussian lines yield under pressure from the French, the Czar turned to Wittgenstein and said, "I don't want to be a witness to this defeat. Order the retreat!" Then spurring his horse he rode off.

When night fell the two allied sovereigns rode slowly toward Reichenbach. Alexander tried to comfort the King of Prussia, who paced in gloomy silence, hardly listening to him. At last Frederick William sighed, "Really, I expected something else. We hoped to march west and here we are, retreating east. . . . If the Lord wants to crown our common efforts, we should confess before the world that it is to Him alone that the glory of success belongs."[1] These words made a powerful impression on Alexander, as if they had sprung from his own heart. For some time he, too, had been seeing the will of God in all events. The greater he felt before men, the smaller he felt before the Creator. Leaning from his saddle he shook the King of Prussia's hand firmly and swore that he shared his opinion.

At Reichenbach Alexander ordered Wittgenstein to continue the retreat as far as Schweidnitz (Swidnica) so as to join reserves coming from Russia. A few days later he once again designated Barclay de Tolly commander in chief of the allied armies.

Napoleon was the victor, yet he could not fully exploit his advantage.

The weakness of his cavalry prevented him from completing the work of his infantry. And he knew only too well that his sources of manpower, in France and in the occupied countries, were not inexhaustible. Again he proposed an armistice; this time the allies hastened to accept. The town of Pleswitz was agreed upon for a meeting of plenipotentiaries. The negotiators were General Count Shuvalov for Russia, General Kleist for Prussia, and General de Caulaincourt for France. Caulaincourt had been instructed by Napoleon to try to break the unity of the allied front by offering Russia important territorial compensations. But for all his efforts, he was unable either to have a private conversation with Shuvalov, who clearly wanted to remain faithful to the coalition, or to obtain a personal interview with Alexander. With great difficulty an agreement was reached providing for a suspension of hostilities starting on June 4. This truce was later prolonged and lasted for two months. "The diplomats have almost nothing to do in these times," said Alexander. "Only the sword can determine the outcome of events." Nevertheless, while preaching war, Alexander did not neglect political maneuvers. From the moment the agreement was signed he understood that this armistice that Napoleon had imprudently accepted would enable the allies to gain strength, to reorganize, and above all to find new supporters among the countries hostile to French supremacy. And indeed, in the interval Metternich leaned toward Russia and Prussia by adopting a common plan of operations against France. England joined the coalition, sending two men to headquarters: Lord Cathcart to treat with Alexander and Stewart to reach an agreement with the King of Prussia. England undertook to pay for the war on condition that "the high contracting parties" should never take it into their heads to negotiate separately with the enemy.

The Reichenbach armistice was followed by a congress in Prague, dominated by Metternich. To persuade the Austrian minister to espouse Russia's position, Alexander had recourse to the charms of his sister, the "delightful madwoman" Catherine, who happened to be on the spot. He wrote to her in French on July 20/August 1, 1813: "I am touched by all the efforts you have made for the *common cause*. . . . I am sorry that you have not yet told me anything about Metternich and about what is needed to make him wholly ours. I have the necessary funds. So don't stint yourself. . . . I authorize you to go ahead with this tactic, the surest of all, wherever it may be required." Catherine set to work immediately. On July 21 she received "the necessary funds." Metternich was easy to persuade, for he had been ready to join the allies in any event. By the time Caulaincourt arrived in Prague the game was already over.

Caulaincourt brought precise instructions from his master: "If they want to continue the armistice, I am ready; if they want to fight, I am equally ready." Now, the proposals made to him by Russia, Prussia, Austria, and England were so humiliating that it was clear they had been designed for the purpose of forcing Napoleon to reject them. "No congress ever had less to do," noted Nesselrode. "Basically, no one wanted peace." The talks broke off. Caulaincourt left Prague empty-handed. In his place there appeared two high-ranking traitors, General Moreau, who arrived from America, and General Jomini, who had just deserted the Grand Army to place himself at the service of the Russians. No doubt they had sensed which way the wind was blowing. Welcomed with open arms, Moreau gave the Czar valuable advice on the best way to defeat his former brothers in arms. Alexander must avoid engagements in places where Napoleon was personally in command, confront him only with very superior forces, and try to beat the dispersed marshals separately. The Czar was enchanted and exclaimed, "Moreau is really a great man! I should like to be Moreau!" At this point Austria officially joined the coalition and Emperor Francis declared war on his son-in-law. Signal fires were lit all along the road from Prague to allied headquarters to announce the end of the armistice.

The Russo-Prussian troops began to move. With the addition of the Austrian army and a Swedish unit sent by Bernadotte, the coalition now had available half a million men, with considerable reserves, against 300,000 French. But having dispersed their forces, they committed only 250,000 soldiers to the battle of Dresden, where the French numbered barely 100,000. Although the allied armies had the numerical advantage, they were badly led by general staffs torn with dissension, and they beat a retreat in the rain. Sinking to their knees in mud, the soldiers groaned and swore in all the languages of Europe. Furious over the incompetence of Schwarzenberg, Moreau told him to his face, *"Sacrebleu, monsieur, I am not surprised that for seventeen years you have always been beaten!"* And turning to Alexander he added, "Sire, that man is going to ruin everything!" Not long after, when the Czar had ridden a few paces off, a French cannonball struck the ground at the very place he had just left. Moreau, who had remained on the spot, had to have both legs amputated, and in the end did not survive. Although Alexander had become increasingly hardened to war from one battle to the next, he showed "much feeling" at the dying man's bedside. But it was chiefly of God that he was thinking. He wrote Prince Golitzin, "This event, while it leaves bitter regret for the person of the general, has produced no other effect on me than to strengthen my belief that God reserves to himself alone the task of directing everything and that *my confidence in Him is stronger than in all the Moreaus on earth.*" The idea was increasingly taking root in his mind that he had been chosen by the Almighty to destroy the spirit of evil incarnated in Napoleon.

But after Dresden Napoleon still seemed invincible. How many peoples would they have to unite against him in order to overthrow him? Suddenly the hand of God parted the clouds and everything grew bright. Hope changed camps. In a few days the defeat of Dresden was forgotten: Oudinot let himself be crushed by the Prussians at Gross-beeren, and Macdonald was beaten at Katzbach (Kochaba); the Russians confronted the troops of General Vandamme at Kulm (Chelmno), and after two days of fighting, Vandamme was taken prisoner with ten thousand men and all his artillery (eighty-two cannon). Alexander was jubilant. It was the first victory that had been won over the French in his presence and thanks to his advice. All his life he was to remember with happiness the glorious hours of Kulm. Before him passed the slow, gray mass of prisoners. At last Vandamme appeared on horseback, surrounded by Cossacks. Dismounting, the general kissed his steed farewell. Alexander greeted him coldly. But when Vandamme made a tentative gesture with his hand giving "the Masonic sign of distress," the Czar changed his attitude and promised to lighten his captivity. On the following day the prisoner was sent to Moscow.[2]

For a few weeks the combatants caught their breath and counted their losses. On the French side the marshals were demoralized and complained of the lack of troops. On the allied side the first successes of the campaign encouraged the three partners to consolidate their union. Each pledged to throw into this battle of giants an army of 150,000 men. On October 16, 1813, their forces were concentrated outside Leipzig, 360,000 allied troops against 185,000 French. In the meantime Bavaria abandoned the Confederation of the Rhine. That was a severe blow for Napoleon. He himself took command of operations. Alexander would have liked to do the same. He admonished Schwarzenberg, whose plan he thought absurd. "Well, Marshal," he said, "since you insist, you will do what you like with the Austrian army, but as for the Russian troops of Grand Duke Constantine and Barclay, they will go to the right of the Pleisse [River] where they ought to be and nowhere else!" During this discussion the King of Prussia and Emperor Francis avoided expressing an opinion, as if the affair did not concern them. The course of events proved the Czar right. All day long there were attacks and counterattacks. Napoleon sent in his cavalry, but it was repulsed by the Cossacks and hussars. Paying no heed to the cannonballs falling around him, Alexander anxiously observed the fighting. The action he had ordered Blücher to take met with great success: Fifty-three cannon were taken from the enemy, and two thousand prisoners. On the other hand, the action of the Austrians, commanded by the obstinate Schwarzenberg, ended in failure. This bloody encounter cost the allies thirty thousand men and the French as many. The Austrian general Merveldt was taken prisoner and dined that evening at the table of Napoleon's aides-de-camp. "I pity you, gentlemen," he said. "You are caught in a mousetrap." Next morning Napoleon sent him to Alexander to propose a new armistice. The Czar refused. The day was spent in more cannonading.

On October 18 the fighting resumed at dawn with increased violence. Alexander surprised his entourage by his steadiness in the midst of the rifle fire and exploding bombs. He rode from one hillside to another followed by his overlarge escort, giving orders, reviving the courage of those who were wavering. In the middle of the battle the Saxons abandoned their position and joined the ranks of the allies. Not long after, the Württembergers turned their guns against the French. Evening fell on a field of corpses. Napoleon had lost twenty thousand men, dead, wounded, or taken prisoner; the allies fifty thousand.

At the end of the engagement the Czar found himself with Frederick William, Emperor Francis, and a retinue of generals on an elevation that would later be known as The Hill of the Monarchs. From this vantage point he observed the last movements of the troops in the twilight mist. His dearest wish would have been to pursue the retreating enemy, but the commanders of the various units pointed out that their decimated, exhausted regiments needed rest. Alexander resigned himself and while the French, defeated at last, withdrew toward the Rhine, he wrote Golitzin, "After a battle of four days under the walls of Leipzig, Almighty God has granted us a brilliant victory over this famous Napoleon. . . . Twenty-seven generals, nearly three hundred cannon, and thirty-seven thousand prisoners are the result of these memorable days. And now we are only two days' march from Frankfurt am Main. You can imagine how I feel." And to Countess Zénaïde Volkonsky he wrote, "It is the Supreme Being alone who has guided everything and to whom we owe all these brilliant successes."

Now it was the King of Bavaria's turn to abandon Napoleon and join the camp that had hope on its side. An unfortunate decision: The victors of Leipzig were so lax and inconsistent in their pursuit of the van-

quished that at Hanau Napoleon routed the Bavarians who had betrayed his cause, then crossed the Rhine and returned to France with
the remains of his army. Metternich's idea was to travel faster than the
Russians so that Emperor Francis could make a triumphal entry into
Frankfurt, the natural capital of liberated Germany. But warming to
the race, Alexander made better time than the Austrians, entered the
city first, and next day had the malicious pleasure of welcoming his
annoyed ally. Thus he showed Europe that Russia took precedence over
Austria and Prussia. Henceforth it was he who was the real head of the
coalition. Already German princes and diplomats crowded his antechamber, as not long before they had crowded Napoleon's.

Shortly after his arrival he learned that on the other side of the
world, in the village of Gulistan, his plenipotentiaries had signed a
treaty with Persia securing for Russia all the territory she had conquered in the Caucasus. In Europe it would be more difficult to get his
way. The allies were not agreed that they should continue the war. His
strongest adversary on that issue was Metternich, who feared both that
if Napoleon were not crushed at once he would rise again, and that if
he were, Russia would have a military and diplomatic triumph that
would be disastrous to the interests of Austria. Personally, Emperor
Francis's minister leaned toward coming to terms with the common
enemy so as to restrain the ambitions of the Czar, whom he found
increasingly arrogant, overbearing, and messianic. On his advice the
allies sent Napoleon an unofficial emissary, Monsieur de Saint-Aignan,
a French minister who had been taken prisoner by the Russians after
the battle of Leipzig. He bore peace proposals contingent on France's
returning to her natural borders. Napoleon agreed to talk. But in Frankfurt, meanwhile, the monarchs who favored war carried the day. During these few weeks' respite the allies had been able to organize the
administration of the occupied territories and to obtain supplies and
equipment for the troops. A joint communiqué announced the resumption of hostilities not against France but against the Emperor of the
French: "The allied powers are not making war on France, but on the
primacy which, to Europe's misfortune and that of France, the Emperor Napoleon has exercised outside the limits of his empire. The
sovereigns desire France to be great, strong, and happy." In the interval
the King of Naples, Murat, at the instigation of Metternich, had come
over to the side of the allies, placing at their disposal a contingent of fifty
thousand men. All that remained was to decide upon the invasion route.

According to the plan that was worked out, the allies' first objective
was to conquer a base of operations in Switzerland. This maneuver

would enable them to outflank Napoleon's forces, but it meant that Swiss territory would have to be violated. At first Alexander was violently opposed to this. On learning that despite his reluctance, the Austrians had gone ahead with the plan, he exclaimed with resentment, "This is one of the unhappiest days of my life." Not long after, however, his scruples subsided and he said to Metternich, "It is success that crowns everything. . . . What is done is done. . . . From the military point of view, it's a good operation."[3] And he wrote his beloved Laharpe deploring the event and laying responsibility for it on "those gentlemen of Bern," who had wanted to draw the allies into their country to stifle any attempt at independence on the part of the other cantons: "Let me tell you that if, along with the work of Providence, any perseverance and energy that I have had the opportunity to exert over the last two years have been useful to the cause of European independence, it is owing to you and your instruction. Your memory has been constantly present in my mind at difficult moments, and the desire to be worthy of the care you took with me, to merit your esteem, has sustained me. . . . I cherish as a sweet consolation the thought that I shall be able to clasp you in my arms and express to you again in person all the gratitude which is in my heart and which I shall feel for you to my grave." When it came time to cross the Rhine from Schaffhausen to Basel, Alexander let the Austrian troops go first, insisting that the Russian Guard await symbolically the first day of the year 1814, according to the Julian calendar. Once again his behavior was determined by a mystical idea. He acted in accordance with signs and numbers and, he thought, with the will of God.

Thus on January 1/13, 1814, having set up temporary headquarters at Basel, he went to the bridge to watch his regiments march by in a storm of rain and snow. To his new diplomatic assistant, Capo d'Istria, a citizen of free Corfu, he defined the agenda for the days to come as follows: "To return to each nation the full and entire enjoyment of its rights and institutions; to place all of them, together with ourselves, under the safeguard of a general alliance, to guarantee ourselves against the ambition of conquerors and to preserve them from it: such are the foundations on which we hope, with the help of God, to make the new system rest. Providence has set us on the road that leads straight to the goal. We have covered part of it. The part that remains for us to travel is bristling with great obstacles. We must smooth them out."

On January 16 he left Basel and at last set foot on French soil. He was extremely moved. Not only as a conqueror but as a student. He owed so much to France for the improvement of his mind! He wanted

desperately to be equal to his conquest. Accustomed from earliest childhood to withstand exposure to the elements, he rode through the icy
wind without a coat, a happy look on his face. In the villages where he
halted he would sometimes get up in the middle of the night and,
preceded only by a lantern-bearer, would walk the dark streets, to
communicate in person his orders to some general startled from sleep.
From the Rhine to the Marne the allies encountered no resistance. The
cities of Strasbourg, Saverne, Epinal, Toul, Chaumont, Lunéville, and
Nancy were quickly occupied. On January 22 Alexander was in Langres
with the King of Prussia and Emperor Francis. There, with transports
of joy, he received the worthy Laharpe, who had come to be present
at his pupil's triumph. But Alexander had other things to do besides
reminisce over his childhood with "the one to whom he owed everything." Once again sharp discussions arose between him and his partners over the best way to finish their business. The Czar favored taking
strong action, while the others, including Castlereagh, Schwarzenberg,
Metternich, and even Nesselrode, Barclay de Tolly, and Volkonsky
leaned toward a peaceful solution. Although they didn't admit it to
themselves, all of them were afraid of a sudden revival of the French,
of another Valmy.* A compromise was agreed upon: They would pursue the war and at the same time propose negotiations to Napoleon; the
French plenipotentiary would be Caulaincourt and the meeting place
Châtillon-sur-Seine.

Meanwhile, alarming reports were reaching Alexander on the
morale of his troops. The Russian soldiers, he was told, no longer understood precisely why they were fighting. In Russia they had been defenders of the motherland. In Germany they had been welcomed as liberators. In France they had no sooner set foot in the country than they had
run into hostility. Here, everyone feared and hated them. The peasants
were frightened by these men come from the north, with their rough
speech, and especially by their auxiliaries—the fierce Cossacks whom
they called "candle-eaters," the Kirghiz and Kalmuks, horsemen of the
steppes with long hair and wild laughter, who swept through the villages like a whirlwind, stealing chickens and pigs, molesting men,
knocking girls down in the straw. To be sure, strict discipline was observed in the towns, in accordance with the Czar's orders, but hamlets
and isolated farms were raided daily. The farmers defended themselves

---

*The site of the first significant engagement in the French Revolutionary Wars, an
inconclusive battle that revealed the superiority of French artillery. (Ed.)

Alexander I as a child.
Anonymous engraving.
*(Bibliothèque Nationale.
Photo B . N .)*

Alexander I.
Engraving by N. Bertrand
(Photo Flammarion)

PAUL I.
Empereur de toutes les Russies.
Couronné à Moscou le 5 avril 1797.

Empress Dowager Maria Feodorovna,
mother of Alexander I. By Ritt. In *Portraits
russes*. *(Bibliothèque Nationale. Photo B.N.)*

Empress Catherine II, grandmother of
Alexander I. Engraving by G. Skorodumov,
after a painting by F. Rokotov. *(Leningrad,
Hermitage Museum. Photo Novosty
Press Agency)*

Paul I, father of Alexander I. Engraving by
A. Radigue, after a painting by J.-L. Voile.
*(Moscow, National Museum of History.
Photo Novosty Press Agency)*

Empress Elizabeth.
By E. Vigée-Lebrun.
(Photo Roger-Viollet)

Alexander I. By Monnier, 1806. In *Portraits russes*. (*Bibliothèque Nationale.*
Photo B. N.)

Grand Duke Constantine, brother of Alexander I. Engraving by F. John, after a painting by H. Benner. *(Bibliothèque Nationale. Photo B. N.)*

Grand Duke Nicholas, brother of Alexander I. Engraving by Jonnot, after a portrait by H. Benner. *(Photo Flammarion)*

Empress Elizabeth. Engraving by Mécou, after H. Benner. *(Bibliothèque Nationale. Photo B. N.)*

Prince Adam Czartoryski. By Olechkevich. In *Portraits russes*. (*Bibliothèque Nationale*. *Photo B . N .*)

Military parade in front of the imperial palace in St. Petersburg in 1812. Anonymous engraving. *(Photo Roger-Viollet)*

Count Michael Speransky. By Tropinin. In *Portraits russes*. *(Bibliothèque Nationale. Photo B.N.)*

Maria Naryshkina, mistress of Alexander I. By Stroely. In *Portraits russes*. *(Bibliothèque Nationale. Photo B.N.)*

Count Alexis Arakcheyev. Miniature. In *Portraits russes*. (*Bibliothèque Nationale*. *Photo B . N .*)

General Prince Kutuzov. Engraving
by Hopwood. (*Bibliothèque Nationale.
Photo Flammarion*)

Russian cavalrymen
at the beginning
of the nineteenth centur
(*Photo Roger-Viollet*)

The three allied sovereigns on horseback: Emperor Alexander I, King Frederick William III of Prussia, and Emperor Francis of Austria. Aquarelle by J. G. Mansfeld, 1816. *(Vienna, Albertina)*

Queen Louise of Prussia. Engraving by Benoist, after a drawing by Swebach. *(Bibliothèque Nationale. Photo B.N.)*

General Bennigsen. Anonymous engraving. *(Bibliothèque Nationale. Photo Flammarion)*

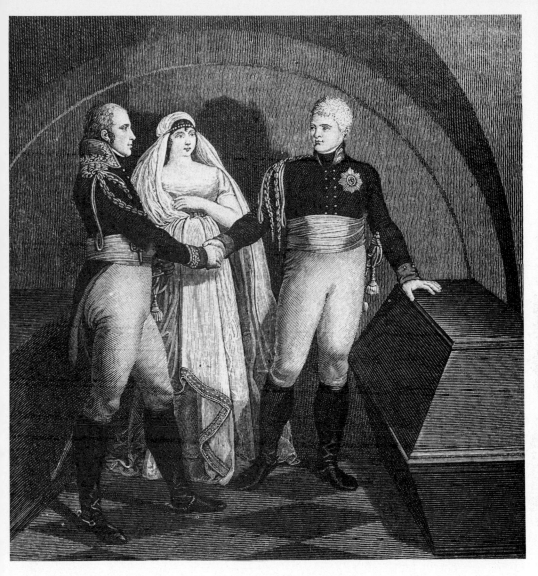

Alexander I, the King of Prussia, and Queen Louise before the tomb of Frederick the Great. After a contemporary engraving. *(Photo Flammarion)*

Alexander I presents the Kalmuks, Cossacks, and Bashkirs of the Russian army to Napoleon at Tilsit. By Bergeret. (*Musée de Versailles. Photo Flammarion*)

Napoleon and Alexander I bid farewell after the Treaty of Tilsit, July 9, 1807. By Serangeli. (*Musée de Versailles. Photo Flammarion*)

The Moscow Kremlin on fire. Drawing by Oldendorp. *(Photo Bulloz)*

The retreat from Russia. Lithograph after Faber du Faur. *(Bibliothèque Nationale. Photo Flammarion)*

The allied sovereigns on the Boulevard
Saint-Denis. By Zippel. *(Paris, Musée
Carnavalet. Photo Flammarion)*

Rostopchin, Governor of Moscow.
Anonymous engraving. *(Bibliothèque
Nationale. Photo Flammarion)*

Russian soldiers in Paris in 1814.
After a contemporary aquarelle.
(Photo Flammarion)

Cossack bivouac on the Champs-Elysées in 1814. Anonymous
engraving. (*Bibliothèque Nationale. Photo Flammarion*)

Louis XVIII in Napoleon's study. By Gérard.
Detail. (*Musée de Versailles. Photo Flammarton*)

Baroness von Krüdener.
After an engraving of 1820.
(*Photo Flammarion*)

The staretz Feodor Kuzmich, who
some believe was none other than
Czar Alexander I living withdrawn
from society. (*Photo Roger-Viollet*)

Caricature of the participants in the Congress of
Vienna. From left to right: Talleyrand, England, the
three allied sovereigns, Holland, and Prince Murat.
(*Bibliothèque Nationale. Photo B.N.*)

Alexander I receives communion four days before his death in Taganrog. Lithograph
by Freeman. (*Bibliothèque Nationale. Photo B.N.*)

as best they could with rifles or pitchforks. Bands of partisans were
formed in the forests to resist the incursions of the enemy.

All this weighed on Alexander's mind while the Congress of Châtillon was going on, but he refused to give up his idea. He repeated to all
comers, "I shall not make peace so long as Napoleon is on the throne."
He had instructed his envoy Razumovsky to entangle the discussions so
as to allow time for military events to clarify the political landscape.
Thus, while most of the plenipotentiaries favored an honorable peace,
the Czar's spokesman refused to negotiate before the unconditional
capitulation of "the tyrant." On every side people were saying that
Alexander, lost in a haze of idle musings, meant to leave it to the French
themselves to choose their future government. "I think our greatest
danger at present," Castlereagh wrote, "is from the *chevalresque* [sic]
tone in which the Emperor Alexander is disposed to push the war. He
has a *personal* feeling about Paris, distinct from all political or military
combinations. He seems to seek for the occasion of entering with his
magnificent guards the enemy's capital, probably to display, in his clemency and forbearance, a contrast to that desolation to which his own was
devoted."[4]

As the discussions continued around the table, feelings ran high and
each participant pulled in his own direction. The Prussian minister
Hardenberg noted in his journal: "Saw the King [of Prussia] and the
Emperor of Russia. Discussion of the plan of operation and disagreement. Stein maneuvering to go straight to Paris, which Emperor Alexander also wishes. The Austrian party is opposed to that. Others don't
know what they want." This last was an allusion to the King of Prussia.
In the end Frederick William yielded to Alexander's prestige: They
would go to Paris and there, in a fraternal spirit, would make the
decisions indicated by circumstances and the divine will. So by order
of the Czar the Congress of Châtillon was broken off and the allied
plenipotentiaries rejoined headquarters, which had been moved to
Troyes.

Meanwhile, without waiting for the Congress to end, the allied sovereigns had met at Chaumont and signed an important treaty providing
for the continuation of the war. Each of the four parties (Russia, Prussia,
Austria, England) had renewed its commitment to supply 150,000 men,
not to enter into separate negotiations with the enemy, and to do
everything possible to ensure the balance of power in Europe. In addition, Castlereagh had promised that during the year 1814 Great Britain
would provide a subsidy of five million pounds sterling to help the
common cause.

Military operations had started up again and were moving with extraordinary speed. Napoleon had appointed Marie Louise as regent and had left Paris to place himself at the head of his army. From the beginning he had "put on his Italian boots"* and disconcerted the allies by the rapidity of his maneuvers. Once Schwarzenberg and Blücher had made the mistake of separating their forces, the first taking the route along the Aube and the Seine, the second following the Marne and the Petit Morin, Napoleon was able to race from one to the other and confront them successively. Blücher was badly shaken up at Champaubert, Montmirail, Château-Thierry, and Vauchamps. Schwarzenberg, who was threatening Fontainebleau, was beaten at Montereau and pushed back to the right bank of the Seine. The allied sovereigns were worried and held a council at Bar-sur-Aube. The King of Prussia and Emperor Francis, who had been quickly demoralized, talked about the necessity of a general retreat. But the Czar was more determined than ever. He insisted that any such order not include Blücher's army, which at all costs must besiege Paris. He threatened to abandon Schwarzenberg's forces, withdrawing all Russian troops, if the other allies refused. Arguing every step of the way with his two partners—who, according to one witness, looked like mere aides-de-camp next to him —he jotted down with a pencil, in French, the ideas that were going through his head: "1) We shall not give battle near Bar-sur-Aube. 2) Blücher will continue his separate movement. 3) The main army will continue its movement via Chaumont to Langres. 4) The continuation of that movement will depend on circumstances . . . "

In the end Alexander managed to impose his will. Blücher's tattered, exhausted men moved on again in the mud. Beaten at Craonne, they dug themselves in on the plateau of Laon from which, despite bloody efforts, Napoleon was unable to dislodge them. The French had taken Reims, but they had lost Soissons, which had been abandoned by its timorous and incompetent commander, a man of the same name as the turncoat Moreau. The surrender of that city compromised Napoleon's strategic plan. But the allies had dispersed their forces and it seemed increasingly risky for them to move on Paris. At this point Alexander received a visit from a representative of the French legitimists, Baron de Vitrolles, secretly sent by Talleyrand. This emissary was the bearer of a letter written in a friendly tone by the Duke of Dalberg, at the

---

*A reference to Bonaparte's brilliant Italian campaign against Austria from April 1796 to April 1797, which was terminated by the Treaty of Campoformio. (Ed.)

dictation of Talleyrand*: "You are walking on crutches; make use of your legs and have the will to do what you are able to do." Vitrolles said that popular sentiment in Paris was running strongly against Napoleon and that the city would joyfully open its gates to the allied armies as soon as they showed themselves on the horizon. But when he expressed the hope that the defeat of the Corsican tyrant would be followed by the restoration of the Bourbons, Alexander stopped him. "If you knew [the Bourbons]," he said, "you would be persuaded that the burden of such a crown would be too heavy for them. . . . Perhaps a wisely organized republic would be more in accordance with the French frame of mind. The ideas of liberty have not germinated for so long in a country like yours without consequences!" Vitrolles could not believe his ears. "The king of the kings who had joined together to save the world was talking about a republic!" he wrote later. After a moment's stupefaction, he collected himself and entreated the Czar to step up his attacks so that he might enter the capital as soon as possible and reestablish the monarchy. The truth was that Alexander was not displeased with this sort of talk. His remark about the possibility of a republican regime in France had been merely a verbal concession to the liberal principles of his youth, a nod in the direction of Laharpe. At heart, he was a determined royalist. "Monsieur de Vitrolles," he said, "the day I arrive in Paris I shall recognize no other ally than the French nation. I promise you that our conversation will have the greatest results."

Yet for the moment between Alexander and Paris stood the unpredictable, elusive Napoleon. On March 20, 1814, Alexander went to Arcis-sur-Aube where, it was said, the French were going to try their last chance. He arrived on the field at dawn, accompanied by his brother Constantine and a large suite. Dismounting from his horse, he took up a position on the highest ground and said, "Well, the Congress of Châtillon is dissolved, the diplomats are washed up, now we have to see what remains to happen." Due to Schwarzenberg's half measures, the fighting remained indecisive. At this juncture Napoleon conceived the plan of marching to Saint-Dizier to cut the allies' supply lines, instead of persisting in the defense of the capital. But he made the mistake of confiding his intentions to Marie Louise in a letter. This letter was intercepted by the Cossacks and transmitted to Blücher, who informed Alexander.

---

*The Duke of Dalberg, a German, had gone into the service of France and become a Councillor of State and Talleyrand's "accomplice."

The Czar had just attended a mass in memory of his father. Thirteen years ago to the day, on March 11/23, 1801, Emperor Paul had been assassinated, with the tacit consent of his son. A painful anniversary. Alexander was still preoccupied with memories of that tragic night when he received the message and summoned his Russian and allied associates. The Austrians stressed the necessity of falling back to the Rhine to protect their rear. The Czar rebelled against this excessive prudence. The next day another letter was seized by his troops, one in which Savary begged Napoleon to return to Paris where royalists were plotting to overthrow the regime. This time Alexander hesitated no longer, and in the town hall of Sommepy, where he had spent the night, he called a council of war. "Now that we have reestablished communications with Blücher," he said to his officers, "should we follow Napoleon to attack him with superior forces or should we march directly on Paris?" "In the circumstances we are in," replied General Toll, "there is only one thing to do. We must advance on Paris by forced marches, with the whole of our army, detaching only ten thousand cavalry against Emperor Napoleon in order to disguise our movement." General Diebitsch offered a few objections but finally sighed, "If Your Majesty wishes to reestablish the Bourbons, the best thing is indeed to march on Paris with all our troops." "It's not a question of the Bourbons," replied Alexander, "it's a question of overthrowing Napoleon!"[5]

Still, at the decisive moment he was seized by a last doubt. Had he underestimated the danger? He confided his feelings later to Golitzin, "In the depths of my heart I had a kind of vague feeling of expectation, the overwhelming desire to entrust everything to the complete discretion of God. The council was still in session; I left it for a moment to go to my room; there my knees bent of themselves, and I poured out my whole heart to the Lord."[6] A few moments of blinding illumination and Alexander was convinced he had the agreement of God. It was the Almighty himself who, having become Russian, was dictating what he should do. Henceforth all was clear. The Czar stood up, adjusted his uniform, returned to the council chamber, and announced his intention of marching on Paris at once.

Immediately afterward he rode out to meet the King of Prussia and Schwarzenberg. He came upon them on the road, dismounted, had a map spread out on the ground, and explained the course of action he favored. Schwarzenberg was hard to convince. But at last the order was given to the main body of the allied forces to make a rush for Paris, while Wintzingerode's cavalry rode toward Saint-Dizier to deceive Napoleon and detain him. The stratagem was successful. Having dispersed the allied cavalry at Saint-Dizier and at Vitry, Napoleon was astonished to learn from intercepted dispatches that it was not the vanguard of the main troops, as he had imagined, but a diversionary detachment sent to keep him amused while the whole mass of Russians and Prussians swooped down upon the capital. "It's a beautiful chess move!" he exclaimed. "I should never have thought a general of the coalition was capable of it!"[7] Then he decided to return to Paris by way of Troyes and Fontainebleau. But it would take time for him to complete this vast southern movement and the allies had a head start that made them masters of the field. Nothing remained between them and the capital but the reduced forces of Marshals Marmont and Mortier, who had been assigned to protect the route. On March 25 Schwarzenberg met them at Fère-Champenoise. Alexander's presence on the battlefield electrified the Russians. It was the cavalry that did all the work. Not a single rifle shot. The soldiers ripped each other apart with cold steel. The Czar and the King of Prussia were swept up in the mêlée. It became clear that the French were defeated. Generals Pacthod and Amey, five brigadier generals, seventy-five cannon, forty-eight hundred men, and the whole convoy fell into the hands of the allies. Hastening their retreat to Paris, Marmont and Mortier reached the Porte-de-Charenton on March 29. During the evening of that day the Czar moved into the chateau of Bondy, a few kilometers outside the capital.

Alexander was elated to be approaching the goal at last, but at the same time he was worried. He didn't yet dare believe in so great a triumph. Suppose the city resisted? Suppose Napoleon returned before it had capitulated? Once again Schwarzenberg trembled for his lines of communication and the Czar for his prestige. Alexander the liberator could not permit himself a defeat at the very gates of Paris. For the hundredth time he assessed his chances. He had available a hundred thousand men, of whom sixty-three thousand were Russians, against a force of about forty thousand for King Joseph, Napoleon's brother. This last figure included the weary troops of Marmont and Mortier, as well as twelve thousand men of the National Guard. Furthermore, the French were in a bad situation politically. Wellington had driven them out of Spain and had occupied Bordeaux; the Austrians were in Lyons; in Paris itself the opponents of the regime were lifting their heads under the leadership of the wily Talleyrand, who contrary to the Emperor's orders had not followed Marie Louise and the King of Rome when they took refuge in Rambouillet. It was with that lame old fox, thought Alexander, that he would have to negotiate.

At dawn on March 30 the battle began. While the cannon thundered around Romainville, the Czar had a French prisoner brought to him, an architect by the name of Peyre who was attached to the general staff of the National Guard. After questioning him about the feelings of the Parisians, Alexander charged him with informing the commander in chief of the French army that the allies had a large force, that they demanded the surrender of the city, and that their enemy was not France but Napoleon. Colonel Michael Orlov, the illegitimate son of one of Catherine the Great's lovers, was ordered to accompany Peyre through the French lines. In entrusting him with this mission Alexander, who seemed strangely overwrought, exclaimed, in French, "Go! I give you the power to suspend fire wherever you judge necessary. I authorize you, without any responsibility, to halt the most decisive attacks and to suspend even victory in order to prevent and stop disasters. Paris, with its defenders dispersed and its great man absent, will never resist, I am deeply convinced of it. But in granting me power and victory, God wishes me to use them only to bring peace and tranquillity to the world. And if we can obtain that peace without fighting, so much the better; if not, let us yield to necessity and fight, for whether by consent or by force, parading down the streets or charging through them, be it in marble halls or on a heap of ruins, Europe must sleep this night in Paris."

Peyre and Orlov rode at once to Pantin, in the thick of the fighting. The two envoys tried in vain to calm the belligerents. The battle was raging all the way from Vincennes to the slopes of Montmartre. Advancing by the eastern route along the Ourcq Canal, the allies took Montreuil, Belleville, Ménilmontant, and the Buttes-Chaumont one after another, and later Aubervilliers and La Villette. From the heights of the Buttes-Chaumont the Czar, the King of Prussia, Schwarzenberg, Blücher, and Barclay de Tolly watched through their field glasses as the regiments moved forward in line. At that distance it was hard to identify the uniforms. The men merged into lines of color, green, red, blue. Through the smoke the bayonets shone like pins. Here and there a banner fluttered like a butterfly. The hill of Montmartre, with its charming windmills, was taken by assault by the troops of General Langeron, a French emigré in the service of Russia. At the Clichy gate Moncey and the students of the Polytechnical School were building a barricade. But they soon realized their efforts were futile against the ever-swelling torrent of assailants.

At the end of the afternoon Marmont signed the capitulation of Paris in an outdoor café in La Chapelle called Le Petit Jardinet. On the allied side negotiations were conducted by Orlov, the Count de Paar, and

Nesselrode. Under the terms of the agreement the members of the French garrison were not to be held prisoner and would be allowed to leave the capital. Couriers galloped in all directions to bring the news to the combatants. One by one the batteries fell still. A great silence descended over the darkening countryside. Then cheers burst from the Russian ranks. Alexander rode to the positions in Belleville and on the Buttes-Chaumont to congratulate his troops.

The next day as dawn was breaking a delegation from the municipality of Paris led by Baron Pasquier, the Prefect of Police, presented itself at the chateau of Bondy. Orlov entered the Czar's room and found him in bed. "What news?" asked Alexander. "I bring you the capitulation of Paris, Majesty," said Orlov. Alexander took the act of capitulation, ran his eye over it, folded the document, slipped it under his pillow, and asked for a detailed account of the interview. On learning that his emissary had already met with Talleyrand, he said with a smile, "It's still only an anecdote, but it may become history." Then he closed his eyes. The excitement of recent days had exhausted him. Even before Orlov backed out of the room he had fallen asleep again.

When he awoke he dressed with the greatest care while the Paris delegation waited in an adjoining room. On this great day he wanted to appear before the French in all his splendor. Now he was sure that he had won the match. Napoleon, having met the advance guards of Marmont and Mortier who had just evacuated Paris, was heading toward Fontainebleau. There he would stay. The tyrant's abdication was no longer in doubt.

At last Baron Pasquier and his colleagues were shown in to the Czar. Pacing up and down the salon of the chateau with a jerky stride, Alexander spoke to them in French with a vehemence that surprised them. "I have only one enemy in France," he said, "and that enemy is the man who has deceived me in the most shameful manner, who has abused my confidence, who has betrayed every oath he gave me, who has brought my country the most iniquitous, the most abominable war. Any reconciliation between him and me is henceforth impossible; but, I repeat, I have only this one enemy in France. For all the French, save him, I have great esteem. . . . Therefore, gentlemen, tell the Parisians that I do not enter within their walls as an enemy and that it rests entirely with them to have me for a friend."[8] Having made this speech, the Czar agreed to state the exact conditions of the occupation: He would ask the city only for necessary provisions, would have his soldiers camp in the open, would leave it to the National Guard to maintain order, and would guarantee respect for persons and property. His deepest feeling at this moment was expressed in a letter to his mother: "If there is one thing I am pleased about . . . it is the way in which God has permitted it to be done, that is, that we come not as conquerors or enemies but as friends."

Once the deputies had been dismissed Alexander instructed Nesselrode to reach an agreement with Talleyrand about the other matters. Not long after, he received a visit from Caulaincourt, who said that on behalf of Napoleon he was ready to accept the conditions that had been worked out at Châtillon by the Russian plenipotentiaries. Alexander replied haughtily that neither he nor his allies were disposed to treat with "that man." This was no time to stoop to idle chatter, just when he was getting ready to make his victorious entry into the capital. Already an equerry was leading up the horse on which he had chosen to show himself to the Parisians. It was a superb light-gray thoroughbred named Eclipse. Caulaincourt bitterly recognized the mount he had given to the Czar a few years earlier on behalf of "that man" from whom no one now wanted to hear another word. The Czar swung up into the saddle. His face radiated nobility, kindliness, happiness. Around him all his aides-de-camp wore joyful expressions. The weather was fine. A historic day was in preparation. At eight o'clock in the morning, Alexander set out on the road to Paris.

X

THE RUSSIANS IN PARIS

The Parisians had not been unduly alarmed by the sound of nearby cannon fire. They had never imagined for an instant that the besieged city could meet the same fate as Moscow. Throughout the fighting, little groups of curious idlers had gathered in the streets of the suburbs, notwithstanding the barriers erected here and there by the National Guard. Some had ventured as far as the lines of riflemen to hear the whine of the bullets. On the boulevards, on the terraces of cafés, an elegant crowd had spent the afternoon commenting on the events, hour by hour. The announcement of the capitulation had been greeted with relief by a population torn between anxiety and curiosity.

On the Russian side the common soldiers felt no hatred for their enemies of yesterday. During the time they had been fighting on foreign soil they had finally forgotten the ravages of war in their own country. As for the officers, most had been brought up by French tutors, and Paris attracted them like the light of the world. They were all making feverish preparations to enter "the modern Babylon." Orderlies were brushing their masters' uniforms, polishing buttons, waxing boots. Many French emigrés had enlisted under the Czar's banners— Polignac, Rochechouart, Montpezat, Rapatel, Lambert, Damas, Boutet . . . They couldn't get over the fact that they were "home again" at last. But their Russian comrades were no less impatient. "We felt that our least gesture would be historic," wrote the Russian general Löwenstern. "For the rest of our lives we would be beings apart, who would always be looked at with astonishment, listened to with admiring curiosity. Supreme happiness to be able to say all one's life, 'I was with the army in Paris!' "

That was what Alexander thought, too, on that clear morning of March 31, 1814, as he rode toward the conquered capital. Leading the procession was the regiment of the Red Cossacks of the Czar; at their heels came the cuirassiers and hussars of the Prussian Royal Guard and the dragoons and hussars of the Russian Imperial Guard. Then came Alexander, the King of Prussia, and Schwarzenberg representing Emperor Francis. They were accompanied by a retinue of a thousand generals of different nations. Among them were old Blücher and Barclay de Tolly, who the day before had been elevated to the rank of field marshal. Behind marched the Austrian and Russian grenadiers, the infantry of the Russian Imperial Guard, and three divisions of Russian cuirassiers.

Alexander had put on the undress uniform of the chevaliers-gardes. He wore the blue cordon of the Order of St. Andrew across his chest. A black belt cinched his waist. Heavy gold epaulets emphasized the breadth of his shoulders. A stiff collar embroidered with gold framed his jaw. His face looked pale, solemn, and benevolent under the big green two-cornered hat decorated with a cascade of cock's plumes. From atop his horse Eclipse, the gift of Napoleon, he observed the people crowded along his route. In the working-class suburbs the attitude of the French seemed to him reserved, fearful, even hostile. But starting from the Porte Saint-Denis the atmosphere grew warmer. According to the terms of the armistice, the regular French army had left the city during the night, leaving only the National Guard. Rigged out in their blue uniforms with red epaulets, they were lined up on either side of the way, making a path for the men they had been fighting the day before. Behind their backs swarmed a vast crowd of Parisians. Heads appeared at every window. Curious onlookers had climbed up into trees, on top of carriages, and even onto rooftops. Some doffed their hats before the Czar, others applauded. Alexander waved to them and smiled. Women waved their handkerchiefs as a sign of welcome. Here and there a white sheet hung from a window as a symbol of the royalist sentiments of the owner of the house. Now, the allied army included so many nationalities and so many different uniforms that, to avoid mistakes between defenders of the same cause, both officers and men had been ordered to wear white armbands. The many legitimists among the onlookers interpreted these white armbands as a demonstration of support for the Bourbons. During a halt in the procession the Czar said in a loud voice, "I do not come as an enemy, I come to bring you peace and commerce!" He was answered with cheers. A citizen pushed aside the National Guardsmen, took a step forward, and cried, "We've been waiting for you a long time!" "If I didn't come sooner it is the bravery of your troops that is to blame!" Alexander replied in French. The shouts redoubled, "Long live Alexander! Long live the Russians! Long live the allies!"

At this moment Alexander felt himself beautiful both physically and morally, pleasing to men and to God. "His face expressed a mixture of deep emotion and unreserved joy," noted Madame de Chastenay.[1] As the troops advanced down the boulevards, enthusiasm grew. One would have thought the French had found another motherland—Russia. A few ladies from the fashionable faubourg Saint-Germain distributed white rosettes to the passersby, shouting, "Down with the tyrant! Long live the Bourbons!" But clearly their profession of faith did not meet with much response.

At the entrance to the Champs-Elysées the Czar and his retinue halted to pass the troops in review. Behind Alexander some ladies of fashion, overexcited by the spectacle, climbed up on the horses of the officers belonging to the imperial escort. They wanted to get a closer look at "the Agamemnon of peoples." The Czar smiled at them and pointed them out to his neighbors. "Let's hope there won't be another rape of the Sabines," said Schwarzenberg.

For five hours—from ten o'clock in the morning until three in the afternoon—the crowd watched the parade of Russian and Prussian troops in full dress uniform. The appearance of the nearly twenty thousand Cossacks and Kalmuks raised a murmur of amazement: Asia on the Champs-Elysées. Four hundred cannon passed, their wheels making an earsplitting din. Even the orderlies, dressed in hand-me-downs, had been gathered in a special formation to swell the numbers. Now the Parisians knew where they stood: With such forces in the capital the allies had nothing to fear from Napoleon.

Just before the end of the review, Alexander decided where he would stay. He had originally planned to move into the Elysée Palace, but he was told that the building might be mined. The Tuileries Palace being hardly safer, he decided on the residence of Prince Talleyrand, close at hand on the Rue Saint-Florentin. It was there he went, on foot, as soon as the last soldier had passed before his eyes.

In a salon on the second floor, "the Eagle's salon," with windows giving on the corner of the Rue Saint-Florentin and the Rue de Rivoli, a meeting was immediately held, attended by the sovereigns of Russia and Prussia, Schwarzenberg, Talleyrand, the Duke of Dalberg, Nesselrode, and Pozzo di Borgo. Shortly after, Baron Louis, General Dessolle, and Abbé de Pradt were invited to sit at the conference table. True to his principle, Alexander declared himself open to all suggestions regarding the political future of France: a regency under Marie Louise, the installation of Bernadotte on the throne, the return of the Bourbons, a republic . . . Baron Louis, speaking of Napoleon, cried, "That man is nothing but a corpse, only he doesn't stink yet!"[2] Supporting this point of view with greater delicacy, Talleyrand declared sententiously that, the notion of Napoleon being excluded, "the republic was an impossibility, the regency or Bernadotte an intrigue, the Bourbons alone a principle." This remark struck Alexander, who felt he was hearing the voice of France speaking through the Prince. Still, he stressed that the monarchy could not be restored without "the necessary agreement of all the French." That was no problem: Talleyrand promised to obtain the consent of the Senate. And indeed, no later than the next day, April first, sixty-four hastily assembled senators elected a provisional government, to be presided over by Talleyrand. At the Hôtel de Ville the General Council and the Municipal Council blasted Napoleon's conduct and adopted the following resolution: "The two Councils declare that they formally renounce all obedience to Napoleon Bonaparte and express the most ardent wish that the government of the monarchy be reestablished in the person of Louis XVIII." The value of 5 percent government bonds, which had fallen to forty-five francs, shot up.

That evening at the Opera, Alexander attended a performance of *La Vestale* and saw beneath him a superbly dressed audience and everywhere white rosettes. During the intermission the actor Lays came downstage and sang a verse improvised to the tune of the popular song "Le Roi Henri":

> *Vive Alexandre!*
> *Vive ce roi des rois!*
> *Sans rien prétendre,*
> *Sans nouns dicter de lois,*
> *Ce prince auguste*

> *A ce triple renom*
> *De héros, de juste,*
> *De nous rendre un Bourbon.*

> Long live Alexander!
> Long live the king of kings!
> This victorious commander
> No harsh conditions brings.
> Making no demands on us,
> Laying no commands on us,
> This prince in whom we trust
> Has three claims to renown:
> He's a hero, he is just,
> He gives the Bourbons back their crown.

There was a burst of applause, the royalists embraced each other, and Alexander, much moved, bowed majestically. Perhaps at that moment he recalled another theater, the one in Erfurt, where six years earlier he had received the same ovation because in full view of the audience he had clasped the hand of Napoleon.

At the Comédie Française a tumultuous audience obliged Talma to read a poem in honor of Louis XVIII. Next day pedlars were hawking an engraving by Benoist bearing the legend:

> *D'un vainqueur généreux la sagesse profonde*
> *Rend la France à ses rois, donne la paix au monde.*

> A generous victor's wisdom brings
> Peace to the world, France to her kings.

Street urchins would come up to Russian officers on the sidewalks, stretch out their hands for coins, and sing:

> *Que le bon Dieu maintienne*
> *Alexandre et ses descendants*
> *Jusqu'à ce que l'on prenne*
> *La lune avec ses dents!*

> Now we pray the Lord divine
> Keeps Alexander and his line
> On Russia's throne until the night
> When from the moon we take a bite.

Some feeble verses honoring the occupiers caught on and were recited in public places as soon as a foreign uniform appeared:

> *Que j'aime à revoir sur ces bords*
> *Les fiers guerriers de la Russie!*
> *Parmi nous, ces enfants du Nord*
> *Sont encore dans leur patrie:*
> *Redoutables dans les combats,*
> *Grands, généreux, pleins de vaillance,*
> *A ce titre ne sont-ils pas*
> *Les meilleurs amis de la France?*

> How I love to see Russians step forth
> Every day on the banks of the Seine!
> These proud warriors, sons of the North,
> In our midst find a homeland again.
> Since in war they are steadfast and daring,
> Since they're generous, valiant, and true,
> Are we not justified in declaring
> They're the best friends that France ever knew?

Even Rouget de Lisle, the author of the *Marseillaise,* stooped so low as to flatter the Czar in a clumsy, pompous poem:

Sois le héros du siècle et l'orgueil de l'histoire,
Punis de l'Occident l'exécrable oppresseur,
Aux Français consolés, fais chérir la victoire,
Rends aux Bourbons leur trône, à nos lys, leur splendeur.

Be the hero of the age, the pride of all history.
Punish the abominable oppressor of the West!
Make the French, now consoled, rejoice in your victory,
Give the Bourbons back their throne, raise once more our lily crest.[3]

Under this avalanche of bouquets, Alexander was beginning to think that all of France looked upon the Romanovs and the Bourbons with equal affection. But what was Napoleon planning to do? The impetuous young Sosthène de La Rochefoucauld had tried in vain to tear down the Emperor's statue from the top of the column in the Place Vendôme. He had been followed up the column by another individual who had slapped the bronze effigy, to the cheers of a little group of hotheads.

Without a doubt, the defeated Emperor was preparing a countermove from Fontainebleau. To beat him to it, the Senate pronounced him deposed, accusing him of having "violated his oath and interfered with the rights of peoples by levying men and taxes in defiance of constitutions."

When Alexander greeted the senators who had just dismissed their former master, he stressed the necessity of basing the French government on "strong, liberal foundations." Actually he had no liking for the Bourbons but was bowing to what he perceived to be the popular will. In any event, the next moment he received Caulaincourt, come from Fontainebleau with offers of negotiation. In three words he rejected them. So long as Napoleon had not officially abdicated, he refused to hear him. And still guided by Providence, he declared that he nursed no personal hatred against Napoleon, that he even pitied him with all his heart, and that he pardoned him for the devastation of Russia. He said he was ready to let the deposed sovereign choose his place of retreat, on condition that it be neither in France nor in Italy. He even offered Napoleon hospitality in his own country. "If he comes to Russia," he said to Caulaincourt, "I shall treat him like a sovereign. If he were to trust me, he would realize, more in Russia, perhaps, than anywhere else, how sensible I am to the duties imposed upon me by the character and misfortunes of a great man. He has misunderstood me, and the wrong he has done to himself explains the wrong he has done to Europe: the welfare of our peoples demands that we take precautions . . . but I shall have no more resentment against him on the day when all that is settled. I open doors for you: choose." But in fact, though in a burst of eloquence he had invited Napoleon to settle in Russia, he was already thinking of a quite different residence: the island of Elba.

Faced with Alexander's refusal to engage in further dialogue, Napoleon decided to risk his all. At Fontainebleau he had sixty thousand men. Tough, seasoned troops, who dreamed of marching on Paris. Politically, he could hope for support from Austria, which he thought would decide in his favor out of regard for Marie Louise. Once again he tried to persuade the marshals to follow him. But they were tired and discouraged and refused to resume the fight. On April 4, under pressure from Ney, Oudinot, and Lefebvre, Napoleon resigned himself to abdicating in favor of his son, with Marie Louise becoming regent. Caulaincourt, Ney, and Macdonald were assigned to take the act of conditional abdication to Alexander.

They reached Paris at night in a driving rain. The Czar received them at once and listened attentively to the proposals they brought. In his eyes these proposals had the advantage of removing Napoleon from the scene without more bloodshed. As for Louis XVIII, he did not necessarily have to be placed on the throne, in spite of the agitation of the royalists. Already Alexander was hesitating in the midst of a divided France. How many parties there were in this country seething with intrigues—Bonapartists, legitimists, republicans! How calm and united Russia seemed compared to the political cauldron of France! "I have no particular feeling about the Bourbons; I don't know them," the Czar told the plenipotentiaries. "I shall communicate your proposals to my allies and I shall support those proposals. I too am eager to be done with this." Then he dismissed his interlocutors, who left with the impression that they had come out on top. They made an appointment for the following day, April 5. But in the meantime Marmont's army corps, commanded by General Souham, had passed the Austrian outposts and gone over to the side of the allies. Ney, Macdonald, and Caulaincourt were already aware of the betrayal, but the Czar had not yet heard the news. As the discussion resumed, Alexander was very gracious. Then suddenly an aide-de-camp slipped into the drawing room and said a few words in His Majesty's ear. The Czar started imperceptibly. What he had just learned upset all his ideas. Once again, while he had been debating within himself what decision to make, the finger of God had pointed out the right direction to him. By deserting their master's cause, Souham and Marmont had shown that the French army was not entirely devoted to Napoleon. Under these conditions, it would be absurd to yield. "That settles the question," murmured Alexander, as if speaking to himself. And he said to Pozzo di Borgo, "You see, it is the will of Providence! Providence reveals itself, declares itself, no more doubt, no more hesitation!" Nevertheless, he reserved his decision until the following day to have time to consult Frederick William and Schwarzenberg. There was no doubt about the verdict: The allies would not "treat either with Napoleon or with any member of his family." It was unconditional abdication they demanded.

Abandoned by all, Napoleon gave in and on April 6 drew up the act that was expected of him: "The powers having declared that the Emperor Napoleon was the sole obstacle to the reestablishment of peace in Europe, the Emperor Napoleon, faithful to his oaths, declares that he renounces, for himself and his children, the thrones of France and Italy, and that there is no sacrifice, even that of his life, which he is not ready to make in the interest of France."

That same day the senators and deputies met to "freely call to the throne Louis Stanislas Xavier of France, brother of the last king." The common people knew nothing about this new monarch, who had taken refuge in England, except that he was said to be good-natured, fat, and afflicted with gout. One thing was certain: With him, there would be no more war. In the opinion of many, that was the essential point. As for Napoleon, Alexander was tending to him solicitously. He proposed that his unfortunate adversary become the sovereign of the island of Elba and specified that Louis XVIII was to provide the man he was replacing with an annual income of two million francs.

Throughout these negotiations the Czar had felt the Lord's presence hovering over him. The fact that events of such importance had taken place during Holy Week seemed to him an additional proof of divine intervention. Moreover, by extraordinary coincidence, the Russian Orthodox Easter fell upon the same day as the Catholic Easter that year. Was it not a providential sign of reconciliation among nations? Much impressed by this circumstance, the Czar scrupulously observed the fast and went to pray every day in the little Orthodox chapel that had been hastily set up in a neighboring house. Every time he appeared in the street he was surrounded, touched, cheered by dozens of joyful passersby. He began to wonder whether he was not the one the French should have chosen as king.

To watch over his dear Parisians he had appointed General Osten-Sacken governor of the city and named three commandants including the Comte de Rochechouart, a French emigré in the service of Russia. He wanted the Russian troops to be imbued with the same religious spirit as their master, so he had Osten-Sacken make the following announcement: "His Imperial Majesty hopes and believes that throughout Holy Week no Russian officer will allow himself to defy the rules of the Church by going to the theater. Any Russian who attended performances would be immediately brought to the attention of His Imperial Majesty."

On April 10, Easter Sunday, to the astonishment of the Parisians, Alexander had an Orthodox mass celebrated on the Place Louis XV.* An altar had been raised on a platform at the place where Louis XVI's head had fallen under the knife. After reviewing the troops, the Czar and the King of Prussia climbed the steps of the platform, where all available Orthodox priests were already gathered. The assembled soldiers and officers of the infantry took off their hats and knelt on one knee. The cavalry remained on horseback but with bare heads and

---

*The present Place de la Concorde.

sabers down. While the worship service went on, Alexander enjoyed the strange scene—the bearded, mitered priests in their gold chasubles; the banners, icons, and censers; the grave chanting in Old Slavonic— and all this in the heart of Paris, just a few steps from the Seine. The enormous crowd who had come to attend the ceremony reinforced his idea that everything he did was pleasing to the French. He wrote to Golitzin describing this "Te Deum": "It was a solemn, moving, awe-some moment for my heart. [I had] led my Orthodox warriors from the depths of their cold Nordic homeland to . . . the very spot where the royal victim succumbed to popular fury. . . . It was as if the sons of the North were performing the funeral rites of the King of France. . . . Our spiritual triumph achieved its full effect. I was even amused to see French marshals and generals pushing and shoving to kiss the Russian cross."

But Metternich, who arrived in Paris that same day, thought that there was nothing of the religious mystic about Alexander. "I found the Emperor of Russia in a very reasonable frame of mind," he wrote to Emperor Francis. "He talks much less nonsense than I should have thought. . . . Moreover, he can scarcely contain his joy at the turn events have taken; but our success does exceed everything one could have hoped." The only thing Metternich held against Alexander was that he had permitted Napoleon to withdraw to the island of Elba. Would the tyrant stay quiet there? Alexander swore that he would, that Napoleon would never go back on a commitment he had made before the whole world. "One cannot doubt the word of a soldier and a sovereign without insulting him!" he exclaimed. Metternich smiled ironically, and when the moment came to sign the document, he said to the Czar, who was watching him anxiously: "I shall set my name at the bottom of a treaty that in less than two years will bring us back onto the battlefield."[4]

On April 20, in the courtyard of the chateau of Fontainebleau, Napo-leon bade a heartbreaking farewell to his old comrades in arms and left for exile. From London Grand Duchess Catherine, who had lost her husband, the Duke of Oldenburg, in 1812 and had sought distraction by traveling in Europe, wrote in French to her brother Alexander, "I congratulate you, my friend, on the great news of Napoleon's abdica-tion. It is hard to become accustomed to the idea, and assuredly there was never a more sudden transition than the one from the most horrible and bloody war to the most perfect peace. The joy here is like delirium, and your name is blessed as it should be: the city is to be illuminated for three days." Alexander was flattered to learn that his fame had spread as far as England.

In Paris, meanwhile, the Russians were settling down. At first the Cossacks had bivouacked under the trees along the Champs-Elysées, and the Parisians had come out with their families to stare at the "savages from the steppe," crowded around their campfires. Their huts were made of bundles of straw supported by lances planted in the ground. They dried their clothes on lines strung between the branches. Their little horses were tethered everywhere, eating the bark off trees. Around them was a pervasive odor of fur, tallow, and horse manure. Paying no attention to the strollers, the men would pick lice, play cards, sleep with their heads resting on their saddles. Almost all were tanned and bearded, with high cheekbones. They could not have aroused more curiosity if they had come from the moon. Now, however, after Napoleon's abdication, the Champs-Elysées had emptied. The elite units were divided among various barracks: Babylone, Rueil, Grenelle . . . The others were billeted on the outskirts of town. A monotonous, rigorous life began for the soldiers. As Alexander was afraid that his troops might indulge in excesses in a great city full of temptations, he tightened discipline. Restricted to quarters most of the time, the victors began to feel like prisoners of the vanquished. They also complained about the bad food (how could one do Russian cooking in France?) and all the reviews they had to participate in to dazzle the crowds. "Our Emperor," wrote General Nikita Muraviev, "was so prejudiced in favor of the French that he gave the Parisian National Guard orders to arrest our soldiers if they met them on the street. This resulted in not a few brawls, in which we generally got the best of it. But this way of treating the men also induced them to desert."

While the soldiers had no contact with the local population and did not participate in the life of the capital, it was different for the officers. Furnished with billeting orders, most of them had their room and board in private homes. The cold reception they were accorded there at first soon gave way to cordiality. Friendships were formed. Flirtations began. The Russian uniform was at a premium among the ladies of high society. Drawing rooms in the faubourg Saint-Germain opened their doors wide to the members of the Russian nobility. At a reception given by the Comte de Rochechouart a chorus of the chasseurs of the Imperial Guard sang national songs that delighted the French guests. When supper was over the master of the house offered a toast to the return of Louis XVIII. The party broke up at four in the morning, and Grand Duke Constantine, who was one of the guests, declared that he had enjoyed it more than any court ball.

The officers of humbler origins took pleasure in strolling on the boulevards, frequenting the theaters, laughing at the jokes of a public entertainer, lunching in fashionable restaurants, taking in the sights while sipping a demitasse at a café, or seeking an amorous adventure at the Palais-Royal, gathering place of all the beauties of easy virtue. The more serious-minded visited the museums, went into raptures over the stained-glass windows of Notre-Dame, talked with disabled veterans at the Invalides, admired the sunset from the top of Montmartre, and made excursions to Saint-Denis, Versailles, Saint-Cloud, and even as far as Ermenonville, where the memory of Jean-Jacques Rousseau stirred sensitive hearts. Some felt the ferment of ideas in the capital like a kind of electric current. Infected by "the French contagion," they discovered the need to discuss the great problems of the day with profound thinkers. They were more attracted to political and literary circles than to high society. As the sons of an autocratic country, they felt a guilty intoxication talking about liberty with the sons of the Revolution, even if just now France had become a kingdom again. Prince Volkonsky met Benjamin Constant and Madame de Staël; Nikita Muraviev made the acquaintance of Sieyès and Abbé Grégoire; Lunin visited Saint-Simon. Lastly, many of the Czar's officers were introduced into the French Masonic lodges. There they found a tolerance, an independence of mind that astounded them. Whether their hosts in these secret associations were for the Bourbons, Napoleon, or the republic, they seemed to be filled with the same concern for humanity and human dignity. The Russians had mixed feelings in their presence. They were proud of their sovereign but ashamed of their regime. They loved their country but deplored its backwardness. They had come "to teach a lesson" but discovered they were ready to be taught. "The French do not consider their monarch to be Providence on earth, as the Russians do," noted Mikhailovsky-Danilevsky, a regular visitor in the French Masonic lodges, and before the "Worshipful Master" of one lodge he took an oath to "hate tyrants." Nicholas Turgenev, secretary to Baron von Stein, even offered a toast to the emancipation of the Russian serfs. "Where better than in a meeting of true Masons," he exclaimed, "could one utter such a wish? Is not the idea of Freemasonry the same as that of cosmopolitanism and fraternity? . . ." And he noted in his journal, "Many Russians will go back to their country having observed that serfdom is not indispensable to civil order and the prosperity of kingdoms."[5]

The Russian officers would have been glad to prolong their stay in Paris, but Alexander was in a hurry to have done with French affairs. Nothing could be concluded, however, before Louis XVIII returned to his capital. And he was long in coming. On April 13 his younger brother, the Comte d'Artois, showed up as a forerunner, wearing the uniform of the National Guard. Then Emperor Francis arrived in great pomp, which irritated the Parisians: The father of Marie Louise should show more discretion in triumph. Finally, on April 29, Louis XVIII arrived in Compiègne. Before leaving England he had sent the Regent a letter that was printed in the London *Times:* "It is to the advice of Your Royal Highness, to this glorious country and to the determination of its inhabitants that, after the will of Divine Providence, I shall always attribute the reestablishment of my house upon the throne of its ancestors." Not a word about the hospitality extended to him in Russia as the Comte de Provence or about the bloody sacrifices made by the soldiers of the Czar to bring about Napoleon's downfall. None the wiser for his exile, Louis XVIII seemed to consider all the efforts of the allies on his behalf as no more than his due. Fearing that his arrogant attitude would make the people angry, Alexander sent his aide-de-camp Pozzo di Borgo to him with a letter advising him to be considerate of the feelings of the French army and to envision a liberal regime for the country. "There exist," wrote the Czar, "a national will, a few opposition parties, and some undecided opinions, over which moderation alone can triumph, if one does not wish to produce new disturbances at a time when what is needed is calm and consolidation. . . ."

Louis XVIII sent such an evasive reply to this message that Alexander was annoyed and had Fouché draft a note on the necessity of respecting twenty-five years of glory and of keeping the tricolor flag. He himself took this note to Compiègne. He was received there with a coldness that dumbfounded him. Without rising from his armchair, the heir of Saint Louis, swollen with fat and with pride, indicated a chair to the heir of the Romanovs. While the Czar was talking to him he showed no interest in his remarks; then all of a sudden breaking out of his reserve, he uttered a few words on how beneficial it would be for France to have a legitimate sovereign at the head of the nation again. Later, when Alexander went to take possession of the lodgings set aside for him, he crossed through the three sumptuous apartments of the Comte d'Artois and his sons the Duc d'Angoulême and the Duc de Berry before arriving, by way of a labyrinth of dark corridors and winding staircases, in the modest rooms of the governor of the palace, which had been assigned to the Emperor of all the Russias. Alexander, who had intended to spend the night at Compiègne, immediately asked that his carriage be brought round as soon as dinner was over. At dinner time Louis XVIII entered the dining room first, and when a servant presented a dish to the Czar, he cried in a sharp voice, "Over here, if you please!" Alexander got the message: The lessons were all designed to make him feel that notwithstanding his victory, he was of little consequence in the presence of "the first prince of Christendom." "Louis XIV at the height of his power," the Czar said later, "would not have received me differently at Versailles; one would have thought it was *he* who had just put *me* back on my throne. The reception he gave me made the same impression on me as if a bucket of ice had been thrown at my head. . . . We northern barbarians are more courteous in our country."[6] And next day, when someone expressed the hope that the Bourbons had returned to France "corrected of their errors," he answered, "Not corrected, and not correctable!"[7] He was also to say, "Those people will never last."

Still, for better or worse, he had to accommodate to this majestic tub of lard. Only one condition: Before returning to Paris Louis XVIII would have to accept the constitution voted by the Senate, providing for a kind of English-style parliamentary monarchy. On May 2 at Saint-Ouen, secure in the knowledge of his legitimacy, the King made a declaration by which, instead of subscribing to the constitution as it had been drafted by the senators, he promised the people basic freedoms, national representation, and equality before the law. That meant that while he renounced all forms of absolutism, he rejected the principle of popular sovereignty, which was incompatible with the idea of a dynasty. The declaration was followed not by a constitution but by a charter *granted* by the King to his subjects and dated the nineteenth year of his reign (counting from the death of Louis XVII). Alexander was satisfied with this solution, which was a compromise between a monarchy and a republic.

On May 3, the day after the declaration of Saint-Ouen, Louis XVIII made his entrance into a Paris decorated with white flags and painted-cardboard shields bearing the royal fleurs-de-lis. The crowd cheered the obese old man seated in his barouche, who lifted his big three-cornered hat from time to time with a bored gesture. As a courtesy, the military governor of the city, Osten-Sacken, had ordered that no allied uniform be seen that day on the streets. In spite of the demonstrations organized by a few royalists, in his own capital Louis XVIII enjoyed far less popularity than Alexander. Lodged in the Tuileries, he found it painful to hear people everywhere singing the praises of the Russian sovereign, whom he mockingly called "the little king of Paris."[8] Alexander, who meantime had moved into the Elysée Palace, felt only mistrust and repulsion for the new master of France. He almost regretted Napoleon, whom he admired even as he detested him. When the question was raised—with the greatest discretion, of course—of a possible marriage between his sister, Grand Duchess Anne (the one Napoleon had also wanted to wed) and the Duc de Berry, he opposed the notion, preferring not to have any family connections with Louis XVIII whose throne, he thought, was not firmly enough established.

On the other hand, he was full of consideration for those close to Napoleon. It was as if he had contributed to the restoration of the Bourbons for reasons of state while remaining sentimentally attached to the memory of his former enemy. He made a courtesy visit to Rambouillet, the provisional residence of Marie Louise. He was even more attentive to Josephine. Almost every day he went to Malmaison to meet Napoleon's repudiated wife. There he turned on all the charm of his conversation and smile. The idea of pleasing a woman who had captivated "that great man" excited his imagination and tickled his vanity. He also paid assiduous court to Josephine's daughter, Queen Hortense, whom he admired for her blue eyes, her dainty feet, and her long past as a coquette. One day in an amiable mood he said to her with a sigh, "I arrived in Paris full of animosity against your family and it is only in the midst of that family that I find life sweet." He even managed to have Louis XVIII create her Duchesse de Saint-Leu. To Josephine also he poured out speeches full of respectful affection. One evening he was walking with her in the park of Malmaison when she suddenly shivered. She was wearing a ball gown and, warmed by dancing, had wanted a breath of fresh air. Now she didn't feel well. Not long after, on May 29, she died from the consequences of that chill. The Czar spent the night near the room where she lay dying. He attended the funeral with a large retinue and had a detachment of his Guard pay military honors to the deceased.

Since France had chosen to be governed by a Bourbon, Alexander thought it necessary to gather around the new monarch all those who had served the preceding regime. Otherwise the country would be thrown into chaos, and that would quickly endanger the stability of Europe. Therefore, despite his antipathy for Louis XVIII, he tried to rally the former supporters of the Emperor to the King. He flattered defeated marshals with compliments and danced with their wives at society functions, which further enhanced his personal popularity. He was liked by both sides: by the legitimists because he had helped to restore the monarchy, by the Bonapartists because he respected the glory of their idol. While the old King stayed shut up in the Tuileries, Alexander rode out almost every day without an escort, responded to the greetings of onlookers, visited public establishments, took an interest in hospital patients, went to the Champs-Elysées to assess the damage done by the Cossacks to the lawns and trees so as to make just reparation, and kept making serious or amusing remarks that were immediately reported in the newspapers. To a passerby who stopped him to thank him for his affability toward even the least citizen, he replied, "Isn't that what sovereigns are made for?" Looking at the statue of Napoleon at the top of the column in the Place Vendôme, he remarked, "If I had reached such heights I'd be afraid it would go to my head." When it was suggested that he change the name of the Pont d'Austerlitz, he said, "No, it's enough that I have passed over that bridge with my army."[9]

He received a delegation from the Institute very graciously.* In the drawing rooms of Madame de Staël, who had just returned to Paris with politics boiling in her head, he posed as a champion of peace and freedom. He coolly deplored the subservience of the French press and declared, to the astonishment of his compatriots, that the Russian press was perfectly independent. In the same way, he said to Madame de Staël in a mellifluous voice, "With God's help, serfdom will be abolished under my reign." He announced to Lafayette that he would take the most energetic stand against the slave trade. Moved to tears, Madame de Staël wrote, "I wish with all my soul for everything that can raise up this man who seems to me to be a miracle of Providence sent to save liberty, which is threatened on all sides." Chancellor Pasquier noted, "Emperor Alexander is becoming very popular. One could see that everything emanated from him, that everything depended on him. His ally, the King of Prussia, went unnoticed; he was seldom seen, he avoided showing himself in public, and when he did so it was always with an air of timidity that could not make him stand out." Even Chateaubriand, whose patriotism had been so wounded when the allies entered Paris, now wanted to meet Alexander. He wrote, "Inwardly thunderstruck and overwhelmed, as if they had torn my French name from me and replaced it with the number by which I was henceforth to be known in the mines of Siberia, at the same time I felt my exasperation growing against the man whose glory had reduced us to this shame." Chateaubriand had expressed that exasperation in his pamphlet, *De Buonaparte et des Bourbons,* which he felt should have earned

---

*The Institut de France, founded in 1795, includes five learned academies of the sciences, arts, and humanities. (Trans.)

him the right to be honorably received by Alexander. But Alexander disappointed him by his extreme reserve. Instead of the expected compliments, Chateaubriand heard that men of letters should not meddle in politics. The Czar was being true to his policy of magnanimity: He could not pardon a French author for having bitterly denounced so illustrious a man in defeat. And again he scored a point with the Bonapartists.

Nevertheless, the statue of Napoleon was finally taken down from the Vendôme column and replaced by a white flag until such time as a statue of Peace could be erected on top. The diplomats had been working for weeks to lay the groundwork for that peace. On May 30, 1814, a treaty was signed that stripped France of her conquests since 1792, and practically restricted her to the geographical limits of the old monarchy. This was a cruel blow to national pride. Talleyrand's concessions to the allies were considered scandalous. It was whispered that Louis XVIII had been "brought back in the foreigner's baggage train." In the opinion of the diplomats, however, France had by no means been strangled by her conquerors. Thanks to Alexander's energetic intervention, she had no forced contribution or indemnity to pay. In spite of Stein's insistence, the Czar also refused to let Alsace and the fortresses of the Rhine be returned to Prussia. And with supreme unselfishness, he decided that the defeated would not be required to restore the art treasures they had carried off as booty in the course of their campaigns. According to him, these masterpieces had found an ideal home on the banks of the Seine, where they would be more accessible than anywhere else for Europeans to admire.

Alexander's entourage considered him too benevolent toward the French and complained that Russia was getting no territorial advantage in exchange for the blood shed and the sufferings endured. In reality, Alexander had already rewarded himself handsomely at Poland's expense and was counting on the forthcoming congress at Vienna to obtain from his allies official recognition of the annexation. Meanwhile, he was careful not to show his cards and plied the Poles with fair words and demonstrations of friendship. When Czartoryski arrived in Paris the Czar gave him a fraternal welcome that reminded him of their youth. Alexander permitted the Polish regiments, which had remained loyal to Napoleon to the end, to return to Poland "with drums beating" and with their "arms, baggage, and colors." Grand Duke Constantine became their commander. When General Sokonitski asked him if the Polish soldiers could keep their national cockades, he replied, in French, "Yes, and I hope that you will soon wear them with the certainty that you will keep them forever. It is true that I shall have many difficulties to overcome, but you see me in Paris and that is enough. I am wiping the slate clean, and although I should be justified in complaining of many individuals of your nation, I want to forget everything. You are brave men, you have performed your duty faithfully." To a delegation of Polish officers he further declared, "The two neighboring nations, drawn together by language and customs, once united should be friends forever." At a dinner at General Krassinski's he drank a toast to "the brave Polish nation." At a ball at Princess Jablonowska's he asked Kosciusko, who had been a refugee in France ever since the partition of Poland, if he did not wish to return to his country. The old soldier answered that he would not go back to his native land until it had been liberated. At these words the Czar, with an angelic smile, said in a loud voice so as to be heard by the officers around them, "Gentlemen, we must arrange things in such a way that this gallant man can return to his country." And he said to Laharpe: "How can a decent man resign himself to not having a country? If I had been a Pole I should have yielded to the temptation to which they succumbed. My intention is to return to them as much of that country as I can and to give them a constitution that I shall reserve the right to expand in proportion as they inspire my confidence." The naïve Laharpe was greatly moved and confided to a friend, "Those words still echo in the depths of my heart and I delight to recall them as I gaze upon his bust and portraits."

Alexander appeared conciliating, but he knew how to "speak a Napoleonic language" when necessary, as Beugnot put it: "It must be done, it must; orders have been given."[10] As Louis XVIII continued to delay publication of the constitution promised to his subjects, the Czar told him that he would remain in Paris until that obligation had been fulfilled. Grudgingly, the King gave in and set the date of June 4 for the solemn proclamation of the charter.

What lay in store for France? Alexander was skeptical: He felt that one could not "found a solid throne on the ruins of the Revolution." Moreover, he was disappointed in Talleyrand and angry with him. Although Talleyrand had been completely devoted to the Czar when the Russian troops entered Paris, in a few weeks he had found a way to declare his independence. Pozzo di Borgo described him as follows in a letter to Nesselrode: "He is a man like no other, he spoils, rearranges, intrigues, governs in a hundred different ways every day. The interest he takes in others is in direct proportion to the need he has of them at the moment. Even his civilities are one-day investments made in the expectation of exorbitant returns." Having once been infatuated with the French diplomat, Alexander now treated him coldly. He refused to receive him for a farewell audience and said bitterly of him, "That man, by his conduct, sacrifices his country and his friends to his ambition."

Informed of the Czar's feelings toward him, Talleyrand wrote him, all sweetness and light: "I did not see Your Majesty before his departure and I make bold to reproach him for it with the respectful sincerity of the most affectionate attachment. . . . I foresaw your destiny and felt that, Frenchman though I was, I could associate myself with your plans because they would always be magnanimous. You have completely fulfilled that lofty destiny. . . . You have saved France, your entry into Paris signaled the end of despotism. . . . Who can flatter himself that, so soon after so great an upheaval, he understands the mood of the French? The French, in general, have been and will be fickle in their impressions. . . . This changeableness will soon incline them to repose considerable confidence in their sovereign: ours will not abuse that confidence."

Alexander set out for London the day before the Senate and the Legislative Body were to hold a joint session to adopt the charter. He left behind him the memory of an enlightened monarch, full of clemency and delicacy. Recalling the Czar's stay in the capital, Chateaubriand wrote, "He seemed astonished by his triumph; with eyes full of emotion he looked about at a population which he appeared to consider superior to himself: it was as if he felt himself a Barbarian in our midst, as a Roman felt ashamed in Athens. Perhaps also he was thinking that these same Frenchmen had appeared in his burning capital; that now his soldiers were in turn masters of Paris, where he might have found some of the extinguished torches by which Moscow had been delivered and consumed. The thought of destiny, of changing fortune, of this pitiful condition common to both peoples and kings, must have made a profound impression on a mind as religious as his."

And indeed, the long national war with its alternating despair and enthusiasm, its military and diplomatic intrigues, its displaced borders, its arches of triumph and avalanches of corpses, its court balls and campfires, had profoundly marked Alexander's character. To superficial observers he still had the same handsome face, the same polished speech, the same elegant bearing as on the eve of the French troops' entrance into Russia. But behind the unaltered appearance a great change had taken place. Imperceptibly, the petted grandson of Catherine II, the gentle pupil of Laharpe, the liberal young Czar who had been hailed at his accession as "an angel robed in purple" had become, through the vicissitudes of his life, a man whose thoughts were filled with God but who found no solace in Him. While he was intoxicated with glory, there were moments when he was suddenly struck by the vanity of human greatness. He was unable to give up the pleasure of being honored and fêted everywhere, yet he had only sadness and anxiety in his heart. Sometimes it seemed to him that no earthly satisfaction would ever quench his tormenting thirst for the absolute.

Nevertheless, when he left Paris on June 3, 1814, he was looking forward to another great joy the journey held in store for him: His sister Catherine was impatiently awaiting him in London and predicting that he would have an even greater personal success there than he had enjoyed in Paris. "When has there ever been a conquering monarch whose character could be cited as his first virtue?" she wrote him, in French. "I must tell you, it is delightful to hear everything that people are saying about you, and in spite of the high praises they add, 'Nothing is exaggerated, you have to know what a soul he has.' Don't scold me, I'm only telling you this because I'm bursting with it. You will see for yourself if I'm exaggerating!"

As soon as the Czar had left, the allied regiments began evacuating Paris. Their departure was so discreet that one would have thought they were preparing a surprise maneuver. After two months of occupation, the French were again masters in their own house, with a king who, thanks to the blunders of the former emigrés, was already being discredited in the eyes of the public.

XI

THE CONGRESS
OF VIENNA

When he disembarked at Dover, Alexander realized that the English were as infatuated with him as the French. The crowds cheered him. They unhitched the horses from the barouche in which he was sitting with the King of Prussia and pulled the carriage through the streets of the city. But if the people were with him, the same was not necessarily true of the government. In Paris the Czar had noticed that the English diplomats objected to his views on Poland. He hoped that his presence in London would be enough to convince the Regent* and the public that he should be left a free hand in the Slavic territories. As usual, he counted on his charm and on God to help him in this enterprise.

But in London he discovered a political milieu that was more di-

---

*George Augustus Frederick, ruling in place of his father, George III, who had become blind and mentally unbalanced by 1811. He would be crowned George IV on his father's death in 1820. (Ed.)

---

vided than he had supposed. His bustling, harebrained, imperious sister Catherine had not found favor with the cold British court or the Tories then in power and had allied herself out of spite with the Whig opposition party. Mixed up in all the intrigues involving the royal family, she had welcomed to her drawing room Lord Grey and Lord Holland, and by so doing had set the Regent violently against her.

Brother and sister were reunited in an effusion of reciprocal affection and admiration. Far from criticizing Catherine for her imprudent political scheming, Alexander approved her conduct. Had not he himself posed in Paris as the champion of liberal ideas? Had he not compelled Louis XVIII to grant his people a charter? Here as there, he wanted to be considered a broad-minded sovereign. Apartments had been prepared for him at St. James's Palace, but Catherine urged him to refuse them and to live more simply with her, at Pulteney House. She a sured him that the people hated the Regent and would be grateful to the Czar for having declined his official hospitality. And indeed, Alexander had hardly arrived at Pulteney House when he realized that his sister had been correct. While he was waiting for a visit from the Prince Regent, an enthusiastic crowd gathered in front of the house. Twenty times he had to appear on the balcony to respond to the ovations of the English. But still his distinguished visitor did not come. At last, after three hours, the Czar was informed that His Royal Highness had decided not to venture into this densely populated district where his presence might "provoke disturbances." Catherine triumphed. Amused by the Prince Regent's timidity, Alexander went to visit him first, at Carlton House, and came back more convinced than ever of his sister's extraordinary perspicacity.

Like her, he surrounded himself with notorious Whigs. To astonish them with his liberalism, he even asked Lord Grey to submit to him a plan for "the creation of an opposition in Russia." After this audience, his puzzled interlocutor said to Metternich, "Is the Czar thinking of introducing a parliament in Russia? If he is determined to do so—and I shall be careful not to urge it upon him—he won't have to worry about creating the opposition; he will certainly not lack for one."[1] Nothing more was ever said, of course, about this ideal "opposition." Some plans are all the better for being left unexecuted—that's the poetry of politics.

Alexander also met the most eminent leaders of the community of Quakers, discussed religious questions with them, attended one of their meetings, and invited them to St. Petersburg. He talked with the famous philosopher and jurist Jeremy Bentham and questioned him about the possibility of revising Russian legislation. When he received an honorary doctorate from Oxford University, he said he regretted that he had not defended a thesis, to which the Rector replied, "Sire, you have defended your thesis against the oppressor of peoples more brilliantly than any other Doctor of Laws in the world would have done." Careful to maintain his popularity, he often showed himself in Hyde Park on horseback, in English uniform, and bowed to the admirers who applauded him. With his sister he visited Westminster, St. Paul's, Greenwich, the Royal Exchange, and the British Museum, and attended the races at Ascot. All their evenings were given over to banquets, balls, and gala performances. Lord Castlereagh and Lord Liverpool organized official dinners in their honor. The leaders of the opposition, Lord Grey and the Duke of Devonshire, did likewise.

While the Prince Regent refrained from appearing at the society gatherings of the Whigs Alexander made a point of doing so. "The magical effect produced by the presence of the Emperor," wrote Princess de Lieven, "and the cheers which accompanied him everywhere made the most humiliating contrast possible for the Regent. He was angered and deeply wounded and very soon came to think of Alexander only as a rival." Having invited Alexander to a review at Hyde Park, the Regent purposely arrived an hour late. Alexander responded by arriving two hours late at a court reception, and to explain the delay to the fuming Regent he said that he had been detained at the home of Lord Grey, the most intransigent leader of the opposition. When Lady Jersey, a guiding spirit among the Whigs, invited him to a ball on June 15, the Regent arranged to keep him at Oxford so that he could not return to London until the sixteenth at three o'clock in the morning. The Czar barely took time to change his clothes, arrived at Lady Jersey's in the first light of dawn, and danced the Scotch reel until five. As always, he had no trouble reconciling the pursuit of grand designs with the glitter and pretense of society life. By flouting the Regent in London, as he had flouted Louis XVIII in Paris, Alexander felt he was winning the esteem of the population.

Policy, however, was made at court, not in the street, and while the Czar was busy showing himself to advantage in public, behind his back Castlereagh and Metternich were preparing a joint objection to Russia's thinly disguised annexation of Poland.

Besides, the Londoners' interest in Alexander was gradually losing its edge. The curiosity seekers turned to more spectacular Russians, like the rough leader of the partisans, the Cossack general Platov, who now appeared in the streets with his escort of bearded, fiery-eyed horsemen. From countless little signs the Czar could tell that his star was fading, not only at court but in society. A great banquet at the Guildhall, at which seven hundred guests gathered around the Emperor of Russia, the King of Prussia, and the Prince Regent, only accentuated the general uneasiness. Although served on gold plates, the dinner was lugubrious. Italian singers did their best to charm the guests, but Grand Duchess Catherine, who detested music, abruptly asked that the artists be silent. Her demand threw the company into confusion. Alexander, who was hard of hearing, didn't understand the embarrassed murmurs all around him. Suddenly, he couldn't wait to leave this country that was so proper, cold, and stiff.

He took ship again at Dover on June 26, sailed to Calais, traversed Holland amid acclamations, and arrived in Bruchsal, in Baden, where he found his wife, whom he had not seen for eighteen months. Her whole Badenese family was gathered there. Shy, distant, and proud, the Empress Elizabeth had earlier refused to join her husband in Paris. "If in Paris I could have seen only the royal family and those who have always been devoted to it, that would have made me happy," she wrote. "But I should have had to see a very mixed society, people whom I despise, and I should not have been able to hide my feelings. Lastly, I should have been afraid to show my face before a public as different from ours, as sharp-eyed and as spoiled as that of Paris."

In the little German town the Czar had restful conversations with Laharpe, Baron von Stein, and a few intimate friends. Far from the pomp and ceremony of London, he relished the pleasures of simplicity. But fame found him out in his retreat. A delegation of four high Russian dignitaries came to offer him, in the name of the Senate, the Holy Synod, and the Council of State, the appellation "Alexander the Blessed." A monument would be erected for the occasion and a medal struck, both inscribed *From grateful Russia to the restorer of sovereigns.* Though in Paris and London Alexander had received every homage with evident satisfaction, here he shied away from the honor. It was as if, unlike the trinkets he had been given by the French and English, this Russian consecration was too heavy a weight for him to bear; as if he were afraid that to accept it would be to offend God by his presumption; as if the sin of pride did not exist abroad but became mortal in Russia. He ordered Chichkov, who begged him not to disappoint the nation by refusing, to draw up an evasive reply: "May you erect a monument to me in your hearts, as I erect one for you in my own heart! May my people bless me as I bless them! Long live Russia, and may the divine benediction fall upon her and upon me!"

No statue, no medal: But among the people the appellation, which had a nice ring to it, was to remain attached to the person of the liberator of the motherland. Foreseeing an apotheosis when he returned to Russia, Alexander wrote to the Governor of St. Petersburg, "I have heard that you were making all sorts of preparations to welcome me. Having always detested that sort of demonstration, I think it would be more inappropriate now than ever. The Almighty alone is the source of the glorious events that have put an end to the bloody fighting in Europe. Before Him we must all bow. Make it known everywhere that I absolutely will not tolerate any demonstration of welcome or any reception when I return."

In St. Petersburg, where the municipal authorities had prepared magnificent ceremonies in honor of the sovereign, all gatherings were hastily canceled and the framework for the various arches of triumph was taken down. On July 13/25 Alexander arrived in his capital early in the morning, without fanfare or procession, and went to the Cathedral of Kazan to pray. Everyone who came near him was struck by his look of depression.

No doubt he was satiated with glory. Having reached the summit, he found there was now nothing left for him to desire. The vanity of the noblest human enterprises deprived him of all incentive and brought him nearer to God. Nevertheless, a few days later he agreed to attend an entertainment that his mother had organized for him, with great pomp, at the "Palace of Roses." He appeared there in ill humor, distracted, distant. A choir sang him a cantata, with words written by the old poet Derzhavin: "You have returned, you, our benefactor, our modest angel, the ray of light in our hearts."

Instead of thanking the author, Alexander talked to him about his worries: The country was ravaged, everything was in ruins, finances were shaky.

For the reconstruction he would need energetic men. He recalled to public service the inevitable Arakcheyev, who for some time had been resting at his estate of Gruzino: "It is time for us to work," he wrote him. "I await you impatiently." He accepted the resignation of the venerable Count Rumiantsev, Chancellor of the Empire, and replaced him with his associate Nesselrode; he retired Secretary of State Chichkov, who was in poor health, and appointed Olenin as his successor; he dismissed Count Rostopchin, the Governor of Moscow, whose swaggering he had always detested.

Before he retired Chichkov drew up, at the Emperor's request, a manifesto of gratitude to the Russian nation. When Alexander read the draft he bristled at two passages: First, in listing the various classes of society the author mentioned the nobility before the army, which was unjust in view of the services the valiant soldiers had just rendered the country; second, he had dared speak of the good relations between landowners and peasant serfs "based on reciprocal advantages." These were two opinions the Czar could not tolerate. Chichkov changed the document to suit His Majesty but noted, "These unfortunate prejudices against slavery in Russia, against the nobility and, in general, the whole ancien régime, are the work of the Laharpes and other young men raised on French ideas who, as companions of the Czar's youth, only turned his eyes and heart away from our dress, language, customs, in short from everything Russian."[2]

The manifesto was published on August 30, 1814, and two days later Alexander left the capital to go to Czarskoye Selo and thence to the Congress of Vienna. Just before climbing into his carriage, he sent a note to Arakcheyev: "Au revoir, my dear friend, I have worked all night and am leaving at once."

On the way to Austria he stopped at the Czartoryskis' in Pulawy, declared that for him it was "a choice and favorite place," kissed the hand of the dowager Princess, called her "maman," and exclaimed to her sons, who were much affected, "Poland has three enemies: Prussia, Austria, and Russia, and one friend: me!" Having tossed off a few vague promises, he left again at night, for, he said, he had to gallop "like a courier."

On September 25, 1814, he made his entrance into Vienna, accompanied by the King of Prussia, and took up residence in the imperial palace, the Hofburg. He had made a few brief notes in French on his ideas about the negotiations to be undertaken: "For Russia: the duchy of Warsaw. At worst, I agree to yielding only Posen up to a line drawn from Thorn to Peysern and, from there, along the Prosna as far as the border of Silesia, and the district of Kulm up to the Drewenz, excepting a radius around Thorn."[3] And to justify his claims he wrote, "It is just that my subjects should be indemnified for so many sacrifices and that a military border should preserve them forever from a new invasion." However, he had no intention of simply annexing Poland. What he wanted was that the grand duchy of Warsaw, expanded to include the territories allotted to Prussia and Austria at the time of partition, should become an independent kingdom of which he would proclaim himself king. In short, Poland would be Russian without being Russian. It would be bound to Russia only by the person of its sovereign. It would be autonomous geographically but not politically. One head for two Slavic countries. What could be wiser? In exchange for these concessions,

Austria would receive "the north of Italy as far as the Ticino and Lake Maggiore, Venezia, the Tirol, Salzburg, the Inn Valley, and Dalmatia." As for Prussia, it would be granted a strip of Saxony as compensation, the rest being ceded to the house of Weimar and the house of Coburg.

This distribution satisfied none of the partners. From the beginning of the negotiations, Alexander encountered opposition from Austria, England, and even France. Yes, to the Czar's amazement, the nation he had just defeated dared to contradict him, through Talleyrand. No sooner had the Prince arrived in Vienna than he was transformed from beggar to equal participant. He had managed, in his own words, to "seat himself at a place of honor" at the conference table. His first exchange with the Czar was so sharp as to verge on insolence. Speaking of the advantages that each nation would derive from the new treaty, Alexander said, "I shall keep what I occupy!"

"Your Majesty will wish to keep only what is legitimately his," retorted Talleyrand, stiffening his neck under his big cravat, while the corners of his mouth turned down in an expression of cold contempt.

"I am in agreement with the great powers," declared the Czar.

"I do not know if Your Majesty counts France among those powers," murmured the diplomat.

"Yes, certainly. But if you do not want each of us to have what suits him, what is it you desire?"

"I put right first and what suits people afterward."

"What suits Europe is right."

"This language, Sire, is not yours, it is foreign to you and your heart disavows it."

"No," the Czar cut him short, "I repeat, what suits Europe is right!"

"Europe! Europe! Poor Europe!" groaned Talleyrand, knocking his head against the wall paneling in feigned despair.

Later, as Alexander was inveighing against those who, like the King of Saxony, had betrayed the European cause by supporting Napoleon, "that Frenchman" said to him, "Sire, that is a question of dates and the effect of the confusion into which people may have been thrown by the circumstances." Was this a venomous allusion to the Russian attitude at the time of the Treaty of Tilsit? Alexander turned pale at the stinging retort. The truth was that Talleyrand could not allow Poland to become a branch of Russia. In his view that would mean "creating a danger for Europe so great and so imminent that if the execution of such a plan could be prevented only by force of arms, one should not hesitate for a moment to take them up." Moreover, he feared an expansion of the power of Prussia, augmented by a piece of Saxony. Lord Castlereagh for his part would accept a kingdom of Poland if necessary, but with no dynastic link with Russia. As for Metternich, he thought that a reconstitution of Poland under the aegis of the Czar would represent a threat to Austrian Galicia and, by suddenly expanding Russia, would disrupt the European balance of power. Alexander fought the three diplomats —French, English, and Austrian—angrily and stubbornly. He was assisted in his task by a seven-man delegation of whom only one, Count Razumovsky, was authentically Russian. The rest of the team consisted of three Germans, a Pole, a Corsican, and a Greek.[4] This diversity of backgrounds pleased the Czar, who considered himself the most international of sovereigns.

Alexander refused to be worn down by the fatiguing discussions. He shouted to Talleyrand, "I thought France owed me something. You always talk to me about principles. Your public law means nothing to me. I don't know what it is. What do you think all your parchments and treaties matter to me?" And again: "The King of Prussia will be King of Prussia and of Saxony, as I shall be Emperor of Russia and King of Poland. The extent to which France is accommodating to me on these two points will be the measure of the extent to which I myself shall be accommodating to her, and on everything that may interest her."[5] Coming away from one meeting of the committee, he muttered with irritation, "Talleyrand acts as if he were the minister of Louis XIV!" He likewise railed against Metternich and told him to his face, "You are the only man in Austria who would dare speak to me in a rebellious tone!" Another time he threw his sword on the table and demanded that the Austrian minister give him satisfaction in single combat. Emperor Francis was stunned at the idea that a monarch who ruled by divine right should challenge to a duel a simple nobleman who had only recently been elevated to princely station. "Heavens, what times we live in!" he exclaimed, and took it upon himself to mediate the dispute. The Czar of Russia and the Austrian statesman did not cross swords, but from that day forth Alexander avoided the receptions given by Metternich, and when he met him in a drawing room pretended not to see him.

Meanwhile, Talleyrand was pursuing his work of subversion. On January 3, 1815, his conversations resulted in a secret alliance of France, Austria, and England, aimed against Russia and Prussia. Delighted to have sown discord among the former allies, Talleyrand wrote to Louis XVIII, "The coalition has been dissolved and dissolved forever." Alexander was so far from suspecting what had been plotted behind his back that he was again considering the possibility of a marriage between Grand Duchess Anne and the Duc de Berry. At the same time, without letting it be known, he was getting ready to accept the formation of a Poland that would not include Poznania and Galicia. He knew now that he could not obtain more without resorting to war, and he cared too much about his image as a champion of universal peace to launch into such an adventure.

While the conference table was the scene of angry confrontations, the drawing rooms were given over to the pleasures of feminine society. "The congress dances but takes not one step forward," said the Prince de Ligne. From the moment the negotiations opened Vienna had become an international caravansary teeming with kings and loose women, diplomats and pickpockets, princesses and merchants. Not a room could be found to rent in town. Each participant in the Congress had with him both male and female assistants charged with keeping an eye on the other plenipotentiaries. In addition to these amateur spies, of course, there were the regular spies of the Austrian police. Secret reports piled up in offices. Every reception or entertainment was an opportunity for informers. The most charming women tried to extract confidences from their partners as they danced, chatted, or made love. In theater boxes and bedrooms, between smiles or between embraces, each strove to worm secrets from the other. Among the army of ladies serving as volunteer informers, there were some who were in a class with the professionals: Talleyrand's beloved niece Dorothée, the Duchess of Kurland, and her sister, the Duchess of Sagan. As for the Czar, his best source of information was the licentious Princess Bagration. She tried to seduce Talleyrand, who rejected her. She proclaimed in spite that he was a dreadful sight, "with his eyes like a dead fish's and his heavy lids that he keeps lowered like the roof over a shop-window." He said in turn of this sharp-eared trollop: "She has a way of listening to secrets over her leg that must be a strain sometimes."[6]

In the midst of this sparkling chaos, Alexander the mystic found himself perfectly at ease. After great thoughts, little frivolities were restful to him. From trifling and jesting he drew extra energy for conducting public affairs. No doubt in Russia he would have shown himself less fond of worldly amusements. He was of that breed of men who are serious at home and dissipated abroad. To him, exoticism was both a stimulus to excesses and an excuse for them. He had insisted that Empress Elizabeth join him in Vienna, but his attentiveness was all for others. He attended all the receptions, flitted about in all the salons, laid himself out to charm all the pretty women. When the ball opened with the traditional polonaise, he led the dancers and enjoyed the sense of being followed by so many admiring glances. Wearing his close-fitting military tunic with the stiff embroidered collar, his thighs molded in white knee breeches, his calves encased in high patent-leather boots with pointed toes, he would glide and twirl with perfect ease to the sound of the music. Nearing forty, he had a face as attractive as ever: a rounded oval with a fresh complexion, bright eyes, narrow lips, a balding forehead, hair carefully arranged on the top of his head, and wavy sideburns like silk floss on his cheeks. Every morning he washed his face with a piece of ice to tone his flesh. Being somewhat nearsighted he used a lorgnette, and his slight deafness made him bend his head gracefully toward his interlocutors. When conversing with women he was courtly in the extreme, and the variety and warmth of his compliments even made some of them doubt his sincerity. Certain ladies found him almost "too kind." In turn, or simultaneously, he took a fancy to Princess Gabrielle of Auersperg, "the virtuous beauty"; Countess Caroline Szechenyi, "the coquettish beauty"; Countess Sophie Zichy, "the vulgar beauty"; Countess Esterhazy, "the astonishing beauty"; Julie Zichy, "the dazzling beauty"; and Countess Saaran, "the beauty of youth." To this collection of pretty Viennese women were added Metternich's two friends, the Duchess of Sagan and Princess Bagration, widow of the hero of 1812 who had fallen at Borodino, as well as a number of young women of less importance. According to the report of a detective, "at supper at Charles Zichy's, Alexander and Countess Vbrna discussed the question of whether it took a man or a woman more time to dress, and to find out they made a wager and withdrew to disrobe. Countess Vbrna won."

Most of the time the flowery compliments and the parlor games were of no consequence. Fond of light touches, amorous glances, and courtly allusions, Alexander was content to hear the rustle of romance. Police reports were full of consistent observations: "Of all the society ladies he has seen, Princess Léopoldine Liechtenstein is the one whom Alexander likes most. It is said in this connection that he shows himself to be very much a Russian, for he likes women of ice." And again: "Alexander pays much attention to Princess Esterhazy, Sophie Zichy, and Princess Auersperg. He dances and talks a great deal with Princess Liechtenstein and the young Szechenyi. The first two already believe that they have caught him in their nets; but the others recognize that for Alexander, here, as in Frankfurt and elsewhere, it is purely a flirtation." However, the spies assigned to the Czar by the Austrian Minister of Police, Baron Hager, noted that at night he sometimes slipped into the town house where the ravishing Princess Bagration was staying and stole out again three hours later. Some also claimed they had seen him walking rapidly down a dark corridor of the Hofburg toward the rooms occupied by two of his wife's ladies-in-waiting.[7] In any case, the whole congress was swept up in a whirlwind of amorous adventures, and the Austrian police were so busy they didn't know which way to turn. In a jumble of observations they noted that "Lord Stewart has again spent the whole night at the Sagan woman's," that "the affair between François Palffy and la Bigottini is coming to an end," that "Wellington has brought his mistress, Grassini, here," and that Prince Volkonsky received at his home every evening a young lady by the name of Josephine Wolters, "often dressed as a man."[8] As for the Czar's sister, Grand Duchess Catherine, "the dear madcap" was deep into an affair with Prince William of Württemberg, whom she wished to marry. Around the palaces, in the parks, in outdoor cafés the same mood of abandon reigned. People danced and dallied to the sound of violins while the diplomats tried to settle the fate of Europe.

Even the virtuous Empress Elizabeth felt her head spinning. Long since abandoned by the Czar, she had just met again in Vienna her old admirer, Prince Adam Czartoryski. Age had left its mark on her features, but Czartoryski found her just as disturbing as during their first meetings. He wrote in his journal, "I see her here very changed, but to me she is still the same from the point of view of her feelings and mine (they have lost some of their warmth but are still strong enough so that the prospect of not seeing her at all is painful to me). I have seen her only once so far. Having been rather ill received, I am having a bad day. . . . Second meeting. New obligations are imposed. She is, as always, an angel. Her letter. . . . She is still my first and only object of adoration. . . . Exchange of rings. . . . I desire her happiness and am jealous of that happiness; I adore her to distraction and yet. . . . This long uncertainty, this resistance, these continual disappointments and these twenty years of waiting; the tragedy of a single infidelity has upset certain very delicate principles. But that is no excuse for me, for I have forgiven her with all my heart and she is worthy not of forgiveness but of love, respect, adoration." The Empress, for her part, wrote her mother complaining that she was obliged by her situation to "sacrifice the true happiness of my life to the legal order, by separating myself from the being whom, for the fourteen best years of my existence, I have been accustomed to regard as another self."[9]

Thus the love relations between the Empress and Prince Czartoryski, which had been broken off in 1807 at the time of Elizabeth's affair with the cavalry ensign Okhotnikov, resumed with fresh ardor on the banks of the Danube. He had "forgiven her with all his heart" for her former infidelity, and she again considered him the incarnation of "the true happiness of her life." To be sure there was considerable romanticism in this reciprocal passion, and it was held in check on both sides by a sense of duty. As physical relations between them were forbidden, their feeling for each other only grew more intense. They played a game in which each hurt the other by refusing the surrender they both desired. The temptation grew stronger every time they met. "Czartoryski continues very much in favor with the Empress," stated a police report of October 3, 1814. Did they remain prisoners of their principles to the end, or did they finally yield to their passion? It may be supposed that in course of time Elizabeth let herself be persuaded by her lover and that the Czar was informed of it. Indeed, while betraying his wife in private, Alexander became increasingly harsh with her in public, as if he were satisfying some old grudge against her. The reports of the Austrian police mentioned many insults that Alexander inflicted on his wife: "Note to Baron Hager, January 2, 1815. This is what they are saying at Etienne Zichy's: 1) that last Friday Alexander forced his poor wife to go to the ball at Princess Bagration's. The Empress reluctantly obeyed and the sofa on which she sat down was in such bad repair that it broke under her; 2) that on Saturday there was a family dinner at Alexander's during which he horribly abused the Empress, her brother, and her sister. They say that the Empress will not return to Russia but will go to her brother's in Karlsruhe."

A second police report, dated February 5, 1815: "The Empress of Russia . . . whose union is so unhappy, never dines with the Emperor or with her sisters-in-law, the Grand Duchesses. . . . It is said that she will not return to St. Petersburg. If that is really so, the fact will make a profound impression in the capital, where the Empress is very popular and much beloved."

A little later, another report of the same nature: "At the last ball at Bagration's, when the Empress of Russia entered and people exclaimed, 'Oh, how beautiful she is! She certainly is a fine woman!' Alexander, stung to the quick and thinking this was a criticism of him, said quite audibly, 'Well, *I* don't think so! That's not my opinion at all!' "

Elizabeth bore everything without a murmur and even found excuses for her husband's coldness. "I must say in fairness that the Emperor has been nice to me," she wrote her mother. "He proposed of his own accord that I should dine with him more frequently, and even in private when I am alone. One must judge things according to individual characters, and that is a great deal for him."[10]

The beauty, dignity, and discretion of the disdained wife were the admiration of those around her, despite their habitual inclination to backbiting. Madame de Staël saw her as "the angel of Russia," and the Comte de La Garde wrote, "Endowed with a bewitching face, her eyes reflected the purity of her soul. She had the most beautiful ash-blond hair, which she usually left floating on her shoulders. Her figure was elegant, supple and flexible, and even when she was masked her bearing betrayed her in an instant. With a charming character she combined a lively, cultivated mind, the love of fine arts, and a boundless generosity."[11]

Although she had never had a taste for society, with the discipline of her rank she attended all receptions. At certain balls the ladies wore thirty million francs' worth of jewels. On October 18, 1814, for the anniversary of the battle of Leipzig, there was a great gala evening in the Prater, during which Alexander drank to the health "of the people and the army." The commemorative celebration continued the next day at the palace of the Russian ambassador, Count Razumovsky. At a table set for 360 guests the imperial couple received all the high personages of Europe and all superior officers of the allied armies—two emperors, four kings, thirty reigning princes. Emperor Francis was placed on Elizabeth's right, while the Czar, seated next to the Empress of Austria, tried vainly to converse with her: They were both half deaf, but not in the same ear. On December 6 an indoor riding ring was transformed into a ballroom to celebrate Grand Duchess Catherine's name day. The guests admired Russian dances performed in national costume. Supper was served on fifty tables with six places each, by the light of a forest of candles. The Czar and Czarina regaled their guests with the rarest gastronomic specialties: sterlets from the Volga, oysters from Cancale and Ostend, truffles from Périgord, oranges from Palermo, pineapples from the imperial greenhouses in Moscow, strawberries from England, and grapes from France. In addition, each guest had before him a plate of cherries that had been brought from St. Petersburg in the dead of winter and had cost one silver ruble apiece. The Comte de La Garde wrote in wondering admiration, "In truth, I can scarcely believe my own memories when I look back on that splendid prodigality." After supper the dancing resumed. As usual, Alexander joined in the exercise and flirted with his successive partners. "As for the emperor of Russia, he dances while Rome is burning," wrote E. Cooke, Castlereagh's secretary.

Underneath all this frenetic social and political activity lay a single obsession shared by all the allies: Napoleon. He might be relegated to his island for now, "playing Robinson Crusoe," as the Prince de Ligne said jestingly, but Talleyrand continued to demand that the Corsican be moved far from the Mediterranean coast. As a place of internment he proposed the Azores, "five hundred leagues," he said, "from all land." Wellington, who had just arrived in Vienna, was of the same opinion. Metternich, however, thought that before deporting the fallen emperor elsewhere they must wait for him to commit some rash act that would serve as a pretext. As for the Czar, he was categorically opposed to considering a new place of detention for his former enemy, and for two reasons: First, from the reports of his spies of both sexes he guessed that a secret treaty had indeed recently been signed among England, Austria, and France against Russia and Prussia; second, he had just learned from Talleyrand that Louis XVIII had rejected the possibility of a marriage between the Duc de Berry and Grand Duchess Anne. Forgetting that he himself had formerly been hostile to this union, he became indignant that this gouty kinglet, set upon the throne thanks to the efforts of Russia and the allies, should consider a Romanov unworthy of his nephew! This new affront reawakened Alexander's rancor against the Bourbons and made him more sympathetic toward Napoleon, who at least had always shown himself to be an honest adversary. His affectionate correspondence with Queen Hortense and his daily walks through the streets of Vienna arm-in-arm with her brother, Prince Eugene de Beauharnais, were a disguised reply to the insults he received from the Tuileries. "By what right," he said, "should this man be dragged away from the island of Elba, which he received last year by treaty?"

Discussions of Napoleon's future were shattered by a piece of news that struck the congress like a bolt of lightning. During the night of March 6, 1815, Metternich received a message that the ex-Emperor of the French had left his island for an unknown destination. At eight o'clock in the morning he hastened to Emperor Francis who, staggered by the news, ordered him to go at once to the Emperor of Russia and the King of Prussia. For the first time in three months of diplomatic coldness, Metternich went to see the Czar. When he heard what had happened, Alexander declared without hesitation that he was ready to strike back. In the face of the common peril, the disagreements of yesterday were forgotten and the coalition came together again as a matter of course. Then the Czar said magnanimously to Metternich, "We still have a personal difference to settle. We are both Christians; our holy law commands us to pardon offenses. Let us embrace and let all be forgotten."[12]

Within the hour, the members of the congress met to examine the situation. Since Alexander had always maintained that there was no risk in leaving Napoleon on his island, he felt himself in the position of the accused. It was to Alexander that the captive had broken his word. He resented this action personally, all the while admiring Napoleon for having taken it. What daring! He said reproachfully to Wellington, "How could you have let him leave his island?" The Englishman replied imperturbably, "Why did you put him there?" They did not yet know the intentions of the returning exile. Talleyrand believed, or pretended to believe, that he would land in Italy and throw himself upon Switzerland. Metternich cut him short, declaring, "He will go straight to Paris." They all hoped that if Napoleon set foot on French soil he would be arrested as soon as he took the first step, without striking a blow. But could the Bourbons count on the loyalty of the French people? Certain ministers doubted it, and the following days proved them right. After Napoleon landed in the Gulf of Juan, near Cannes, he advanced rapidly toward Paris; the towns opened enthusiastically before him. Peasants cheered him, soldiers refused to fire upon him, and Marshal Ney, after promising to "bring the usurper back in an iron cage," met his Emperor at Auxerre and went over to his side. Louis XVIII, abandoned by all, fled to Ghent.

When Napoleon moved back into the Tuileries on March 20, 1815, he discovered in the files of the Ministry of Foreign Affairs the text of the secret treaty of January 3, 1815, which the King, in his haste, had forgotten to take with him. Delighted with his find, he instructed the Secretary of the Russian legation, Butiagin, who had stayed in Paris, to deliver the document to the Czar in Vienna, so as to open his eyes to the duplicity of his so-called allies and to induce him to enter into direct negotiations with France. Alexander, who had long suspected his partners' hypocrisy, first gave way to violent anger. Capo d'Istria saw him striding up and down his study and noticed that his ears were abnormally red. But the Czar soon regained his self-control. Having summoned Metternich, he asked him if he knew "this document." As the Austrian Chancellor stood mute with shock, Alexander declared that the time for diplomatic trickery was past and that the allies must unite in common combat against the usurper. Then, walking up to the fireplace, he threw the document into the fire. Similarly, to the King of Bavaria, who came to offer him his apologies, he said, "You were drawn into it, I no longer think about it."

But together with the copy of the treaty, Butiagin had given Alexander a letter from Queen Hortense begging him to look more favorably upon Napoleon: "The entire nation is devoted to the Emperor, but it wants peace and [Napoleon] will be wise enough to follow the dominant opinion on that question, for he has already discovered—and the Bourbons are an example of it—that one can remain a sovereign only by not separating one's cause from that of the nation. . . . People are waiting impatiently to know the intentions of Emperor Alexander; they say that it is in his interest to be at peace with France, that he need never fear that he will be troubled on the Polish question. . . . [Napoleon] promises a liberal constitution and freedom of the press; in a word, he wants to satisfy everyone, and if he failed to do so he could not remain in place. . . . If you are our friend, all will be well." In short, Napoleon had returned from Elba with the soul of a lamb.

In spite of the affection he felt for his correspondent, Alexander remained adamant. Besides, on March 25 he had already signed the declaration of the eight powers condemning Napoleon's conduct: "Napoleon Bonaparte has placed himself outside civil and social relations and, as the enemy and disturber of world peace, has delivered himself up to public justice."

By a new pact of alliance, the Czar committed himself to raise 150,000 troops and not to lay down his arms until the common enemy had been definitively crushed. The total allied forces were to come to 800,000 soldiers. The Russian army, which had evacuated France the year before, received orders to set out again for the banks of the Rhine.

In Vienna the party was over: no more balls, no more banquets. In the reception halls the chandeliers were extinguished. The orchestras were out of work. The pretty spies had nothing to do. The congress completed its work in haste. In the general disarray, Russia obtained the grand duchy of Warsaw except for Poznan, Bromberg (Bydgoszcz), and Thorn, which were left to Prussia as compensation for the continuing independence of Saxony. In addition, the Tarnopol region, which had been ceded to Russia in 1809, was restored to Austria, and Krakow was declared a free city. Alexander took the title of King of Poland and reserved the right to give that state, which was to "enjoy a separate administration," "the internal development he judged appropriate." "The duchy of Warsaw, with the exception of the parts for which other provision has been made, is united to the Russian empire," the document read. "It will be bound to it irrevocably by its constitution, to be possessed by His Majesty the Emperor of all the Russias, his heirs and successors in perpetuity." And to avoid any misunderstanding, the Czar wrote in French to the President of the Polish Senate, Count Ostrovsky: "In assuming the title of King of Poland, I have wanted to satisfy the wishes of the nation. The kingdom of Poland will be united to the empire of Russia by the provisions of its own constitution, on which I wish to base the happiness of the country. While the crucial consideration of general peace has made it impossible for all the Poles to be united under the same scepter, I have at least tried to alleviate the hardships of separation, insofar as possible, and to obtain for them everywhere the enjoyment of their nationality."

Treaties followed one after another: The territory of Genoa was ceded to the King of Sardinia; a constitutive act established the new German Confederation; the Austrians were strengthened in the Lombardo-Venetian kingdom; on June 9, 1815, the plenipotentiaries signed the Final Act that fixed forever the conditions of the great partition of Europe.

Two weeks before the official closing of the congress, Alexander left Vienna to move closer to the Rhine. After brief stays in Munich and Stuttgart, he settled down in the little town of Heilbronn, near the place chosen for the future headquarters of his army, there to await the arrival of his troops. Since the return of Napoleon he had felt a deep anxiety that was no longer only political but also religious. How could God, who was manifestly on the side of the allies, have allowed the devil to come out of his box? What was one to think of the French, who acclaimed a despot whom Alexander had had so much trouble ridding them of? Was it necessary once again to spill the blood of Russian soldiers to reestablish the Bourbons on the throne? Was not the Almighty punishing the Czar for having amused himself too much in Vienna? Assailed by all these questions, Alexander sought answers to them in the pious books sent to him by his friend Koshelev. After the pomp and splendor of Vienna, Stuttgart, and Munich, he thirsted after solitude and meditation. He would have liked to find at his side a superior being, a kind of guardian angel who would understand him and point out to him the path leading upwards. A year before, in Bruchsal, Mademoiselle Stourdza, the future Countess Edling, lady-in-waiting to the Empress, had presented to him the celebrated mystic Jung-Stilling, a disciple of Swedenborg. He regretted that he had exchanged only a few innocuous words with that great mind. But the same Mademoiselle Stourdza had once spoken to him of her friend, Baroness Julie von Krüdener, an exceptional woman capable of bringing light to the most tortured souls. Only recently Madame von Krüdener had given evidence of an extraordinary gift of prophecy by announcing in a letter the forthcoming return of Napoleon: "The storm is approaching; those lilies which the Eternal had preserved, that emblem of a pure and fragile flower that broke an iron scepter, because the Almighty wished it so, those lilies which should have summoned men to the love of God, to repentance, have appeared only to disappear. The lesson has been given, and men, more hardened than ever, dream only of tumult."[13] These words still rang in the memory of Alexander, who had learned of the message from Mademoiselle Stourdza. There was no question that Baroness von Krüdener bore within her the living word of God. Why could he not speak with this inspired person now? Where was she at the moment?

While he was wondering about her one evening in the silence of his study, Prince Volkonsky came to announce with an air of annoyance that a Russian visitor requested an audience with His Majesty, despite the lateness of the hour. It was Baroness von Krüdener. Increasingly inclined to superstition, Alexander was dazzled as by a ray of light falling from heaven. "You can judge of my astonishment," he said later to Mademoiselle Stourdza. "I thought I was dreaming. . . . I received her immediately, and as if she had read my soul, she spoke strong, consoling words to me which calmed the inner turmoil which had obsessed me for so long."[14]

In fact, long before Alexander met Julie von Krüdener, he had learned all about her from people around him. The daughter of a Livonian gentleman of very old family, Baron von Vietinghof, and widow of an eminent Russian diplomat, she had had a very eventful love life, had traveled all over Europe, living in Italy, France, Germany, and Switzerland, had formed friendships with Chateaubriand, Bernardin de Saint-Pierre, Madame de Staël, Benjamin Constant, Queen Hortense, and Queen Louise of Prussia, and had published in Paris a sentimental novel entitled *Valérie*. After the death of her husband and the loss of part of her fortune, she had gradually turned away from the handsome officers and brilliant diplomats who until then had occupied her thoughts and excited her senses. With the approach of old age she now found peace only in the practice of religion. She had developed a passion for the doctrines of Swedenborg and considered herself called upon to regenerate humanity by serving as an intermediary between the material world and the spiritual world. When she came to visit Alexander she was sure of bringing him the divine illumination he needed to lead his people.

Although at fifty she was a faded creature with irregular features, a blotchy complexion, a pointed nose, and a blond wig, Alexander was conquered as soon as he saw her. After having courted so many beauties in Vienna, the Czar should not have felt any attraction for his nocturnal visitor. And indeed, he did not think of her as a pleasing woman or one whom he might charm. That was not what he was looking for. With an agreeable shiver he felt the intensity of her look, heard the inflection of her authoritarian voice. He had recently received from Koshelev a mystical book, translated by Labzin from German, entitled *A Cloud over the Sanctuary*. The work was so difficult that he had been unable to understand it. He spoke of it to Madame von Krüdener and effortlessly, on the spot, she explained to him the meaning of the most obscure passages, then launched into a sermon that left him speechless. In a harsh tone she pointed out his errors, reproached him for his pride, accused him of not having been able to repent before God. "No, Sire," she cried, "you have not yet approached the God-man like a criminal who comes to ask for mercy. You have not renounced your sins and have not humbled yourself before Christ. And that is why you have not found inner peace!" This allusion to the assassination of Paul I shook Alexander, who did not know how to reply. For nearly three hours the prophetess berated her distraught sovereign in a ringing voice. No one had ever dared to treat him like this. It hurt. It was good. He bent his head and burst into sobs. Fearing that she had gone too far, Madame von Krüdener justified herself by invoking the will of God. "I have only fulfilled a sacred duty toward you," she said. "Fear nothing," replied Alexander, "all your words have found a place in my heart." And he asked her to follow him everywhere to sustain him with her edifying conversation.

Very quickly she reinforced in him the idea that he was the "White Angel," Napoleon's rival, and that sooner or later the "Black Angel" would succumb to the blows of his righteous adversaries. Then it would be up to the Czar to apply to universal politics the principles of primitive Christianity. Laharpe, who was worried about the meddling of this visionary, wrote his former pupil that he disapproved of the new "crusade" against France. Alexander immediately sent him a sharply worded reply: "To bow to the spirit of evil is to consolidate his power, it is to offer him the means of establishing his tyranny in a more terrible way than the first time. We must have the courage to combat him and, with the help of divine Providence, of unity and perseverance, we shall reach a happy outcome. Such is my conviction."

While preparations were being made for the great confrontation between the allied armies and the reconstituted army of Napoleon, Alexander left Heilbronn for Heidelberg, where he moved into the little house of the Englishman Pickford. Henceforth it was there that he would await the arrival of his troops. Madame von Krüdener came to join him. She lived with her daughter, her son-in-law, and her friend, the preacher Empaytaz, in a peasant hut nearby. Every evening Alexander went to her house, read the Bible by her side, listened to her commentaries, her advice, and the account of her visions, and bent his head when she addressed to him some of the vehement reproaches of which she had the secret. She was poor and, while claiming to be disinterested, willingly accepted financial help from the Czar. Many notes he sent to Golitzin mentioned subsidies to be paid anonymously to Madame von Krüdener and her family; she gratefully referred to him as her "celestial banker." By her side he claimed to feel "the power of the grace and spirit of Jesus." His dream, the old dream of his youth, would have been to retire to a hermitage. But he had to look after the affairs of the world.

The Belgian campaign was getting organized. Wellington was already in Brussels with 90,000 English, Hanoverians, Dutch, and Belgians; Blücher was in Namur with 120,000 Prussians. Large Austrian and Russian forces were heading toward France. As soon as they arrived the offensive would begin. While the allies were discussing strategy at headquarters, Napoleon decided to attack before their reinforcements arrived. On June 15 he crossed the Sambre and routed the Anglo-Prussian armies at Ligny. Stunned by this defeat, the allies met in a council of war to work out plans for a counterattack. Their anxiety was of short duration. On June 22 they received news of the decisive victory of Wellington and Blücher at Waterloo. With mystical fervor Alexander declared: "I am a great sinner, but the Lord is willing to make use of me to bring peace to the nations."

Events moved quickly: Napoleon abdicated for the second time, the capital of France was opened to the Prussians, Louis XVIII could return. Alexander was burning to be back in Paris himself to seal the victory of good over evil. Abandoning Madame von Krüdener, he left with only a detachment of Cossacks as escort and recklessly crossed two hundred versts of a country that the allies had not yet pacified. His faith in Providence assured him that he would not be attacked en route.

XII

THE HOLY ALLIANCE

On July 10, 1815, Alexander arrived in Paris and moved back into the Elysée Palace. Within half an hour he received a visit from Louis XVIII, who had come home to the Tuileries. This time the King was very gracious and the Czar gave him a good welcome. While he still had a personal aversion to the pretentious Bourbon, Alexander was more than ever convinced of the necessity of a rapprochement between Russia and France. Since his allies had betrayed him and the final victory over Napoleon had been won without the assistance of Russian troops, he had felt lately that his position in the coalition was unstable. True to his ideas, he meant to present himself as the protector of the French people. When the two sovereigns parted after an hour's conversation, Alexander was wearing across his chest the blue ribbon of the Order of the Saint-Esprit.

Five days later Napoleon, having failed in all his enterprises, embarked on the *Bellerophon* and entrusted his destiny to the generosity of England. "I come, like Themistocles, to sit at the hearth of the British people," he wrote. That "hearth" was to be called St. Helena.

In Paris, meanwhile, the royal power was being strengthened, with the support of Talleyrand and Fouché. The new Prefect of Police, Decazes, had his hands full maintaining order in a population that was demoralized, ill fed, a prey to the violence of armies of occupation. There was only a small Russian detachment in the capital, but Blücher's and Wellington's troops were there in force. The Prussians proved especially arrogant and brutal. They camped in the Tuileries, in the Luxembourg gardens, on the parvis in front of Notre-Dame. At night they went marauding, saber in hand, at the octrois of the city. Blücher himself incited them to the worst acts of extortion, as if he were trying to revenge himself upon civilians for the defeats that had been inflicted on him in former days by soldiers. In reprisal, he even decided to blow up the Pont d'Iéna (Jena), which he found guilty of bearing the name of a victory of Napoleon over the Prussians. Preparations had already been made for the explosion when Talleyrand attempted to intervene. "I'd like Monsieur de Talleyrand to be on it at that moment [when the bridge blows up]," replied the irascible Blücher. Louis XVIII informed him at once that it would not be Monsieur de Talleyrand but the King himself who would go up with the bridge.* Alexander was outraged by Blücher's crudeness and also protested. In the end the Pont d'Iéna remained standing but became the Pont de l'Ecole militaire, to satisfy, said Talleyrand, "the barbarous vanity of the Prussians."

Still concerned with consolidating the throne of Louis XVIII in the midst of a battered and divided people, the Czar tried to convince his skeptical allies that no further amputations of French territory should be made. Further, he pretended to know nothing about the excesses of the extremists, the "white terror" that reigned in the provinces and compromised the prestige of the monarchy. For the royalists, sworn enemies of the Bonapartists, were already in full cry after liberals, constitutionists, the wavering, all who did not share their fanatical opinions.

The Czar found this second stay in Paris less enjoyable than the first. Perhaps he had aged; perhaps he had grown blasé; or perhaps the frivolous French had lost their charm for him. In any event, in spite of reading the Bible, he increasingly inclined to melancholy. The feeling of the inevitability of fate had taken such deep root that he would walk the streets of Paris alone, in defiance of all prudence. Some of the passersby doffed their hats to him. But no one cried, "Long live Em-

---

*It is supposed to be Talleyrand who suggested this proud answer to Louis XVIII.

peror Alexander!" anymore. He could also be seen on horseback, with his equerry, on the paths of the Champs-Elysées. When he went out in a barouche he was accompanied by two French lackeys and was driven by a French coachman. Englishmen, Prussians, and Russians took turns guarding his residence.

A month after he had moved into the Elysée Palace a division of Russian grenadiers and another of cuirassiers made a triumphal entry into the city. But during the parade certain units made a mistake and fell out of step. This fault assumed inordinate proportions in the Czar's mind. He saw it as an insult to his honor, to the greatness of Russia. All the stupid severity of Gatchina rose up in him again. In the very manner of his father, he flew into a rage against two colonels whom he judged guilty and had them placed under arrest in the palace itself. General Ermolov pointed out to him in vain that on the day in question the palace guardpost was manned by British troops. "So much the worse for [the colonels]!" he cried. "Their shame will only be the greater!" Another time, when Volkonsky was unable to find a certain document, Alexander shouted in his face, "I'll send you to a place you won't be able to find on your maps!"[1] Witnesses to the scene were dumbfounded; they saw before them the specter of Paul I in one of his moments of fury. Toward evening, when the Czar had put his hand on the document again, he calmed down, summoned Volkonsky, and said to him with a laugh, "Admit that you were at fault. Let us make peace!" "You reprimand me in front of everyone, Sire," said Volkonsky, "and you make peace when we are alone."

Notwithstanding this carping concern for the way he was served and these sudden fits of anger over trifles, Alexander continued to believe that he was inspired by Christ. Having brought Madame von Krüdener to Paris, he settled her in the Hôtel Montchenu at 35 faubourg Saint-Honoré, near the Elysée Palace. He would go to see her almost every evening, slipping into the house by a secret door opening onto the Champs-Elysées. He would have hardly crossed the threshold when he heard the Baroness saying to him, in a trance, "My brother in Christ, I thank you for having come. Let us pray, let us pray for divine mercy to be with us." In a great, dark drawing room, dilapidated and sparsely furnished, he would attend a prayer session and an improvised sermon. They would read Holy Scriptures, comment on the sweet teachings with tears in their eyes, and talk about the best way to conduct politics in a manner pleasing to God. Little by little, under the influence of his hostess, Alexander came to have a distaste for the society life he had been so fond of in Vienna. Now he took pleasure not in dallying to the sound of violins but in engaging in interminable, incoherent conversations studded with biblical quotations; not in flirting with a pretty woman but in communing with a faded, voluble person for whom, late in life, sacred love had replaced profane love. "Alexander is the chosen of the Lord," wrote Madame von Krüdener. "He walks in the paths of renunciation. This spiritual bond, created by God, increasingly gains strength. When he is obliged to go out into society from time to time, it is never to a play or a ball. He told me that such things had the same effect on him as a funeral."

But sometimes at the home of his spiritual guide he met French celebrities who had come to visit her either out of curiosity or in the hope of getting close to His Majesty. Among her guests were the Duchesses de Bourbon, de Doudeauville, and de Duras; Madame Récamier, Madame de Genlis, Michaud, Benjamin Constant, and Bergasse, Mesmer's disciple. Lamartine submitted to the high priestess of the Hôtel Montchenu an epistle dedicated to "the wise man who wears a crown," and Chateaubriand, whom she patronized, begged the Czar to "dethrone the Revolution after having dethroned our oppressor."[2] Nevertheless, the author of the *Génie du christianisme (The Genius of Christianity)* was not to remain long under the spell of the mystic lady. "Madame von Krüdener had invited me to one of those sessions of celestial sorcery," he wrote later in his *Mémoires d'outre-tombe (Memoirs from Beyond the Tomb)*. "Although I am a man of dreams and fancies, I hate unreason, abominate the nebulous, and despise charlatanism. The scene bored me: the more I tried to pray, the more I felt the barrenness of my soul. I could find nothing to say to God, and the Devil was tempting me to laugh." But Chateaubriand did respond to the luminous serenity of the Czar.

Alexander was indifferent to these contacts with a few brilliant representatives of the salons and the world of letters. When he was asked to intercede with Louis XVIII to obtain a pardon for General La Bédoyère and Marshal Ney, he contented himself with sighing, in Madame von Krüdener's presence, "What's the use of being so harsh? What do they hope to accomplish? . . . If justice has its claims, charity makes its own demands." But he said not a word to the King and let the two men be shot for rallying to Napoleon's cause when they had been ordered to arrest him after his return from the island of Elba.

To impress his allies by a display of Russian military force and to strengthen his hand at the final negotiations, Alexander decided to organize a gigantic review in the plain of Vertus, 120 versts east of Paris, near Epernay. This was the very site of the battle of Châlons, the famous "Catalaunian fields" where in 451 the Roman general Aetius had stopped the hordes of Attila. Participating in the demonstration were seven cavalry divisions and eleven infantry divisions, 150,000 men in all, with 540 cannon and ninety-six generals. The Czar had personally planned every detail of the troop movements. For weeks his entire general staff had been in a fever of activity. Preparations would not have been made with more intensity, or more apprehension, for a great battle. The dress rehearsal, held in the presence of His Majesty and the young Grand Dukes, went off without a hitch. The next day distinguished foreigners began to arrive in camp: Emperor Francis, the King of Prussia, Wellington, Schwarzenberg; innumerable marshals, generals, and princes come from Paris, the Hague, Berlin, and London; and, of course, the perennial Baroness von Krüdener, flanked by her daughter, her son-in-law, and Empaytaz. All the houses in Vertus and the surroundings had been requisitioned to lodge the important guests. It was Fontaine, Napoleon's favorite architect, who had decorated the tents intended for councils and banquets. The camp, brightly lit and gay with flags, besieged by a swarm of itinerant pedlars, looked like a fairground crowded with soldiers. Among the white tents could be seen all the uniforms of Russia. The trumpeters and drummers were practicing in the woods. From the last foot soldier brushing his coat to the highest general reviewing his marching orders, every man was gripped by the same anxiety: if only Alexander was satisfied with the performance!

On September 10, in splendid weather, the review began before the Czar's guests assembled on a hill. For the first time, Grand Duke Nicholas commanded a brigade of grenadiers and Grand Duke Michael an artillery unit. At the head of the army was Field Marshal Barclay de Tolly. The interminable review dazzled all the connoisseurs. At a signal given by artillery fire, the dotted lines of men broke up, lengthened, turned, joined, separated. Not one error in the maneuver. The soldiers marched like automatons. Even the horses kept perfect alignment and seemed to nod their heads in time. One regiment replaced another, differing only by the color of their uniforms. As soon as the drums and fifes fell silent, the guests could hear the sound of this vast movement, like the roar of a river. When the troops had formed into squares again, artillery salvos shook the earth and the landscape was obscured behind puffs of smoke. Under cover of this cloudy screen, the army hastily evacuated the drill ground. After twelve minutes of intensive firing, silence returned, the veil of smoke parted, and the plain appeared deserted. None of the allies had expected this last exploit. Wellington declared, "I would never have believed that an army could be brought to such perfection!" And Alexander exclaimed enthusiastically, "I see that my army is the first in the world and that there is nothing it cannot do!"

Seated in a court barouche—a carriage and four with two postilions —Madame von Krüdener was beaming. A straw hat topped her false blond hair. The attentions with which she was surrounded made her feel as if she were the heroine of the day, the true Empress of Russia, with the Emperor, her mystical bridegroom, at her side. "I saw at the head of the army the man of great destinies, the man prepared before the ages and for the ages," she wrote. "The Eternal had summoned Alexander and, obediently, Alexander had answered to the call of the Eternal." She did not suspect that this apotheosis presaged her own decline. On that day the Czar had already resolved to separate from her. Perhaps he was tired of her; perhaps he had seen through her. In any event, he did not yet let her know that he was finished with her. The same evening she reigned over the dinner he gave for three hundred of his guests. The next day, St. Alexander's day, with the allied sovereigns she attended the "Te Deum" celebrated out of doors by seven priests on seven altars before 150,000 troops ranged in seven squares. A banquet for the senior officers followed. Alexander congratulated them upon the good performance of their regiments, announced that he was conferring the title of Prince upon Field Marshal Barclay de Tolly, and promised the soldiers that they would soon return home. "That day was the finest day of my life," he said to Madame von Krüdener. "Never shall I forget it. My heart was filled with love for my enemies. I was able to pray fervently for all of them, and weeping at the foot of Christ's cross I asked for the salvation of France."[3]

Having reached this point of religious exaltation, Alexander turned his thoughts to reinforcing the decisions of the great powers—Russia, Prussia, and Austria—by a solemn declaration of international fraternity and submission to the commandments of the Bible. Thus, he thought, the political alliance would be matched by a mystical alliance that would give it its true significance. For a long time he had been convinced that a sovereign could guide his people only by having constant reference to divine will. His conversations with Madame von Krüdener had only confirmed this belief. He roughed out on paper the outline of a sacred agreement to be called "the Holy Alliance," the final drafting of which was entrusted to Stourdza and Capo d'Istria. This treaty was unprecedented in the history of European diplomacy. In accordance with the Czar's instructions it began with an invocation to "the Very Holy and Indivisible Trinity." Its signatories pledged to take as their only rule of conduct "the precepts of justice, charity, and peace, which, far from being solely applicable to life, should on the contrary have a direct influence on the decisions of princes." The text that followed spelled out the full significance of this statement: "In conformity with the words of the Holy Scriptures, which command all men to look upon each other as brothers, the three contracting monarchs shall remain united by the bonds of a true and indissoluble fraternity, and, considering themselves as compatriots, on all occasions and in all places they shall lend each other assistance, help, and aid; regarding themselves as the fathers of their subjects and armies, they shall guide them in this same spirit of fraternity by which they themselves are animated so as to protect religion, peace, and justice." Lastly, the three allied princes affirmed that they were "delegated by Providence to govern the three branches of a single family."

Alexander was very proud of this confused, bombastic document designed to unite three sovereigns of rival faiths—Catholic, Russian Orthodox, and Protestant. The King of Prussia readily agreed to sign a profession of faith that recalled to him the words exchanged ten years before, at night, beside the tomb of Frederick the Great at Potsdam. Emperor Francis first showed some reluctance to launch into mysticism but soon yielded to pressure from Metternich, who referred contemptuously to the treaty as an "empty, echoing monument." In reality, the Chancellor of Austria immediately foresaw a way in which he could utilize the Holy Alliance for practical ends. The sovereigns' duty to help each other so as to make peace reign among nations carried with it, for each, an invitation to crush revolutionary plots not only in his own country but also in his neighbor's. By posing as champions of the legal order they would turn themselves into the policemen of Europe. The same thought had very probably occurred to Alexander. His love for perfect alignment and for the tranquillity of peoples readily inclined him to a kind of paternalistic oppression. The God to whom he prayed wore a gendarme's uniform. It would seem that the Czar, always a secret man, always of two minds and with tangled motives, hid political calculation behind a sincere idealism. Simultaneously and effortlessly he was both wily politician and religious mystic. Besides, was it not again the Lord that he was honoring in serving Russia? Everything was mixed together in his head—territorial conquests and Bible teachings, the wine of banquets and the wine of communion.

The pact of the Holy Alliance was signed on September 26, 1815, by the Czar, Emperor Francis, and the King of Prussia. France, Sweden, Spain, and the kingdoms of Naples and Sardinia were to join in later. Insular England, always mistrustful, would refuse politely; the Sultan obviously could not participate in a league formed under the sign of the cross; and the Pope, who was also invited to subscribe to the pact, declined because the document that was submitted to him did not take into account the distinctions between faiths.

When one has climbed to such heights, it is difficult to come down again to base, material questions. The more elevated the principles, the more disappointing their application. However, after the treaty of the Holy Alliance, Alexander had to attend to the treaty with France, which had been defeated a second time. He had written in his own hand a note stating that to dismember France again would be incompatible with the plan for the balance of power in Europe. He had to defend this view against the representatives of Prussia, who were demanding Flanders, Alsace, Lorraine, Franche-Comté, Burgundy, Savoy, and Saarland. On the Czar's advice, Louis XVIII threatened to abdicate if the allies mutilated his kingdom. "I shall refuse to be the instrument of the ruin of my people, and I shall step down from my throne rather than consent to tarnishing its ancient splendor by an unprecedented humiliation," he wrote to Alexander on September 23, 1815. Communicating this prearranged letter to his allies, the Czar commented, "I knew this would happen: now we are in more trouble than ever. Louis XVIII is renouncing his throne and he is right to do so. France no longer has a king. Find her another one if you can. As for me, I shall not meddle in an affair that could have been avoided. Besides, it is time for me to go home and for all that to come to an end."[4]

After much bargaining, Prussia, Austria, and England yielded in part. France retained the borders of 1790. She was charged with war reparations in the amount of 700 million francs, of which 100 million were for Russia, and forced to accept the temporary occupation of her territory by an army of 150,000 men. In addition, contrary to what had been decided at the time of the first Treaty of Paris, the allies demanded the restitution of the works of art which Bonaparte had stripped from the museums, palaces, and churches of the countries conquered by his troops. The final agreement was not signed until November 20, 1815. At the end of the negotiations, Austria had extended its dominion over the major part of Italy, Prussia had doubled its territory and was installed on the Rhine, and England had become the queen of the seas. As for Russia, although the congress did not grant it any territorial advantage, it kept Finland, which it had earlier taken from Sweden, and Bessarabia, which had been ceded in 1812 by Turkey. Furthermore, its dynastic union with the new kingdom of Poland placed it in direct contact with the Germanic countries and associated it in a way with the destiny of Europe. One last satisfaction for Alexander: Talleyrand, whom he could no longer endure, was removed from his post by Louis XVIII. The new King was anxious to please the allied plenipotentiaries and in any event was himself tired of his presumptuous minister. The services Talleyrand had rendered at the Congress of Vienna were forgotten. There remained only a man who, in the eyes of Louis XVIII, had made the mistake of thinking himself indispensable and of having introduced to the court the despicable Fouché, a former member of the regicidal Convention. Talleyrand's replacement was the Duc de Richelieu, a French emigré and the ex-Governor of Odessa, who two weeks before, at the review at Vertus, had still been wearing a Russian uniform.[5] On learning of this appointment, Talleyrand sneered, "A good choice, assuredly: he knows the Crimea better than any other man in France."

Finally Alexander left Paris for Prussia, dissatisfied both with his allies, who were too greedy, and the French, who were too fickle. Of France, where he had just spent four months, he said bitterly, "On that land live thirty million cattle possessed of the gift of speech, without rights, without honor: How can it be otherwise where there is no religion?"[6] And he wrote to his dear Catherine, "So here I am, away from that accursed Paris!"

Berlin gave him a triumphal welcome. During a huge banquet, he rose at the same time as the King of Prussia and announced the engagement of his younger brother, Grand Duke Nicholas, to Princess Charlotte. Cheers greeted this new token of friendship between two peoples who had fought side by side.

On October 27/November 8 Alexander continued his journey. When he crossed the border of the kingdom of Poland that he had created, he put on a Polish uniform and replaced the star of St. Andrew on his breast with the decoration of the White Eagle. It was thus attired that he entered Warsaw, on horseback. His escort was composed almost exclusively of Polish generals and magnates. In Saxony Square he passed in review Polish regiments wearing the national cockade, while the crowd shouted, "Long live Alexander, our King!" The next day, at the Czartoryskis' residence, he opened the ball with Prince Adam's mother. Moved to tears by this honor, she noted in her journal that same evening, "Poland existed, there was a King of Poland wearing a national uniform and the Polish decorations. I have a motherland and I shall leave it to my children."

To win the affection of his new subjects, Alexander gave them many tokens of his esteem and benevolence. He restored the property that

had been sequestered from Poles who had served under Napoleon's
flag, awarded several Polish officers the title of aide-de-camp, distributed financial aid out of his own purse, created a royal court in
Warsaw and chose the chamberlains, masters of ceremonies, and ladies-
in-waiting from the Polish aristocracy. He went to visit Princess Domi-
nique Radziwill, whose husband had died fighting the Russians, appeared in the uniform of the Polish light calvary at the home of the
Princess of Württemberg, Prince Adam Czartoryski's sister, danced
with her, and "abandoned himself to gaiety." "The Emperor is deified
here," wrote General Ermolov to one of his friends. "No one can resist
him in anything." But although high society was delighted with its new
King, there were many Poles who continued to regard the Russians as
occupiers, even enemies. They muttered demands for the restoration
of Mogilev, Vitebsk, Volhynia, Podolia, and Lithuania, and anxiously
awaited the constitutional charter promised by the Czar.

He signed it on November 15/27, 1815. On the whole it was very
liberal, providing for national representation, a direct vote with only a
modest property qualification, independence of the press, a guarantee
of certain personal rights, exclusive use of the Polish language in the
administration and army, abolition of confiscation and deportation, and
so on. Paradoxically, the Czar thus granted the Poles what he refused
the Russians. But, he thought, the Poles had long experience of a constitutional regime, while in Russia such an innovation would lead to mad
dreams and rumblings of rebellion. What he wanted to do was try out
on Poland a treatment that later, after careful preparation, could be
applied to Russia. Little Poland would be a kind of experimental labora-
tory for its huge neighbor, which for some time yet would be maintained under an autocratic regime. The Poles' reaction to the constitution of 1815 was nonetheless lukewarm. They had hoped for better.
Also, they wondered about the exact nature of the relationship between
the new kingdom and the old empire, with a common sovereign at their
head. Was it a union founded on his person or on political reality?

There remained to appoint a viceroy who would represent Alexander on the spot. The man best qualified to occupy this high post was
obviously Prince Adam Czartoryski. Because of his friendship for the
Czar, his profound knowledge of Polish affairs, his background as a
member of the Secret Committee, his stay at the headquarters of the
allied troops, and his participation in the Congress of Vienna, he had no
equal in the eyes of the Russians as well as the Poles. But it was precisely
his distinction, his intelligence, his independence of mind that worried
the Czar. He was afraid that so dynamic a viceroy would replace the

King in the esteem of his fellow citizens. Moreover, he could not forgive Czartoryski for certain abrupt reactions, certain disrespectful remarks, which indicated a temperament disinclined to obedience. Lastly, he no doubt held it against Czartoryski that in Vienna he had renewed his romance with the Empress. In any event, Alexander needed someone less colorful, a man who would execute orders, not give them. Accordingly, without informing anyone, he decided to appoint as viceroy the worthy old one-legged general Zajaczek, who had commanded the Polish troops under Napoleon. To avoid any discussion, he did not announce his intention until the eve of his departure from Warsaw, and, as with Speransky, he sacrificed the victim without warning, in a private interview. Summoned to the Emperor's study in the middle of the night, Czartoryski received the blow with ill-concealed resentment. "It happened toward two o'clock in the morning," wrote General Mikhailovsky-Danilevsky. "I was in the antechamber of the imperial study with Prince Volkonsky and Secretary of State Martchenko. Suddenly Prince Czartoryski burst out of the study and began to pace up and down the room, looking distraught. Not only did he pay no attention to us, he did not even bow to us. He was as if beside himself, probably because of the wound to his pride that he had received."

The next day Czartoryski swallowed his rage and accepted as a consolation prize the presidency of the Senate.

When he finally left the capital of Poland, Alexander stopped in Vilna, which was especially illuminated in his honor and which displayed a transparent signboard proclaiming, in French, *Gratitude and confidence.* In St. Petersburg, on the contrary, where he arrived at night, there was no flattering inscription to welcome him. Once again, he had refused all honors, but actually no one had thought of celebrating his return. Empress Elizabeth, who had come back from her travels the day before, awaited him at the palace. He saw her again without giving the least sign of emotion. His thoughts were elsewhere. A fervent admirer of the Czar, Joseph de Maistre, wrote to his government: "The great soul has at last returned to its great body. The Emperor has arrived!"

From his first days back, the persons close to Alexander noted that "the great soul" was particularly somber. It was as if after a period of artificial excitement, the accumulation of honors had led him to satiety, disenchantment, melancholy. He leaned toward a carping severity. Officers were forbidden to wear civilian clothes when off duty. Discipline in the regiments was reinforced. Since numerous cases of conversion to Catholicism had been observed in high society, the Jesuits were

driven out of St. Petersburg and sent to Polotsk. It was a far cry from
the dream of the Universal Church dear to Madame von Krüdener.

Having left the prophetess in Paris, Alexander had completely detached himself from her. Not that he had renounced mysticism, but he
no longer needed the Baroness to help him walk in the paths of the
Lord. She had given him the necessary start. Her role was ended. Yet
she still wrote him interminable, delirious missives, in French. He was
flattered by this correspondence but also bored by it. Always the same
entreaties and the same ecstasies. Rambling, incomprehensible nonsense: "If you knew, Sire, how He loves you, you could not resist Him
in anything. . . . If you were unable to respond to His great views, the
Lord would not have called you to the noble task of vanquishing the
dragon and leading the peoples. . . . Before the ages, God prepared a
path for each of us. . . . He says Himself that He gives nations for a
Chosen One! . . . Being at the head of God's people . . . judge how
purified you must be by grace." And also: "You who are so great, and
yet such a child, I tell you without the slightest doubt that you will not
be able to advance without me as long as God wills that it should be I;
this has so often been my experience as a spiritual guide." Not receiving
the reply she expected from Alexander, Madame von Krüdener traveled about Switzerland and Germany, always short of money. Having
preached the good word all across Europe, she returned, disillusioned,
to her family's castle in Livonia.

As usual, Alexander had tired of his infatuation as quickly as he had
formed it. Madame von Krüdener was a part of his experience abroad.
Now he was home again, in Russia. Facing Russian problems. On December 25, 1815, he solemnly announced to his country that the Holy
Alliance had been concluded. The Holy Synod immediately ordered
the text of the treaty to be posted on the walls of churches and recommended that priests base their sermons upon it. But in Alexander's view
that was not enough. To enlighten the people as to the true significance
of the politico-mystical pact for which he had been responsible, on
January 1, 1816, he published a scathing manifesto. In this document
—though he thanked his subjects for the courage they had displayed
during the war—he attributed to God alone all the successes obtained.
Commenting on the events of which he had been the inspired hero, he
inveighed against defeated France; denounced Paris as a hotbed of
insurrection, vice, and perpetual corruption; called Napoleon a com-
moner, a foreign bandit, and a malefactor; and accused him of what, to
an autocrat, was the ultimate outrage: having "usurped the right that
belongs to God alone to command all men as a despot." "No human

tribunal can pronounce a sentence heavy enough for such a criminal,"
the manifesto continued. "Not having been sufficiently punished by a
mortal hand, he will present himself drenched in the blood of peoples
before the terrible tribunal, in the face of God, when each receives
retribution for his acts." Astonished and dismayed, those around the
Emperor wondered if this man exploding with the violence of a be-
nighted priest was the same who in Paris had used elegant language to
the representatives of Louis XVIII. It was as if, on his return to Russia,
he had gone back a century in time. Instead of basing his positions on
precise political considerations, he constantly invoked the struggle between the spirit of good and the spirit of evil, Providence, the Word,
the Almighty. His concept of monarchy was becoming theological and
patriarchal. Horrified by these new tendencies in his former pupil,
Laharpe wrote to him, "Your manifesto of January 1 has just been
reprinted here and is being widely distributed. I should be tempted to
think that this is because of certain epithets which were found very
shocking. In their distress, [the French] still loved to look to the man
who had proved the most generous of their enemies. It seems that this
last consolation is to be taken from them. There are times when I no
longer doubt that people are conspiring against the glory you acquired
in 1814."

Alexander was not in the least moved by this reproach. Why should
he concern himself with public opinion when he had God on his side?
He wrote, in French, to his sister Catherine, "You ask me, dear friend,
what I am doing? Still the same thing, that is, accustoming myself more
and more to bow to the decrees of Providence, and already finding a
kind of satisfaction in my complete isolation." Sometimes he thought
that his was the isolation of Moses, leader of the chosen people.

XIII

MYSTICAL SOCIETIES
AND MILITARY
COLONIES

In August of 1816 Alexander went to Moscow, which was rising again from its ruins. The city was one vast construction site, with new houses standing next to charred heaps of rubble. "One must seek out the devastated places," wrote the Empress, "so quickly is the city being rebuilt and becoming in part more beautiful than before. I wish this news could be brought to Napoleon. . . . In St. Petersburg strangers are struck by the city's appearance of youth and regularity; here, irregularity bears witness to a long succession of centuries, and there is an air of antiquity which inspires respect and admiration."[1]

The Czar was welcomed to the Kremlin with wild enthusiasm. He gave 500,000 rubles to the poor and 150,000 rubles for the reconstruction of the palace of the Nobles' Club. However, members of his entourage were surprised that on the anniversary of Borodino he did not think it necessary to visit the battlefield or to hold a commemorative service for the repose of the heroes' souls. Had he forgotten the price of victory? Persons close to him noted that he was less and less inclined to tell about memories of the patriotic war. Lately his mind had been turned wholly toward the future. And even, more precisely, toward the hereafter.

Nothing in his past would seem to have predisposed him toward divine aspirations. In his youth at the court of Catherine II, surrounded by skeptics, he had hardly taken any interest in problems of faith. His religious instruction had been entrusted to the liberal, Anglophile archpriest Samborsky, and he remembered from it nothing but a pleasant tissue of legends. His father Paul, although personally inclined to mysticism, had inculcated in him only the love of parades. After the regicide Alexander had felt terror, despair, and remorse, but without coming closer to God. Having himself become Emperor and as such administrative head of the Orthodox Church, he had proved respectful of rites, no doubt, but indifferent to dogma. It was the great fire of Moscow that, by his own admission, had "shed light in his soul."

Having appointed his old friend Prince Golitzin to the post of Procurator of the Holy Synod, Alexander had gradually fallen under his pious influence. Once worldly and frivolous, Golitzin had discovered in his new functions the true meaning of life. He had urged Alexander to read the Bible, and the Czar had received a dazzling revelation from it. Another person who had pushed him to seek spiritual perfection was Koshelev, Grand Master of the imperial court. Koshelev, who was much attracted to occultism, had studied the greatest exponents of initiatory wisdom: Saint-Martin, Lavater, Swedenborg, Jung-Stilling. He had corresponded with leaders of the Quakers and the Moravian Brethren. In close accord with Golitzin, he had founded the Russian Bible Society, modeled on the British and Foreign Bible Society. Alexander had immediately agreed to become an honorary member. "May the Almighty let His blessings fall on this institution," he wrote Golitzin. He ordered that the society be given a capital of twenty-five thousand rubles and an annual subsidy of ten thousand rubles. At his urging the Metropolitan of St. Petersburg, Ambroise, and the Metropolitan of Kiev, Serapion, agreed, like it or not, to sit as vice-presidents of the society beside the Protestant minister Pitt, the delegate from the British Bible Society. With the exception of the Superior-General of the Jesuits, who had declined the invitation, the Russian Bible Society included the leaders of all Christian communities in the country. It soon had 189 chapters scattered throughout the empire. Its proclaimed goal was to combat superstition among the people and to reveal to them the evangelical truth behind the rites. For this purpose the Holy Scriptures were translated into the many languages of Russia. But the clergy opposed imme-

ALEXANDER OF RUSSIA

diate publication of a Russian version, and the faithful had to content
themselves, like their fathers, with the Church Slavonic text.

Having become a kind of official institution, the Bible Society soon
deviated from its initial mission. Before long its members were offering
up ecstatic prayers in Quaker fashion. Since the ordeals of the patriotic
war of 1812, many representatives of Russian high society had been
turning with fascination to all forms of mysticism. The national Church,
frozen in tradition, could not quench their tormenting thirst for the
absolute. Deeply religious but afloat in vague yearnings, they yielded
to the attraction of Freemasonry, Martinism, Illuminism, and Pietism.
Golitzin and Koshelev were both Freemasons. Alexander shared their
humanitarian ideas, but being the Lord's Anointed, he could not submit
to the symbolic trials of the initiation or be a simple "fellow" in a lodge.
As an outside sympathizer, he received the secret teachings without
being admitted into the brotherhood. These secret teachings were akin
to those that had been dispensed to him by Madame von Krüdener:
Lost in a corrupt world, man must shake off his crude, sensual envelope
and draw near to God. Not one act of ordinary life could escape that
rule. Even foreign policy and internal administration fell within the
jurisdiction of the Bible. "Russia is not a nation, it is a church," wrote
a contemporary, Countess Bludov.

A church with dozens of different chapels, many varied beliefs,
extraordinary bursts of piety and no cohesion. More and more people,
drawn to the mysterious or troubled by spiritual anguish, broke away
from the official religion to join sects. Some of these sects mixed mysticism with sadistic orgies. A certain Kondrati Selivanov presided over
gatherings of *Skoptsy* or eunuchs, who were soon joined by curious
spectators—dignitaries, officers of the Guard, ladies of fashion, merchants. He greeted his followers from a raised, gilded throne in the
house of the wealthy merchant Solodovnikov and, claiming that he was
"the dwelling-place of the Holy Ghost, proceeding from the Father to
the Son," predicted the future, distributed blessings, and gave advice.
A row of sumptuous carriages with four or six horses each would be
drawn up in front of his door. Golitzin and Kochubey visited him frequently. His prophecies were reported to the Czar, who took no offense
at them; any search for God, he thought, was to be respected. He
expressed this feeling in a letter to Marquis Palucci, the Governor of
Riga, who had made some difficulties for the troublesome Baroness von
Krüdener and her friends. "Why disturb the tranquillity of people who
are only concerned with praying to the Eternal and who do no harm
to anyone?" wrote the Emperor. "Leave Madame von Krüdener and

the others in peace, for what does it matter to you if a particular person prays to God in one fashion or another? In that regard each acts according to his conscience and is responsible only to Him. It is better to pray in any way than not to pray at all." The Czar's tolerance extended even to the Old Believers, to the *Molokhanes* (milk drinkers), who were close to the English Methodists, and to the *Dukhobors*, who recognized neither priests nor rites nor dogma nor marriage and relied solely on the Bible.

There was so much religious ferment that the French embassy reported as follows: "A number of society women—most of them reformed from a wanton past—are now seeking the excitement of mysticism. They write to the Emperor, they gather to read *Le Pur Amour*, Madame Guyon's *Théologie astrale*, Fénélon's *Maximes des Saints*, the works of the Bavarian illuminist Jung-Stilling, and those of the famous Saint-Martin. The court bookseller, Saint-Florent, told me that he could not keep up with the demand for these works. While dissemination of the Bible, without commentary, leads to the overthrow of all beliefs, the mysticism which one is supposed to reach through this Biblism leads to the conviction that the perfect security of the soul in the love of God renders unimportant the actions of the body, even those which were commonly held to be the most guilty."[2]

One of Selivanov's followers, Catherine Tatarinova, founded a separate community with rites resembling those of the whirling dervishes. Her mother, Madame de Buxhoewden, the former governess of the Czar's children, had an apartment in Mikhailovsky Palace. She placed it at her daughter's disposal for pious meetings with Bible readings, songs, dances, and various transports. Catherine Tatarinova was very close to the Bible Society, and the fervent admirers she received included the inevitable Golitzin and Koshelev. Dressed in a white chemise she would spin in front of them like a top, and when on the verge of exhaustion she would speak in a breathless voice about the celestial visions that visited her. The Czar granted her an annual pension of six thousand rubles and was not above consulting her on the esoteric meaning of certain passages in the Old and New Testaments.

The only ones who did not benefit from the imperial benevolence were the Jesuits. A first measure had driven them from St. Petersburg in 1816, when the celebrated abbé Nicolle, director of the lycée of Odessa, had lost his job after he refused to create a little Bible Society among his pupils. In March of 1820 all the Jesuits, numbering 380, had to leave Russia. Thus the country lost some able pedagogues but at the same time rid itself of indefatigable converters.

Absorbed in his cloudy ruminations, Alexander grew indifferent to the internal affairs of the country and decided to delegate full administrative responsibility to a trusted, tough associate. He immediately chose his old friend from the Gatchina days, the terrible Arakcheyev. Being himself unstable, idealistic, wavering, high-strung, and irritable, he saw in Arakcheyev—that rock so firmly embedded in reality—a kind of complement to his reveries. Even the man's physical appearance inspired his confidence. He would have been suspicious of a fellow who was too attractive. This one looked like a workman's tool. Stooping, with his thick hair in a crew cut, a low forehead, thin tight lips, a thick nose shaped like a shoe and cold eyes, he lacked all social graces. He had scant education, no manners, and vulgar tastes. Separated from his legitimate spouse, he had taken as his mistress a sailor's wife, one Anastasia Minkina, a fat, coarse, licentious woman who was particularly fond of pornographic drawings. On his beautiful estate of Gruzino there was a pavilion where one could press a spring and a series of obscene pictures would appear. He also collected libertine books: *Tendres Etreintes conjugales et plaisirs pris avec les maîtresses (Tender Connubial Embraces and Pleasures Taken with Mistresses)* . . . But Arakcheyev's true passion was work. Taciturn and cruel, scarcely able to write a report without making spelling mistakes, he invented detailed rules and enforced their application with a strictness that amounted to obsession. Subordinates trembled in his presence; he insulted them, mocked them, struck them. He derived more intense pleasure from humiliating them than from making love. Rarely appearing in society, he knew the aristocrats despised him and he enjoyed taking them down a peg. "He has against him everyone who counts here and everyone who serves those who count," wrote Joseph de Maistre. "He tramples on everyone!"

In relation to the Czar Arakcheyev was, as he himself put it, "faithful without flattery." Alexander knew that he had in him a servant who would never defect and never be indiscreet; an automaton ready to assume all the responsibilities that the Emperor refused to take, an umbrella that would protect His Majesty during downpours. In a short time Alexander found that he could no longer do without Arakcheyev's company. He made long visits to the general's estate at Gruzino and admired the arrangement of the grounds, the well-raked paths, the neatly pruned trees, the white turrets, the imperial emblems everywhere. Here each blade of grass, each pebble, each peasant was in his place. Canes kept in salt were used to punish guilty servants. Or else a collar with iron points was placed around their necks. Not surprisingly, no one made any mistakes. To Alexander, this was the image of paradise. When he left Arakcheyev he would write him friendly, almost affectionate letters. Their common past at Gatchina in the days of Paul gave their relations a tinge of frank military camaraderie. Arakcheyev, a coward on the battlefield, was a peerless commander in the barracks. He had a passion for drill, for cleanliness in the rooms, for the correct cut of uniforms. Alexander cheerfully joined in his insanely perfection-ist demands. When it came to his regiments, the Czar found no detail negligible. The copper buttons were his *idée fixe*. He wanted his sol-diers to hold their breath during reviews, "so that they will not be seen to breathe." His heart found peace, his nerves relaxed at the sight of symmetry. Even at work, it pained him to see an unsharpened pencil or one file sticking out beyond the others. In his study he liked to look at the two identical mantelpieces, one bearing a bust of Juno, the other a bust of Minerva, the quill pens, the inkstands, immutably arranged, the little tables all exactly the same, all covered with green cloth, one for each minister. But most of the time it was Arakcheyev alone who was received in the monarch's study. All the business of the empire passed through his hands. Though he held no portfolio, he had the power of a dictator. Men belonging to the most varied parties called him a "cursed serpent," a "monster," the "evil genius of Russia." His associates said of him that he was "industrious as an ant and venomous as a tarantula." Under his influence Alexander resolutely turned his back on the liberal ideas of his youth. The God to whom he prayed henceforth was a God of order and oppression. Discipline became one of the prime concerns of government. Some whispered that you would think you were back in the days of Paul I.

In February 1816, Karamzin, the official court historian, arrived in St. Petersburg to submit to the Czar the first eight volumes of his *History of Russia*. Despite repeated requests, he could not obtain an audience. After he had waited for ten weeks, a remark of Arakcheyev's was reported to him: "Karamzin doesn't seem to want to meet me." Finally the historian understood that in order to see the Czar he had to obtain the consent of the guard at the door. He therefore went to visit Arakcheyev, who told him, "Having had a simple deacon for my tutor, I am an ignorant man. My role is to execute the will of the Emperor. If I were younger, I would take lessons from you. Now it's too late." Two days later Karamzin was received by His Majesty, who granted him sixty thousand rubles for the printing of his work, the Order of St. Andrew, and the rank of Councilor of State. Speransky himself, the Czar's friend of former days, now the Governor General of Siberia, was not readmitted to the Council of State until he had humbly begged the protection of the man who had always been his enemy.

Count Razumovsky's request to retire having been granted, the Ministry of Public Education, which he had headed, was merged with the Ministry of Ecclesiastical Matters under the single authority of Prince Golitzin. This merger was based on the idea that all teaching should proceed from religion. The Bible became the sole source of knowledge. "They want to make lay education Christian; they will only increase the number of hypocrites," wrote Karamzin to his friend Dmitriev.

But Alexander's great idea, ardently espoused and developed by Arakcheyev, was the "military colonies." Reading an article by the French general Servan de Gerbey, *Les Forces frontières des Etats* ("The Border Forces of States"), the Czar had felt the shock of revelation. The point was to keep soldiers with their families in time of peace and at the same time to combine the work of the soldier with that of the muzhik, who would be given military training. Allotted fifteen hectares (thirty-seven acres) of ground, each farmer would maintain one soldier together with his family and his horse. Thus peasants would become soldiers while continuing to till their lands, and soldiers would share field work with peasants. All of them, soldiers and peasants alike, would wear the same uniform and be subject to the same discipline. Since they would feed themselves, these numerous troops would cost the state nothing.

A first attempt of this kind had already been made in the region of Mogilev in 1810, but it had been interrupted by the war. In 1815 the Czar went back to the plan and made Arakcheyev responsible for its execution. Starting in 1816 part of the province of Novgorod, where Arakcheyev's estate was situated, was converted into a bivouac. The provinces of Mogilev, Kherson, Ekaterinoslav (Dnepropetrovsk), and Slobodsko-Ukraïnski were likewise turned upside down according to imperial directives. Soon one-third of the army was established in these provinces. The process was simple: A regiment was moved into a district, and automatically all the inhabitants of that district became soldiers. Divided into companies, battalions, and squadrons, they constituted the reserves of the unit that had been settled on their soil. Shoulder-to-shoulder with their new brothers in arms, they worked in the fields and spent the rest of their time learning to march in step. It was in uniform and to the sound of the drum that they went off to push their ploughs and wield their scythes. Arakcheyev, a specialist in leveling and in supervised leisure activities, destroyed the picturesque, wretched villages, replaced the isbas with symmetrical cottages, and shaved the muzhiks' beards. They were taught their new role with blows of the stick. Marriages were decided upon by the military authority and often the choice was made by drawing lots. Obligatory coupling. Not one widow, not one old maid. Rebellion on the grounds of sentiment was unacceptable. A fine was imposed on women who did not give birth often enough. From the age of six, boys were enrolled among the army children. Thus their freedom was alienated forever. Arakcheyev ordered for them clothing of three different sizes. "As soon as these clothes are ready," he wrote the Emperor, on May 27, 1817, "I shall have them distributed in all the villages and I shall give the order for all the children to appear in this uniform on the same day and to wear it at all times in all their work." These instructions were followed to the letter. He went in person to the villages and enjoyed the spectacle of his miniature army. "Only a few old women wept," he wrote the Czar.

In the pink or blue cottages, all identical, all with the same little porch painted red, the same little white boundary-posts, the same little rows of slender birches, lived families in uniform. The rooms were tidy, an inventory of the furniture hung on the wall in a frame. At regular intervals inspectors came to check the condition of the equipment. The sweeping of courtyards, the washing of floors, the care of cattle, the lighting of stoves, the nursing of children, the polishing of the copper buttons, every act of daily life was provided for and described by an article of the regulations. For the least infraction—the cane. Alexander liked all this. His dream would have been to see Russia transformed into one vast military colony, each citizen having his place in society, his role, his uniform and no personal ideas.

But while the military colonies delighted the Emperor, they were the despair of those who were forced to live in them. In this convict-prison dedicated to precision, all private life was abolished. The peasants, accustomed to their filth, their laziness, their servitude, had difficulty adjusting to their new houses, new clothes, new masters. Military obedience seemed harder to them than civil obedience. The muzhiks protested, entreated, fled, hid in the forests, sent delegations to the Empress Dowager and Grand Duke Constantine. When Grand Duke Nicholas passed through, a few hundred wretched peasants came out of a wood and burst forth into lamentations. Four young women who had been forced to marry threw themselves at the feet of Alexander himself and implored his clemency. The Czar's reply was categorical: "The military colonies will continue to exist, even I had to cover the

route from Petersburg to Chudovo with corpses." And he told the
ambassador of Saxony, "I have already made my will prevail in far more
difficult matters and I mean to be obeyed in this one."

On August 24, 1819, Arakcheyev sent the Czar a report on a rebellion that had occurred in the colony of Chuguyev. The uprising had
reached such proportions that the military tribunal had been obliged
to pronounce 275 death sentences. Arakcheyev flattered himself that
he had attenuated these sentences, "after asking the advice of Almighty
God" and "prompted by the feelings natural to a Christian." Enlightened by the Lord, he had decided that the guilty would not be shot but
rather "passed twelve times under the rods between the rows of a
battalion of a thousand men." In fact, this left the strongest of the
condemned only a slim chance of survival, in agonizing pain. Arakcheyev magnanimously limited the torture to forty ringleaders. When
the others had asked for mercy, he "thanked" the Almighty for bringing
them to reason and promised to ask imperial clemency on their behalf.
"The events here have greatly perturbed me," he wrote the Czar. "I
will not conceal from you that some of the criminals who were most full
of hate died after the application of their sentence. I am beginning to
be very weary of all that." On reading this letter, gentle, angelic Alexander was seized with insane anger against the troublemakers. He
could not tolerate having common muzhiks, barefoot beggars, presume
to cross him. His sympathy went not to the victims but to his friend
Arakcheyev, who had suffered so much in condemning them. "On the
one hand," he wrote him, "I can understand what your sensitive soul
has undergone in these circumstances. On the other hand, I can appreciate the clearsightedness you have demonstrated in these grave
events. I thank you sincerely and with all my heart for the trouble you
have taken." Not only did he say nothing about pardoning the rebels
who had repented, but he even insisted, with a sigh, on the necessity
of continuing to carry out the sentences. "The conjuncture is no doubt
painful," he concluded. "But since, unfortunately, it has not been possible to prevent these deeds, there remains no other means of getting out
of the situation than to let the violence and severity of the laws take
their course." The executions were therefore resumed, and according
to a report by the French chargé d'affaires Malvirade, 160 men met
death under the blows. In addition, twenty-six women were passed
under the rods and sent to Orenburg, and fifty-six officers were given
disciplinary sentences.

The next year there was another rebellion. This time it was not a
collection of ignorant muzhiks who raised their heads but the Czar's

favorite regiment, the one he had commanded as heir to the throne, the illustrious Semeonovsky. The soldiers of this elite unit were commanded by Colonel Schwarz, a brutal, dull-witted man, who demanded of them a superhuman precision in maneuvers and who considered no violence excessive if it served to obtain this mechanical regularity. According to the dispatch of one diplomat, "he made his soldiers work barefoot so as to economize on shoes, he tarred their mustaches, spat in their faces, drove them to exhaustion, knocked them down."[3] During the night of October 16, 1820, the men of the company known as "His Majesty's" of the first battalion told their captain that they could no longer endure Schwarz's methods. They were immediately arrested for insubordination and imprisoned in the Fortress of St. Peter and St. Paul. The next night the soldiers of the four other companies rebelled in turn and demanded that their comrades be freed. Encircled by the loyal troops, they committed no violence and were likewise imprisoned in the dungeons of the fortress. All things considered, it was an ordinary mutiny provoked by the brutality of a commander detested by his men. But the Semeonovsky regiment was the most prestigious unit of the Guard, and the insurrection had taken place in the capital itself. In the absence of the Czar, the military authorities had not been able to convince the soldiers to return to the ranks. Alexander angrily assessed the effect this event would have on public opinion in Russia and abroad: These insurgents in uniform had insulted him in front of all Europe. He did not believe it had been a spontaneous act: "No one in the world will ever convince me," he wrote Arakcheyev, "that the soldiers rose up of their own accord, solely on account of Colonel Schwarz's cruelties." Obviously politics was behind it. Revolutionaries wanted to destroy the Russian army. He confided in Metternich, who was in Troppau (Opava) with him, and Metternich in turn noted in his *Mémoires:* "The Czar believes there is a reason why three thousand Russian soldiers have abandoned themselves to an act which is so inconsistent with the national character. He goes so far as to imagine that it is radicals who did the deed, in order to intimidate him and make him return to St. Petersburg. I am not of his opinion. It would be too much to believe that in Russia the radicals could already dispose of whole regiments. But this proves how much the Emperor has changed."

As soon as he returned to St. Petersburg, Alexander sanctioned the verdict of the military tribunal that had judged the mutineers of the Semeonovsky regiment. All soldiers and officers who had been found innocent would be sent to provincial garrisons to meditate upon the crime of their comrades. As for the others, the ringleaders, the judgment stipulated: "His Majesty the Emperor, in consideration both of the long detention under remand of the men hereafter named and of their combat records, deigns to spare them the ignominious sentence of the knout and to order that each of them shall receive six thousand blows of the cane, after which they will be sent to forced labor in the mines."

Relieved at having settled the fate of these wretches, Alexander wrote to Golitzin, in French, "I abandon myself completely to God's guidance, to his decisions, and it is He who directs and disposes all things. I merely follow in total submission, persuaded that He can lead me only toward the goal which His economy has determined for the common good." The Czar felt even more justified in his intransigence because all Europe was seething with revolutionary ferment: This very year the Duc de Berry had been assassinated in Paris; the year before, in Germany, the writer Kotzebue, who was generally considered to be a spy for the Russian government, had been struck down by a student; in Spain, in Italy, popular feeling was running high. Alexander feared contagion. And so it was with increased suspicion that he considered the social and intellectual life of the capital.

After the war the great town houses had opened their doors again. Every evening the nobility gathered in one or another of these princely mansions, while lines of carriages waited in the streets. On the second floor, in drawing rooms lit by a thousand candles, women laden with diamonds danced with men in uniforms blazing with decorations. Few civilian dress coats were to be seen turning to the strains of the orchestra. Seated apart would be the cardplayers, not even hearing the music. "In ninety houses out of a hundred they play at cards," wrote General Mikhailovsky-Danilevsky. "I have hardly greeted the hostess when I find myself with cards in my hand. Before going in to supper they sit down for a game of whist. And it is not only the elderly who do this, but the young people as well."

Theater was another craze of St. Petersburg society. The halls were filled to overflowing. People in the different boxes bowed to one another while waiting for the curtain to rise. Lorgnettes, fans, cordons, stars of orders, epaulets, and diadems glittered like so many spangles on the moving mass of spectators. All the young officers sprang to attention as soon as a general came down the aisle. Whether dancers, singers, or actresses were on stage, every spectator had his idol. The government approved of this sort of entertainment: Persons who are taking a keen interest in whirling tutus and vocal arabesques cannot at the same time concern themselves with politics.

But besides agreeable, innocent artistic expressions like Didelot's ballets, in which the dancers Kolosova and Istomina were applauded; besides the comic operas distinguished by the beautiful voices of Catalini and Madame Dangeville-Vanderberghe; besides the French vaudevilles and Russian comedies, there was also the activity of the poets, which it was harder to monitor. The poets had imagination and a taste for independence, all the more dangerous because their works were not always published but circulated clandestinely in hundreds of anonymously made copies. Some young authors formed a mock society called the *Arzamas* to preach the spirit of initiative and the use of modern language, as opposed to Chichkov's *Besseda,* a party of writers and art devotees who tried to uphold the archaic tradition in literature. At meetings of the Arzamas there appeared alongside Zhukhovsky, the celebrated and universally respected representative of Russian romanticism, a newcomer with thick lips, frizzy hair, and sparkling eyes: Alexander Pushkin, who was a descendant on his mother's side of "Peter the Great's Negro." His epigrams ridiculing society people and high dignitaries made his companions at these merry evenings laugh until they cried. Before long, freed from the French influence, he was to dazzle his contemporaries by the entirely Russian originality of his talent. Beside him stood illustrious older men: Karamzin, respected and admired for his monumental *History of Russia;* Glinka, the poet-patriot; Krylov, the writer of fables; and Griboyedov, whose comedy *The Misfortune of Being Too Clever,* forbidden on the stage, was known to all thanks to innumerable handwritten copies. As many as forty thousand such copies may have been passed from hand to hand and read in secret at private gatherings. It really seemed as if the severity of the authorities stimulated the writers' talents. In St. Petersburg as in Moscow heads were bubbling with ideas, pens sped over paper. The Arzamas society was followed by the society of "The Green Lamp," whose members talked a great deal about literature and women, and sometimes about politics. Still more serious were the philosophical clubs, such as "The Young Men of the Archives," whose members mused over the thought of Schelling. During their discussions they forgot the meannesses of daily life and tried to plan a better future for their country and for humanity.

All this idle talk was faithfully reported to Arakcheyev by his spies. He informed Alexander and urged him to strengthen police surveillance and censorship. In 1818 a committee was created in the Ministry of Public Education for the purpose of establishing "a salutary harmony among faith, science, and the authority of the State." Its main objective was to remove from circulation all writings "which contradict Christi-

anity," all "vain conjectures about the formation and transformation of
the earth," and all medical treatises which did not give sufficient place
to "man's spiritual nature" and "the Providence of God." On order of
the committee, many volumes were burned and certain foreign books
were stopped at the border. Works that mentioned, even indirectly,
liberal institutions or popular movements were banned: Notable among
these were Aristotle's *Politics,* Madame de Staël's *Dix années d'exil*
(*Ten Years of Exile*), and even Lamartine's *Méditations poétiques,*
which had delighted Empress Elizabeth. A short treatise on the dangers
of eating certain mushrooms was proscribed because mushrooms were
a favorite item on Lenten menus, and the same censor attacked a pale
poem by an unknown author that struck him as blasphemous. The poet
sang of the "celestial smile" of his beloved, hoped to "play his lyre for
her, lying at her feet" and concluded: "Oh! how I should like to give you
my life!" The censor's retort: "A woman's smile cannot be described as
celestial, the pose chosen by the poet is humiliating for a Christian and,
if he sacrifices his life, what will remain for God?" When another
rhymester wrote, "With you, in the calm of the wilderness, unknown
to all, I should like to attain felicity," the censor objected: "That is a
dangerous thought. The author gives up continuing to serve the Czar
so as to be with his beloved; felicity is not to be acquired in the company
of a woman but through evangelical faith."[4] Pushkin, a rising star, was
accused by Miloradovich, the Governor General of St. Petersburg, of
having composed several subversive poems including the *Ode to Liberty;* he was expelled from the capital and transferred to the south of
Russia. Even writers as orthodox as Karamzin and Glinka, the founder
of the *Russian Messenger,* had to defend themselves against harassment
by the censors.

At the same time it was muzzling poets, historians, and journalists,
the central authority extended its control over education. Under Magnitsky, a former associate of Speransky's who had opportunistically become a strong supporter of Arakcheyev, the universities were
"purified" one after another. The first was the University of Kazan,
where twelve professors were dismissed because their teaching was not
sufficiently based on the Holy Scriptures. The students, forced to attend
services, were graded on how fervently they prayed. The works of
Voltaire, Rousseau, and Kant were removed from the library. The conservative Bossuet became supreme arbiter in matters relating to the
study of history. The Rector Nikosky opened his course in higher math-
ematics by demonstrating the symbolic value of the hypotenuse "as a
sign of the meeting, in a right angle, of truth and the things of this

world, of justice and love." Not long after, he asked his students to consider two triangles that "with the help of God" were equal to a third.

From Kazan the movement of "moral cleansing" spread to the Universities of Kharkov, Moscow, and St. Petersburg. A professor in the capital was fired for having explained "philosophical systems without immediately refuting them," another for having dared to say that "the lands tilled by free peasants yield better harvests than the others." Even the imperial lycée of Czarskoye Selo, which had been founded by Alexander and which counted Pushkin among its most famous pupils, did not escape the housecleaning. Professor Kunitzin, whom Pushkin loved so much, was dismissed for having spread "shocking arguments that were made fashionable by the too-famous Rousseau." These draconian measures discredited the educational establishments in the eyes of the young. Before long only forty students remained in the University of St. Petersburg, and less than fifty in the University of Kazan. In July 1822 the University of Dorpat was forbidden to admit students who had already attended foreign universities. A few months later all Russians were prohibited from studying abroad, in Heidelberg, Jena, or Würzburg. Finally it was made illegal, throughout the country, to teach political science or to discuss the natural rights of man.

But it was not enough to keep an eye on literary circles, universities, and salons. Illiterate though they were, the muzhiks might still hear what they should not. Local authorities were ordered to seek out suspicious persons "who lead the peasants astray by holding out the dangerous bait of a freedom for which the nation is not prepared."[5] In 1822 the right of landowners to exile their serfs to the provinces of Siberia, a right they had lost in 1809, was restored.

Nevertheless, Alexander went on pretending to be interested in the possibility of freeing the peasant masses. Playing to the gallery, he exclaimed, in French, "I want to bring the nation out of the state of barbarism in which it has been left by the traffic in men. If civilization were sufficiently advanced, I should abolish this slavery, even if it cost me my head!" In 1816 he had instructed General Kisselev to prepare a memorandum for him on the gradual abolition of serfdom in Russia. When he received the document, he complimented the author on his good intentions, then sent it to the Archives, where it was buried under other papers. It was the same with the work of the commission assembled in Warsaw, under the presidency of Novosiltsev, to draft a constitution for Russia. The Byzantine debates were dominated by a French jurist, Monsieur Deschamps. The final document was submitted to the Czar, who approved it but had no intention of ordering its implementation. He had only to dream of a liberal policy in order to feel its benefits immediately in his conscience. When he talked he recaptured the illusion that he was still twenty years old and all heart; when he acted he was forty again: weary, irritable, autocratic, and terrified of change. Arakcheyev drew him ever deeper into despotism and rigid conservatism.

Although Arakcheyev was the Emperor's faithful confidant, he was pained that his competence extended only to civil and military affairs. When the Czar wished to lift his soul toward the higher realms of mysticism, it was not Arakcheyev whom he summoned but Golitzin and Koshelev. With these two "visionary old men" he would hold mysterious secret meetings that lasted for hours and from which he would emerge misty-eyed with melancholy joy. Arakcheyev, who was kept apart from their conversations, was as furious as a betrayed wife. He could not accept being excluded from an important part of Alexander's concerns. Obviously, although he sincerely believed and practiced his religion, he was not sufficiently educated to discuss theological problems with his master. Yet he sensed the danger in Alexander's abandoning the country to the magic of the sects. As a true Orthodox believer, he reasoned that the Church was the surest support for the monarchy and that everything that weakened one weakened the other. The Bible Society and the various assemblies of illuminati were diverting a fraction of the people from the official Russian religion. Let the Czar beware: Chaos in religious thought might well be the prelude to chaos in political thought. To increase his hold over Alexander, Arakcheyev undertook to reveal to him the scandalous excesses provoked by the energumens whom Golitzin and Koshelev protected. Alexander, friend of the theosophists, suddenly caught sight of the abyss gaping before them all—any searching, any innovation in faith as in matters of government was dangerous. Decidedly, Arakcheyev, with his rough common sense, was irreplaceable. On the advice of the father of the military colonies, Catherine Tatarinova, the hallucinating lady who had once fascinated the Czar, was turned out of Mikhailovsky Palace. The brilliant eunuch Kondrati Selivanov, who had conceived the unfortunate idea of having a young officer of the Imperial Guard—the nephew of General Miloradovich—castrated during an initiation ceremony, was banished from the capital and packed off to a monastery in Suzdal. Baroness von Krüdener had meantime returned to St. Petersburg and sought to regain Alexander's favor. "I know, Sire, that I am a trouble to you, perhaps that I offend you," she wrote him. "But should I offend God? Must I not obey Him, must I not tell you everything that you should know? At least my conscience will be at peace." Irritated by his former friend's many requests for money, by her awkward intercessions on behalf of the insurgent Greeks, and by her never-ceasing oracles, the Czar sent her an eight-page handwritten letter in which he accused her of having failed in her duties as a "loyal subject and a Christian" and invited her to retire to her estates. Offended, she left for Livonia and sent His Majesty a last message: "They are tormenting you, they have even separated me from my brother! May you rise again greater than ever before and follow the celestial Bridegroom under the banners of the Cross, may you see it placed above the Church of St. Sophia and worship Jesus Christ on the steps of the mosque, which will have become the temple of the living God."* Alexander didn't answer. When Franz von Baader, whose mystical teachings had so impressed him, wanted to come to St. Petersburg to visit his disciples, he made him wait three months in Riga for authorization to continue his journey. After which the illustrious traveler was expelled without explanation and lost the pension he had enjoyed as correspondent of the Ministry of Public Education.

To complete the destruction of all supporters of "the Pietist hysteria," Arakcheyev very shrewdly decided to make an alliance with two representatives of the high Russian clergy: Seraphim, the new Metropolitan of St. Petersburg, and more importantly, the archimandrite Photius, a thirty-year-old monk of very little learning who was nevertheless filled with an explosive fanaticism. Tall, thin, with an emaciated face and a little reddish beard, Photius terrorized people he spoke to with the magnetic brilliance of his gray eyes, his jerky gestures, and his inspired words. An ascetic ready for any mortification, who wore a hairshirt and an iron belt under his frock, he had won the confidence of Countess Anna Orlova, niece of Gregory Orlov, the lover of Catherine the Great, and become her confessor. He saw her as "a humble servant of God and the vessel of the mercy of Christ." A virgin at the age of thirty-five, heiress to an immense fortune, this singular lady drove her own troika, rode like a Cossack, and danced like a sylph but fled men; nourished herself on roots and was fervently devoted to pious exercises. All the money, all the connections at her disposal she placed at the service of Photius. Did she go so far as to succumb to the temptation of this holy man with the fiery temperament? Some members of

---

*Baroness von Krüdener was to die in 1824, in the Crimea, where she had tried to found a colony that would be a "model of heaven."

her entourage claimed that she did, but she indignantly denied it. Her
union with Photius, she said, was entirely spiritual. Like her, he was
obsessed with only one thing: Satan's constant enterprises against
human beings. He saw the devil in his dreams and cursed him. But that
was not enough. Since he had met Anna Orlova he had felt called upon
to combat evil in the world around him; to unmask and punish the
Voltairians, the Martinists, the Freemasons; to decapitate "the seven-
headed hydra of illuminism." A kind of Russian Torquemada, the
spokesman for a wrathful God, he launched anathemas against the
enemies of strict Orthodoxy. The clergy, troubled by the heretical passions let loose around the throne, recognized this raging preacher as
their best defender. As for Golitzin, he never even suspected that when
Photius stormed against the false spiritualism of current society, it was
really himself and his followers the monk was denouncing.

Cleverly working to drive a wedge between the Czar and his chief
mystical confidant, Arakcheyev persuaded His Majesty to grant the
archimandrite an audience. On June 5, 1822, when Photius was introduced into Alexander's presence, he did not even bow. First he looked
around for the icon that, traditionally, should sanctify the room. Discovering it in a corner, he knelt and recited a prayer, then having paid
homage to the "celestial Czar," he rose without haste and bowed before
the "earthly Czar." Moved by so much pious serenity, Alexander de-
voutly kissed the hand of his visitor, made the sign of the cross several
times, and said, "For a long time, Father Photius, I have wanted to see
you and receive your blessing." "Peace be with you!" responded
Photius. "May God inspire you!"

The Czar made him sit beside him, and Photius spoke to him in a
grave voice of the dangers that Church and throne faced from all these
heretics protected by the sovereign's close collaborators. Alexander was
shaken by his apocalyptic eloquence. It was God Himself who was
ordering him to take a different road. By following Golitzin and Koshelev he had been led astray into Protestantism, illuminism. After two
hours of conversation he fell to his knees before the monk, raised his
eyes humbly to the waxen face with the short beard, and begged his
blessing. "When I saw Prince Golitzin again," wrote Photius, "I told him
nothing of the secret words I had exchanged with the Czar."[6] As a
reward for his wise counsel, Alexander gave the archimandrite a pecto-
ral cross studded with diamonds, while the Empress Dowager made
him a gift of a gold watch. But these presents did not turn his head. He
scorned luxury, lived on oatmeal, and drank only a decoction of water
hemlock. His reputation as a miracle worker spread through all classes

of society. Countess Anna Orlova worshiped her mentor; he treated her roughly. When he returned from celebrating an office, she would wipe the sweat from his brow and take off his boots. The Czar visited him at his monastery, and an inscription was carved in the main church, on an elbow-high balustrade separating the choir from the nave: *Here Emperor Alexander, accompanied by Count Arakcheyev and other persons of the court, prayed, kneeling beside Photius.*[7]

It was not long before Photius's intervention with Alexander showed results. On August 1, 1822, an imperial edict ordered Kochubey, who was still Minister of the Interior, to "dissolve the secret societies of every denomination, such as the Masonic lodges." This unexpected verdict stunned thousands of "brothers," including high dignitaries of the empire. No one could understand the Czar's sudden severity toward a humanitarian organization whose ideas he had once shared. It was whispered that he had been driven to it by the discovery of a "plot" instigated by the Polish and English Masons. But Russian lodges had done no harm. Why dismantle them? "Russian Freemasonry had no other purpose than to do works of charity and to give its members the opportunity to spend time pleasantly," wrote General Mikhailovsky-Danilevsky. "Now that the lodges are closed, we are deprived of the only places where one could gather without playing cards." Labzin, the editor of a mystical gazette, *The Children of Zion,* made no secret of his despair. "What's the good of all that?" he asked. "Today they close the lodges and tomorrow we shall be forced to return to them. The lodges have done no harm to anyone. As for the secret societies, they continue to exist without the lodges. Does not Koshelev organize secret meetings at his house? Does not Prince Golitzin attend them? The devil only knows what they do there!" For this insolent language, Labzin was relieved of his functions as vice-president of the Academy of Fine Arts and exiled to a provincial town far from the capital. He was to die in 1825 in abject poverty.

The publication of *The Children of Zion* was forbidden. The different mystical associations were dispersed. But how could one combat friendly little gatherings in private drawing rooms? Cautiously, secretly, persons thirsting for the ideal sought opportunities to meet. In hiding they talked about God and politics. Meanwhile the naïve Golitzin, whose prestige had been greatly shaken by the imperial decision, remained at his post without suspecting the cabal that was threatening him. He continued to trust his best assistant Magnitsky who, foreseeing the forthcoming disgrace of the Minister of Ecclesiastical Matters and Public Education, plotted against him in the shadows. And over their heads Arakcheyev, attentive, patient, and full of hate, pulled the strings.

Early in 1824 one of Golitzin's protégés, the preacher Gossner, published *Der Geist des Lebens (The Spirit of Living)*, an exegesis of the New Testament, in a Russian translation by Popov. Pouncing on the book, Photius discovered that it revealed a revolutionary, satanic spirit. He drew it to the attention of Chichkov and the new Minister of the Interior, Lanskoy, who judged that the book was indeed an insult to the Church. The Committee of Ministers examined the affair. Gossner was invited to leave Russia. His work was burned. The censors who had failed to condemn the blasphemous text were handed over to justice. Photius, overwrought by these events, had visions commanding him to go forward. A council of war was held at the house of the very pure "virgin girl" Anna Orlova, attended by the archimandrite, the Metropolitan Seraphim, Arakcheyev, Magnitsky, and Chief of Police Gladkov. It was agreed that Seraphim, speaking on behalf of the outraged Church, would ask the Czar to dismiss the Minister of Ecclesiastical Matters and Public Education, Prince Golitzin. But in the presence of the Emperor the Metropolitan spoke without conviction, and nothing came of the interview. Not to be discouraged, Arakcheyev then obtained an audience at the palace for Photius himself. The archimandrite was brought in by a hidden staircase, reserved in the old days for Catherine the Great's lovers. Once again Alexander was shaken to the marrow of his bones by his inquisitorial visitor. "You have sent me an angel from heaven in the person of this saint," he cried, raising his eyes to the ceiling. "He comes to reveal truth and justice to me!" For three hours Photius fulminated against the heterodox. He was so agitated that he was covered with sweat from head to foot. He even said, later, that blood had mingled with his perspiration. Despite this long diatribe, Alexander hesitated to dismiss his minister. Instead he ordered Arakcheyev to go talk to the Metropolitan of St. Petersburg in the presence of Photius. Seraphim blazed up with holy wrath, threw his tall white hat on the table, and declared that he would rather give up his rank than continue to work with Golitzin, the "sworn enemy of Church and State." Whereupon Photius obtained authorization to write to the Emperor setting forth his grievances and proposals. In four successive letters the archimandrite demanded the dismissal of Golitzin, the restoration of the affairs of the Orthodox Church to the Holy Synod, the right to supervise all education, and the dissolution of the Bible Society; "I have told you the will of God," he wrote the Czar. "It is up to you to accomplish it. . . . God vanquished the visible Napoleon who invaded

Russia. He will likewise vanquish the moral Napoleon [Golitzin]. . . . You can strike him down in three minutes, with a stroke of the pen."

Still unable to make up his mind, Alexander asked Arakcheyev to bring about a reconciliation between the minister and his enemies. At last aware of the danger, Golitzin made the first move: He showed up at Countess Anna Orlova's and, in the absence of the mistress of the house, invited Photius to have a friendly talk. He was met by a bristling madman with glittering eyes and foam on his lips who shouted the worst insults at him, while witnesses of the scene trembled and crossed themselves. "If you do not repent, and if those who surround you do not make honorable amends, anathema on you all!" roared Photius. "You, as the leader of the godless, you shall not see God, you shall not enter into the Kingdom of Christ, you and all your people shall be hurled into hell, where you will remain for eternity! Amen!" Golitzin, terrified, fled with head hanging. After he had left, Photius tucked up his cassock, jumped up and down, and shouted at the top of his lungs, "God is with us!"

The next day the incredible news spread throughout the city: The Minister of Ecclesiastical Matters and Public Education had been anathematized by the archimandrite Photius. Foreseeing that the Czar would not disavow the man whom he regarded as "God's emissary," Golitzin offered his resignation. "For a long time, my dear Prince, I have wanted to have a heart-to-heart talk with you," Alexander told him. "The truth is that you have not been successful in the ministry I entrusted to you." On May 15, 1824, Golitzin was relieved of his duties. His portfolio was immediately turned over to Chichkov. The affairs of the Orthodox Church were removed from the jurisdiction of the Minister of Ecclesiastical Matters and Public Education. The Metropolitan Seraphim was appointed President of the Bible Society, which now had no choice but to keep in line. The fallen Golitzin received as compensation the office of Director of the Postal Administration. Arakcheyev, triumphant, became rapporteur for the affairs of the Holy Synod. Photius wrote of him: "He has conducted himself like a servant of God, a defender of the faith and of the Church, a new St. George." The Czar's other associates now had only minor roles. Prematurely weary, Alexander preferred to surround himself with persons who were old and docile. Longuinov, the Empress's secretary, compared this collection of colorless septuagenarians to a Hogarth painting. "They are a kind of gerontocracy dozing around the helm of State," wrote another contemporary. "The old men—Tatishchev, Lobanov, Lanskoy, Chichkov—are more like the ghosts of ministers than real ministers. Keeping watch in their place there is only Arakcheyev, hated by all."[8]

The more enemies this faithful adviser made, the more the Czar appreciated him. He was relieved that the duel between Arakcheyev and Golitzin had ended in victory for the former. In his view, these two men, though very different in nature, had in common the same narrow-mindedness and the same devotion. One saw everything from the angle of religion, the other from the angle of order on earth. One symbolized the Russia of the mystics, the other the Russia of the police. These twin tendencies, toward messianism and discipline, were ones that Alexander felt deep inside himself. He reconciled the censer and the knout, the Kingdom of God and Siberia. It was piety alone that made him want an obedient nation. And he did not doubt that Arakcheyev would help him in his task with all the necessary severity. The founder of the military colonies, who late in the day had suddenly assumed the role of champion of the true Orthodox faith, thus became a kind of vice-emperor at Alexander's side.

XIV

THE SECRET SOCIETIES

After the definitive victory of the allies over Napoleon, Russia's military prestige was so great that certain European diplomats suspected Alexander of wanting to expand his domain. But he was determined more than ever to remain within his borders. His geographical gains satisfied his conscience with regard to his illustrious predecessors, Peter the Great and Catherine the Great. After all, he had appropriated Finland and Bessarabia, he had acquired territory in the Caucasus by the voluntary submission of Georgia and Mingrelia, he had obtained, by the Treaty of Gulistan signed with Persia, the shores of the Caspian Sea with the province of Dagestan and the cities of Derbent and Baku, and he had extended Russian protection to Poland. What more could he desire? The patriotic war he had conducted with determination to the end had bled the nation white. Henceforth he would think only of restoring ruins and purifying hearts. His ambitions were no longer warlike but moral. And this desire for peace, order, and holiness he wanted to see shared by all the governments in the world. At each meeting with a foreign ambassador, he obstinately repeated his desire for universal harmony. "People do not know Russia," he said to Count Lebzeltern, Austria's new ambassador to St. Petersburg. "They were too busy with the colossus that threatened the life of all [France under Napoleon]; now that it has been destroyed, they turn their gaze toward another colossus [Russia], without thinking that one was malevolent while the other is conservative and has no other thought than the general good. . . . I have seen war from too close up not to detest it, I am tired of it. All the glories it brings in its brilliant moments are only the pleasures of personal vanity and pride, and they can never balance the horrors that accompany it. I have as my goal a quite different kind of pleasure, that of looking after my internal affairs and my subjects. That is my first duty to God as a sovereign and as a man, and never shall I undertake a war unless I am provoked into it, never for personal interest, especially if it might harm the interests or the rights of my brothers."[1] After an interview with the Czar the French ambassador, the Comte de Noailles, wrote to the Duc de Richelieu: "It would be a great mistake to consider the Emperor's passion for drilling and military details as an indication of the ambitious views and warlike intentions of this Prince. The predilection for military means and theories must be entirely separated from the predilection which leads men to put them into practice. The sovereign of this country is quite willing to be the arbiter of Europe, but he has no thought of becoming its conqueror."[2]

To Alexander, however, there could be no "arbitration of Europe" without a strong authority as guardian and overseer. In his mind the Holy Alliance was designed to safeguard both the peace between countries and, inside each country, the social order that was threatened by the consequences of the French Revolution. For the Declaration of the Rights of Man, which had aroused his enthusiasm in his youth, he had now substituted the Apostles' Creed. He could not speak or write a sentence without invoking the Almighty. He now based his political conduct not only on the interest of the country but on a higher morality of which he was sole judge. In his opinion, Good was the concept of monarchy by divine right as it existed before 1789; Evil was everything that tended to oppose it. Metternich encouraged him in this way of thinking. As Chancellor of a country made up of disparate pieces, Metternich could not tolerate a doctrine that preached the right of peoples to self-determination. He feared an awakening of the different nationalities that would lead to the dismemberment of the Hapsburg Empire. Shrewdly, he persuaded Alexander that all the autocratic

states, including Russia, should beware the machinations of revolutionaries who were secretly swarming over their territory. To respect the
will of God, one had to take action against them. Putting aside the
resentment he had harbored against Metternich since their altercation
at the Congress of Vienna, Alexander suddenly discovered in the Austrian minister an ally after his own heart. Eagerly he embraced his
views. During the great international meetings that followed, the wise
Capo d'Istria tried in vain to moderate his master's theocratic tendencies. Alexander had mounted the horse of the Apocalypse.

The first of a series of congresses took place at Aix-la-Chapelle (Aa-
chen) in September, November 1818. The secondary states that had
signed the Holy Alliance were excluded from these conferences and
were merely informed of the decisions of the great partners. England
participated in the deliberations as an exception, and Alexander insisted that the Duc de Richelieu be present as the representative of
France. The Czar would have liked to see a very close union among the
allies, who would commit themselves to coming to one another's aid in
case of any threat to their present regimes. The British delegate, Lord
Castlereagh, indignantly opposed this potential intervention by a third
party—even a friendly country—in the internal affairs of its neighbors.
"Nothing would be more immoral," he said, "or more prejudicial to the
character of government generally than the idea that their force [the
force of kings and nations] was collectively to be prostituted to the
support of established power without any consideration of the extent to
which it was abused."[3] Beaten on that point, Alexander did win his case
for the reemergence of France. In his opinion, by prolonging their
military occupation of the country the allies ran the risk of "hurting the
pride of peoples, of deepening their wounds, of further alienating them
from a dynasty which they might accuse of being responsible for their
troubles." Despite great reluctance, the allies finally agreed to withdraw their troops from French territory and to cancel the French debt,
which still amounted to 263 million francs, including 42 million owed
Russia. France, allowed to join as an equal with the four other great
powers (Russia, Prussia, Austria, England) that claimed to be "inspired
by God," came out once for all from the shadows of political punishment. The event was consecrated by a brief visit to Paris by the Czar
and the King of Prussia, reviews of Russian troops at Valenciennes and
Maubeuge, and a dinner at the table of Louis XVIII. Back at Aix-la-
Chapelle for the end of the congress, Alexander learned from his spies
of a Bonapartist plot against him. The conspirators were planning to
kidnap him on his way to Brussels and force him to sign a proclamation

ordering that Napoleon be freed and that his son accede to the throne under the regency of Marie Louise. The Czar, who more than ever placed his trust in Providence, was not worried by this threat. To make it easier for possible kidnappers to recognize him, he even wore for his journey a three-cornered hat decorated with enormous white plumes. Despite this distinctive sign, no one made so bold as to attack him. True, a great number of gendarmes served as escort for his barouche, and some of them, disguised as peasants, kept an eye on the villages along the route.

On his return to Russia, Alexander learned the painful news of the death of his favorite sister, the flamboyant Catherine, who in January 1816 had become Queen of Württemberg. It was said she had succumbed to influenza. She died on December 28, 1818. The Czar's grief was profound and silent. The court went into mourning. "I can only regard this death as one of those inexplicable blows of Providence for which one cannot account," Elizabeth wrote her mother.

But politics very quickly regained the ascendancy in Alexander's fevered mind. While the French plot had turned out to be imaginary, there were other sinister movements throughout Europe that were very alarming. In Germany the youth continued to make trouble; in Italy the Carbonari, a patriotic organization, was spreading its poison every day; in Spain Ferdinand VII had been forced to restore the constitution granted in 1812; in Naples a veritable revolution had broken out, and the King, yielding to popular discontent, had likewise granted a constitution; in France, after the assassination of the Duc de Berry, the whole "intellectual underworld" was in ferment.*

Alexander could not forget that in other countries he had always posed as a champion of constitutional regimes. Had he not promoted the Charter in France? But today, logically, he should leave behind the dreams of his youth. As a signatory of the Holy Alliance, he had become the defender of the Christian order against the supporters of atheistic liberalism. "The same disorganizing principles," he wrote in French to Golitzin, "while they are enemies of the throne, are directed even more against the Christian religion: They are only the practical application of the theories preached by Voltaire, Mirabeau, Condorcet, and all

---

*The assassination in 1820 of the Duc de Berry, as he left the Opera, was the act of a somewhat deranged loner, a certain Louvel. But it served as a pretext for the ultramonarchists to obtain the dismissal of Decazes, considered too weak a minister, and the return to authoritarian policies that were anathema to the liberal opposition.

those self-styled philosophers known under the name of Encyclopedists. . . . Have no illusions, there is a conspiracy among all these societies: they all spread out and communicate with each other—I have
irrefutable proof of it in hand—and all these anti-Christian sects, which
are founded on the principles of the so-called philosophy of Voltaire,
have sworn relentless vengeance upon all governments."

It was clear to Alexander that a vast international organization was
stretching its tentacles across Europe. Its central committee was
located, naturally, in Paris. Metternich affirmed it and the Czar believed it. The successful coup that the French had brought off in 1789
in their own country they now wanted to reproduce in the rest of the
world. In June 1821 an eminent diplomat, Monsieur de La Ferronnays,
described the political climate in France as the Czar analyzed it: "The
violence of our discussions, the insolent audacity of the principles which
people sometimes dare proclaim from our tribunes, the crimes and
conspiracies of which France has been the scene for the last eighteen
months, the especially well-established idea that it is in Paris that the
revolutions in Italy and Spain are planned and directed—all this has
become a powerful weapon in the hands of Metternich to excite the
fears of the Emperor."[4] Nevertheless, for the time being Alexander was
not contemplating interference in French political life. As long as Louis
XVIII was firmly seated on his throne, with a team of reactionary ministers around him, the movements of public opinion could be tolerated
by the allies. But it was necessary to keep a close watch on the degree
of restlessness among the people. Thus the Czar had been very disturbed by the action taken by his brother-in-law, the King of Württemberg: That foolish prince had seen fit to abolish serfdom in his country
and to grant his people the constitution promised in 1813. Another
brother-in-law had likewise disappointed Alexander by his weakness of
character in the face of the demands of the common people: The Prince
of Orange, husband of Grand Duchess Anne and future King of Holland, had rashly granted his subjects freedom of the press, which, of
course, they had immediately put to bad use. An energetic intervention
by the Czar, in October 1816, put an end to the "abuses" by tightening
up censorship and clamping down on liberal circles with police surveillance.

But these slight rents in the sacred mantle of the Holy Alliance were
as nothing compared to the insolent manifestations of Evil in Italy and
Spain. The danger was so great that on October 20, 1820, a congress
met in Troppau, in Silesia. Alexander went to it accompanied by Capo
d'Istria. He had expressed his personal feeling a few weeks earlier, in

French, in a speech opening the second Diet of Warsaw: "The spirit of evil is trying to resume its disastrous sway; already it hovers over part of Europe, already it is piling up crimes and catastrophes." Upon seeing Metternich again he had the comforting feeling, according to the Austrian minister, that he was meeting "an old comrade in arms." Alexander was now convinced that only the Chancellor of Austria could help him behead the revolutionary hydra. How could he have once opposed the policies of this admirable man? More than ever he wanted to march shoulder-to-shoulder with him under the banner of the Holy Alliance. In a burst of friendly feeling he exclaimed to his attentive listener, "You don't understand why I am no longer the same; I'm going to tell you. Between 1813 and 1820 seven years passed, and I feel as if those seven years were as long as a century. In 1820 I would not do for any price what I did in 1813. It is not you who have changed, it is I. You have nothing to repent; for myself, I cannot say the same!"

It was in the middle of the congress that he received news of the rebellion of the Semeonovsky regiment, which only strengthened his conviction that forceful measures were necessary. This manifestation of the "satanic spirit" in his own country drew him even closer to Metternich. Having settled the fate of the mutineers in Russia, he turned with increased rage to the mutineers in Europe. Only the wise Capo d'Istria exercised some restraint on his despotic impulses. Metternich sensed in this prudent adviser a moderating element that might thwart his own strategy and wanted to create a rupture between him and the Czar. But Alexander kept his assistant with the vague awareness that while he was an irritation he also provided necessary protection.

There were no violins and women in Troppau, any more than there had been at Aix-la-Chapelle. No entertainment, no dancing. Only work. The weather was vile. The little town was sinking into the mud. "The ground in Troppau is as soft and slippery as butter," wrote Metternich. "We flounder in it as in chocolate ice cream. As one cannot step out of doors without sinking in up to one's knees, the municipality has had some thousands of planks laid on the ground in a row. They make a narrow but very convenient path. . . . Emperor Alexander goes for a walk every day on these planks. Naturally, all the men going in the opposite direction splash through the mud, while when he meets women coming the other way he plunges into it himself to let them pass, unless they forestall him by sacrificing themselves."

At last the allied plenipotentiaries drew up an official memorandum defining their attitude in the face of all the revolutionary tendencies: "The powers," it read, "have the right to take, by common accord, precautionary measures against States in which political changes brought about by rebellion are (if only by example) inimical to the legislative power, especially when that spirit of restlessness is communicated to neighboring States by emissaries charged with propagating it." Despite the refusal of France and England to sign this threatening text, King Ferdinand of Naples was summoned to Laibach (Ljubljana) to consult on joint punitive action to be taken in his country. Delighted with this first concrete result, Alexander wrote to Princess Sophie Mestcherski, "We are concerned here with a highly important but highly difficult task. Our purpose is to counteract the empire of evil, which is spreading rapidly by all the occult means at the disposal of the satanic spirit which directs it. The remedy we seek is above the puny power of man. Only the Saviour, through the power of His divine word, can provide the means. Let us therefore invoke Him with all the fullness and fervor of our hearts, so that He may deign to shed His Holy Spirit upon us."[5]

At the new congress, which opened in Laibach on January 8, 1821, efforts were made to work out concrete measures. In the meantime, Capo d'Istria's prestige on the diplomatic stage had fallen. Under pressure from Metternich, the Czar was becoming irritated with this pusillanimous adviser who pulled at his coattails when he wanted to go forward. To bring order to Europe, Austria had drawn up an army of ninety thousand men; Alexander promised to send ninety thousand Russian soldiers to help them if necessary. General Ermolov was called to Laibach to take command of the Czar's army of intervention, but the Russian troops only stood by in readiness. The Austrians were sufficient for the task. Crossing the Po, they reduced Naples to obedience. Shortly afterward they also crushed the insurrection in Piedmont. Ermolov was relieved: "Without doubt," he wrote, "no commander of an army has ever been so satisfied as I am not to have taken part in a war." Although the Russians had not moved, Metternich was now sure of their military collaboration in case of need. "Russia does not lead us," he wrote. "It is we who lead Emperor Alexander, for several quite simple reasons. He needs to be advised, but he has lost all his advisers. He regards Capo d'Istria as a chief among the Carbonari. He distrusts his army, his ministers, his nobles, and his people. Now in that situation, one does not lead."

The following year the allies gathered at the Congress of Verona to examine the affairs of Spain. Speaking through Chateaubriand, Louis XVIII's new plenipotentiary, France declared herself ready to reestablish order beyond the Pyrenees by force. The Czar was delighted with this proud language, discovering in the romantic writer a soul with the same true ring as his own. Sure that he would be understood, he told Chateaubriand grandiloquently, "There can no longer be English, French, Russian, Prussian, or Austrian policy; there is only a general policy which, for the salvation of all, should be accepted by peoples and kings alike. It is up to me to be the first to demonstrate that I am convinced of the principles on which I founded the Alliance. . . . What could tempt me? . . . Providence has not placed 800,000 soldiers at my orders in order to satisfy my ambition but in order to protect religion, morality, and justice, and to make those principles of order prevail on which human society rests."[6] In support of this proclamation he once again offered the cooperation of the Russian army in any action of reprisal against the troublemakers. Fortunately, again this was only empty talk and the regiments never left their barracks.

But the Russian officers were growing increasingly uneasy over the Czar's willingness to send his troops everywhere to stifle spontaneous movements of revolt. They were afraid that they, the natural defenders of the motherland, would be turned into an international police force. Immediately after Laibach General Vassilchikov, the commander in chief of the Guard, had warned Prince Volkonsky of the reluctance of the Russian military elite to play a repressive role in far-off lands. "You do not know the extent to which liberal ideas are spreading among us," he had written him. "Don't answer me with the worn-out phrase, 'Silence them!'—too many tongues are wagging for them to be stilled. The revolution already exists in men's minds, and the only way to save the ship is not to put on more sail than the force of the wind allows."

In spite of almost unanimous disapproval, echoes of which reached him from Russia, Alexander persisted in his intention of being the pure crusader for the cause of monarchy throughout the world. The demoniacal spirit, formerly personified by Napoleon, had been split into many parts and was now incarnated in thousands of revolutionaries. Having fought the Grand Army in uniform, the Czar owed it to himself to fight a new Grand Army in civilian clothes. "I say that the present evil," he wrote Golitzin, "is even more dangerous than the devastating despotism of Napoleon, since the present doctrines are far more appealing to the multitude than the military yoke under which he held it . . . You recommend that I divest myself completely of my own will and place myself in God's hands. It is to that idea that all my thoughts are dedicated."

But there came a time when the word of the Almighty no longer sounded distinctly in Alexander's ears. Suddenly obliged to face the problem of Greece, he hesitated. Shortly before leaving for Laibach he had learned that one of his young aides-de-camp, Prince Ypsilanti, a Greek, had crossed the Prut with a few supporters recruited in Russia and had sent out a call for rebellion against the Turkish oppressor. Bands of mountain men armed with old flintlocks and sabers had enthusiastically joined him, and the revolt had spread like wildfire to Peloponnesus and Attica. Soon Byron brought the light of his genius to the Hellenic ranks. Pushkin, exiled in Kishinev, dreamed of imitating him. The struggle continued in fits and starts, a barbarous struggle marked by sudden raids and by massacres of the civilian population.

In Russia everyone was in great excitement over this holy war. What was the Czar going to do? Could he, the defender of the Christian faith, let his Orthodox brothers be hacked to pieces? Alexander was in a dilemma: Religion ordered him to intervene on the side of the Greeks, but his horror of insurrection prompted him to condemn these same Greeks for rising up against their Turkish masters. He had already told Capo d'Istria that he didn't want to hear about new difficulties with Constantinople on the subject of liberating the Moldavians, the Walachians, and the Serbs: "All that is a very good idea, but in order to make something of it we would have to fire cannon, and that is something I will not do. We've had enough of wars on the Danube, they demoralize the armies. Besides, peace is not yet consolidated in Europe, and the makers of revolutions would like nothing better than to see me grappling with the Turks."

This time Capo d'Istria returned to the charge with greater determination. A Greek by birth, he felt that he was serving both the country of his ancestors and the greatness of Russia by demanding that the Czar take energetic action against Turkey. Even his enemies recognized him as a man of courage and intelligence, perfectly informed on affairs in Europe and in western Asia. But Alexander dug in his heels against his minister who was drawing him into a war. He knew that he could not count on his allies to support him in a possible expedition. In vain had he cried to the French ambassador, "Look at the map! What is needed is to have a fine French fleet force the entrance to the Dardanelles and come to join hands with us in St. Sophia!" Not France, nor England, nor Austria would respond to his approaches.

In the end, good relations among the great powers were more important to the Czar than the sufferings of a few thousand coreligionists. Metternich persuaded him that Ypsilanti was in league with the Italian Carbonari and that if the Greek insurrection triumphed it would spread to neighboring nations. The Czar acquiesced, and Capo d'Istria was disavowed. The Chancellor of Austria said ironically of Alexander, "If ever anyone turned from black to white, it is surely he!" And: "Emperor Alexander is a firm believer in my school." As an apt pupil of his new Austrian friend, the Czar stated, "If we answer the Turks with war, the managing committee in Paris will triumph and no government will remain in place." And he wrote Golitzin, "There is no doubt that the impetus for this insurrectional movement was given by the same central committee, directly from Paris, with the intention of creating a diversion in favor of Naples and of preventing us from destroying one of Satan's synagogues established solely for the purpose of propagating and spreading his anti-Christian doctrine." So much the worse for the Orthodox Greeks, for Russia's traditional policy since Peter the Great and Catherine the Great, for all the liberals in St. Petersburg and Moscow: Alexander informed the Porte that he was personally hostile to all subversion and that he desired only that the treaties signed between the two countries should be maintained. Prince Ypsilanti was publicly condemned and removed from the ranks of the Russian army. After his troops were dispersed by the Turks, he took refuge in Austria, where he was imprisoned. Capo d'Istria told the Emperor that under these circumstances he could not continue to head the Ministry of Foreign Affairs. "Very well," said Alexander, "since it is necessary, let us part."

Thus disappeared the only man capable of holding his own against Metternich.* He was replaced by the young and pliant Nesselrode, who submitted entirely to Austria's views. "The principle of evil has been rooted out," Metternich exclaimed cheerfully; "Count Capo d'Istria is finished for the rest of his days. . . . Europe will be delivered from a great danger with which it was threatened by the influence of that man." And he reported to Emperor Francis, "The present Russian cabinet has destroyed at one blow the great work of Peter the Great and all his successors. Everything is on a new basis here, and what Russia loses in moral force the Porte gains."

Among the Russians there was consternation. "Too bad that the likable and intelligent Capo d'Istria is leaving us," wrote Karamzin. "There are few men of that sort. Europe has buried the Greeks. May God raise the dead." Grand Duke Nicholas's young wife, the former Charlotte of Prussia who had taken the Russian name Alexandra Feodo-

---

*Capo d'Istria left St. Petersburg for Ems in mid-August 1822. Then he went to Switzerland and settled near Geneva. In 1827 he became the first president of liberated Greece and died by an assassin's hand four years later.

rovna, allowed herself to criticize her brother-in-law's decision publicly. "I told the Emperor," she wrote, "that the cause of the Greeks could not be compared to that of the other revolutionaries; it seems to me that it is just and noble and fit to arouse enthusiasm in the minds of the young." The Czar felt more and more isolated, discredited, spurned, like a traitor to the sacred cause of his country. He admitted to Lebzeltern that his policy was "not the one which Catherine followed, not the one which the army and the public would wish." Lebzeltern wrote Metternich, "The Greek affair is finished in the eyes of the Emperor. He fully appreciates all the bad aspects of his position. Dignity, honor, the interests of his empire and of his august person have been sacrificed. The reputation of Russia has declined in the last three years and the country knows that. . . . The Porte at last dares to defy her." And Monsieur de La Ferronnays, analyzing the internal situation of the country, noted, "It is not easy to follow the course of a cabinet which has no definite direction, whose system, plans, and decisions are as uncertain, inconstant, and variable as the character of a prince who is no doubt prompted by the noblest sentiments and the purest intentions but who—in the exaggerated fear of allowing himself to be influenced or dominated, wanting to see and do everything by himself and by himself alone—loses his way in the immensity of details, a prince who, to avoid placing his trust in the wrong persons, promises himself to accord it to no one and consequently puts at the head of his cabinet men who are in open and obvious opposition as to principles and sentiments, a prince, finally, who believes he can subject the politics and ambitions of his century to the abstract mystical rules which he himself takes for the basis of his private conduct."[7]

Indeed, Alexander's sole consolation in failure came from God, whose designs he continued to believe he was executing. His mind constantly returned to the mystical significance of the murder of his father and of his personal struggle against Napoleon. Those were the two great events in his life. And now his rival for glory was no more: The "prisoner of Europe" had passed away on St. Helena on May 5, 1821. When he mused on the past, Alexander wondered whether Napoleon had not been the ideal enemy for him, a friendly enemy. To him, the man had represented both something to resist and something to lean on. When the support gave way, he had lost his balance. Suddenly he found himself unsteady on his feet, the only one of his kind, surrounded by dwarfs.

The Czar was overwhelmed by the futility of all these struggles, these intrigues, these deaths. He had greatly aged. His eyes were sad, evasive. At every moment he thought people were whispering behind him, criticizing some fault in his dress. He would get angry with the people around him, demand explanations, apologies. "Tell me the truth," he growled to General Kisselev; "perhaps there is something comical about the back of my uniform, for I saw you and your two comrades sneering when you looked at me." "It was painful to see such weaknesses in a man so distinguished in heart and mind," noted Grand Duchess Alexandra Feodorovna. And the subtle Monsieur de La Ferronnays, who observed the sovereign on every occasion yet despaired of finding the key to his personality, described him as follows: "What becomes more of an enigma to me every day is the character of Emperor Alexander. . . . A conversation with him always leaves the most favorable impression. You leave him persuaded that this prince combines the noble qualities of a true knight with those of a great sovereign and a man of keen mind endowed with the greatest energy. He reasons wonderfully well; he presses arguments; he explains his position with the eloquence and warmth of conviction. And when it is all over, experience, the history of his life, and the things one sees every day warn you not to trust it. Repeated acts of weakness prove to you that the energy he puts into his words is not always present in his character; but, on the other hand, this weak character can have an unexpected burst of energy and anger, and that may suffice to make him suddenly take the most violent decisions, the consequences of which are incalculable."[8]

Curiously enough, the devotion to high principles that in his youth had shaped Alexander's thinking about internal policy (his dream of liberating the serfs and of making his subjects equal before the law) manifested itself again, late in life, in his conception of foreign policy (fraternity among the monarchic nations in the observance of Christian precepts). But just as in internal policy Alexander's aspirations had resulted in a harsh tyranny exemplified by the military colonies, so in foreign policy they had found expression in the Holy Alliance, an instrument of repression aimed at any and all subversive tendencies in Europe. Like his grandmother Catherine II, after a period of illusion, he had recognized that French republican principles could not be applied to rough Russian reality. He had unconsciously followed the same route she had taken, starting with the idealism of the Encyclopedists and ending with a reinforced autocracy. Everything that as a youth he had criticized in her, he now discovered in himself, fully developed, justified, necessary. He was pained by this reincarnation in his own flesh of a despotic old woman. At other times—more rarely—it was the obtuse, militaristic spirit of Paul I that possessed him. His thoughts always seemed to be dominated either by his grandmother or by his father. But where was he himself in the midst of this extreme confusion? Was it possible that Alexander I did not exist?

Stirred by contrary passions, he could not find his center of gravity. For the last few years he had not felt at ease anywhere. He had a restless desire to be always on the move. It seemed to him that the best defense against his inner torment was to get away from his usual surroundings. As soon as a congress abroad was proposed, he rushed to attend it, as if in escaping from his palace he escaped from himself. But these journeys beyond the borders were not enough. Hardly a month passed without his undertaking a long trip across Russia. He went to see Moscow, the martyred city, Kiev, Warsaw, Riga, Bessarabia, Odessa, the Crimea, Taganrog, the shores of the Sea of Azov, Rostov-on-Don . . . Wild races by night and by day, over roads full of potholes. The strain of these expeditions brought the Czar a kind of intoxication. When he visited his empire he had his fill of ovations, genuflections, speeches, parades. He admired the number and diversity of the people subject to his law. He persuaded himself that a country so vast and so rich in men and natural resources was destined one day to lead all other nations.

And in reality, despite the terrible upheaval of the Napoleonic wars and the levying of 900,000 recruits in three years, it seemed as if Russia was being pushed toward the future by the irresistible force of all its energies. The number of factories was increasing; in Moscow alone, hardly reconstructed after the great fire, there were a dozen spinning mills. Serfs who owned small manufacturing enterprises grew rich and bought their emancipation, paying a high price to their masters; there were a growing number of free laborers in industrial jobs; the level of wages was rising again. The beautification of St. Petersburg was going forward. Twelve million rubles were spent just on the construction of the red granite quays in the capital. Transactions on the stock exchange amounted to two hundred million rubles annually, and the commercial activity of the port on the Neva had never been so brilliant. In Bessarabia there was such an influx of "colonists" that the population doubled in six years; in Odessa, which had been proclaimed a free port, merchants of all nationalities were doing business. Scientific expeditions were prospecting the mineral wealth of the Caucasus and the Urals; the reestablishment of maritime trade with England had expanded the market for wheat; only agriculture trailed behind, the feudal system of serfdom giving very poor practical results.

Despite this revival of industry and trade, the mood of the nation was somber. The shadow of Arakcheyev hovered over the country, and the repression of liberal ideas was the despair of the young. Everyone in Russia who read, thought, or dreamed was now hostile to the government. Only opportunists crowded around the throne. "People continually and almost openly attack the hold which religious ideas have over the monarch and compare them to a kind of fanaticism," wrote a French diplomat, Monsieur de Malvirade, in 1819. And Longuinov, the Empress's private secretary, noted, "It is in the order of things that revolution should take place in our country sooner or later, since all of Europe has been through it. You will see that the conflagration will break out because of these military colonies: even today it would take only a spark to set everything ablaze."

The decree of 1822 closing the Masonic lodges and dissolving similar societies had only strengthened the secret resistance to oppression in certain circles. Opponents to the regime were recruited especially among the military elite. The Napoleonic wars had taken many Russian officers to the heart of Europe, Germany and France, and they had caught the fever of liberal ideas. Comparing the lot of the people in the conquered countries and in their own country, they had been seized with shame at Russia's unpardonable backwardness. After their return home they had found it hard to endure the degradation of the masses, the spying on private life, the harshness of military service. "It was with a pang of bitterness that we rediscovered at home serfdom, the misery of the people, the persecution of liberals," wrote one of them, Yakushkin. "When they had come into contact with the French liberals, our officers, without being aware of it, had taken over their way of thinking and their taste for representative institutions," observed another, von Wiesen. "Now they blushed for their country humiliated by tyranny. Had Russia emancipated Europe only to remain herself in slavery?" Still another, the most notable of all, Pestel, concluded, "Everywhere we saw thrones restored and overthrown. Our minds became accustomed to revolutions, to their possibilities, their benefits. . . ." These young men, whose heads were full of theories they had heard expounded in progressive circles in the occupied cities, dreamed of a social upheaval that, without bloodshed, would institute a humane civilization in Russia. Their role, they thought, had not ended with the fall of Napoleon. Having served their motherland in time of war, they should devote themselves to her in time of peace. In the beginning they set forth these ideas with an openness and candor that astonished the publicist N. Turgenev. "The officers of the Guard," he wrote, "especially attracted attention by the freedom and boldness with which they expressed themselves, caring very little whether they were speaking in a public

place or in a drawing room, whether those who heard them supported
their doctrines or opposed them." As heroes of the patriotic war, they
thought they were safe from prosecution. But the fear of spies soon
taught them prudence, and they grouped themselves in secret societies.
The earliest of these was the "Union of Salvation." Chief among its
members were the two Muraviev brothers (Artamon and Nikita),
Prince Sergei Trubetskoy, Sergei and Matthew Muraviev-Apostol, Paul
Pestel, and Prince Valerian Golitzin. Later the society expanded and
took the name of "Union of the Public Good." Most of its members, who
quickly came to number two hundred, belonged to Freemasonry. Their
discussions were high-minded and confused. According to one of them,
Lorer, their goal was "to spread education, combat abuses, sacrifice
personal interest to the happiness of humanity, and try to hold the most
modest posts in order to make justice triumph by setting an example
of disinterestedness." As soon as a practical proposal was made, these
idealists fought it as being too daring. They were only happy in the
pleasant mists of the imagination. "The end," they liked to say, "does
not justify the means."

However, a program gradually emerged from this tumult. It provided that serfdom be abolished, that citizens be equal before the law,
that the great decisions of government be made openly, that the mo-
nopoly on the sale of spirits be abandoned, that the duration of service
for soldiers be reduced in peacetime, and so on. These pious wishes
could not satisfy a man as fiery as Pestel. At his initiative a revolutionary
group formed within the "Union" with the purpose of overthrowing the
monarchy. Pestel even went so far as to envisage assassinating the Czar
and wiping out the whole Romanov family. After the rebellion of the
Semeonovsky regiment, a number of its officers were sent far from St.
Petersburg and incorporated in line regiments stationed in the Ukraine.
Pestel and the two Muraviev-Apostols were among them. When they
arrived at their new post, they created the "Southern Society," while
in the capital the old "Union of the Public Good," deprived of some of
its leading spirits, became the "Northern Society."

The ranks of this Northern Society were rapidly swelled by an influx
of officers from the general staff, the Horse Guards, the navy, and the
regiment of grenadiers. The president, Nikita Muraviev, drafted a plan
for a constitutional monarchy that left great powers to the Czar but also
provided for an assembly of national representatives. In the south,
Pestel's friends were more radical. They wanted no part of a monarchy,
hereditary, elective, or constitutional. Only a republic would suit them.
They preached direct action. But they had no more idea than the others

how to go about creating an uprising in a disciplined army and an amorphous population.

Needless to say, all this talk behind closed doors did not escape the government spies. General Vassilchikov, the commander in chief of the Guard, presented Alexander with a detailed report on the intentions of the conspirators. His chief of staff, Benckendorff, wrote a memorandum on his own account indicating the goals of the associations and the names of their principal members. It would have been easy for Alexander to launch a vast dragnet as soon as he saw the documents. All these wriggling young people would be caught in its meshes. But at the moment of acting he was gripped by a strange inhibition. He had sacrificed the Masonic lodges without hesitation, but he did not feel the courage to strike down so many officers with mad aspirations. In the list submitted to him he found the names of devoted functionaries, captains who had covered themselves with glory in battle, the most brilliant ornaments of Russia. A few sentences in Benckendorff's report reassured him. "In conclusion," he read, "we may say that these hotheads have been mistaken in their mad hope for a general action. With the exception of the capital, where, as in every capital in the world, there are many who are ready to be set on fire, we can state with certainty that Russia is not thinking of a constitution. . . . The Russians are so well accustomed to the present regime, which enables them to live calmly and happily and which corresponds to the local situation, the circumstances, and the soul of the people, that the mere idea of a change seems inconceivable to them."

While General Vassilchikov was questioning the Czar as to his intentions regarding the associations of officers, Alexander hardly listened to him. He was suddenly overwhelmed by fond memories of Speransky, Laharpe, Czartoryski, the Secret Committee—all the friends of his distant past. Recalling the idealistic days of his youth, he had a sense of bewilderment. For a few seconds it seemed he no longer coincided with himself. What a distance between the liberal adolescent he had been and the sorrowful, mature man who held this indictment in his hand! At last he said, in French, "My dear general, you who have been in my service since the beginning of my reign know that I shared and encouraged these illusions and errors." And after a long silence he added, "It is not for me to deal severely with them."

XV

TAGANROG

Fond as the Czar had been of the company of women in his youth, he was completely indifferent to it in middle age. The war years had separated him from his mistress, the beautiful Maria Naryshkina. Since then she had traveled a great deal in Russia and abroad, accompanied by a princely retinue, had had affairs with other men, and had thus lost the hold over Alexander that "the power of habit"[1] had given her. Learning that she was about to return to the capital, he wrote in French to his spiritual adviser, Koshelev, to reassure him as to his intentions: "I cannot defer saying a word to you about the arrival of Madame Naryshkina in St. Petersburg. I hope you know my present state too well to harbor the least anxiety about me in that connection. Besides, even if I had still been a man of the world, it would have taken no special virtue on my part to remain completely aloof from this person after everything that has happened on her side. Yours, heart and soul, in our divine Master." Touched by grace, and perhaps also by fatigue, he no longer wished to yield to the temptations of the flesh. When Alexander saw his former favorite again, he felt only the embarrassment of a guilty memory. With her white dress, her smile, her perfume, she belonged to a false world in which he no longer had a place. While she tried to recapture the playful tone of their conversations in the old days, he talked to her about moral regeneration in the shadow of the cross. The only remaining bond between them was their daughter, Sophie Naryshkina. Having no living children by the Empress, Alexander was very attached to this pretty little person of eighteen, who was elegant, educated, aware of her true parentage, and preparing to wed Count Shuvalov. But she suffered from consumption, which was growing disturbingly worse. Every day, morning and evening, the Czar received in his study a bulletin on her health. On June 23, 1824, while he was getting ready to attend artillery maneuvers, he learned that Sophie was dead. He burst into sobs, weeping so freely that, according to his doctor, Tarassov, "the whole front of his shirt, on his chest, was wet." A quarter of an hour later, he recovered his self-control, put on his uniform, had his horse led up, and left for the review. The next day he wrote to Arakcheyev, "Don't worry about me. It is God who has willed it, and I am able to submit. I shall bear my affliction with resignation and I pray God to fortify my soul." He had hardly sent the letter when he went to Gruzino in person to find distraction from his sorrow by inspecting the military colonies. They were his favorite enterprise, the one of which he was proudest. He intended to abolish the taverns in these paradises of discipline, a grave problem that he discussed with Arakcheyev. "I hope the Almighty will allow us to complete this work successfully and that He will deign to help us with it," he said.

In spite of the pleasure he took in seeing the soldier-farmers working in uniform, he could not forget his Sophie, who had died just before she was to have been married. Curiously, this mourning brought him closer not to his former mistress but to his wife, as if by striking him, God had wanted to bring him back into legitimate paths. Elizabeth, always understanding, wept with her husband over the death of his child born of another woman. Having sobered down herself, no longer hoping to arouse the admiration of any man, she had dismissed past infidelities from her mind and now longed only for quiet conjugal harmony. Faded and thin, with feverish eyes and blotchy cheeks, she counted only on mutual understanding to hold Alexander. "I no longer dream of the possibility that my face could be counted for anything," she said. "What remains of my desire to please relates entirely to moral qualities."

Having been pulled in so many different directions for so long, the Czar had a sense of finding refuge with her. The love that was long since dead between them was succeeded by affection. At Czarskoye Selo the couple arranged moments to be alone together. Elizabeth wrote in French to her mother, "Since my apartment is too cold at this time of year and is, moreover, separated from the Emperor's by even colder rooms, he has forced me, by appealing to my feelings, to move into a part of his apartment, three rooms arranged with perfect elegance. It was really touching, the combat between our two noble souls before I agreed to accept this sacrifice. The next day after dinner I went for a sleigh ride with the Emperor until nightfall. After which, he wanted me to sit with him in his study while he attended to business."

There were some who deplored the couple's new understanding because the Emperor, liking to withdraw with the Empress, isolated himself from the court and sometimes failed in his duty to appear in public. When Elizabeth wanted to slip into the Czar's apartment at the Winter Palace, she made her way through secret passages and so evaded the curiosity of her entourage. Yet there was nothing passionate about their meetings. They read the Bible and talked freely about family matters and political concerns. During these conversations she was all sweetness and he felt free from all constraint. "One would think," she wrote her mother, "that I wanted to boast about that which is prescribed by human and divine laws, but there are so many rivalries [in the imperial family] that I am reduced to thinking of myself sometimes as Alexander's mistress, or as if we had been married secretly."

Reading of these chaste relations between husband and wife, the Margravine of Baden wondered whether her imperial son-in-law, enlightened by the Lord, was still "capable of feeling sexual impulses." She said so bluntly in a letter to her daughter. But Elizabeth did not need to have physical relations with her husband in order to be happy. When the Czar left for one of his tours of inspection across the empire, she was forlorn: "Here I am, left alone again, all alone, in this family in which I find not a shadow of affection." When he wrote her from Moscow that he regretted his absence, she was as excited as a schoolgirl: "He told me that he had wished I was there. Alas! I should have liked nothing better and it would have been so easy!"

Early in 1824 Alexander was confined to his bed with a high fever. At the same time he was suffering from an attack of erysipelas in his left leg, already injured in a fall from his horse. Elizabeth felt sorry for him but was at the same time delighted to have this opportunity to show her devotion. She spent hours at the patient's bedside, her eyes fixed on the face full of suffering. On January 31 she wrote her mother, "The day before yesterday the Emperor said something to me that was very sweet to my ears and which I can share only with you, Mama. He said, *You will see that I shall owe my recovery to you,* because he thinks he owes the first tolerably good night he has had to a bolster I had given him for his head, which was paining him extremely." And again: "This time of trials has been shortened by the real affection the Emperor showed me; he seemed to be pleased to have me do little things for him, he allowed me to sit by him while he slept and to serve him at his lunch."

As soon as the Czar recovered he succumbed again to his craze for travel, visiting the principal localities in European Russia. He returned exhausted to Czarskoye Selo and had hardly gotten over the strain of the journey when he was dumbfounded to learn of a terrible catastrophe that had just struck his capital. On November 7, 1824, the Neva, driven by southwest gales, had swelled, overflowed its banks, and rushed through the lower parts of St. Petersburg. The furious waves swept the walls of the Winter Palace, surged into the cellars of town houses, broke up wooden huts, tore away bridges, and carried off pellmell cattle, horses, abandoned carriages, and pieces of furniture that crashed into each other in the raging current. More than three hundred houses were destroyed and five hundred persons perished, caught in the rising waters. A similar but smaller flood had occurred in 1777, the year of Alexander's birth. The superstitious saw this coincidence as a sign of divine wrath. The Czar himself was painfully struck by it. He went to inspect the damage and wept on seeing the disaster. The crowd surrounded him, groaning. A man came forward and cried, "God is punishing us for our sins!" "No," replied Alexander, "He is punishing me for mine."

He sincerely believed it. As on every occasion when fate dealt him a blow, the ghost of his father came back to haunt his memory. He had a confused feeling that his crime of patricide-by-consent poisoned even his noblest actions. Even his victory over Napoleon, which should have earned him the indestructible gratitude of his subjects, had, in a way, turned against him. No matter what he did, he was not understood, not loved by his people. His faithful correspondent the Rector Parrot, outraged by the repressive measures he had taken in every area, wrote him frankly and gravely, in French, "Do you feel happy, Sire, in this fog of mistrust which at all times hampers your natural movements, which forces you to feel your way, testing the ground at every step, which places a weapon against your most faithful subjects in the hand that would like to strew only benefactions, which paints the young people in the blackest colors, those young people whom yet you love, in spite of the hatred and fear of them which people seek to inspire in you?"

Alexander was weary of these reproaches, which he thought unjustified. Besides, power no longer interested him. Having discovered how empty political satisfactions were, he returned to the dream of his youth: to renounce the throne, retire to an isolated spot in the country, and there end his days in prayer and meditation among the humble. He was not concerned about the problem of succession. Normally, the crown would pass to his brother, Grand Duke Constantine, the dynastic heir. But the latter's marriage to Grand Duchess Anna Feodorovna had been annulled by an imperial manifesto on March 20, 1820, and on May 14 of the same year he had married Countess Joanna Grudzinska, later created Princess Lowicz. This morganatic union presupposed, of course, that he abandoned his right to govern the empire. Having received Constantine's letter of renunciation, Alexander turned to his other brother, Nicholas, third son of Paul I. This robust, energetic young man of rather limited intelligence had married a Prussian princess and now, at the age of twenty-seven, was the father of a healthy boy (the future Alexander II, born in 1818) and several girls. Although Alexander had no liking for Nicholas, he recognized that he had all the qualities needed to rule Russia. A manifesto announcing the change in the order of succession was drafted by Archbishop Philaret, but after having examined the document and revised it, Alexander decided not to publish it, so as not to stir up public opinion prematurely. The solemn act was given to Philaret in a sealed envelope with the following superscription in the Emperor's hand: "To be kept in the Cathedral of the Assumption with the State papers until further orders from me; in case I should die without having given other instructions, the present envelope should be opened, before anything else is done, by the Archbishop of the diocese of Moscow and the Governor General of Moscow, at the Cathedral of the Assumption." For greater security copies of the manifesto were also secretly entrusted to the Council of State, the Holy Synod, and the Senate. Clearly Alexander wanted to announce simultaneously his retirement and the name of his successor. He had spoken of the matter beforehand to Constantine. "I want to abdicate," he had told him. "I no longer have the strength to bear the burden of government. I am informing you now so that you may have time to think about what you will have to do on that occasion." Then he revealed his intentions to Nicholas and his wife, the chief interested parties. "You seem astonished," he had told them, "but know that my brother Constantine, who has never cared about the throne, is more than ever determined to renounce it formally, making his rights pass to his brother Nicholas and his descendants. As for me, I am determined to give up my functions and retire from the world. Now more than ever Europe needs

young sovereigns in all the energy of their strength." "Seeing us ready
to burst into sobs," wrote Grand Duchess Alexandra Feodorovna, "he
tried to comfort and reassure us, saying that this would not happen
immediately, that years would pass before he put his plan into execution, and he left us alone, in the state that can be imagined." Similarly,
Alexander confided to Nicholas's brother-in-law, William of Prussia: "I
shall abandon the throne when I am fifty. . . . I know myself too well
not to feel that in two years I shall no longer have the physical and
mental strength to govern my immense empire. . . . My brother Nicholas is a reasonable and understanding man, just the proper person to
guide the destiny of Russia down the right road. On his coronation day
I shall be in the crowd massed at the foot of the great staircase of honor
in the Kremlin and I shall be the first to shout hurrah."

For the present, Alexander, at age forty-seven, led a gloomy existence shut up in his palace. He only went out to inspect the Guard. The
only ministers he received were Guriev of Finance and Nesselrode of
Foreign Affairs. All other reports about his empire passed through the
sinister Arakcheyev. He would gladly have left the management of the
country to him, but he was still restrained by the awareness of the
mission he had received from God. Whenever he had a moment's
solitude, he knelt before the icons to pray. In time he came to have large
calluses on his knees.[2] The diplomats tried in vain to approach him. The
audiences he granted them were increasingly rare. And underneath his
customary graciousness they could detect a bitter disenchantment.
"Religion orders us to submit when the hand of God weighs heavily
upon us," he said to La Ferronnays. . . . "I try to submit, but I am not
afraid to let you see my weakness and distress."

His prestige had fallen so low that some people already dared to
criticize his acts aloud in the salons. "I recall the complaints about the
weakness of Emperor Alexander I toward Metternich and Arakcheyev," wrote Koshelev. "The old men, the middle-aged, and above
all the young—in a word, almost everyone—condemned his policies at
every turn. Some feared revolution, others ardently desired it and
placed all their hopes in it. The discontent was violent and general. I
shall never forget a soirée attended by Ryleyev, Prince Obolensky,
Pushin, and a few others. . . . Ryleyev read us his patriotic thoughts and
everyone spoke very freely of the necessity of *having done with this
government.*"* Informed of this disaffection, Alexander noted on a
piece of paper: "There are rumors that the deadly spirit of free thinking

---

*In French in the text. Pushin was a friend of Pushkin's.

or liberalism has spread, or at least is spreading, in the army; there are secret societies and clubs all over which have emissaries assigned to propagate their ideas."

Nevertheless, while he recommended increased surveillance of intellectual and military circles, the Czar did not order any investigations or arrests. Beyond everything else he was preoccupied with the health of the Empress. She had caught cold, she was coughing, she had a rising fever that alarmed the court physicians. "I saw the Emperor in great anxiety and touching affliction," wrote Karamzin to Dmitriev. "He loves [the Empress] tenderly. God grant that they may live a long time together in that deep love." And Alexander wrote to Karamzin, "To be sure, my wife's health has improved somewhat, but not enough to ease my mind. The persistent coughing torments her greatly and, what is more serious, prevents the application of a medication intended to calm the beating of her heart and arteries."

In the beginning of 1825 some improvement could be discerned in the patient's condition and Alexander decided to go to Poland to inaugurate the third Diet of Warsaw. Before he left he had a change made in the constitutional charter of that country: Henceforth the sessions of the Diet would no longer be public, except for opening and closing meetings. It was a first turn of the screw. Still, the Russians could not forgive their sovereign for having granted the Poles institutions he had refused his own people. Alexander was accused of having a soft spot for a nation that had always been inclined to anarchy and the hatred of Orthodox religion; he was warned against any notion of restoring the Lithuanian provinces to that foreign state. At the same time, the Poles were angry with the Emperor for opposite reasons: they blamed him for the amputation of their territory, which without Krakow and Danzig (Gdansk) was not geographically viable; for repeated violations of the constitution; for the presence of Russian troops in the kingdom; for the surveillance exercised over all their internal affairs; for the appointment of the harsh and impetuous Grand Duke Constantine as head of the Polish army. In this new post Constantine had proved a worthy disciple of his father, Paul I. He even resembled him physically, with his flat nose, fierce eyes, and shrill howls, which made him seem, it was said, like "a raging hyena." A stickler for order in military drill and the cut of uniforms, he terrorized the Poles with his demands. "My lord the Grand Duke seems to have acquired a hatred for this country and everything that goes on in it," Czartoryski wrote the Czar. "And that hatred is growing at an alarming rate. . . . The nation, the army, nothing finds favor in his eyes. . . . My lord does not even abide by the military laws which he himself has confirmed. He insists on introducing beatings among the troops, and he gave the order for them yesterday, without regard for the unanimous representations of the Provisional Government." And Czartoryski concluded, "An enemy could not do more to harm Your Imperial Majesty." Of course Alexander had no intention of removing his brother or even of lecturing him simply because he had ordered a drubbing for a few soldiers. But he was forced to realize that by trying to satisfy both the Russians and the Poles he had angered everyone. One more failure.

On May 1/13 Alexander opened the solemn session with a speech in French: "Representatives of the kingdom of Poland, may you proceed to your deliberations calmly and free from all influence. The future of your country is in your hands." At the closing meeting a month later he declared, again in French and in the same inspired tone, "Believe that I shall know how to show my gratitude for the expressions of confidence that have marked your present meeting. They will not have been wasted. They have made a deep impression on me which will always be joined to the desire to prove to you how sincere my affection is for you and how great an influence your conduct will have on your future." In his close-fitting uniform, with the cordon of the Polish Order of the White Eagle across his chest, he still looked dashing, and the ladies in the audience went into raptures. "In the seven years I had been at court," wrote his doctor, Tarassov, "it was the first time I had seen Emperor Alexander with this look of superterrestrial greatness. His angelic gaze expressed at once power, perspicacity, modesty, and benevolence." However, to astute observers this hollow speech added nothing, changed nothing. Once again, Alexander had contented himself with putting on a show.

When he returned to Russia in June 1825, he found his wife in very weak condition. Could it be the beginning of consumption? She was coughing more and more and complained of heart spasms. "They are not accidental palpitations," she wrote her mother. "It is an almost habitual pulsation, which I have had for a number of years, sometimes stronger, sometimes weaker, not precisely in the heart but below." The doctors feared that the cold, damp climate of St. Petersburg in autumn would be bad for the patient and advised that she be taken to a warm country. Italy or the south of France would be most suitable, but the Empress said she hated the idea of being stared at by crowds of foreigners; she did not want to leave Russia; in that vast empire there must surely be a place with a mild climate. After much debate the doctors decided on Taganrog, on the Sea of Azov. "I confess I do not understand how the doctors could have made such a choice," Volkonsky wrote to a friend. "As if there were no more agreeable spot in Russia!" And in truth, Taganrog was nothing but a village lost in marshy terrain under a brutal sun, where a raging wind swept the deserted streets. No matter, the medical profession had pronounced itself and Alexander did not argue. He decided to accompany his wife on her journey and not to return to St. Petersburg until the new year.

One day while he was preparing for the departure, he received in his palace on Kamenny Island a young man of English descent named Sherwood, who was a lieutenant in the uhlans and bore a letter of introduction from Arakcheyev. Without that high recommendation Alexander would never have agreed to see so unimportant a personage, alone in his study. Sherwood, unflustered in the presence of the sovereign, spoke his piece. He stated that some officers in the regiments in the Ukraine, with a few accomplices in St. Petersburg, were preparing an uprising in the army to overthrow the regime and drive Alexander from the throne. "Yes, your suppositions are probably correct," said the Czar. "But what do those people want? Are they so unhappy?" "In overfed dogs, comfort breeds rabies!" replied Sherwood, stating that he could not supply more details concerning the conspiracy but asking for permission to pursue his research. Alexander very calmly authorized him to undertake a thorough investigation, under the guidance of Arakcheyev. He held out his hand for the informer to kiss and dismissed him. He said not a word to his entourage about the revelations he had received. Actually, they only confirmed his earlier impressions. All reports were consistent: The ground beneath his feet was being undermined. He took no notice. To Golitzin, who was urging him to make public the manifesto changing the order of succession to the throne, he answered simply, "Let us rely on God: He will know how to order things better than we mortals." And when Karamzin told him, "Sire, your years are numbered, you can no longer postpone matters, and you still have so many things to do so that the end of your reign may be worthy of its beginning," he declared that he still intended to give Russia "a fundamental law." Those close to him were surprised that he was so serene in the midst of the general anxiety. It was because he was looking forward to his journey with great joy.

To prepare the lodgings they would share in Taganrog, Alexander left St. Petersburg ahead of his wife, during the night of September 1, 1825. His barouche, drawn by three horses and driven by his bearded coachman Elie Baïkov, passed through the deserted city plunged in darkness. At four o'clock in the morning he had the carriage stop in front of the monastery of St. Alexander Nevsky. Forewarned of his visit, the Metropolitan Seraphim, the archimandrites, and the monks greeted him on the parvis. He entered the Cathedral of the Trinity, knelt before the shrine of St. Alexander, heard a nocturnal office, and rising to his feet again, asked to see an old cloistered monk, Father Alexis, who enjoyed a reputation for holiness. The monk received him in his cell, which was shaped like a sepulchral crypt. The little room was lit by a single lamp burning before the icons. On the floor stood an open coffin, which served as a bed, with a shroud for a cover. 'Look," Father Alexis said to him, "here is my bed, and it is the bed of all of us. We shall all lie down in it one day, Majesty, and we shall all sleep there for a long time." Alexander prayed beside the ascetic, who was emaciated by fasts and penitences, then had a long conversation with him. When he left him, heavy in spirit, he said, "Certainly I have heard many eloquent sermons in my life, but none has stirred me so much as the words of this old monk. How I regret that I did not know him sooner!" Then he passed bareheaded between two rows of monks with bowed heads, received the blessing of the Metropolitan, climbed back into his barouche with eyes wet with tears, and sighed to the assembled brotherhood: "Pray for me and for my wife."

On September 13 he arrived in Taganrog and started fitting out the house that had been set aside for the imperial guests. It was a modest structure of brick under a rough coat of plaster, topped by a green roof and having only a raised ground floor. Inside was a rather large room for receptions and meals. To the right two rooms for the Emperor; to the left eight little low-ceilinged rooms reserved for the Empress. The servants were lodged in the basement. Situated between a muddy courtyard and a neglected orchard, the house had only a few windows giving on the sea. The furniture was of the simplest. Alexander organized the arrangement of the rooms, saw to it that curtains were hung, and personally drove in nails to put up paintings and engravings.

On September 23 he climbed into a "sleeping carriage" and went to meet his wife at the last relay. Starting from that day, it was the couple's second honeymoon, according to Volkonsky. They would walk through town together and respond graciously to the greetings of passersby. Or they would drive out to see the surrounding countryside, stopping on the steppe in front of old Scythian tombs and watching the Tatars' camel caravans as they slowly passed. When Elizabeth expressed regret that there was no view of the sea from the municipal garden, the Czar immediately ordered a path to be cut leading to the open water. At every turn he asked his wife, "Are you comfortable? Is there nothing you need?" He took his meals with her, apart from their attendants. Those attendants were very few in any event: General Diebitsch, Prince Volkonsky, Longuinov, Elizabeth's secretary, five doctors, a dozen servants, and a few subalterns including two topographers. The topographers were to accompany the Emperor on his forthcoming journey to Astrakhan, the Caucasus, and Siberia. But for the time being no one thought of going anywhere. Elizabeth delighted in this newfound conjugal intimacy. She liked everything, even the flat, bleak landscape, even the ugly little houses of this provincial town populated by Greeks and Tatars. She wrote to her mother, "Recently I asked the Emperor to tell me when he expected to return to St. Petersburg, because I preferred to know so that I could prepare myself for the idea of this departure as for an operation. He answered: 'As late as possible, I'll see. But in any case, not before the new year.' That put me in a good humor for the whole day." Foreseeing how lonely she would be in Taganrog after he left, he said to her, "I think that even if it were possible to send you someone from the family, outside of me you don't need anyone." And she concluded joyfully, "I was pleased to see him so convinced that he was everything to me."

Yet Alexander sometimes returned to his dark thoughts, his irritation, his mistrust. Once he found a pebble in a biscuit that was served to him and took offense, wondering if someone was not trying to poison him, demanding that the strange object be analyzed. He calmed down only when the Scottish doctor Wylie declared that it was indeed a little stone that had stuck to the dough while it was baking. On September 22 he received a letter from Arakcheyev informing him that the peasants of Gruzino, driven to desperation, had murdered the adviser's mistress, Anastasia Minkina. Immediately Arakcheyev, mad with grief and rage, abandoned all affairs of state, transmitting his powers to General Euler. "Farewell," he wrote the Emperor, "remember your former servant. It was the house serfs who cut my beloved's throat, at night, and I do not yet know where I shall go to lay my sorrowful head, but I shall leave here." That very day the Emperor sent him a long letter of friendship and condolence: "You write that you want to go far away from Gruzino but that you don't know where to go. Do come to me. You have no friend who loves you more. We are completely alone here. You will live with us in whatever way you like. The conversation of a friend who shares your grief will assuage it a little. But I entreat you by everything that is most sacred, remember the motherland, think how precious—how necessary, I may say—your services are to it, do not forget that the country and I are as one." The archimandrite Photius was ordered to bring the unfortunate lover the aid of religion. But

Arakcheyev did not let himself be moved either by the monk's sermons or by Alexander's invitation. He stayed in Gruzino and sought consolation for his sorrow in torments inflicted upon his servants. Even those who had not participated in the murder were tortured because he suspected them of having been gratified to learn of his beloved's death. Despite repeated appeals from His Majesty, he refused to return to affairs of state. His public life, he said, was over.

Abandoned by this irreplaceable adviser and beset with many urgent problems, Alexander was seized with discouragement. General de Witt, the commander in chief of the southern troops, had come to Taganrog and confirmed the existence of a dangerous plot. On his advice the Emperor instructed Colonel Nikolaev to join Sherwood and pursue the investigation on the spot, "with the necessary prudence."

Faced with all these people who talked to him about a conspiracy and trembled for his life, Alexander suddenly felt in the same situation as his father, Paul I, in the last months of his reign. Except that he did not have beside him a criminal son who protected the conspirators. It was strangers who wanted to dethrone him. So, on the whole he was better off than his progenitor. There were moments when he thought of taking terrible reprisals, but most of the time—from weariness or piety?—he preferred to abandon himself to the will of God. Let come what might.

Count Simon Vorontzov urged the Czar to go on an inspection tour of the Crimea. Alexander was not displeased by this means of escape from Taganrog and his cares. On the afternoon of the day before his departure, while he was working in his study, a cloud hid the sun and the room suddenly grew dark. He ordered his valet Anissimov to bring candles. A little while later, after the sky cleared, Anissimov ran in to take them away. The Czar expressed surprise at his haste; the valet replied that in Russia candles lit in full daylight were a bad omen, for they recalled the wake around a dead man's bed. The Czar shuddered and murmured, "You are right. I think as you do. Take the candles away." This incident left him with a profoundly uneasy feeling. His natural inclination toward superstition prompted him to interpret the most trivial events of his life as signs emanating from God. All of a sudden he no longer wished to leave. "I could very well do without this journey," he said in French to Elizabeth. "I should much rather stay quietly like this. . . . But everything is already arranged, people are expecting me, I have to go through with it!"[3] Shaking off his apprehension he set out, on October 20, 1825, with a retinue reduced to the essential.

He visited all the picturesque spots on his itinerary, admired the German and Dutch colonies that had recently been established in the region, spent the night in Simferopol, then went to the estate of Count Vorontzov. He told Volkonsky: "Soon I shall settle in the Crimea to live there like a simple mortal. I have served for twenty-five years; at the end of that time every soldier gets his retirement. . . . You too will retire. You will be my librarian." He dined at Alupka and was pleased to sample the local wines, the products of French vines brought from Bordeaux and Champagne. Then, sometimes on horseback, sometimes on foot, over roads that were scarcely passable, he explored the neighboring countryside. Those in his entourage begged him to take care of himself, but he took a bitter pleasure in exhausting himself in this desert landscape. On October 27, after breakfasting in Balaklava, he mounted again to take a hilly shortcut to the monastery of St. George. When night fell the temperature suddenly dropped. A cold wind sprang up. Alexander was wearing only a light cloth uniform. He shivered but refused to stop to put on a coat. When he reached Sevastopol he had a dizzy spell, asked for hot tea, and refused to eat dinner. The next day, mastering his malaise, he resumed his tour, visiting barracks, fortifications, churches, hospitals, mosques, synagogues, one after the other. He even presided over a circumcision ceremony in a Tatar house. His duty as a Russian monarch commanded him, he thought, to take an interest in all the races, religions, and customs of his empire. It was by treating all his innumerable children with the same kindness that he would best perform his role of a father unifying the whole country. What was the use of travel if it was not rewarded in the end by mutual understanding?

On the road to Orekhovo Alexander met the courier Maskov, who was bringing him dispatches. After taking possession of the papers, he ordered Maskov to follow him. As always, his barouche rolled at a dizzying speed. Dashing after it, the courier's post chaise struck a mound and overturned, and Maskov was killed on the spot. Tarassov, left behind at the scene of the accident, did not reach Orekhovo until near midnight and found his sovereign in a disturbing state. Alexander stood shivering in front of a fireplace where great logs were burning. "What a calamity!" he said. "I pity that man."

The following day he had the disagreeable experience of being present at a scuffle between the civil Governor of Ekaterinoslav and Archbishop Theophile: the administration exchanging blows with the Church. Alexander was painfully affected by this scandal, and in spite of his fatigue and nausea, he summoned the two opponents to lecture them separately. On November 4, when he reached Mariopol, he had a fever so high that his teeth were chattering. After hesitating a long time, Dr. Wylie made him drink a glass of rum punch, put him to bed, and smothered him under the covers. Alexander passed a very restless night, but next morning he berated the doctors who advised him to rest for a few hours. He was only ninety versts from Taganrog, the Empress was expecting him, he gave the order to harness the horses.

When he reached his destination he refused to go to bed, but the doctors found his condition increasingly alarming. Wylie thought it might be a "bilious gastric fever" and ordered laxatives and strong purgatives. The temperature did not come down, the patient's complexion was yellowish, his deafness was increasing noticeably. Nevertheless, he tried to work. "It has become such a habit with me that I can no longer do without it, and my head is empty when I am not doing anything," he said to the Empress. "If I left my post, I should have to devour whole libraries, otherwise I'd go mad." He read the Bible, trembling with emotion. It was not until November 9 that he authorized Volkonsky to inform the Empress Dowager and Grand Duke Constantine of his illness. Elizabeth wrote to her mother, "Where is there refuge in this life? When you think you have arranged everything for the best and are going to be able to enjoy it, there comes an unexpected trial that robs you of the power to appreciate the good with which you are surrounded. This is not a complaint—God reads in my heart—it is only an observation which I have made a thousand times and which is now justified for the thousandth time by the event." She had forgotten the infidelities, the humiliations, the indifference of the old days and was already magnifying in her mind the man who had shared her life for so long and whose affection had returned to her in his declining years.

On November 10 for the first time Alexander lost consciousness when he got out of bed. When he regained his senses he was very weak and hardly spoke. The next day Wylie noted in his journal, in French, "The illness continues. The bowels are still very impure. When I talk to him about bleeding and a purge, he is furious and does not deign to speak to me." He fainted again as he was getting ready to shave. He fell from his chair. They raised him up, bathed his temples with eau de cologne, and put him to bed. He did not even try to get up. On the days that followed Wylie observed a drowsiness in his patient, "which is a very bad sign." He wrote, "Everything is very bad, although he has no delirium. I wanted to give him some muriatic [hydrochloric] acid with his drink." The Czar refused. Perhaps he was afraid they were trying to poison him. The idea of political murder, which had haunted his youth, returned with force during his last moments. Having been under Wylie's care until now, he had Tarassov called in and asked him to replace his colleague who, he said, needed rest. Tarassov did so, but he had no idea either what to do to relieve the patient. Considering the Emperor lost, he advised the Empress to summon a priest. Curiously, Alexander had not expressed this desire himself, although he was a sincere believer. No doubt even at the height of his fever he had never felt in danger of dying. Elizabeth sat down at her husband's bedside and said gently, "I should like to propose to you my own remedy, which brings its benefits to all. I know better than anyone that you are a great Christian who observes all the rites of our Orthodox Church. I advise you to have recourse to the medicine of the soul." Skeptical at first, Alexander had the doctors called and asked Wylie if it was true that his illness had become so extremely grave. Wylie was flustered but confirmed it. "What a sad office was mine to inform him that his dissolution was at hand, in the presence of Her Majesty the Empress, who had gone to suggest to him a sure remedy: *Sacramentum,*" he noted in his journal. Very calmly the Emperor turned toward his wife and said, "I thank you, my dear. Give orders. I am ready."

What were his thoughts, on the threshold of death? For a long time he had wanted to rid himself of the burden of the crown, the burden of life. Had the moment come for him to take leave of all that? Yes, no doubt, since the doctors said so. And then? What would he find behind the black curtain? It was impossible that this man who was so deeply religious should not have thought with terror of what awaited him in the other world. Doubtless God would take into account his good intentions and his piety. But what did sublime thoughts and brilliant actions weigh in the scales against the corpse of an assassinated father? And if by some miracle he recovered? Oh! then he would retire to some wilderness, as he had said a hundred times, to live as a hermit, unknown to all.

On November 15 the archpriest of the Cathedral of Taganrog, Alexis Fedotov, presented himself at the bedside of the patient. Alexander came out of his torpor, asked to be left alone with the minister of God, and made long confession. Then he took communion in the presence of the Empress, his close advisers, the doctors, and the valets. Having fulfilled his religious duties, he kissed his wife's hand and said to her, in French, "Never have I felt a greater pleasure, and I thank you for it very much." Finally, addressing the doctors, he stammered, "Now, gentlemen, do your work. Give me the remedies that you judge necessary."

Toward evening Tarassov applied thirty-five leeches to the patient

behind his ears and on the back of his neck, and placed cold compresses
on his forehead. Alexander's condition seemed to improve. It was a brief
remission. Clearly the end was near. Only Elizabeth refused to believe it.
Plunged into deep unconsciousness, the dying man recovered his wits
only when she bent over his bed and spoke in his ear. He took her hand,
pressed it on his heart, then turned toward the icon and recited prayers
in a low voice. Toward evening on November 18 Tarassov observed in
the Czar symptoms of cerebral congestion. He gave him something to
drink from a spoon. Alexander had difficulty swallowing. His breathing
was now only a smothered snore. As no food passed his throat, the doctors
administered two enemas of broth "made with Smolensk wheat flour."
At ten o'clock Elizabeth came back to sit by her husband. In her left hand
she held the right hand of the dying man. Tears streamed down her face.
She waited, motionless, for life to depart. But the hours passed, the night
slipped away in a funereal silence, and Alexander was still breathing.
The clergy ordered public prayers.

The next day, November 19/December 1, 1825, the crowd, eager
for news, assembled on the square in front of the imperial house, under
a gray, rainy sky. At ten minutes to eleven in the morning, Alexander,
the Czar "blessed by God," gave his last sigh without having regained
consciousness. He was forty-seven years and eleven months old. Elizabeth rose from the chair where she had spent so many hours watching;
she knelt and prayed; then, making the sign of the cross, she kissed the
dead man's forehead, closed his eyes, and tied her own handkerchief
around his chin.

Returning to her own room, she took a pen and with her eyes
drowned in tears wrote her mother, "Ah Mama, I am the most
wretched creature on earth! I only wanted to tell you that I exist, after
the loss of that angel who was martyred by illness and who, nevertheless, always had a smile or a kind look for me, even when he recognized
no one. . . . I am engulfed in grief, I do not understand myself, I do not
understand my destiny." Two days later: "It is a continuous pain, a
feeling of desolation to which I sometimes fear my religion may succumb. Oh my God! it is almost beyond my strength. If only I had not
received so many caresses from him, so many tokens of affection, almost
up to the last moment! And I had to see expire this angelic creature who
retained the faculty of loving after he had lost that of understanding.
What am I to do with my will, which was entirely subject to him, with
my life, which I loved to devote to him?" To the Empress Dowager,
Alexander's mother, Elizabeth addressed the following letter, also in
French, "Dear Mama, our angel is in heaven and I on earth; of all those

who weep for him, I am the most unhappy creature. May I soon join him! . . . Here is some of his hair, dear Mama. Alas! why did he have to suffer so much? But his face now wears only the expression of the contentment and benevolence which are natural to him. He seems to approve what is going on around him. . . . So long as he is here, I shall remain here. When he leaves, if it is possible, I shall leave, too. I shall go with him as long as I can." Later, speaking of the appearance of the dead man, she wrote to her mother again, "The first two days he was young again and handsome. . . . On the first day he even had a cheerful expression of such lively satisfaction that it seemed he was going to get up with all the habitual vivacity of his movements, and yet, at the last moment, what a cruel change!"

While the house echoed with sobs and funeral chants, nine doctors from the court and the garrison proceeded to an autopsy. The specialists noted that most of the organs were in perfect condition. No cerebral lesions were indicated. A report was drawn up and signed by all the participants.* The next problem was to embalm the corpse. Tarassov and Wylie pleaded respect for the deceased as a reason for refusing to participate in the macabre task. The others rolled up their sleeves and set to work, with big cigars in their mouths to combat the odor. Beside them, aromatic herbs were cooking in a pot. But in Taganrog certain necessary ingredients were lacking, even clean towels. The heart, the brain, the intestines were deposited in a silver vessel like a big sugar-bowl. "The doctors," wrote Schenig, a member of the household staff, "turned the body over like a piece of wood and I was able to examine it with curiosity and emotion. I have never seen a man so well made. The hands, the feet, all the parts of the body could have served as models for a sculptor. The skin was extraordinarily delicate." The work lasted all night. Then they dressed the Czar in a general's uniform, with all his decorations pinned on his chest, laid him out on an iron bed, and, as his face was already beginning to darken despite the embalming, they hastened to give him absolution and covered him all over with a muslin veil. Officers of the garrison kept watch in the room. The priests relieved each other every two hours. From time to time one of those present raised the veil and wet the Czar's face with a sponge soaked in alcohol. The heat in the room was suffocating. Three enormous church

*It is impossible to determine from the document the exact cause of the Emperor's death. According to certain experts, it was probably a disease of the liver followed by a cerebral complication.

candles mixed their odor with those of balsam and of decomposing flesh. "This putrid smell clung to our uniforms for three weeks," noted Schenig. "After two days, as I raised the muslin veil of the deceased, I pointed out to Dobbert [one of the doctors] that an end of the cravat was sticking out from beneath the Czar's collar. He pulled on it and found with horror that it was a piece of flesh." Wylie, alerted, had the windows opened and a bucket of ice placed under the bed. Finally, the Czar was laid in a double coffin of lead and wood, but without a cover, and exposed on a platform in a room hung with black cloth. Every day the Czarina climbed up on to the platform but refused to draw aside the transparent shroud. "He who was so fastidious about his person," she said, "would not have liked anyone to look at him when he must have been so changed."[4] She would kiss her husband's forehead through the veil and stay by him for some ten minutes.

Prince Volkonsky was overwhelmed by the responsibility that fell to him. The death of a czar so far from his capital was an exceptional event in the history of Russia. It was almost as if he had died abroad. There was no tradition to rely on in this strange circumstance, not the least directive coming from on high, and if he took personal initiative, there was every chance of making a mistake. While waiting for the body to be sent across Russia to St. Petersburg, Volkonsky had to see to all the preparations, alone. "At two thousand versts from the capital, in an out-of-the-way corner of the empire, without any local resources, with enormous difficulties to procure the least thing necessary in the circumstances, I am obliged," he wrote, "to send couriers in all directions, to make decisions, and even draw up plans and sketches of the way the ceremony should proceed. If I were not here, I wonder how they would manage, for everyone around me has lost his head."

In St. Petersburg, too, everyone had lost his head, starting with Grand Duke Nicholas. It was on November 27 in the church of the Winter Palace, during a mass held for the recovery of the Emperor, that he learned from a courier that his brother was dead. Alexander had indeed told him that he considered him as his successor, but without revealing to him the existence of the manifesto. Thus, ignorant of the definitive dispositions taken by the deceased, Nicholas swore an oath of allegiance to Constantine and invited his entourage to do likewise. All official bodies and principal regiments immediately did as they were asked.

In the meantime, news of Alexander's death had also reached Constantine who, secure in the knowledge that he had renounced the throne, had sworn an oath of allegiance to Nicholas. The result was a short interregnum: Russia had two Czars, each as legitimate as the other. Although Prince Golitzin had confirmed to Nicholas the contents of the manifesto, the Grand Duke refused to ascend the throne before he had had a personal interview with his brother and urged Constantine to come to him in St. Petersburg. Constantine considered the journey unnecessary and begged his brother to accept power. Couriers galloped at top speed between St. Petersburg and Warsaw. Given the importance of the affair, the third brother, Grand Duke Michael, acted as intermediary between the two others who, with noble self-denial, were passing the crown of Russia back and forth between them like a football.

At last, on the evening of December 12, Nicholas received by messenger the categorical refusal of Constantine either to reign or even to bestir himself from Warsaw. Let those in high places solve their problems without him. The time had come for Nicholas to invite the troops who had just sworn allegiance to his brother to swear allegiance to himself. He was not unaware of the danger he was incurring by thus calling upon rough, simple men to go back on their word. Moreover, he had been warned that an insurrection was brewing: The secret associations meant to take advantage of the army's uncertainty and move into action. "On the morning of the day after tomorrow," wrote Nicholas to General Diebitsch, "either I shall be Emperor or I shall have ceased to breathe. I sacrifice myself for my brother, happy if I can accomplish his will. But what will become of Russia? What will the army do?"

And on the morning of December 14, 1825, a few officers who were members of the Northern Society did indeed rouse their men to revolt, claiming that Nicholas was a usurper. The regiment of the Moscow Guard and a regiment of grenadiers came out of their barracks and ranged themselves threateningly on the Senate Square near the monument to Peter the Great. These groups were soon joined by sailors from the ships of the Guard. A crowd of onlookers gathered. Some shouted, "Hurrah for Constantine!" Others went further, "Long live Constantine and the Constitution!" under the impression that the constitution was Constantine's wife. The troops loyal to Nicholas formed ranks opposite the rebels. The Emperor himself arrived in the square. Count Miloradovich, Governor of St. Petersburg, tried to harangue the mutineers. He was killed by a pistol shot. The Horse Guards, who supported the new Czar, started to charge at close range. But their mounts slipped on the icy ground and they were repulsed by heavy fire. Then Nicholas reluctantly decided to bring up the artillery. A few cannonballs sufficed to disperse both onlookers and rebels. In a split second the scene became a rout, a massacre. Master of the situation, Nicholas wrote to his brother, "Dear, dear Constantine, your will has been done: I am Emperor, but at what a price, great God, at the price of the blood of my subjects!"

That very night, on his orders, the arrests began. Spies communicated the names of the ringleaders to the commission of inquiry. One hundred twenty suspects were thrown into prison and summoned before a High Court composed of members of the Council of State, the Senate, and the Holy Synod. The tribunal condemned the five men chiefly responsible to death by hanging, the others to forced labor in Siberia.* Thus ended the affair of those whom people were already calling the "Decembrists." Commenting on the illusions of these high-minded revolutionaries, most of whom came from great families, Count Rostopchin said, in French, "Ordinarily, it is the shoemakers who make revolutions in order to become great lords; but in our country it was the great lords who wanted to become shoemakers."

During the disturbances of the interregnum, Alexander's mortal remains had stayed in Taganrog amid a murmur of daily prayers. Every evening around seven o'clock Elizabeth went to the church where the coffin was exposed, and bowed. "I can still find a little consolation only here, where *his* spirit seems to surround me more than elsewhere," she said. It was only on December 29, 1825, that the funeral convoy left the town. The Empress, too weak to face the long journey, remained behind. She wrote to her mother, "All the earthly ties between us are broken. . . . Childhood friends, we walked together for thirty-two years. We traversed together all the periods of life. Often separated, we always found each other again in one way or another. On the true road at last, we tasted only the sweetness of our union. It was at that moment that he was taken from me."

Each time the cortege stopped for the night the coffin was placed in a church. From time to time it was opened to check if the corpse was still there, a report was written, and the cover was screwed back on. It was the Czar's usual coachman, Elie Baïkov, who drove the team. Even in the middle of the steppes peasants flocked to prostrate themselves. When the procession entered towns troops presented arms. Cannon were fired. Sometimes the people went ahead of the hearse and unharnessed the horses to pull it along themselves. What did all these weep-

---

*The five men condemned to death were Paul Pestel, Sergei Muraviev-Apostol, Michael Bestuzhev-Riumin, Conrad Ryleyev, and Peter Kakhovsky.

ing people think of the Czar who had just left them? If they called to mind the actions of his life, they saw not an ascending line but a dramatic, incoherent zigzag. Surrounded with delirious love at the time he ascended the throne, he had disappointed all hopes by applying not one of the liberal measures promised. He had regained popularity after his victory over Napoleon. But once back in Russia, he had again betrayed the confidence of the nation by authoritarian conduct. Allegedly enlightened by God, he had become the champion of repression abroad and at home. While invoking Christian charity, he had instituted the Holy Alliance and the prisons known as military colonies. As his remains passed, his subjects wondered whether they should weep for the shining czar of the early years or rejoice at the death of an aging despot. Unable to dissociate the pupil of Laharpe from the protector of Arakcheyev, they felt as if they were bowing before two dead men at once, enclosed in the same box.

All those who had come into contact with Alexander had been struck by his ambiguous character. He had been nicknamed "the sphinx of the North," "the crowned sphinx," "the sphinx uncomprehended even in his tomb." Had he himself known who he was? Was not his tragedy that he had constantly dreamed of doing good without being capable of it? Yes, throughout his life he had feared that which he wanted to accomplish. Worried by the disturbances that accompanied the least innovation, most often he had stopped halfway. Two steps forward, three steps back. Metternich would write of him, with insight, "Moving from one form of worship to another, from one religion to another, he stirred up everything and built nothing. Everything in him was superficial, nothing went deep." And Chateaubriand: "Whatever high qualities the Czar may have had, ultimately he was disastrous to his empire. . . . He sowed seeds of civilization and then wanted to crush them. Pulled in different directions, the people did not know what was being asked of them, what was wanted of them—thinking or mindlessness, passive obedience or legal obedience, movement or immobility. . . . He was too strong to employ despotism, too weak to establish liberty."[5] Chateaubriand also said, "The Emperor of Russia had a strong soul and a weak character."[6]

Thus the chants of the clergy rose toward an enigma. With majestic slowness, from stage to stage, from mass to mass, Alexander, the man of two faces, the inveterate traveler, traversed his empire for a last time. The gloomy journey lasted two months. On February 28, 1826, Emperor Nicholas received the procession at Czarskoye Selo and accompanied his brother's remains to the church of the palace. The next day, at his request, Dr. Tarassov opened the coffin, removed the mattress of aromatic herbs that covered the body, brushed the uniform, changed the gloves, wiped the face, combed the hair of the deceased. When he had finished, the members of the imperial family—and they alone— were admitted to the ceremony of final farewell. The priests and local officers were kept outside. Sentries were posted at the doors. One by one, the privileged approached the coffin and kissed the forehead and hand of the corpse. It was unrecognizable. According to Tarassov, the skin of his face had turned to a "pale brown." On seeing him, the Empress Dowager exclaimed in French in a dramatic voice, "Yes, it is my dear son, my dear Alexander. Ah! how thin he has grown!"

From Czarskoye Selo the body was transported with great pomp to St. Petersburg. The sky was gray, snowflakes whirled in the icy wind. Emperor Nicholas, Grand Duke Michael, foreign princes, all enveloped in black cloaks, tramped behind the hearse. The ceremony was the same as for the interment of Peter the Great. An endless stream of generals, dignitaries, priests, and monks moved to the sounds of a fu- neral march toward the Cathedral of Kazan. A platform had been set up in the nave. The crowd was allowed to file in front of the catafalque. But, contrary to Russian custom, the coffin remained closed, for Em- peror Nicholas was afraid to expose the decomposed face of the dead man to the eyes of his subjects. Six days later, on March 13, 1826, there was another procession to take Alexander's remains from the Cathedral of Kazan to the Fortress of St. Peter and St. Paul, where it was to be interred. A snowstorm descended upon the city and slowed the prog- ress of the convoy. Nevertheless, at two o'clock in the afternoon, artil- lery salvos announced that the Czar "blessed by God" had returned to the earth. Metternich remarked, "The novel is over, history begins."

Not long afterward, Elizabeth finally decided, despite her extreme lassitude, to leave Taganrog with a small suite for St. Petersburg. "I am ill in body and soul," she wrote her mother. The Empress Dowager was to meet her daughter-in-law in Kaluga. On May 3 when Elizabeth reached Belev, the provincial seat of Tula, in the heart of Russia, she gave up the idea of continuing her journey and stopped in hastily prepared lodgings. She was so exhausted that she had difficulty speaking and could not bear the light of candles. "Her eyes were dull and sunken," wrote her secretary, Longuinov, "the veins under her eyes were blue and swollen like nuts, which made her nose so large that it seemed not to belong to her face. Her complexion seemed very flushed and her chin hung down leaving the mouth open." The doctors in her escort took the patient's pulse, gave her some medicine, and withdrew.

She refused the services of Mademoiselle Tison, her lady's maid. Toward four-thirty in the morning, when Mademoiselle Tison returned to the room to make sure that the Empress was resting, she found her dead in her bed. The autopsy revealed heart failure. Again a funeral cortege set out for St. Petersburg. On June 21, 1826, Elizabeth's coffin was lowered into the crypt beside the coffin of Alexander.

EPILOGUE

It was inevitable that Alexander I, the sphinx of the North, would not disappear without leaving behind him a wake of mystery. His death in a remote part of the empire after an illness as brief as it was strange, his long-delayed return to St. Petersburg, his interment without the people's having been permitted to see his face in the open coffin, as was the tradition—all this was disturbing, to say the least. Hardly had the funeral chants died away when rumors spread throughout the country. It was said that the Czar had not died at Taganrog but had boarded an English yacht to go to Palestine, to the holy places, or that he had been kidnapped by Cossacks, or that he had left secretly for America. The people who spread these various versions were in agreement on only one point: A soldier whose face and figure resembled the Czar's had been placed in the coffin in his stead to deceive everyone.

Gradually the gossip subsided. But ten years later, when the legend seemed to have lost all vitality, there appeared in Krasnoufimsk, in the province of Perm, an old man with an imposing presence named Feodor Kuzmich. As he had no papers and told the local authorities that he knew nothing of his origin, he was condemned to twenty lashes and deported to western Siberia. There he lived humbly, working from time to time in a factory, sheltered by peasants whom he astonished with his knowledge of the Scriptures, his gentleness of character, and his excellent advice. His reputation for holiness intrigued a merchant, Khromov, who took him under his protection and built him a little house in the vicinity of Tomsk. Freed from all care, Feodor Kuzmich devoted himself entirely to meditation and prayer. Many notables of Tomsk came to see him in his retreat. All of them were surprised by his inspired look, his broad education, and his knowledge of important political events. He seemed to have known great statesmen, spoke respectfully of Metropolitan Philaret of Moscow and the archimandrite Photius, referred with emotion to Kutuzov's victories, talked of the military colonies, recounted the triumphal entry of the Russian armies into Paris. All his visitors came away convinced that he was a very high personage of the empire who was living under the guise of a peasant. Some of them, without really daring to say so, found he had a resemblance to the late Emperor Alexander. He was tall and broad shouldered, with light blue eyes, regular features, a bald forehead and a long white beard. While he did not limp as the Czar had, he was, like him, slightly deaf. In addition, he had the same way of standing with one thumb slipped under his belt. Dressed in a loose shirt of white linen that came down to his calves and pants of the same material, he carried himself with as much dignity as if he were wearing a uniform. Eminent prelates, such as the Bishops of Tomsk and Irkutsk did not hesitate to make the journey to converse with the venerable old man. The eldest son of Alexander II, Nicholas Alexandrovich, then heir to the throne, and Grand Duke Alexis Alexandrovich, the younger brother of Alexander III, visited him in turn. However, when a soldier cried out in Feodor Kuzmich's presence, "It's our Czar, our father Alexander Pavlovich!" the latter retorted quickly, "I am only a vagabond. Be quiet, or you're liable to go to prison!" Until his last breath he claimed to know nothing of his birth. To those who begged him to reveal his true name, he replied, "God will recognize his own."

He died on January 20, 1864, at the age of eighty-seven, venerated by all. To Khromov, who had given him every attention during his last years, Feodor Kuzmich was a saint, a staretz. He obtained permission from the local ecclesiastical authorities to bury his former pensioner within the grounds of the monastery of St. Alexis in Tomsk and to erect over his grave a cross bearing the inscription, *Here rests the body of the great staretz Feodor Kuzmich, blessed by God.* Now, this was the very appellation that Alexander had officially received after his victory over Napoleon. Next, Khromov had the local press spread the account of predictions and miracles attributed to the deceased staretz: his curing of the sick by the laying on of hands, the soft perfume that emanated from his beard, the light that illuminated his home without the help of any candle. Twice Khromov went to St. Petersburg—once under the reign of Alexander II and once under Alexander III—to talk with high personages and entrust a few relics to them. A portrait of the holy man was sent to Alexander III, who, it was said, kept it in his study. The grave of Feodor Kuzmich became a place of pilgrimage. Grand Duke Nicholas, the future Emperor Nicholas II, stopped on his way back from a journey to Japan in 1891 to bow before the memorial stone. An elegant chapel was built on the spot by a member of the Council of State, Galkin-Vraskoy. In the little house of the staretz, now transformed into a museum, a portrait of Alexander I was hung on the wall; on St. Alexander's day an office was celebrated in the cottage by the priest of a neighboring church. The whole population of the area was convinced that it was indeed the Czar who had come to this region to end his days humbly under the eyes of God. A first biography of Feodor Kuzmich, published in 1891, gave no information about his existence until 1836, the year when he had appeared in Siberia. A third edition of the same book, in 1894, gave two portraits of the old man, a view of his cell, and a facsimile of his handwriting. A few graphologists thought they saw a vague similarity to the writing of Alexander I. With time the thesis of the false death of the Czar gained more and more adherents. Those who support this version base their belief on a series of observations that are not to be lightly dismissed. They are as follows:

Several times Alexander had declared his intention of abandoning power and retiring to some peaceful place. He had even fixed the age at which he meant to leave the throne—when he was around fifty. When he arrived in Taganrog, in November 1825, he was forty-seven. The notes of witnesses of his illness are often contradictory. For example, on November 28, Dr. Tarassov wrote that the Emperor had spent "a quiet night," while on the same date, Dr. Wylie spoke of a "restless" night, the sovereign's condition becoming, according to him, "worse and worse." The report of the autopsy bears the signature of nine doctors, but in his *Mémoires* Dr. Tarassov, who had drafted the document and whose name appeared at the bottom of the last page, claims not to have signed it. Might someone have forged his signature? Moreover, the examination of the brain revealed lesions caused by syphilis, a disease with which Alexander was not afflicted. Lastly, in 1824 the Czar had suffered an erysipelas of the left leg, but it was on the right leg that the doctors who performed the autopsy observed traces of old wounds. The fact that despite the embalming the dead man's face quickly became unrecognizable, the fact that the people were not allowed to file by the open coffin, the fact that the Empress did not accompany her husband's remains to St. Petersburg, the fact that the Czarina's journal breaks off a week before the death, the fact that Nicholas I ordered most of the documents relating to the last years of his brother's reign to be burned, are all so many arguments marshaled by those who believe Alexander survived. To support their position they also cite certain reports that when, on orders from Alexander III, the sarcophagus was opened by Count Vorontzov-Dashkov, he found the coffin empty. In 1921 the rumor even spread that when the Soviet government had an examination made of the remains of the sovereigns buried in the Fortress of St. Peter and St. Paul, the investigators likewise noted the absence of any corpse in Alexander's coffin. No official confirmation has corroborated this report, but most of the members of the Romanov dynasty, who took refuge abroad after the Bolshevik revolution, believed that Feodor Kuzmich and the conqueror of Napoleon were one and the same.

However, in the front rank of those who held a contrary opinion stands a grandnephew of Alexander I, Grand Duke Nicholas Mikhailovich. He gained access to the secret archives of the imperial family, and after some hesitation pronounced himself firmly convinced that the Czar had died in Taganrog. "If one reflects upon Alexander's character and inclinations," he wrote, "one cannot find in them the least taste for a metamorphosis of this kind. Even less can one find any disposition to inflict upon himself gratuitously, at an already advanced age and in completely extraordinary conditions, privations and mortifications of all kinds. . . . Not only does it defy all logic to accept the likelihood of such a legend, but also there exists not the least argument nor the least appearance of proof in favor of such a hypothesis."

Indeed, it seems highly unlikely that after such an affectionate reconciliation with his wife, the Czar should have abandoned her on an impulse when he knew that she had tuberculosis and had only a short time to live; equally unlikely that, having nurtured this plan for a long time, he should not have taken pains to settle the question of his succession; lastly, unlikely that he could have had a "similar" corpse brought to him without awakening the suspicions of his entourage. To accept the notion of a body's being substituted in Taganrog one would have to imagine a macabre charade in which some thirty persons participated: officers, doctors, secretaries, ladies-in-waiting, and Empress Elizabeth herself. Did she not watch over the patient until his last moments? Did she not close his eyes? After his death did she not write heartrending letters to her mother, to the Empress Dowager, to her close friends? Could all that have been merely a cynical parody of mourning on her part? Did her very tears serve only to allay suspicion? And what about the report of the autopsy performed on Alexander's body, signed by the doctors? What about the many verifications of the contents of the coffin on the journey from Taganrog to St. Petersburg, all with certificates to support them? And what about the written and oral testimony of all those who had lived intimately with the Czar during his dying hours? Is it conceivable that so many pious people hid the truth after having attended masses for the repose of the soul of a man whom they knew to be alive? Such complicity would have verged on sacrilege.

Besides, after Empress Elizabeth was interred, even she did not escape a myth similar to the one about Alexander. Popular rumor claimed that she had not died but that in 1840, under the name of Vera the Silent, she had taken refuge in a convent in the province of Novgorod. Having taken a vow never to speak, she was supposed to have died in 1861 without having revealed her origin. Struck by the delicacy of her features and the elegance of her manners, the nuns around her are supposed to have recognized her from the beginning as the allegedly deceased Empress. If she had had a secret destiny like her husband's, people said it was because both of them had the same repentance for the murder of Paul I.

Grisly conjuring tricks, sham burials, ultimate masquerades—it is all out of some gothic tale. But if Alexander really died in 1825, who was the staretz buried in the monastery of St. Alexis in Tomsk? Impostures are frequent in the history of Russia. The Russian people have a fondness for personages who miraculously come back to life: the false Dmitris, the false Peter IIIs, the false Ivan VIs, the false princesses. Siberia has always swarmed with mystical prophets, unfrocked priests, and refractory monks living as hermits. Feodor Kuzmich might well have been simply one of those ascetics who had broken with society. Grand Duke Nicholas Mikhailovich, who had studied the question, leaned toward identifying him as an illegitimate son of Emperor Paul I, the naval lieutenant Simon Veliki; others think he was an officer of the chevaliers-gardes, Uvarov, who is supposed to have left his home in 1827; still others, without giving a name, imagine that he must have been a member of the Russian aristocracy who wanted to flee his milieu.

Thus not only Alexander's life but also his death offer an enigma to future generations. While he was unable to lay aside his crown and withdraw from the world as he had so often wished, popular superstition, seizing upon his shade, has given him in legend the end for which he hoped.

NOTES

I. MONSIEUR ALEXANDER

1. Masson, *Mémoires secrets sur la Russie.*

III. THE REIGN OF PAUL

1. Madame de Lieven, *Mémoires.*
2. Manuscript of K. P. Kovalevski, "Après la mort de Paul Ier," quoted by Schilder, *Emperor Alexander I, His Life and Reign.*

IV. THE SECRET COMMITTEE

1. Dispatch of April 16, 1801. Cf. Constantin de Grunwald, *Alexandre Ier, le tsar mystique.*
2. Adam Czartoryski, *Mémoires.*
3. Letter in French from Empress Elizabeth to her mother, dated March 13 and 14, 1801.

4. Countess Edling, *Mémoires*.

5. Grand Duke Nicholas Mikhailovich, *Le Comte Paul Stroganov*.

6. Cf. Constantin de Grunwald, *Alexandre Ier, lé tsar mystique* and Waliszewski, *Le Règne d'Alexandre Ier*.

7. Schilder, *Emperor Alexander I, His Life and Reign*.

V. THE BAPTISM OF FIRE

1. Czartoryski, *Mémoires*.

2. Ibid.

3. Letter in French dated July 7, 1803.

4. Cf. Constantin de Grunwald, *Alexandre Ier, le tsar mystique*.

5. Czartoryski, *Mémoires*.

6. Ibid.

7. Voyeikov, a participant in the campaign of 1805–1806.

8. Schilder, *Emperor Alexander I, His Life and Reign*.

9. Ibid.

10. Ibid., notes.

11. *Archives Stroganov*. Cf. Grand Duke Nicholas Mikhailovich, *Le Comte Paul Stroganov*.

VI. TILSIT

1. Grand Duke Nicholas Mikhailovich, *Le Comte Paul Stroganov*. Letter in French.

2. According to Bennigsen's *Notes*, quoted by Schilder, *Emperor Alexander I, His Life and Reign*.

3. Cf. Constantin de Grunwald, *Alexandre Ier, le tsar mystique*.

4. Ibid.

5. Cf. Schilder, *Emperor Alexander I, His Life and Reign*.

6. Armand Lefebvre, *Histoire des cabinets de l'Europe pendant le Consulat et l'Empire*.

7. Journal of the Prince of Mecklenburg, heir apparent, quoted by Waliszewski, *Le Règne d'Alexandre Ier*.

8. Cf. André Castelot, *Napoléon*.

9. Mikhailovsky-Danilevsky, quoted by Schilder, *Emperor Alexander I, His Life and Reign*.

10. *The Diaries and Letters of Sir George Jackson*, quoted by Schilder, ibid.

11. Cf. Schilder, *Emperor Alexander I, His Life and Reign*.

12. Ibid.

VII. EMBRACES AT ERFURT

1. Duc de Rovigo, *Mémoires*.
2. Ibid.
3. Cf. Schilder, *Emperor Alexander I, His Life and Reign*.
4. General de Caulaincourt, *Mémoires*.
5. Cf. Constantin de Grunwald, *Alexandre Ier, le tsar mystique*.
6. Ibid., and Schilder, *Emperor Alexander I, His Life and Reign*.
7. Ibid.
8. Cf. Schilder, *Emperor Alexander I, His Life and Reign*.
9. Cf. André Castelot, *Napoléon*.
10. Cf. André Castelot, *Talleyrand*.
11. Metternich, *Mémoires*, quoted by Schilder, *Emperor Alexander I, His Life and Reign*.
12. Cf. Vandal, *Napoléon et Alexandre Ier*.
13. Ibid.
14. Ibid.
15. Thibaudeau, *Le Consulat et l'Empire*.
16. Letter from Rostopchin to Vorontzov, quoted in *Archives du prince Vorontzov*.
17. Words reported by the Empress Dowager in a letter to her daughter Catherine dated December 23, 1809, quoted in *Correspondance d'Alexandre Ier avec sa soeur*, introduced by Grand Duke Nicholas Mikhailovich.
18. Ibid., letter in French dated December 23, 1809.
19. Cf. Joseph de Maistre, Countess Fredro, Adami, Waliszewski.
20. Cf. Schilder, *Emperor Alexander I, His Life and Reign*.
21. Ibid.
22. Ibid.
23. Cf. Waliszewski, *Le Règne d'Alexandre Ier*.
24. Cf. Schilder, *Emperor Alexander I, His Life and Reign*.
25. Ibid.
26. Ibid.
27. Cf. Constantin de Grunwald, *Alexandre Ier, le tsar mystique*.
28. Schilder, *Emperor Alexander I, His Life and Reign*.

VIII. THE PATRIOTIC WAR

1. Letters in French.
2. Report from Count Saint-Julien to Metternich.
3. Ibid., February 10, 1812.

4. Letter in French dated March 31, 1812.

5. Letter to Suchtelen dated April 5, 1812.

6. General de Caulaincourt, *Mémoires*.

7. Cf. Villemain, *Souvenirs contemporains: M. de Narbonne*, and Schilder, *Emperor Alexander I, His Life and Reign*.

8. Cf. Grand Duke Nicholas Mikhailovich, *L'Empereur Alexandre Ier*.

9. Cf. Comtesse de Choiseul-Gouffier, *Mémoires*.

10. General de Caulaincourt, *Mémoires*.

11. Letter in French, written in June 1812.

12. Letter in French dated June 11, 1812.

13. Countess Edling, née Stourdza, *Mémoires*.

14. Madame de Staël, *Dix Années d'exil*.

15. Waliszewski, *Le Règne d'Alexandre Ier*.

16. Letter in French dated September 6, 1812.

17. Cf. Constantin de Grunwald, *La Campagne de Russie—1812*.

18. Cf. André Castelot, *Napoléon*, and Schilder, *Emperor Alexander I, His Life and Reign*.

19. Letters in French dated December 1812 and October 1813.

20. Schilder, *Emperor Alexander I, His Life and Reign*.

IX. THE FRENCH CAMPAIGN

1. Schilder, *Emperor Alexander I, His Life and Reign*.

2. Cf. Mikhailovsky-Danilevsky, *Journal de 1813*.

3. Metternich, *Mémoires*, and Waliszewski, *Le Règne d'Alexandre Ier*.

4. *Correspondence, Despatches, and Other Papers of Viscount Castlereagh*, second Marquess of Londonderry, ed. his brother, Charles William Vane, Marquess of Londonderry (London: William Shoberl, 1852) vol. IX, p. 212. (Trans.)

5. Cf. Schilder, *Emperor Alexander I, His Life and Reign*, and André Castelot, *Napoléon*.

6. Cf. Grand Duke Nicholas Mikhailovich, *L'Empereur Alexandre Ier*.

7. Metternich, *Mémoires*.

8. Chancellor Pasquier, *Mémoires*.

X. THE RUSSIANS IN PARIS

1. Madame de Chastenay, *Mémoires.*
2. Cf. Schilder, *Emperor Alexander I, His Life and Reign.*
3. "Lines to His Majesty the Emperor of Russia," published by *Le Siècle* in 1848.
4. Metternich, *Mémoires.*
5. Quoted by Constantin de Grunwald, *Alexandre Ier, le tsar mystique.*
6. Comte de Villele, *Mémoires.*
7. Cf. Schilder, *Emperor Alexander I, His Life and Reign.*
8. Ibid.
9. Cf. Chateaubriand, *Mémoires d'outre-tombe.*
10. Beugnot, *Mémoires.*

XI. THE CONGRESS OF VIENNA

1. Metternich, *Mémoires.*
2. *Notes, opinions et correspondance de Chichkov,* cf. Grand Duke Nicholas Mikhailovich, *L'Empereur Alexandre Ier.*
3. Schilder, *Emperor Alexander I, His Life and Reign.*
4. Ibid.
5. Talleyrand, *Correspondance* and *Mémoires.*
6. Cf. Jean Orieux, *Talleyrand.*
7. Noted by Mikhailovsky-Danilevsky.
8. Cf. Brian-Chaninov, *Alexandre Ier.*
9. Cf. Constantin de Grunwald, *Alexandre Ier, le tsar mystique.*
10. Letter in French dated February 2, 1815.
11. Cf. Constantin de Grunwald, *Alexandre Ier, le tsar mystique.*
12. Metternich, *Mémoires.*
13. Letter in French.
14. Countess Edling, *Mémoires.*

XII. THE HOLY ALLIANCE

1. Mikhailovsky-Danilevsky, *Journal inédit de 1815.*
2. Cf. Constantin de Grunwald, *Alexandre Ier, le tsar mystique.*
3. Empaytaz, *Notice sur Alexandre Ier.*
4. Countess Edling, *Mémoires.*
5. Baron de Damas, *Mémoires.*
6. Reported by General Mikhailovsky-Danilevsky.

XIII. MYSTICAL SOCIETIES AND MILITARY COLONIES

1. Letters in French dated October 1 and 6, 1817.
2. Cf. Constantin de Grunwald, *Alexandre Ier, le tsar mystique.*
3. Dispatch from Monsieur de Gabriac, November 8, 1820, cf. Constantin de Grunwald, *Alexandre Ier, le tsar mystique.*
4. Cf. Skabichevsky, *Essai sur l'histoire de la censure russe,* quoted by Waliszewski.
5. Cf. Constantin de Grunwald, *Alexandre Ier, le tsar mystique.*
6. Account by Photius, quoted by Schilder.
7. Cf. Waliszewski, *L'Empereur Alexandre Ier.*
8. F. F. Viegel, *Notes.*

XIV. THE SECRET SOCIETIES

1. Dispatch dated August 19, 1816.
2. Cf. Constantin de Grunwald, *Alexandre Ier, le tsar mystique.*
3. C. K. Webster, *The Foreign Policy of Castlereagh 1815–1822,* (London; G. Bell and Sons, 1958; first published in 1925), page 151. (Trans.)
4. Cf. Constantin de Grunwald, *Alexander Ier, le tsar mystique.*
5. Letter in French dated November 4, 1820.
6. Chateaubriand, *Le Congrès de Vérone.*
7. Dispatch dated November 26, 1821, cf. Constantin de Grunwald, *Alexandre Ier, le tsar mystique.*
8. Ibid.

XV. TAGANROG

1. Joseph de Maistre's expression.
2. Report of Dr. Tarassov.
3. Letter from Empress Elizabeth to her mother dated December 12, 1825.
4. Grand Duke Nicholas Mikhailovich, *L'Impératrice Elisabeth.*
5. Chateaubriand: *Le Congrès de Vérone,* chapter 31.
6. Ibid.

CHRONOLOGY

	EVENTS IN RUSSIA AND THE LIFE OF ALEXANDER	PRINCIPAL EVENTS IN OTHER COUNTRIES
1777	*December 12:* Birth of Alexander	Lafayette in America
1778	Rimsky-Korsakov becomes the favorite of Catherine the Great	*June 17:* French open hostilities against England in support of American War of Independence
1779	*April 27:* Birth of Constantine, Alexander's brother	
1780	Catherine breaks with Rimsky-Korsakov; Lanskoy becomes her favorite	Maria Theresa of Austria dies
1781	Alexander's parents travel in Europe	Cornwallis surrenders at Yorktown
1783		Treaty of Paris ends American

	EVENTS IN RUSSIA AND THE LIFE OF ALEXANDER	PRINCIPAL EVENTS IN OTHER COUNTRIES
		War of Independence. Second Pitt ministry in England
1784	Laharpe takes over education of Alexander and Constantine. Lanskoy dies, Ermolov becomes Catherine's favorite	
1785	Ermolov disgraced; Mamonov becomes Catherine's new favorite	
1786		Death of Frederick II (the Great) of Prussia, accession of Frederick William II
1788	Russia imposes its protectorate over Poland. Sweden attacks Russia and threatens St. Petersburg	American Constitution takes effect
1789	Mamonov repudiated by Catherine, who takes on Zubov as her favorite. Russia breaks diplomatic relations with France	George Washington becomes President of United States. Riots in France, opening of the States-General, storming of the Bastille, with abolition of aristocratic privileges
1791		Louis XVI of France attempts to flee and is taken prisoner
1792		Revolutionary France declares war on Austria. Battles of Valmy, Longuy, and Verdun. Trial of Louis XVI
1793	*January 23:* Second partition of Poland. *September 28:* Alexander marries Louise of Baden, who is baptized Elizabeth	France declares war on England, Holland, and Spain. Louis XVI, who formed the first coalition with Austria and Prussia, is executed. The Terror in France
1794	Adam Czartoryski becomes the friend and confidant of Alexander	9 Thermidor in France, fall and execution of Robespierre, end of the Terror
1795	*September:* Treaty of St. Petersburg for an Anglo-Austro-Russian alliance.	French-Austrian armistice. Beginning of the directorate in France. Bonaparte crushes the

	EVENTS IN RUSSIA AND THE LIFE OF ALEXANDER	PRINCIPAL EVENTS IN OTHER COUNTRIES
	October: Third partition of Poland. Alexander befriends Alexis Arakcheyev	royalists in French civil strife
1796	Birth of Nicholas, Alexander's brother, future Czar Nicholas I. Death of Catherine the Great. Accession of Paul I, Alexander's father	Bonaparte's Italian campaign
1797	*April:* Coronation of Paul I in Moscow. Formation of a liberal circle of friends around Alexander. Alexander's wife, Elizabeth, begins liaison with Adam Czartoryski. Anglo-Russian commercial treaty. Paul I, after a few months of liberalism, does a complete reversal	Death of Frederick William II of Prussia, accession of Frederick William III. John Adams is President of United States
1798	Paul I declares war on France	Formation of the second coalition against France
1799	Birth of Marie, daughter of Elizabeth, Alexander's wife. Adam Czartoryski is sent abroad to Sardinia by Paul I. Failure of Russian campaign against France and subsequent rapprochement followed by the breaking of diplomatic relations between Russia and England. First plot against Paul I fails	Coup d'état by Napoleon Bonaparte
1800	Pahlen plot against Paul I develops. Russia and the Scandinavian countries form league of neutral nations. Paul I prepares punitive expedition against British India	Battle of Marengo. French-Austrian armistice
1801	Alexander accepts passive role as accomplice in plot against his father. Paul I is assassinated. *September:* Alexander is proclaimed Czar.	Treaty of Lunéville. Signing of the Concordat in France. Jefferson becomes President of United States. Beginning of the peace talks between

	EVENTS IN RUSSIA AND THE LIFE OF ALEXANDER	PRINCIPAL EVENTS IN OTHER COUNTRIES
	Signing of an agreement with England and reestablishment of diplomatic relations with France and Austria	England and France
1802	Formation of the Secret Committee. In Memel, Alexander meets Frederick William III of Prussia and Queen Louise. Russia has itself recognized by Turkey as the protector of the Rumanian kingdoms	Treaty of Amiens, reestablishing peace in Europe. Napoleon is named Consul for life
1803	Alexander takes Maria Naryshkina as his mistress. Issuance of the ukase about serfdom. Alexander proposes to mediate in the Anglo-French conflict. Russia occupies Georgia	Breaking of the peace of Amiens. Napoleon occupies Belgium and Hanover. England reestablishes the continental blockade. France sells America the Louisiana Territory
1804	Birth of Sophie, daughter of Maria Naryshkina and Alexander. French-Russian defensive alliance. After the assassination of the Duc d'Enghien, Russia breaks diplomatic relations with France. Treaty of alliance between Russia and Austria. Russo-Persian War	Execution of the Duc d'Enghien in France. Promulgation of the Napoleonic Code. Napoleon crowned Emperor of the French
1805	Russo-Swedish alliance. Russo-English alliance. *August:* Russia enters the third coalition with England and Austria. Kutuzov's army, having joined the Austrian forces, has some success against the French in Moravia and Austria. *November 3:* Potsdam convention between Russia and Prussia. *December 2:* Battle of Austerlitz, a bad defeat for the Russian army. *December 4:* Armistice	French-Austrian hostilities. Third coalition against France. Capitulation of Ulm. Napoleon occupies Vienna. Battle of Austerlitz

EVENTS IN RUSSIA AND THE LIFE OF ALEXANDER	PRINCIPAL EVENTS IN OTHER COUNTRIES
between France and Austria under whose terms Russia must leave Austrian territory at once	

1806 Birth of Elizabeth, daughter of Alexander and his wife. *May–September:* French-Russian peace negotiations. Alexander prepares for war while negotiating. Prussia joins Russia and England to form what will be known as the fourth coalition. *July:* Secret agreement between Russia and Prussia. *November–December:* Russian army enters Prussian territory. *December 14:* Russian victory over the French at Pultusk

— Battle of Jena. Occupation of Berlin and Warsaw. Continental blockade

1807 Alexander leaves St. Petersburg to rejoin his armies. Battle of Eylau, where Benningsen, beaten by Napoleon, succeeds in salvaging the army. *June 14:* The Russian army is crushed by Napoleon at the Battle of Friedland and has to retreat. *June 25:* Start of Tilsit negotiations with the signing of an armistice between Russia and France. The two Emperors meet on the Neman. *July 7:* French-Russian treaty for offensive-defensive alliance

— Beginning of the war in Portugal. Embargo Act in United States

1808 Death of Elizabeth, Alexander's daughter. Napoleon has Talleyrand tell Alexander he is going to repudiate Josephine and ask for the hand of one of Alexander's sisters. The

— Napoleonic troops in Spain

	EVENTS IN RUSSIA AND THE LIFE OF ALEXANDER	PRINCIPAL EVENTS IN OTHER COUNTRIES
	Russian court declines, politely. Reestablishment of a secret police in Russia. Russia invades Finland. *September:* Meeting of Alexander and Napoleon at Erfurt turns to the advantage of the Russians	
1809	Prince Schwarzenberg arrives from Vienna to ask for Russian neutrality in any French-Austrian conflict, but Russia declines, citing treaty with France. *April:* Russo-Turkish war resumes. *May:* Feeble fighting by Russians on Austrian soil, side by side with French troops. *October:* Treaty of Vienna displeases Russia. Peace with Sweden. Speransky and Capo d'Istria become Alexander's advisers	Battle of Wagram; fall of Vienna. Napoleon divorced from Josephine. Madison becomes President of United States. Repeal of Embargo Act. Passage of Non-Intercourse Act
1810	*December 31:* Alexander breaks the continental blockade. France and Russia prepare for war	French-Swedish peace. Sweden declares war on England. Napoleon marries Marie Louise
1811	Russo-Prussian military convention. Russian army crushes the Turks	
1812	Alexander leaves St. Petersburg for Lithuania to be near his armies. *April 5:* Offensive-defensive alliance with Sweden. *June 2:* Secret convention with Austria. *June 18:* Treaty of Stockholm between Russia and England. *June 24–25:* The army of France crosses the Neman and takes Vilna. *July:* Declaration of the War of National Salvation against the invader. *July 18:* Treaty of Orebro	United States Congress declares war on Great Britain

	EVENTS IN RUSSIA AND THE LIFE OF ALEXANDER	PRINCIPAL EVENTS IN OTHER COUNTRIES
	among Russia, Sweden, and England. *August:* Kutuzov named commander in chief. *August 17:* Fall of Smolensk. *September 5–7:* Bloody but indecisive battle of Borodino. Kutuzov decides to abandon Moscow, which gives him time to regroup. *September 14:* Moscow falls to Napoleon without a fight. *September 15–18:* The burning of Moscow. *September-October:* Napoleon, with his army weakened, starts talks with Kutuzov and Alexander but without success. *October 19:* Start of retreat of Napoleonic army. Confrontation at Maloyaroslavets, favorable to the Russians. *November 26–28:* Crossing of the Berezina and disastrous retreat of the remnants of the Grand Army, beyond Russian borders. *December 25:* Celebration of the Russian victory. Alexander decides to pursue Napoleon into Europe	
1813	*January 31:* Austro-Russian armistice. *February 9:* Russian troops occupy Warsaw. *February 28:* Russo-Prussian Treaty of Kalisz. *March:* The Russians take Hamburg and Dresden in triumph, beside the King of Prussia. *May 20–21:* Austro-Russian defeat at Bautzen. *June 4:* Armistice that will last two months. *June:* Treaty of Reichenbach among Russia, Prussia, Austria, and England. *July 7:* Defeat of the allies at Dresden, Russian victory at Kulm. *October 18:*	Prussia declares war on Napoleon. Austro-Russian alliance. Battles of Lützen and Bautzen. Austria declares war on Napoleon. General coalition. Battles of Dresden, Leipzig; Napoleon withdraws beyond the Rhine. Wellington lands in the South of France

EVENTS IN RUSSIA AND THE LIFE OF ALEXANDER	PRINCIPAL EVENTS IN OTHER COUNTRIES
Victory at Leipzig, with over 100,000 deaths; Alexander becomes virtual head of the coalition. *November:* Russo-Persian Treaty of Gulistan ensures Russia all her conquests in the Caucasus	

1814 *January 13:* Russian advance guard crosses the Rhine. *January 16:* Alexander enters France. *February 11–March 19:* Congress of Châtillon, resulting in a compromise for pursuing war and negotiations simultaneously. *March 30:* Capitulation of Paris. *April 6:* Unconditional abdication of Napoleon, as demanded by Alexander. *May:* Alexander forces Louis XVIII to promulgate a charter to his people. *June:* Alexander leaves Paris for Baden, where he will meet Elizabeth. As soon as he leaves Paris, the allied troops begin to evacuate the city. *September 25:* Alexander arrives in the Austrian capital for Congress of Vienna, where he has a liaison with Princess Bagration while Elizabeth has a reunion with Adam Czartoryski

Louis XVIII proclaimed King of France in Bordeaux. Abdication of Napoleon, who goes to Elba. British burn Washington, D.C. Hartford Convention. *November 3:* Opening of the Congress of Vienna. Treaty of Ghent ends war between United States and Britain

1815 Relationship based on mysticism between Alexander and Baroness von Krüdener, a "prophetess." *March 6–7:* The various plenipotentiaries at the Vienna congress learn of Napoleon's escape from Elba. *March:* Napoleon returns to Paris and has sent to Alexander proof of the betrayal of Austria and England, who had signed a

Congress of Vienna creates the state of Luxembourg and the Kingdom of the Netherlands (including Belgium). Union of Sweden and Norway. Liberal rebellion in Spain. The French exhume Louis XVI and Marie Antoinette. Battles of Ligny and Waterloo. Second abdication of Napoleon. Louis XVIII enters Paris. Napoleon leaves France for St. Helena.

EVENTS IN RUSSIA AND THE LIFE OF ALEXANDER	PRINCIPAL EVENTS IN OTHER COUNTRIES
secret treaty of January 3, excluding Russia and Prussia. *March 25:* Renewal of the Chaumont pact by the allies, this time united in the fight against Napoleon. *June 9:* Final act of the Congress of Vienna, fixing conditions for partition of Europe and ceding the Grand Duchy of Warsaw to Russia. Alexander becomes King of Poland. Russian troops are recalled into Europe and the allies prepare for a confrontation. *End of June:* After Waterloo, Alexander rushes to Paris with a detachment of Cossacks. *July 10:* Alexander in Paris, reestablishes himself in the Elysée Palace. *September 26:* Establishment of the Holy Alliance among Russia, Prussia, and Austria. *November 27:* Alexander signs the constitutional charter of Poland, which becomes the Kingdom of Poland under Russian suzerainty, which it will remain until 1915	

1816	Grave economic troubles in Russia after the war, but Alexander turns to more metaphysical issues	
1817	Arakcheyev becomes Alexander's principal aide and administrator. Numerous provinces are transformed progressively into military colonies	Monroe becomes President of the United States
1818	Cultural and social life of Moscow offends Alexander. Arakcheyev strengthens police surveillance and censorship	United States forces under Jackson invade Florida

	EVENTS IN RUSSIA AND THE LIFE OF ALEXANDER	PRINCIPAL EVENTS IN OTHER COUNTRIES
1820	Rebellion in the Semeonovsky regiment in St. Petersburg. *October:* Alexander participates in the Congress of Troppau with other members of the Holy Alliance, but under the influence of Metternich he sacrifices the best interests of Russia	Missouri Compromise in the United States
1821	At the Congress of Laibach, Alexander promises Metternich Russian military support	Austria represses the national liberal revolution in Italy. Peru becomes independent and Venezuela is liberated. Greek war of independence against Turkey. Triumph of the reactionaries in France. Napoleon dies
1822	Reestablishment of the right of lords to consign serfs to Siberia, a right abolished in 1809. Imperial edict ordering "the dissolution of all kinds of secret societies of whatever denomination, such as Masonic lodges." Alexander participates in a reunion of the Holy Alliance at the Congress of Verona. Greece asks for his aid in fight against the Turks, and he refuses	Famine in Ireland. United States recognizes newly independent Latin American republics
1824	*January:* Alexander suffers an attack of erysipelas. *June 23:* Death of Sophie, daughter of Alexander and Maria Naryshkina. Rapprochement of Alexander and Elizabeth. *December:* Elizabeth is ill. Archimandrite Photius demands the dismissal of Golitzin and Alexander consents; the Metropolitan Seraphim becomes head of the Bible Society and Arakcheyev heads the Holy Synod	Death of Louis XVIII of France, accession of Charles X

EVENTS IN RUSSIA AND THE LIFE OF ALEXANDER	PRINCIPAL EVENTS IN OTHER COUNTRIES
1825 *September:* Alexander and Elizabeth in Taganrog for their health. *November 4:* The Czar comes down with a high fever. *November 19:* Alexander dies in Taganrog. *December 29:* Cortege leaves Taganrog for St. Petersburg	John Quincy Adams becomes President of the United States
1826 *March:* Cortege arrives in St. Petersburg. *May:* Elizabeth dies, in Belev, having never returned to the capital	

BIBLIOGRAPHY

PRIMARY SOURCES

Boutourline, S., *Histoire militaire de la campagne de Russie en 1812*, 2 vols. (Paris, 1824).

Caulaincourt, General de, *Mémoires* (Paris, 1933).

Centrarchiv of the USSR, *The Rising of the Decembrists*, 11 vols. (Moscow), in Russian.

Chateaubriand, Vicomte François-René de, *Les Mémoires d'outre-tombe*, centenary edition (Paris, 1948).

—— *Le Congrès de Vérone* (Paris, 1838).

Chastenay, Madame de, *Mémoires*, 1771–1815 (Paris, 1896).

Chichkov, Admiral Paul, *Mémoires* (Paris-Bucharest, 1909).

Choiseul-Gouffier, Comtesse de, *Mémoires historiques sur l'empereur Alexandre Ier et la Cour de Russie* (Paris, 1829).

Clausewitz, C. von, *La Campagne de 1812 en Russie* (Paris, 1906).

Czartoryski, Prince A., *Mémoires et correspondance avec l'empereur Alexandre Ier*, 2 vols. (Paris, 1887).

—— *Alexandre Ier et le prince A. Czartoryski* (Paris, 1865).

Dubrovin, *Letters des principaux personnages du règne d'Alexandre Ier* (St. Petersburg, 1883).

Edling, Countess, *Mémoires* (Moscow, 1880).

Fusil, Louise, *L'Incendie de Moscou et la Retraite de Napoléon* (Paris, 1817).

—— *Souvenirs d'une actrice*, 2 vols. (Paris, 1841).

Golovina, Countess B., *Souvenirs* (Paris, 1910).

Gretch, N. N., *Recollections* (St. Petersburg, 1886), in Russian.

Hortense, Queen, *Mémoires* (Paris, 1927).

Karamzin, N., *Works and Unpublished Correspondence* (St. Petersburg, 1862), in Russian.

—— *Correspondence with I. Dmitriev* (St. Petersburg, 1866), in Russian.

Krasnok, *Opinion d'un officier russe sur Paris en 1814.*

Kurakin, Prince, *Memories of the Journey of Princess Kurakin and Memories of Madame Vigée-Lebrun* (1903), in Russian.

Kutuzov, Field Marshal, *Collection of Documents and Materials* (Moscow, 1947–1950), in Russian.

Labaume, E., *Relations circonstanciées de la campagne de Russie* (Paris, 1814).

La Garde-Chambonas, Comte A. de, *Souvenirs du Congrès de Vienne, 1814–1815* (Paris, 1901).

Laharpe, F. G. de, *Mémoires* (Paris, 1864).

—— *Le Gouverneur d'un prince* (Lausanne, 1902).

Langeron, General Comte de, *Mémoires* (Paris, 1902).

Maistre, Joseph de, *Correspondance diplomatique, 1811–1817* (Paris, 1860).

—— *Les Soirées de Saint-Pétersbourg* (Paris, 1922).

Maria Feodorovna, Empress, *Lettres à l'empereur Alexandre Ier* (Moscow, 1911).

Metternich, Prince de, *Mémoires et documents*, 8 vols. (Paris, 1880–1884).

Mikhailovsky-Danilevsky. *History of the Emperor's First Campaign against Napoleon* (St. Petersburg, 1844), in Russian.

—— *History of the Campaign of 1814 in France* (St. Petersburg, 1845), in Russian.

—— *Memoirs on the Campaign of 1813* (St. Petersburg, 1834), in Russian.

—— *Recollections, Notes of 1815* (St. Petersburg, 1831), in Russian.

—— *L'Empereur Alexandre Ier et ses collaborateurs en 1812, 1813, 1814 et 1815.*

Nesselrode, Count, *Lettres et papiers*, 6 vols. (Paris, 1904–1907).

Ortenberg, *Mémoires sur la campagne de 1813 en Allemagne.*

Pasquier, Chancellor, *Mémoires* (Paris, 1895).

Potocka, Countess, *Mémoires* (1924).

Puibusque, Vicomte de, *Lettres sur la guerre de Russie en 1812* (Paris, 1816).

Rapports diplomatiques du comte Lebzeltern, ministre d'Autriche à la cour de Russie (St. Petersburg, 1913).

Recueil de la Société impériale d'histoire de Russie, vols. 2, 3, 5, 6, 21, 23, 31, 33, 41, 44, 54, 70, 77, 82, 83, 89, 112, 119, 121, 127.

Relations diplomatiques entre la France et la Russie avant l'année 1812, in Russian and French.

Rochechouart, Comte de, *Souvenirs de la Révolution* (Paris, 1889).

Rostopchin, Count, *Oeuvres inédites publiées par la comtesse Lydie Rostoptchine* (Paris).

Savary, Duc de Rovigo, *Mémoires* (Paris, 1889).

Ségur, Comte Philippe-Paul de, *Histoire de Napoléon et de la Grande Armée* (Paris, 1873).

—— *Histoire et Mémoires.*

Speransky, *Projets et notes.*

Staël, Madame de, *Dix Années d'exil* (Paris, 1904).

Stedingk, Count, *Mémoires posthumes* (Paris, 1844).

Surugue, Abbé, *Lettres sur la prise de Moscou en 1812* (Paris, 1823).

—— *Les Français à Moscou* (Moscow, 1819).

Sverbeyev, D. N., *Memoirs, 1799–1826*, 2 vols. (Moscow, 1899), in Russian.

Talleyrand, Prince Charles-Maurice de, *Mémoires* (Paris, 1891).

—— *Lettres inédites de Talleyrand à Napoléon* (1889).

—— *Correspondance inédite du prince de Talleyrand et du roi Louis XVIII pendant le Congrès de Vienne* (1881).

Tarassov, D., *Emperor Alexander I, Personal Recollections* (Petrograd, 1915), in Russian.

Turgenev, Nicholas Ivanovich, *Journal et Lettres.*

Viegel, F. F., *Memoirs* (Moscow, 1864–1865), in Russian.

Vitrolles, Baron de, *Mémoires et relations politiques* (Paris, 1884).

Wilmot, Catherine, *Lettres de Russie, 1805–1807* (Leipzig, 1876).

SECONDARY SOURCES

Babkin, V. I., *Recruitment among the People during the National War of 1812* (Moscow, 1962), in Russian.

Bariatinsky, Prince V., *Le Mystère d'Alexandre Ier* (Paris, 1929).

Bourquin, M., *Histoire de la Sainte-Alliance* (Geneva, 1954).

Brian-Chaninov, *Alexandre Ier* (Paris, 1934).

—— *Histoire de Russie* (Paris, 1929).

Capefigue, M., *La Baronne de Krüdener, l'Empereur Alexandre Ier et les traités de 1816* (Paris, 1866).

—— *Diplomates européens* (Paris, 1843).

Castelot, André, *Bonaparte* (Paris, 1967).

—— *Napoléon* (Paris, 1968).

—— *Joséphine* (Paris, 1964).

—— *Talleyrand ou le cynisme* (Paris, 1980).

Chulkov, G., *Les Derniers Tsars autocrates* (Paris, 1928).

Decaux, Alain, *Les Grands Mystères du passé* (Paris, 1964 and 1971).

Eynard, Charles, *Vie de Madame de Krüdener,* 2 vols. (Paris, 1849).

Golubov, *Bagration, Glory of the Year 1812* (1943), in Russian.

Grunwald, Constantin de, *Alexandre Ier, le tsar mystique* (Paris, 1955).

—— *L'Assassinat de Paul Ier* (Paris, 1960).

—— *Trois Siècles de diplomatie russe* (Paris, 1945).

—— *La Campagne de Russie, 1812* (Paris, 1963).

Haumant, Emile, *La Culture française en Russie (1700–1900)* (Paris, 1913).

Hermant, Abel, *Madame de Krudener, l'amie du tsar Alexandre Ier* (Paris, 1934).

Houssaye, Henry, *1814* (Paris, 1888).

—— *1815,* 3 vols. (Paris, 1893–1905).

Korf, Baron M., *The Life of Count Speransky,* 2 vols. (St. Petersburg, 1861), in Russian.

Kudriashev, K. V., *Alexander I and the Mystery of Feodor Kuzmich* (Leningrad, 1923), in Russian.

Ley, Francis, *Alexandre Ier et sa Sainte-Alliance* (1975).

Lubimov, Leon, *The Mystery of Emperor Alexander I* (Paris, 1931), in Russian.

Madelin, Louis, *Histoire du Consulat et de l'Empire,* 16 vols. (Paris, 1954).

Masson, Frédéric, *Le Comte Paul Stroganov* (Paris, 1909).

Matveyev, N., *Life in Moscow before the Invasion of 1812,* in Russian.

Melgunov, S., *Affairs and People of Alexander's Reign* (Berlin, 1923), in Russian.

—— *Freemasonry in the Past and in the Present*, 2 vols. (St. Petersburg, 1915), in Russian.

Miliukov, Seignobos, and Eisenmann, *Histoire de la Russie*, 3 vols. (Paris, 1932).

Nadler, N., *Emperor Alexander I and the Idea of the Holy Alliance*, 2 vols. (Riga, 1886–1892), in Russian.

Nicholas Mikhailovich, Grand Duke, *L'Empereur Alexandre Ier: essai d'étude historique*, 2 vols. (St. Petersburg, 1912), in Russian and French.

—— *L'Impératrice Elisabeth, épouse d'Alexandre Ier*, 3 vols. (St. Petersburg, 1909).

—— *Correspondance de l'empereur Alexandre Ier avec sa soeur Catherine* (St. Petersburg, 1910).

—— *Le Comte Paul Stroganov*, 3 vols. (St. Petersburg and Paris, 1905).

—— *The Dolgoruky Princes, Associates of Emperor Alexander I* (St. Petersburg, 1901–1902), in Russian.

—— *The Legend of the End of Emperor Alexander I in Siberia in the Guise of the Staretz Feodor Kuzmich* (St. Petersburg, 1907), in Russian.

Olivier, Daria, *L'Incendie de Moscou* (Paris, 1964).

Orieux, Jean, *Talleyrand* (Paris, 1970).

Paléologue, Maurice, *Alexandre Ier, un tsar énigmatique* (Paris, 1937); English translation: *The Enigmatic Czar: the Life of Alexander I of Russia*, trans. Edwin and Willa Muir (New York: Harper & Row, 1938), reprinted 1969 by Archon Books) (Trans.).

Pirenne, J. H., *La Sainte-Alliance*, 2 vols. (Neuchâtel, 1946 and 1949).

Platonov, S., *Histoire de la Russie* (Paris, 1929).

Pypin, A., *The Social Movement under Alexander I* (St. Petersburg, 1885), in Russian.

Rain, Pierre, *Alexandre Ier, un tsar idéologue* (Paris, 1913).

Saint-Pierre, Michel de, *Le Drame des Romanov* (Paris, 1967).

Schilder, N., *Emperor Alexander I, His Life and Reign*, 4 vols. (St. Petersburg, 1890–1904), in Russian.

—— *Emperor Paul I* (St. Petersburg, 1901), in Russian.

Semevsky, *Count Arakcheyev and the Military Colonies* (St. Petersburg, 1871), in Russian.

—— *The Political and Social Ideas of the Decembrists* (St. Petersburg, 1901), in Russian.

Shubinsky, *Characters and Anecdotes from the Life of Emperor Alexander I* (St. Petersburg, 1877), in Russian.

Shumigorsky, E., *Empress Maria Feodorovna, 1759–1828* (St. Petersburg, 1892), in Russian.

Skabichevsky, A., *Essay on the History of Russian Censorship* (St. Petersburg, 1892), in Russian.

Soloviov, S., *Emperor Alexander I, Politics and Diplomacy* (St. Petersburg, 1877), in Russian.

Tarlé, E., *The Continental Blockade* (Moscow, 1913), in Russian.

—— *La Campagne de Russie, 1812* (Paris, 1950).

Tatishchev, S., *Alexandre et Napoléon* (Paris, 1891).

Turgenev, N., *La Russie et les Russes,* 2 vols. (Paris, 1847).

Troyat, Henri, *Catherine la Grande* (Paris, 1977); English translation: *Catherine the Great,* trans. Joan Pinkham (New York: E. P. Dutton, 1980) (Trans.).

Tulard, Jean, *Napoléon ou le mythe du sauveur* (Paris, 1977).

—— *Napoléon, proclamations, ordres du jour, bulletins de la Grande Armée* (Paris, 1967).

—— *Le Mythe de Napoléon* (Paris, 1971).

—— *Napoléon et l'Empire,* ed. Jean Mistler (Paris, 1968).

Vandal, A., *Napoléon et Alexandre Ier,* 3 vols. (Paris, 1891–1896).

Waliszewski, K., *Le Règne d'Alexandre Ier,* 3 vols. (Paris, 1923–1925).

—— *Le Roman d'une impératrice: Catherine II de Russie* (Paris, 1893); English translation: *The Romance of an Empress: Catherine II of Russia,* trans. anonymous (New York: D. Appleton and Co., 1894; reprinted 1968 by Archon Books) (Trans.).

—— *Autour d'un trône: Catherine II de Russie* (Paris, 1894); English translation: *The Story of a Throne: Catherine II of Russia,* trans. anonymous (Freeport, N.Y.: Books of Libraries Press, 1971) (Trans.).

Zyzkin, *The Mysteries of Emperor Alexander I* (Buenos Aires, 1952), in Russian.

INDEX